I sincerely wish
that you
learn from this
it was a labor of love

All the best,

Steve

P.S. Truth still matters

MW01503016

MINE EYES HAVE SEEN THE GLORY

MINE EYES HAVE SEEN THE GLORY

Religion *and the* Politics *of* Race *in* the Civil War Era *and* Beyond

STEVEN L. DUNDAS

Potomac Books

AN IMPRINT OF THE UNIVERSITY OF NEBRASKA PRESS

All rights reserved. Potomac Books is an imprint of the
University of Nebraska Press.
Manufactured in the United States of America.

Library of Congress Cataloging-in-Publication Data
Names: Dundas, Steven L., author.
Title: Mine eyes have seen the glory: religion and the
politics of race in the Civil War era and beyond / Steven
L. Dundas.
Description: [Lincoln, Nebraska]: Potomac Books, an
imprint of the University of Nebraska Press, 2022. |
Includes bibliographical references and index.
Identifiers: LCCN 2022005306
ISBN 9781640124882 (hardback)
ISBN 9781640125407 (epub)
ISBN 9781640125414 (pdf)
Subjects: LCSH: Slavery—United States. | Religion and
state—United States—History. | Racism—Religious
aspects—Christianity. | Slavery—Religious aspects—
Christianity. | United States—Race relations. | United
States—Religion. | United States—Politics and
government. | BISAC: HISTORY / United States / Civil War
Period (1850–1877) | SOCIAL SCIENCE / Ethnic Studies /
American / African American & Black Studies
Classification: LCC E184.A1 D86 2022 | DDC 973.7/1—dc23/
eng/20220609
LC record available at https://lccn.loc.gov/2022005306

Set in New Baskervill ITC Pro by Mikala R. Kolander.

To my wife, Judy, who has endured over thirty-nine years of my military service, frequent long-term deployments separations, and my constant desire to read, study, and write about history, often leaving her lonely and frustrated. I could not have produced this without her patience, input, and editing.

CONTENTS

ILLUSTRATIONS

Illustrations

PREFACE

The First Duty

The twenty-third century is an odd place to begin a book about events that were set in motion in the early seventeenth century. I am a historian, retired career military officer, and priest. As a historian I believe the truth, even when uncomfortable or damning, should be told. I take as inspiration a statement by Sir Patrick Stewart, in his role as Captain Jean Luc Picard, in the *Star Trek: The Next Generation* episode "The First Duty." In the story Picard tells Cadet Wesley Crusher, "The first duty of every Starfleet officer is to the truth, whether it's scientific truth or historical truth or personal truth! It is the guiding principle on which Starfleet is based."

The distinguished history professor Timothy Snyder wrote, "To abandon facts is to abandon freedom."[1] Truth matters, but it is human nature to take solace in myths and believe they are true. However, many myths are deadly. The deadliest include American Slavery's "positive good," the "Noble South," the "Lost Cause," the evils of Reconstruction, the good of Jim Crow, and the nonexistence of institutional racism in the United States.

These are lies so big and toxic that one has to call them whoppers. The "Noble South" and the "Lost Cause" are the same kind of lies that Adolf Hitler wrote of in *Mein Kampf*, using the Protocols of the Elders of Zion and the stab-in-the-back myth to eliminate enemies and engineer the Holocaust.

They are intended to destroy truth and create alternative facts. Sissela Bok wrote:

> Deceit and violence—these are the two forms of deliberate assault on human beings. Both can coerce people into acting against their will. Most harm that can befall victims through violence can come to them also through deceit. But the myths of "The Noble South" and "Lost Cause" are gargantuan lies perpetrated for over a century and a half that led to countless acts of violence and discrimination against Blacks. They are corrosive, destructive and an assault on the rights of all Americans.[2]

When I put what I read into the context of the era, the authors, and their motivations, I ask three questions: Why this? Why me? Why now? This helps to identify myths and falsehoods embedded in prior histories. The proper academic term for this is "historiography," which I believe should be a required subject in all disciplines. As the late James Loewen observed,

> Anything who knows the history of the Civil War and its aftermath and who talks with members of the public quickly grows frustrated. Most recent high school graduates, many history and social studies teachers, and even some professional historians whose training is in other areas hold basic misconceptions about the era. Questions about why the South seceded, what the Confederacy was about, and the nature of its symbols and ideology often give rise to flatly untrue "answers." In turn these errors persist because most Americans do not know or have not read key documents in American history about the Confederacy.[3]

Another tool is hermeneutics:

> A methodology of interpretation is concerned with problems that arise when dealing with meaningful human actions and the products of such actions, most importantly texts. . . . The crucial point, then, is that any text has an envisioning historical and cultural context and the context of a text is not simply

textual. . . . After all, texts inevitably have a setting—historical, cultural, authorial—on which their actual meaning is critically dependent.[4]

This is particularly important in interpreting the history of American slavery, the Civil War, Reconstruction, and Southern redemption. Much of what we regard as history is based on the twin myths of the "Noble South" and the "Lost Cause," which, in addition to being crude but effective revisionist history and propaganda, act in a similar manner to religious texts. Facts are ignored, and biography becomes hagiography, pervaded by racist narratives. So, it is important for those who read them to use historiography and hermeneutics to differentiate truth from fiction.

Likewise, historical ignorance and the belief of myth becomes a problem when leaders who are indifferent history and immersed in rapidly changing situations, flaunt their ignorance. This is not new; previous world leaders were human beings, too, and humanity is the one constant in human history. In the words of Barbara Tuchman, "Any person who considers himself, and intends to remain, a member of Western society inherits the Western past from Athens and Jerusalem to Runnymede and Valley Forge, as well as to Watts and Chicago of August 1968. He may ignore it or deny it, but that does not alter the fact. The past sits back and smiles and knows it owns him anyway."[5]

Thucydides, in his *History of the Peloponnesian War,* wrote to inform "those who want to understand clearly the events which happened in the past, and which (human nature being what it is) will, at some time or in another and in much the same ways, be repeated in the future."[6] But history proves its critics wrong in showing the consistency of human beings from one era to the next. Thus the "task of historians then does not seem too difficult to describe; it is to trace the ways in which people of Western culture have reflected on the past and what these revelations have told them about human life in the continuum of past, present, and future."[7] As Williamson Murray wrote about Thucydides's successors:

> Notwithstanding, successors of the Hellenic soldiers and politicians about whom he wrote have repeatedly chosen to believe that they are different and that the lessons of the past are irrelevant to their unique circumstances. Why this remains so remains one of the mysteries of the human experience. Perhaps the most compelling explanation is simple generational transition, the conviction of each new crop of leaders assuming power are different from their predecessors and immune from their errors. To paraphrase an old saying, what is new is not new is not necessarily interesting and what is interesting is not necessarily new. Yet, political and political leaders seem driven to repeat the blunders of their predecessors.[8]

This book began as a short chapter in my *Gettysburg Staff Ride* text while I was on the faculty of the Joint Forces Staff College in Norfolk, Virginia. The persistent myths that serve as blinders to properly understanding the Civil War perplexed me, so I decided to research them and share my findings with my students, because military histories of the Civil War, its battles and leaders, often skim over racism and slavery, which is unsurprising, for they deal with strategy, campaigns and battles. But to understand the American Civil War, one has to tackle the elephant in the room that many people want to ignore: American slavery and racism. Slavery ended, but racism did not, and the lingering effects of both are alive and well in the United States.

The propaganda mill of Noble South and Lost Cause proponents are a major problem, much like Holocaust deniers. Therefore, they must be confronted in ways that may seem impolitic. Nevertheless, their falsehoods must be exposed. Systemic institutional racism and discrimination has impacted almost every aspect of American life, religion, and culture since the first Blacks landed at Jamestown in 1619. It was true then and is true now, for the past is not always past—or, as

Mark Twain reportedly quipped, "History doesn't repeat itself, but it often rhymes."

Many early histories of the Civil War were written, funded, or endorsed by the powerful United Daughters of the Confederacy, which promoted the myths of the Noble South and the Lost Cause. Biographers wrote about Southern leaders as though they were saints, surrounding them with miracles and offering no criticism. They denied slavery as the war's cause and successfully changed the narrative by blaming Northerners for making the issue one of states' rights.

The Lost Cause was historic revisionism at its best. It became "history" because most Northerners wanted to leave the war behind and stopped caring about what happened to Blacks. Northern business interests exploited the situation for profit by working with former slave owners and Southern state governments to reenslave Blacks by other means.

The war was about how Americans' views of liberty and slavery influenced their racial attitudes. To slavery supporters Blacks were an inferior or subhuman race, who could never be the equal of whites—not even human, but property. White supremacy and its web of systemic cultural, political, economic, and religious racism remains a powerful part of American life. This makes it difficult to confront racism without pushback by politicians, pundits, preachers, and militants, who, despite their denials, are as racist as any Klansman, Red Shirt, or White Liner.

In my choice of title and cover image, I wanted to emphasize the evil of the system and the role that Blacks played in abolition: Black soldiers who fought for their freedom and that of their still enslaved people; Blacks who fought against a racist insurgency during Reconstruction, Jim Crow, and the civil rights movement; and Blacks who continue the fight for equality today. The image on the cover is a photograph of Sergeant William Carney of the 54th Massachusetts Regiment, the most famous of the African American units of the war. He was awarded the Medal of Honor for his actions at Battery Wagner in July 1863, which is commemorated in the film *Glory*. During the battle Carney was badly wounded but refused to let the American flag fall into the hands of the rebels. The photo of the proud Sergeant Carney posing in his uniform with the flag captures something that many benevolent and sympathetic whites fail to grasp: for Blacks emancipation and freedom are an extremely personal matter, one in which their ancestors' efforts and sacrifices matter, and their unique insights and experiences are often disregarded.

The book's title, *Mine Eyes Have Seen the Glory*, is the first line of Julia Ward Howe's "Battle Hymn of the Republic," which was a favorite of Black soldiers serving in the Union Army. The hymn became an anthem as the aim of the war expanded from restoring the Union to emancipating slaves. When Black soldiers in the Wilderness Campaign began to liberate fellow Blacks from slavery in Virginia, it increased the validity of their participation in the war. Black soldiers saw the war as a crusade for freedom with a profoundly theological meaning, akin to Moses leading the Hebrews out of Egypt during the Exodus. As Sergeant John Brock of the Forty-Third United States Colored Troops (USCT) Infantry Regiment wrote of his experience:

> We have been instrumental in liberating some five hundred of our sisters and brothers from the accursed yoke of human bondage. . . . As several of them remarked to me, it seemed to them like heaven, so greatly did they realize the difference between slavery and freedom. . . . The slaves tell us they have been praying for these blessed days for a long time, but now their eyes witness their salvation from that dreadful calamity, slavery and, what more than they expected, by their own brethren in arms. What a glorious prospect it is to behold this glorious Army of Black man as they march with martial tread over the sacred soil of Virginia.[9]

The sacrifices and dedication of the Black soldiers who fought as members of the USCT and various state raised regiments had an impact a century later. The night before his assassination, Dr. Martin Luther King Jr. gave his "I've Been to the Mountaintop" speech. He concluded with these words: "And so I'm happy tonight; I'm not worried about anything; I'm not fearing any man. Mine eyes have seen the glory of the coming of the Lord."[10]

The book's subtitle, *Religion and the Politics of Race in the Civil War Era and Beyond,* deals with how racism infects American history, from our colonial beginnings until today. Despite emancipation, citizenship, and suffrage, Blacks have seldom enjoyed the full benefits of equality, and throughout our history whites treated Blacks as less than human. The Christian religion was a major factor in American racism and slavery. Southern ministers became the fiercest defenders of slavery, because rich plantation owners sat in their pews. Ideology was less defined; it was mostly racist, but it had economic and pseudoscientific aspects that supposedly proved that Blacks were inferior to whites. Unfortunately, much of this continues today.

Finally, the words and actions of the white supremacists and their defenders were connected to politics, before, during, and after the war. Slavery created a cult of racist true believers. According to Eric Hoffer,

> It is the true believer's ability to "shut his eyes and stop his ears" to facts that do not deserve to be either seen or heard which is the source of his unequaled fortitude and constancy. He cannot be frightened by danger nor disheartened by obstacles nor baffled by contradictions because he denies their existence. . . . And it is the certitude of his infallible doctrine that renders the true believer impervious to the uncertainties, surprises and the unpleasant realities of the world around him.[11]

Since we still contend with the lies of the Noble South and the Lost Cause, I write this book as my "first duty." Immanuel Kant wrote: "It is a duty to tell the truth. The concept of duty is inseparable from concept of right. A duty is what one being corresponds to the rights of another. Where there are no rights there are no duties. To tell the truth is thus a duty: but only in respect to one who has the rights to the truth."[12]

One editorial note: in my use of quotations from the period, I have not for the most part attempted to modernize the English, correct the grammar, or change the colloquialisms used by the original writers. Likewise, I have left in the racist terms— which I find absolutely reprehensible—that the original writers used, in order that the reader experiences the truth of just how deeply racism was embedded in an often mythical American history. I do it also to remind us why many, especially American Blacks and other racial minorities, are offended when those terms are used today. By doing this I preserve the unvarnished history, and I allow the reader to have an emotional gut reaction that they might not otherwise have. A healthy revulsion regarding the crimes against humanity committed by our ancestors is not a bad thing; perhaps if it were taught and received in the proper spirit, we might have the kind of personal reckoning that would prevent their repetition. Unfortunately, it seems that given the resistance to anything approaching it in our current political and religious climate, such a reckoning will be unlikely for at least another generation.

ACKNOWLEDGMENTS

This is my first book, and being a historian without a PhD I kind of feel like a journeyman minor leaguer who makes the major leagues and then has his work praised by historians and civil rights pioneers who are Hall-of-Famers. I am in awe of being where I am today. To paraphrase Yogi Berra, "I'm a lucky guy . . . and I want to thank everyone for making this night necessary."

There are a lot of them, far too many to name here, and I promise not to be like some Oscar winner who has to be ushered off of the stage. Likewise, I don't want this to be boring. So first I want to thank the librarian in third grade who failed me on a test of the Dewey decimal system. She made me mad enough to spend almost every minute that I wasn't in class reading history, geography, science and technology, and biographies. In fact I thank all the librarians both in school and public libraries who tolerated my insatiable need to read the reference books that I couldn't check out and was too honest to steal, even though I am sure that they knew that I was often cutting class to be there. God bless all of you.

I also want to thank my parents, especially my late father, for seeking the truth and having the courage to speak it to people in power. As Leslie Nielsen, playing Lt. Frank Drebin, said in *The Naked Gun 2 ½: The Smell of Fear*, "Truth hurts. Maybe not as much as jumping on a bicycle with the seat missing, but it hurts." That is kind of what that book is about: telling the truth about the roles that slavery, racism, race-based politics, and religion have played in our complex history, and, since I first began writing while teaching at the Joint Forces Staff College five years following my return from Iraq, the role of these subjects in the wars we were fighting in the Middle East—but I digress; this is about acknowledging those who made this book possible.

I want to thank my tenth grade geometry teacher who made the subject so painfully boring that I cut class to go to the library and read the history books in the reference section four days a week and come in on Friday to barely pass all of my quizzes and tests—but that was the 1970s, and she was intent on retirement, not on keeping track of a nerdy Navy Junior Reserve Officers Training Corps (NJROTC) miscreant like me. I wasn't like I was out smoking dope or getting in trouble; I was in the library exploring the past, which happened to include subjects like this one. Likewise, during my junior high and high school years, I spent almost every day of my summer vacations in the city library, going through the reference sections and checking out books every day. Libraries were a place of exploring the places that I could not visit and events that I could not go back in time to observe.

I need to thank my teachers and professors in junior high, high school, college, and seminary. Mr. Silvagio at Stockton Junior High who in ninth grade let me do independent research and occasionally teach certain topics related to the Civil War and World War II in class. Then there was the late Lt. Cdr. J. E. Breedlove, my NJROTC instructor who taught me about honor, the necessity of telling the truth even if it was dangerous, and to critically analyze historic and scientific evidence when studying naval history and leaders.

In college I benefited from the wisdom and knowledge of my professors of history and anthropology at San Joaquin Delta College. First there is Delmar McComb who taught American history and Western civilization. He has remained some forty years later a man whom I could call on at any time. He was my instructor in a history research and writing course that emphasized field research and study in order to write a small book that would be published by the college and placed in the city library. I studied the former USS *Potomac*, Franklin Delano Roosevelt's presidential yacht, which was then in Stockton, allegedly to be restored. I was able to explore every compartment in the ship and research everything about her, President Roosevelt, her connection to events like the Atlantic Charter, and her postpresidential service, including her time as the property of Elvis Presley. After that she was repossessed, used as cover for a drug smuggling operation, and then sank at her berth in San Francisco. She was then raised, repaired, and restored to her presidential service condition and based at Oakland's Jack London Square provides historic tours of San Francisco Bay.

Charles Block brought me to question myths of California history and made going to the locations where California history was made a key part of our learning experience. Through him I found the importance of walking the ground, which has permeated my life ever since. Mike Sealy brought the importance of anthropology into my studies of history.

When I transferred to California State University at Northridge, my primary professor for my junior and senior years and a year of graduate study was the late Helmut Haeussler. I was fortunate to know him. His family emigrated to the United States when he was seven years old; he studied at the University of Wisconsin and enlisted in the army, where he served as an intelligence specialist, interpreter, and interrogator in the Eighty-Second Airborne Division. Instead of going back to the States at the end of the war, he remained to serve as an interpreter and interrogator for the duration of the Nuremberg trials. As a result his classes on German history, Hitler's Germany, and the Holocaust, as well as the vast amount of independent study and research courses where he served as my professor and mentor, introduced me to digging deep into the truth. In this case it was German anti-

Semitism, political and historical myths, and Holocaust denial. The most important thing that I learned far later was that the Confederacy shared a similar history to that of Hitler's Germany: it was a race-based authoritarian state that was willing to fight to the death for its myths of racial superiority and the enslavement or systematic exploitation and extermination of inferior races.

In seminary it was my Church history professor Doyle Young and systematic theology professor Thomas Kilpatrick who forced me to research and seek answers rather than just recite their denomination's doctrines. They exposed me to the complicity of the Southern Baptists in slavery and secession, and the importance of the absolute separation of church and state as taught by early English and American Baptists, something that current Baptists and evangelicals should relearn.

After seminary my clinical pastoral education supervisor at Parkland Memorial Hospital taught me the value of a hermeneutic of superstition, in not taking everything said to me as a chaplain at face value. He taught me that everybody lies, long before *House, MD* made that statement famous. I have kept that in mind in all of my research ever since, even when reading the mail of long-dead people.

After over a decade and a half of deployments and war, I began to reexamine the history of the Holocaust as well as that of American slavery even before I joined the faculty of the Joint Forces Staff College. There I taught mid-grade and senior military officers, as well as members of other federal agencies and Allied nations, the subject of military ethics, inheriting the leadership of the *Gettysburg Staff Ride* from Vardel Nesmith, who retired around the time of my arrival. Dr. Nesmith knew the campaign and battle inside and out, and I was fortunate to be on his final staff ride. At eighty years old he was an inspiration. I only wish that he had published his work. But other faculty, including Rear Adm. John Smith, academic dean Patricia Strait, and too many faculty members to be mentioned here encouraged my work. One told me, "Steve, you are a historian masquerading as a chaplain—not that there is anything wrong with that."

My final acknowledgments are to my tireless literary agent, Roger Williams, who pushed out the manuscript to publishers for three years until Potomac Books of University of Nebraska Press decided to accept it in late 2020. All their staff have been amazing to work with. I have to give a special mention to my copyeditor, Emily Shelton, whose advice and work helped make the book even better than my final manuscript. To paraphrase Stephen King: "To write is human, to edit divine, and, to copyedit, to be divine on steroids." Working with her was an eye-opening experience that will make me a better writer and editor. I have also been inspired and encouraged by many historians, educators, and friends, including James McPherson, Charles Dew, Charles Reagan Wilson, Thomas Patrick Daly, John Fea, Joe Levin, Rick Herrera, Margaret Sankey, LeeAnna Keith, Kris White, Vic Hackley, Allen Guelzo, Elizabeth Varon, Eric Foner, Gary Gallagher, Stephanie McCurry, Gary Wills, Timothy Snyder, the late James Loewen, and many others.

Finally, last but certainly not the least important, is my long-suffering wife, Judy, who has endured every hardship of military and ministry life, yet remained faithful and encouraging, and who helped edit so many of my papers in seminary, my master's thesis in military history, and parts of this manuscript. She has encouraged me to tell the truth even when I received death threats from white nationalists over the past decade. I am sure that the publication of this book will not convert but enrage them. So I end this by quoting Abraham Lincoln, who said, "The best thing about the future is that it comes a day at a time."

Peace.

MINE EYES HAVE SEEN THE GLORY

1

America's Original Sin

Slavery from 1619 to 1790

apt. John Colyn Jope was master of the privateer *White Lion*. She was an English ship with an English crew sailing under a letter of marque from Maurice, Prince of Orange. She and another privateer captured the Portuguese slave ship *Sao Joao Bautista* in the Caribbean. *Sao Joao Bautista* left Luanda, Angola, with 350 slaves, who were chained and shackled side by side below deck. There was little ventilation and scant water or food. Many died, and the survivors were barely alive. Sailors from the privateers boarded the ship and divided the slaves between them. Captain Jope set sail for the Jamestown Colony.

Jamestown, founded in 1607, struggled to survive. The Powhatan nation outnumbered and hemmed them in. In 1610 some colonists defected, knowing that they would be welcomed. Capt. John Smith sought revenge and sent soldiers after them. The soldiers attacked the Powhatan settlement and massacred 15 or 16 in the attack. They burned the village, cut down growing corn, then "took the queen of the tribe and her children into boats, and ended up throwing the children overboard and shoteing owtt their Braynes in the water." They then stabbed the queen to death.[1] Twelve years later, with English settlements growing, the Powhatans attacked and massacred 347 men women and children.

The colonists could not coexist with or enslave the Powhatan, so the colony's leaders decided to exterminate them. They destroyed Powhatan villages and massacred the inhabitants.

FIG. 1. *Landing Negroes at Jamestown from Dutch Man-of-War, 1619.*
Howard Pyle (1853–1911); signed "H. Pyle" in lower left-hand corner.
Harper's Monthly Magazine, January 1901, 172.

But no matter how many the English killed, they were unable to grow corn for sustenance, or tobacco to ship to England.

War made their problems worse. The Powhatans were willing to trade, intermingle, and live peacefully with them, but the colonists refused, even when the Powhatan's aging chief begged them, admitting the hopelessness of his cause and his weariness of war. The colony needed laborers to plant and harvest corn and tobacco, but their skilled workers and artisans found manual labor so beneath them that they would not work unless forced.

The English were latecomers to the slave trade. The Por-

America's Original Sin

tuguese began trading slaves in the 1400s and built bases in Africa to protect their operations, which initially involved the transport of slaves to Europe. The Portuguese and Spanish expanded the trade to the Americas. Christopher Columbus brought about three hundred African slaves to Hispaniola on his second voyage.

> By 1619, more than a century and a half after the Portuguese first traded slaves on the African coast, European ships had brought a million Africans to colonies and plantations in the Americas and force them to labor as slaves. Trade through the West African ports continued for nearly three hundred years. The Europeans made more than 54,000 voyages to trade in human beings and sent at least ten to twelve million Africans to the Americas.[2]

The arrival of the *White Lion* came as an unexpected surprise when she dropped anchor in Jamestown in August 1619. Historian J. Saunders Redding describes what it what it must have looked like to the colonists:

> Sails furled, flag drooping at her rounded stern, she rode the ide in from the sea. She was a strange ship, indeed, by all accounts, a frightening ship, a ship of mystery. Whether she was a trader, privateer, or man-of-war no one knows. Through her bulwarks black-mouthed cannon yawned. The flag she flew was Dutch: her crew motley. Her port of call, an English settlement, Jamestown in the colony of Virginia. She came, she traded, and shortly thereafter was gone. Probably no ship in history has carried a more portentous freight. Her cargo? 20 slaves.[3]

This beginning was a watershed moment: once the import of slaves began, it took 191 years to end and 243 years—culminating in the bloodiest war in U.S. history—to abolish. It took another century for Blacks to receive civil and voting rights protections, only to see them rolled back. As James Loewen writes, "Race is the sharpest and deepest division in American life."[4]

In a letter to Edwin Sandys, treasurer of the Virginia Company of London, Jamestown Colony's secretary, John Rolfe, whose first wife was Pocahontas, detailed the arrival of the *White Lion*:

> About the latter end of August, a Dutch man of Warr of the burden of a 160 tunnes arrived at Point-Comfort, the Comandors name Capt Jope, his Pilott for the West Indies one Mr Marmaduke an Englishman. They mett with the Treasurer in the West Indyes, and determined to hold consort shipp hetherward, but in their passage lost one the other. He brought not any thing but 20. and odd Negroes, which the Governor and Cape Marchant bought for victualls (whereof he was in greate need as he pretended) at the best and easyest rates they could.[5]

The Rising Tide: The Importation of Slaves

The twenty Africans who landed at Jamestown were the first of a rising tide in England's North American colonies. It started as a trickle, but with the exception of times of war between the French and British, the American Revolution, the Napoleonic Wars, and the ban on slavery in 1807 and 1808, it grew with nearly every decade, especially after 1680, when the English colonies

> underwent a massive shift from indentured to slave labor. Some simple statistics drive home that point. Between 1680 and 1750 the proportion of blacks increased from 7 percent to 44 percent in Virginia and from 17 percent to 61 percent in South Carolina "They Import so many Negros hither" wrote Virginia planter William Byrd II in 1736, "that I fear this colony will at some time or another will be called by the Name of New Guinea."[6]

Between 1619 and 1860, some 472,382 African slaves came to North America; another 56,597 came from other locations in the Americas.[7] Between 1619 and 1860, 528,979 people arrived as slaves. For the first hundred years, the majority were transported to the Chesapeake and Tidewater, but by the mid-1700s

America's Original Sin

the Carolinas and Georgia were importing more slaves than the Virginia settlements.

Jamestown was a special case as England's first North American colony. It needed labor, and the need was magnified by the people who settled there. Edmund Morgan has noted that "of the first 105 settlers who started the colony, 36 could be classified as gentlemen. In the first 'supply' of an additional 120 settlers, 28 were gentlemen, and in the second supply of 70, again 28 were gentlemen."[8] The problem was that neither gentlemen nor their families or servants worked, because English gentlemen did not work. Captain John Smith "complained that he could never get any real work from more than thirty out of two hundred, and he later argued that of all the people sent to Virginia, a hundred good laborers 'would have done more than a thousand of those who went.'"[9]

The "skilled workers" who came to Jamestown did not have the requisite skills. Without work and above labor, they joined the loafers of the gentlemanly class. Consequently, the settlers called for indentured servants. However, indentured servants often proved to be more trouble than they were worth. Every indentured servant entitled his master to more land to grow crops. These servants helped sustain the colony, and the tobacco they worked provided a valuable cash export. But, being white, they could escape to another colony and be free.

Depending on where they landed, indentured servants faced radically different work conditions. Some who went to "New England engaged in (or were taught) skilled trades such as black smithing and carpentry. . . . [Most], however, wound up as agricultural laborers, especially in the tobacco fields of Maryland and Virginia."[10] Nearly half of them in the South died before their indenture was over, due to brutal working conditions and the harsh climate.

The number of indentured whites dropped in 1680 as landowners discovered that slaves were a better investment. They were indentured for life and endured harsh conditions better than Europeans. However, being Black, they could not escape to a new place without people assuming that they were escaped slaves.

The Tidewater—the area of Maryland and southeastern Virginia running down the Potomac River to the Chesapeake Bay to northeastern North Carolina—required the most slaves. The climate of the Tidewater was perfect for growing labor-intensive but high-value tobacco. Edmond Morgon described the toils of those involved in tobacco farming: "Tobacco occupied a man nine months of the year, what with sowing, transplanting, weeding, topping, striking, and curing. The remainder of the year he cleared land, fenced, and cut boards for casks."[11] English settlements expanded up the York and James Rivers, as well as the branches of the Elizabeth River. The area had several natural harbors, which made it a hub for the slave trade and the export of tobacco. The Pamlico Sound in North Carolina was important, while the Outer Banks provided a sheltered waterway for the transport of goods and slaves.

Plantation owners were at the top of the social pyramid. Their "semi feudal model required a vast and permanent underclass to play the role of serfs on whose toil the entire system depended."[12] When the number of white indentured servants dried up in the 1680s, slave traders offered a solution: an abundant supply of African slaves. Since slavery was not yet legalized, the colonies enacted laws limiting the rights of Blacks. Among the first was a 1639 decree that "'all persons except Negroes' were to get arms and ammunition—probably to fight off Indians."[13] Before the legalization of slavery, indentured whites and Blacks had similar rights, although Blacks tended to be punished more harshly. They

> lived together, worked together, played together, and sometimes slept together, and ran away together. Landowning Virginians feared the "giddy multitude" (or rabble) for this was a rather heterogeneous lower-class group of lower-class group of servants and slaves, blacks and whites that seemed to threaten the social order. Until the very end of the seventeenth cen-

America's Original Sin

tury, blacks remained too few in number to constitute a distinct threat of their own.[14]

But, even then, industrious Blacks could climb out of their situation, as they did in Northampton County, Virginia, between 1664 and 1667. By 1667 "at least 13 (out of 101) blacks became free landowners, most through self-purchase; in 1668, some 29 percent of the blacks in the county were free."[15] Using methods they used to provide workers for the sugar plantations of Barbados, slave traders procured "people of African descent who would become the permanent property of their masters, as would their children and grandchildren."[16]

Laws were passed to separate the races when slavery was legalized. A "spate of legislation passed during the subsequent century regulated the condition of the growing population of black slaves and set them off from white settlers."[17] Whites who had grown up, worked, socialized, and suffered with Blacks began to view them as less than human. Soon "most white Americans came to assume that blacks were so different from whites that slavery was their natural state."[18] Over the coming decades, perception became reality. Former white indentured servants moved west and south, where many bought land and slaves to build their own empires in the Deep South and Greater Appalachia.

The laws were nefarious and applied to both enslaved and free Blacks. There were no precedents in English law, as England had no slaves, so each colony passed their own. Some were more benign than others, but Virginia provides an example of the way these laws became progressively more restrictive and lethal for Blacks. "In 1661 a law was passed in Virginia that 'in case any English servant shall run away in the company of Negroes' would have to give special service for extra years to the master of the runaway Negro. In 1691 Virginia provided for the banishment of any 'white man or woman being free who shall intermarry with a negro, mulatoo, or Indian man or woman bond or free.'"[19]

In 1662 Virginia enacted a law forcing the children of Black women to serve according to the condition of the mother; in 1667 another "declaring that baptisme of slaves doth not exempt them from bondage"; in 1669 "an act about the casuall killing of slaves"; and in 1680 "an Act for preventing Negroes Insurrections." In 1682 laws were instituted preventing interracial marriage or other relationships leading to the procreation of mixed-race children, a law excusing slave owners from legal action if they killed a slave, and codified punishments for infractions committed by slaves. In 1705 the Virginia Assembly declared "all Negro, mulatto, and Indian slaves . . . shall be held to be real estate and reinforced the stipulation that if a slave was killed the master would remain free of all punishment . . . 'as if such accident never happened.'" In 1723 Virginia enacted laws preventing Blacks from meeting, forbidding them weapons, limiting the increase of free Blacks to those born to free Blacks or those granted freedom by the legislature, and denying Blacks the right to vote. In 1750 Virginia defined the distinctions between slaves and servants and relegated all slaves to the status of property.[20]

Laws were adjusted to serve plantation owners. The Virginia House of Burgesses and Governor had every reason strengthen them, as did the founders of South Carolina and other colonies in the Deep South. South Carolina's plantation oligarchs created a caste system that so disenfranchised poor whites, they controlled all aspects of government. They imported "shipload after shipload of enslaved Africans whom they treated as fixed possessions, like their tools or cattle, thereby introducing chattel slavery to the English world."[21]

The Ordeal of Slaves from Africa to North America

Africans taken from their homelands in West Central Africa—the so-called Gold Coast—endured brutal dehumanization. This type of slavery was unlike that experienced by Africans at the hands of other Africans, or practiced in the Greco-Roman

World. In Europe and Africa slavery existed in its "patriarchal form in which the slave commonly worked to satisfy the needs of a relatively small group of people—as a domestic servant, artisans, scribe, teacher, or warrior. The arrangement thus grew out of and expressed a very primitive division of labor. Generally regarded as subordinate members of the group to which they were attached, slaves generally retained a variety of personal rights; their unfree status, often temporary, was rarely heritable."[22]

Slaves in Africa "tended to be criminals, debtors and captives in war." They retained rights including owning property and marrying nonslaves. Likewise, "it was not uncommon for slaves in Africa to acquire their freedom."[23] For Africans slavery was just another form of labor, not an economic and social institution.

The plight of slaves destined for European colonies began in West Africa. Initially, most sold into slavery were from Upper and Lower Guinea, the Congo, Angola, and Gambia. Many were prisoners of war or criminals being punished for minor infractions or indebtedness. Over time prisoners of war were the majority, and they became an "increasingly the objects of such conflicts, which approached the crudest level of pure slave-raiding adventures."[24] Thus, Africans became complicit in a vile trade they did not completely understand and that offered them short-term benefits. Cooperation in the seventeenth and eighteenth centuries did not stop Europeans from using brutal military force to colonize Africa in the nineteenth century. Captives were driven from the interior by whites and their African partners. Those destined for European colonies were subjected to conditions designed to crush their spirits. As Peter Kolchin has described them, "The marches to the coast, sometimes for 1,000 miles, with people shackled around the neck, under whip and gun, were death marches, in which two of every five blacks died."[25]

In the beginning traders had

considerable cooperation from African rulers and merchants; although ultimately traffic in slaves was based on force, and the transatlantic trade led to increasing disruption of African societies, Africans—no strangers themselves to slavery joined Europeans in buying and selling human property. The African slave trade involved considerable partnership, albeit of an increasingly unequal nature, between white and black traders. Over time the growing demand for slaves put increasing strains on established sources of supply, the trade's center shifted southward and reached deeper into The African interior.[26]

The captives became part of the transatlantic slave trade, in which manufactured goods from Europe including weaponry, furniture, beers, and ales were transported from England to African forts, where African traders exchanged the captives for European goods. Jessica Glickman writes:

As exploration and technological development opened the world, economic markets and goods expanded as well becoming increasingly more specialized. Economic expansion of the slave trade, led to the development of merchant houses dedicated solely to economic enterprises on the African coast. The more the market increased, the more voyages per year ventured to Africa and the Americas. To obtain the greatest profit margins merchants built ships that would best utilize the wind and currents leading to shorter journeys and lower slave mortality rates.[27]

The Voyage to Hell: Slave Ships and the Middle Passage

Once at the forts, slaves were branded, sold, and shoved into pens or cages, they were held with slaves from other regions who did not share a common language until slave ships came for them. John Barbot, a French Huguenot working as an agent for the French Royal African Company in 1678 and 1682, described the conditions of the Gold Coast in the late 1600s:

America's Original Sin

As the slaves came down to Fida from the inland country, they are put into a booth or prison . . . near the beach, and when the Europeans are to receive them, they are brought out onto a large plain, where the ship's surgeons examine every part of every one of them, to the smallest member, men and women being stark naked. . . . Such are allowed good and sound are set on one side . . . marked on the breast with a red-hot iron, imprinting the mark of the French, English, or Dutch companies. . . . The branded slaves after this are returned to their former booths where they await shipment, sometimes 10–15 days.[28]

When a ship arrived, slaves were transported in canoes to the ships. "One slave trader reported that the Negroes 'were so willful and loath to leave their own country, that they have often leap'd out of the canoes, boat and ship into the sea, and kept underwater until they were drowned.'"[29] Olaudah Equiano, the eleven-year-old son, of a village chief, survived and learned enough English to write about it: "I was now persuaded that I had gotten into a world of bad spirits and that they were going to kill me."[30]

Slaves began their voyage "in despondency and panic."[31] But the conditions during the Middle Passage were worse. Slaves were packed into ships and shackled to the decks with as little as ten inches between them the next deck.

Slavery in the Printed Word

The Brooke-type slave ship was commonly used in the mid-to-late 1700s. They could carry more than six hundred slaves on a single trip. Displacing 250 to 300 tons, they were not the largest or smallest ships serving the slave trade. Jessica Glickman describes how William Alfred detailed these ships in an article published in 1778:

As an established painter Alfred was someone who could portray the truth of the slave ship. He was curious to see the condition of slave ships after the establishment of the Dolban Act

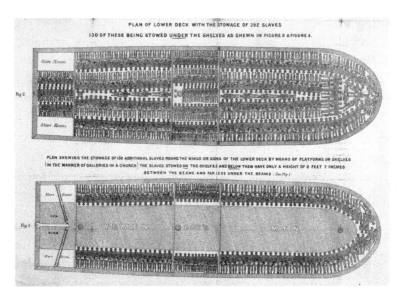

FIG. 2. Plan of British slave ship *Brookes* under the Regulated Slave Trade Act of 1788, by William Alfred, Plymouth Chapter of the Society for Effecting the Abolition of the Slave, ca. 1788. Courtesy of the Library of Congress, LC-USZ62-44000.

in Britain in 1788 (also known as the Slave Trade Act of 1788) The Dolban Act stated that: for every three tons of draft in a vessel only. After visiting the wharf in Liverpool Alfred studied stowage diagrams and completed the image of the plan view of the ship.[32]

A British naval lieutenant accompanied Alfred to take down the specifics of the ship's dimensions. Alfred published the description without appeals to emotion or religion; he sought to show a slave ship in stark forensic detail. It appeared in the popular *American Museum,* was reprinted widely in newspapers, magazines, and books, and used by English and American abolitionists who wanted to end slavery and the slave trade. Most slave ships, however, were built for other purposes and converted for the slave trade. All could carry large numbers of slaves and were well armed and fast, which made them useful again once they had been retired from the slave trade. Since the slave trade spanned three centuries of naval architecture and ship design, many types of ships were used. When the slave trade was banned, speedy Baltimore Clipper types were modified to carry slaves. Before it was banned, such small ships would have been impractical, as they could not carry enough slaves to be profitable; however, speed was essential for outrunning British and American warships enforcing the ban, and they were faster than most warships. Modifications to ships of all types converted to the slave trade included larger kitchen facilities, additional portholes, and sails that deflected air back down to the ship's hatches, to maintain the flow of air below decks.

Regardless of type all had a similar feature: "The holds of slave ships were intensely crowded with rough pallets fitted between decks so that slaves were stacked one atop another. . . . Ships being repurposed for the trade had decks added so that the provisions and cargo could be separate, and more room was designated for the slaves themselves."[33] All were armed with cannons for use against raiders. They also had bulkheads, swivel-mounted cannons, and small arms to allow the crew to put down slave revolts.

Aboard slave ships male prisoners were separated from women and children and loaded like cordwood. One slave trader wrote, "The height, sometimes between decks, was only 18 inches, so that the unfortunate human beings could not be turned around, or even on their sides . . . and here they are usually chained to the decks by their necks and legs."[34] Even under the best conditions, the Middle Passage voyage proved deadly for both slaves and crew members. Under good conditions a ship could reach Barbados in three weeks, but, if complications arose, the voyage could take two months.

The Zong Massacre

If provisions were short, or disease had spread, the ship's master could take drastic action to cover any financial losses, since insurers treated the deaths of slaves in transit differently. In

1781, "when running short of water, the captain of the Zong ordered 132 Africans thrown overboard, because his insurance covered death from drowning but not from starvation."[35]

Venture Smith, a survivor of the Middle Passage, described his voyage in detail: "After an ordinary passage, except great mortality from small pox, which broke out on board, we arrived at the island of Barbadoes: but when we reached it, there were found out of the two hundred and sixty that sailed from Africa, not more than two hundred alive. These were all sold, except for myself and three more, to the planters there."[36] Olaudah Diallo wrote:

> The stench of the hold while we were on the coast was so intolerably loathsome, that it was dangerous to remain there for any time, and some of us had been permitted to stay on the deck for the fresh air; but now that the whole ship's cargo were confined together, it became absolutely pestilential. The closeness of the place, and the heat of the climate, added to the number in the ship, which was so crowded that each had scarcely room to turn himself, almost suffocated us. This produced copious perspirations, so that the air soon became unfit for respiration, from a variety of loathsome smells, and brought on a sickness among the slaves, of which many died, thus falling victims to the improvident avarice, as I may call it, of their purchasers. This wretched situation was again aggravated by the galling of the chains, now become insupportable. . . . The shrieks of the women, and the groans of the dying, rendered the whole a scene of horror almost inconceivable.[37]

Most survivors landed in Barbados while others were transported to the Tidewater or South Carolina. An estimated 1 million to 1.5 million of 10 to 12 million slaves died aboard these hell ships.

When slaves were offloaded, the ships were loaded with raw materials, including tobacco and sugarcane for the trip back to England, where the cycle started anew. This continued until the American Revolution, after which a new triangle developed, with American slave traders traveling from Boston, Philadelphia, and New York on ships loaded with rum, tobacco, and manufactured goods to Africa, where they were exchanged for slaves, returning to the West Indies to trade some slaves for sugarcane before continuing to the United States. The slaves were offloaded, and the cycle began again.

The transatlantic slave trade continued until Parliament and Congress abolished it in 1807 and 1808. The Royal Navy and U.S. Navy established antislave trade patrols in their home waters and off the Gold coast. But smugglers made slave runs to the United States and the Confederacy until the end of the Civil War.

Coming to America: Plantation Slavery and Descent into the Abyss

The form of slavery in the English plantation system was unlike any other in history. Because it supplied low-cost workers for labor-intensive industries such as tobacco, forestry, land clearance, sugarcane, rice, cotton, iron ore, and milling, slavery was essential to the colonies. In the beginning the Tidewater was the center of colonial slavery, but, "by the mid-eighteenth century, slaves accounted for nearly half of Virginia's population. Virginia had changed from a 'society with slaves' in which slavery was one system of labor among others to a 'slave society where the institution stood at the center of the economic process. Slavery formed the basis of the economy, and the foundation of a powerful local ruling class, in the entire region from Maryland south to Georgia.'"[38]

In South Carolina and the Deep South, slavery took on a more brutal character. Unlike the founders of the Northern, mid-Atlantic, and Tidewater colonies, the leaders of South Carolina came from Barbados, not England. Barbados was "the richest and most horrifying society in the English speaking world."[39] The reputation was well earned: "Sugar Production required such strenuous labor that men would not willingly undertake it. Sugar planters . . . had to drive their workers much harder than tobacco planters did. Richard Ligon in the late 1640s was scandalized to see how Barbados planters beat their servants to get the work out of them."[40]

The oligarchs of Barbados set such onerous property requirements for voting that they completely controlled the colony. Many returned to England so wealthy that they purchased estates, received knighthoods, and developed "the most effective colonial lobbying force at the English Parliament ensuring that the imperial tax burden was shifted to others."[41] No amount of indentured labor could meet their demand, so Barbadian rulers implemented the cruelest kind slavery. The sugarcane industry had a massive mortality rate, so slaves had to be replaced far more often than in the Tidewater, "at the rate of about 6 percent a year. It is estimated that between 1640 and 1700 264,000 slaves were imported into the British West Indies. The total black population in 1700 was about 100,000. In the next century, between 1712 and 1762 the importation of 150,000 slaves increased the Black population by only 28,000."[42]

South Carolina's rulers did not "seek to replicate rural English manor life" like their Tidewater neighbors, "or to create a religious utopia in the American wilderness," as settlers in New England attempted; "instead it was a near-carbon copy of the West Indian slave state these Barbadians had left behind, a place even then notorious for its inhumanity."[43] They brought their slaves to South Carolina and pushed them to the limits of human endurance. Slavery was South Carolina's foundation, not an afterthought or later development: "No other Southern regime was as committed to eighteenth-century elitist principles or so resistant to nineteenth-century egalitarian republicanism. South Carolina's balance of despotism and democracy, tipping unusually far toward old-fashioned imperiousness, gave its masters strong confidence in contained, hierarchical dominance, and special contempt for sprawling, leveling, 'mobocracies.'"[44] It was different from other colonies because it

> was a slave society from the outset. . . . "Carolina in ye West
> Indies" was, by its founding charter, a preserve of the West

Indian slave lords. Written by John Locke, the charter provided that a planter could be given 150 acres of land for every servant or slave he brought to the colony; soon a handful of Barbadians owned much of the land in lowland South Carolina creating an oligarchy worthy of the slave states of Ancient Greece.[45]

The heavily wooded swamps and marshlands along South Carolina's coast were terrible ground for growing sugarcane or tobacco. The planters needed a crop suited to the swamps and the streams that meandered through them. The answer to the planter's conundrum was rice, but rice required clearing swamps and building rice paddies, which were expensive to cultivate and harvest, requiring more slaves. Thousands were imported, soon amounting to over a quarter of the population. Slaves cleared tangled forests and constructed rice paddies in the swamps, and more were always needed:

> Because rice fields were so expensive to develop, rice plantations cost several times more than settled than elsewhere in North America. Posh estates, once expensively developed, became almost useless without expensive slaves. Vulnerable sluices and dams had to be incessantly repaired. Thick soils had to be constantly weeded. Golden grains had to be quickly harvested. Compared with the tobacco and cotton black belts, rice swamps, even after development, never attracted as many yeoman nonslaveholders.[46]

Because of its need for slave labor, "South Carolina did not experience a reduction in demand for (or the delivery of) slaves in the third-quarter of the eighteenth century. Throughout the pre-Revolutionary period, slaves constituted a majority of the colony's population—a large majority in the coastal rice producing parishes."[47] About 80 to 85 percent of the populations of these parishes were slaves laboring under inhuman conditions. The planters netted great profits from the golden grain, but "then they secured supplemental treasure. British merchants craved indigo a putrid dye that turned garments a rich blue. Planters found that the hills above unseemly swamps could spawn the unseemly stuff. Slaves, when not needed in the rice fields could be forced to endure the stench, double Massa's profits and help finance Massa's vacation."[48]

Slaveholders pushed into Georgia, then into the future states of Alabama and Mississippi, which became the South's Black Belt, in which slaves far outnumbered whites, and the plantation system flourished through the cultivation of cotton. The Deep South "had a black supermajority and an enormous slave mortality rate, meaning that thousands had to be imported every year to replace those who had died. Blacks in the Deep South were far more likely to live in concentrated numbers in isolation from whites."[49]

South Carolina became the model for the Deep South states. Its oligarchs were

> unusually independent of their plantations but unusually dependent on slaves. Thus did a region 85% Black when whites were most resident become 98% black when white businesses were most active. No other North American Black Belt was remotely this black—a spur to South Carolinas white's special ferocity. No other southern rulers were such idle aristocrats—a source of South Carolina's oligarchic hauteur. . . . Either slavery would enable masters to frolic beyond killing fevers, or emancipation gentlemen feared, would force whites to flee a slaughtering unprecedented in this deadly era.[50]

Slave owners continued to push the institution west, and their "expansionist ambitions would put it on a collision course with its Yankee rivals, triggering military, social, and political conflicts that continue to plague the United States to this day."[51]

America's Original Sin

2

A Struggle to the Death

War Cannot Be Separated from Ideology, Politics, or Religion

The American Civil War was a portent of modern war. Technology increased destructiveness, and opponents moved from limited to near-total warfare. Divided by conflicting concepts of liberty and interpretations of their shared religion, Northerners and Southerners waged a brutal ideological battle undergirded by religion. J .F. C. Fuller rightly called it a struggle to the death:

> At length on 12th April, the tension could no longer bear the strain. Contrary to instructions, in the morning twilight, and when none could see clearly what the historic day portended, the Confederates in Charleston bombarded Fort Sumter and the thunder of their guns announced that the argument of a generation should be decided by the ordeal of war. A war, not between two antagonistic political parties, but a struggle to the death between two societies, each championing a different civilization.[1]

Yet, for another century, defeated Southerners continued the war by other means. A growing white nationalist movement continues to champion the racist goals of the Confederacy even to the point of launching an armed assault on the Capitol. Understanding how racist ideology and religion impact domestic politics and foreign affairs matters. The Civil War era demonstrates how religiously based racism can influence policy, economics, military strategy, and paramilitary terrorism. By studying it leaders can begin to understand how seemingly innocuous conflicts become cataclysmic events with disastrous consequences.

The English military theorist Colin Gray downplays the importance of religion and ideology in future conflicts. He writes, "It is true that, with the minor and probably temporary exception of some aberrant fanatical brands of Islam, ideology has ceased to be a factor in interstate relations . . . However, it is unlikely in the extreme that future Warfare, beyond the challenges posed by some Islamic insurgents, will be driven or even influenced by ideology."[2] However, Gray's argument is ahistorical. Since the Enlightenment many thinkers have minimized the role of ideology in conflicts; according to Edward Luttwak, "as for religious motivations in secular affairs, they were disregarded or dismissed as mere pretense."[3]

While many policy makers, strategists, and futurists minimize its importance religious racial or ethnic ideology still wields influence around the world, including in the United States. As Luttwak writes, "Despite the prevailing intellectual, religion, of course, [has] continued to play a large role in the lives of individuals and societies."[4] Many conservative American Christians want to seize earthly power to usher in the Kingdom of God.[5] Thus "sectarianism keeps claiming center stage, reinforcing or reinventing the radical aspects of American religion."[6] Much is related to the often-symbiotic nature of American faith and democracy.

How Mass Movements Influence Policy

The power of nationalistic, racist, and religious mass movements to capture the hopes of discontented people is underestimated. The 2016 election showed how Donald Trump, a sociopathic and racist candidate who demonstrated none of the moral values traditionally sought after by Conservative Christians played on their fears and hate to win the election. Over 80 percent of Conservative Christians voted for Trump because he exploited their fantasy of establishing a Christian theocracy. Evangelical Christian John Fea of Messiah University argues that "evangelical support for Donald Trump is rooted in nostalgia for a bygone Christian Goden age."[7] As Eric Hoffer writes, "Faith in a holy cause is to a considerable extent a substitute for the lost faith in ourselves."[8] Interestingly, Fea concurs with Hoffer, noting that "most evangelicals were willing to ignore his moral lapses he had, in their way of thinking, the correct policy proposals."[9] We will see closely how these policies represent those of other racist authoritarian states, including the antebellum and Jim Crow South, and likewise, just how much the imagined myth of a bygone Christian golden age is mirrored by the Islamic State of Iraq and the Levant, better known as ISIS, and their belief in reestablishing the golden age of the Caliphate.

Some right-wing movements in Europe that combine religious, nationalistic, and racist attitudes are gaining control in or challenging established democracies where all leaders preach the security of an illusionary past. Dismissing these movements is dangerous. The fear, disappointment, and hatred of people can be manipulated to persuade them to follow an allegedly holy cause. Such mass movements are attractive to the desperate and discouraged, whom authoritarian leaders take advantage of by appealing to their fear and discontent, even provoking otherwise-decent people to violence.

When a mass movement captures the reins of government by channeling fear, they gain support by identifying a devil and offering salvation. According to Hoffer,

> When our individual interests and prospects do not seem worth living for, we are in desperate need of something apart from us to live for. All forms of dedication, devotion, loyalty and self-surrender are in essence a desperate clinging to something which must give worth and meaning to our futile, spoiled lives. Hence the embracing of a substitute will be necessarily passionate and extreme. We can have unqualified confidence in ourselves, but the faith that we have in our nation, religion or holy cause has to be extravagant and uncompromising.[10]

U.S. Supreme Court Justice Robert Jackson, who prosecuted the major Nazi war criminals, warned of fanatical mass movements in his ruling in *American Communications Association v. Douds*, "In our country are evangelists and zealots of many different political, economic and religious persuasions whose fanatical conviction is that all thought is divinely classified into two kinds—that which is their own and that which is false and dangerous."[11]

People process information through their worldview. Many secular or tolerant religious people fail to appreciate the motivations of people who follow political or religious mass movements. As Barbara Tuchman writes, "When information is relayed to policy-makers they respond in terms of what is already inside their heads and consequently make policy less to fit the facts than to fit the notions and intentions formed out of the mental baggage that has accumulated in their minds since childhood."[12]

Many Western leaders fail to realize the importance of the the primal elements of human nature, including religion. Perhaps it is uncomfortable to admit that Western culture is a product of religious beliefs that have informed politics, philosophy, ethics, law, economics, and racial attitudes for two millennia. Maybe we are justifiably appalled and embarrassed by our ancestors' brutality in using religion or racism to punish heretics and unbelievers, and to incite war as justification to subjugate or exterminate "subhuman" peoples.

Samuel Huntington argues that cultural divides will be more important than economics or political ideology in the coming decades: "The revitalization of religion throughout much of the world is reinforcing these cultural differences."[13] This is not only true along the fault lines between the West and Islam, but in the United States, where a form of militant Christianity wages a political culture war against secular humanism and liberalism.

The Army and Marine Counterinsurgency Field Manual discusses how Muslim insurgent groups use the religious ideal of the "caliphate" to create a narrative. Like the Noble South and the Lost Cause, they present myth as history; they promise the caliphate's restoration as an ideal to attract supporters because many Muslims believe a restored caliphate "produces a positive image of the golden age of Islamic civilization."[14] The regeneration of a mythical golden age appeals to religious people of every faith or culture.

Many Americans are unaware of how our ancestors used Christianity to justify subjugating other peoples. Christianity was the heart of the Puritan ideal of a city on a hill, a concept that undergirded the later belief in manifest destiny,which led to genocidal wars against the peoples of our First Nations, the Mexican-American War, and the romantic myths of the Noble South and the Lost Cause. The combination of toxic political ideology, religious fervor, and a belief that one's views mirror God's can be used by the faithful to fuel fires of extremism and to blind followers to the evils they commit in the name of their God.

Manifest Destiny and American Exceptionalism

U.S. foreign policy has nearly always reflected a quasi-religious belief in the importance of spreading Christianity and democracy around the world, but not always in that order. The United States was an anomaly among nations in the early 1800s: while the number of active churchgoers shrank in Europe as the number of skeptics rose as scientific advances and Enlightenment philosophies permeated continental and colonial elites, in the United States the importance of Christianity only grew.

The Second Great Awakening helped shape and define the United States. By the "mid-nineteenth century, from North to South, was arguably Christendom's most churchgoing nation, bristling with exceptionalist faith and millennial conviction."[15] This was especially true of American Protestantism, where "church attendance rose by a factor of ten over the period 1800 to 1860, comfortably outstripping population growth. Twice as many Protestants went to church at the end of this period as the beginning."[16]

Evangelical Christianity came to settlers in vast revival and camp meetings that lasted weeks and were attended by tens of thousands. The Cane Ridge Revival of 1801 was the first and most important. Organized by Presbyterians, Baptists and Methodists joined in the preaching. These revivals became a fixture of frontier life and aided churches willing to "present the message as simply as possible, and to use preachers with little or no education."[17] The awakening made the Methodists and the Baptists the nation's largest denominations. Camp meetings emphasized emotion rather than reason and appealed to common people. The revivals "not only became the defining mark of American religion but also played a central role in the nation's developing identity, independence, and democratic principles."[18]

The West was viewed as a place "where Americans could start over again and the nation fulfill its destiny as a democratic, Protestant beacon to inspire peoples and nations. By conquering a continent with their people and ideals, Americans would conquer the world."[19] The westward expansion satiated the need for territorial conquest and missionary zeal to transform the country and world in the image of Evangelical Christianity. "Manifest Destiny" was the idea of New York journalist John O'Sullivan, who wrote, "Manifest Destiny had ordained America to 'establish on the earth the moral dignity and salvation of man,' to disseminate its principles, both religious and secular abroad."[20]

New York journalist Horace Greeley said, "Go West, young man," and, by the millions, they went. Americans poured westward, into the heartland of the Deep South, the Old Northwest, and across the Mississippi, moving along the great rivers that formed the tributaries of new territories. As they did the "population of the region west of the Appalachians grew nearly three times as fast as the original thirteen states" and "during that era a new state entered the Union on the average of three years."[21]

Nationalism and Evangelical Christianity combined to create the revolutionary idea that America was a "'model republic' that could redeem the people of the world from tyranny."[22] But this belief was infused by white supremacy that fueled the genocide of America's First Nations. James McPherson writes, "By 1850 the white man's diseases and wars had reduced the Indian population north of the Rio Grande to half of the estimated million who had lived there two centuries earlier. In the United States all but a few thousand Indians had been pushed west of the Mississippi."[23] The radical racism of some Americans was expressed in pseudoscientific writings to "find biological evidence of white supremacy," and "radical nationalism" cast Mexicans as an unassimilable mixed race "with considerable Indian and some black blood." The Mexican-American War "would not redeem them, but would hasten the day when they, like American Indians, would fade away."[24]

U.S. Foreign Policy: From Founding to Freedom Agenda

Evangelical Christianity and manifest destiny helped shape domestic policy during the westward movement, while also motivating and justifying America's entry onto the world stage as a colonial and economic power. They undergirded foreign policy as the nation claimed Hawaii, and various Spanish possessions. Woodrow Wilson used the concepts to justify both America's entry into World War I and the taking of former German Pacific colonies after the war's end.

Manifest destiny is still seen in the pronouncements of American politicians, pundits, and preachers who believe that that Christianity and Americanism, religious or not, is essential to American exceptionalism. This was used to justify American foreign policy for over a century, including the factions of former president George W. Bush, as Bush referenced in his 2003 State of the Union address: "Freedom is the right of every person and the future of every nation. The liberty we prize is not America's gift to the world, it is God's gift to humanity."[25] Bush frequently used biblical allusions to justifying the morality of undeclared war. By doing this "Bush made himself a bridge between politics and religion for a large portion of his electorate, cementing their fidelity."[26]

Bush's Christian faith and belief in the ideal of democracy combined to create a mismatch of policy ends and means. Former Israeli ambassador to the United States and historian Michael Oren writes:

> Not inadvertently did Bush describe the struggle against Islamic terror as a "crusade to rid the world of evildoers." Along with this religious zeal, however, the president espoused the secular fervor of the neoconservatives . . . who preached the Middle East's redemption through democracy. The merging of the sacred and the civic missions in Bush's mind placed him firmly in the Wilsonian tradition. But the same faith that deflected Wilson from entering hostilities in the Middle East spurred Bush in favor of war.[27]

Christianity and democracy motivated American Christians to became missionaries, establishing churches, colleges, schools, and hospitals overseas in their zeal to spread the Gospel. U.S. diplomats ensured their protection using the navy, which added fuel to their zeal, and missionaries frequently called upon the government for help. In 1842 Dabney Carr, American ambassador to the Ottoman Empire, "declared his intention to protect the missionaries 'to the full extent of [his] power,' if necessary, 'by calling on the whole of the American squadron in the Mediterranean to Beyrout.'"[28] Such episodes were repeated in the Middle East, Asia, the Pacific, Central America, South America, and Africa again and again.

Pres. William McKinley provided an excellent example of the merger of Christianity and American exceptionalism when he annexed the Philippines in 1898, leading to war in 1899. After Adm. George Dewey's Asiatic Squadron defeated the Spanish fleet at Manila Bay, McKinley wrestled with annexing the Philippines. He was a sincere Christian, and, according to him, he sought God's counsel about what to do. But his faith

A Struggle to the Death

was also built on the Christianity of manifest destiny. He told a group of ministers visiting the White House:

> Before you go I would like to say a word about the Philippine business. . . . The truth is I didn't want the Philippines, and when they came to us as a gift from the gods, I did not know what to do with them. . . . I sought counsel from all sides— Democrat as well as Republican—but got little help. . . . I walked the floor of the White House night after night until midnight; and I am not ashamed to tell you, gentlemen, that I went down on my knees and prayed Almighty God for guidance more than one night. And late one night it came to me this way—I don't know how it was but it came.[29]

As Barbara Tuchman tells McKinley's story, "He went down on his knees, according to his own account, and 'prayed to Almighty God for light and guidance.' He was accordingly guided to conclude 'that there was nothing left to do for us but to take them all, and to educate the Filipinos. And uplift and civilize and Christianize them, by God's grace to do the very best we could by them, as our fellowmen for whom Christ died.'"[30]

McKinley couched his actions in faith, but his decision to annex the archipelago was pure imperialism. He first proposed occupying a few islands and Manila, saying their return to Spain was dishonorable. He rejected a proposal by Carl Schurz to "turn over the Philippines as a mandate to a small power, such as Belgium or Holland, so the United States could remain 'the great neutral power in the world,'[31] or to cede them to France or Germany because 'that would be bad for business.' He rejected Filipino self-rule, as 'they were unfit for self-government.'"[32]

It is doubtful McKinley heard God's voice, but he followed the lead of his adviser's imperialist and business views and annexed the Philippines. He believed it was a rational course of action, but McKinley "was a man made to be managed," considered spineless by Speaker of the House Thomas Reed, who said, "McKinley has no more backbone than a chocolate éclair."[33]

McKinley decided on an imperialism motivated by military and business interests as a gateway to Asian markets, with a bow to Protestant clergy, who saw "a possible enlargement of missionary opportunities."[34] The opportunity was more than McKinley could resist: "The taste of empire was on the lips of politicians and business interests throughout the country. Racism, paternalism, and the talk of money mingled with the talk of destiny."[35] There was brief resistance in Congress, led by William Jennings Bryant, but it crumbled when Bryant, his eyes on the presidency, embraced imperialism.

The peace treaty with Spain sparked an insurrection led by Filipino revolutionary Emilio Aguinaldo. Aguinaldo resisted Spanish rule years before American intervention and was not about to trade one imperialist power for another. The war lasted nearly three years. American forces committed numerous atrocities against defenseless civilians, calling them insurgents and terrorists in official reports and media releases. Some Americans viewed what was done to the Filipinos as a stain on our national honor. Mark Twain wrote, "There must be two Americas: one that sets the captive free, and one that takes a once-captive's new freedom away from him and picks a quarrel with him with nothing to found it on; then kills him to get his land."[36]

Walter Hines Page, editor of the *Atlantic Monthly* at the time, argued that Americans would face greater difficulties by annexing the Philippines.

> A change in our national policy may change our very character . . . and we are now playing with the great forces that may shape the future of the world—almost before we know it. . . . Before we knew the meaning of foreign possessions in a world ever growing more jealous, we have found ourselves the captors of islands in both great oceans; and from our home staying policy of yesterday we are brought face to face with world-wide

A Struggle to the Death

forces in Asia as well as Europe, which seem to be working, by the opening of the Orient, for one of the greatest challenges in human history. . . . And to nobody has the change come more unexpectedly than ourselves. Has it come without our knowing the meaning of it?[37]

Almost instantly America went from a nation of shopkeepers to an imperial power, and most Americans did not realize the consequences. Manifest destiny and American exceptionalism triumphed, and a new day dawned. Subsequent generations of American leaders invoked spreading "freedom and democracy" around the world.

The Continuing Challenge

Since Americans embraced manifest destiny, it has fought wars both great and small. In each one the nation's leaders have invoked God's blessing. Sometimes the United States stood for righteous causes, especially in World War II. However, many were no less than the criminal exploitation of weak nations. Marine general Smedley Butler, a veteran of many small wars,

> spent 33 years and four months in active military service and during that period I spent most of my time as a high class muscle man for Big Business, for Wall Street and the bankers. In short, I was a racketeer, a gangster for capitalism. I helped make Mexico and especially Tampico safe for American oil interests in 1914. . . . In China in 1927 I helped see to it that Standard Oil went on its way unmolested. Looking back on it, I might have given Al Capone a few hints. The best he could do was to operate his racket in three districts. I operated on three continents.[38]

In the war against Al-Qaeda after September 11, 2001, religious motivations contributed to the American response. But long-term occupations in Afghanistan and Iraq against intractable, religiously based insurgencies ended the fantasy that war would be short and sweet: American forces engaged in extended counterinsurgency campaigns against people who resented occupation. In almost every case, American leaders ignored the cultural, religious, or ideological dimensions of the conflicts before taking military action.

For a moment in time, some American military leaders considered the religious and ideological motivations of their opponents. As stated in *The Army and Marine Counterinsurgency Field Manual,* "Ideology provides a prism, including a vocabulary and analytical categories, through which followers perceive their situation."[39] But its lessons were not applied at the higher levels of policy, because many American policy makers see militant Islamic ideology "as a set of theological issues rather than as a profoundly political influence in public life."[40]

Yet, after two decades of unremitting war against enemies for whom religion is at the center of their politics, Americans still misunderstand their Muslim opponents. However, many American Christians do the same as the Islamists, by participating in domestic terrorism, with the view that their faith is more important to their identity than citizenship.[41] Nations created during the postcolonial era "continue to see religion, clan, ethnicity, and other such factors as the markers of community identity."[42] Most of these nations are artificial constructs whose borders were drawn by colonial powers that disregarded these people's cultures, which "have been shaped and forged by centuries of history, by the physical environment, and by their evolving traditions and belief systems."[43]

Americans seldom see the interconnectedness of religion and resistance; in this we err. Even if the religious cause is built upon mythology, it is often—in the words of baseball legend Reggie Jackson—the "straw that stirs the drink." To ignore, minimize, or misunderstand that fact dooms our efforts. This is not simply an Islamic problem. It a part of our history from colonial times to now, and it is true around the world. Such policies will continue because people hate looking in the mirror. It is uncomfortable to admit that the face that we see is

A Struggle to the Death

like that of our opponents, especially those who are willing to commit genocide in the name of their God.

Regardless of whether one's worldview is religious or secular, we have to honestly examine ourselves, our culture, and our history if we are to understand the world that lies beyond us. If we do not, the result will be more tragedy. Relegating a country's crimes to the past blinds people to those crimes and causes us to misread events in tragic ways. As Barbara Tuchman so eloquently puts it, "Strong prejudices and an ill-informed mind are hazardous to government, and when combined with a position of power even more so."[44]

To understand the motivations of people motivated by barbaric religious beliefs, we need only examine our not-too-distant past. This must include the ideas of manifest destiny, American exceptionalism, and "America First," as well as our religious justifications for imperialism, genocide, unjust wars, slavery, and the religious and pseudoscientific beliefs that justified the black codes and Jim Crow.

3

I Hate Them with Perfect Hatred

Religion, Ideology, and Modern War

Political ideology founded upon religion has motivated of some of the most brutal wars in history. The belief that God sanctions the killing of his enemies is nothing new; as the Psalmist wrote, "I hate them with perfect hatred; I count them mine enemies" (Ps. 139:22). As such enemies of God are deserving of His wrath. Thus, any sense of moderation is lost as the executors of God's vengeance commit unimaginable atrocities.

Nationalism buttressed by religion was at the heart of the Thirty Years' War waged by France and Sweden against the Hapsburg Empire. The war devastated Germany, and the longer it lasted the less the initial religious reasons that provoked it mattered. In its final and most destructive stages, to France's Cardinal Richelieu, Spain's Ferdinand II, Gustavus Adolphus of Sweden, and generals like Wallenstein the war had "become little more than an excuse in a struggle for power."[1]

J. F. C. Fuller has described the Thirty Years' War as a "gladiatorial encounter for power. The peasants revolted, soldiers alone could live, and soon hordes of starving women and children, like packs of jackals followed the armies. . . . Battles were won and lost and entire regions depopulated, until, slowly out of the agony, the desire for peace gathered Protestants and Catholics about the Emperor and a semblance of national unity began to appear."[2] Though the opponents were motivated by religious nationalism, "the war devastated Europe while failing to settle the matter of religion."[3]

In 1648 the Peace of Westphalia restored calm to a war-ravaged Europe as the Second English Civil War began, with equally brutal religious hated motivating the opponents, especially Oliver Cromwell. But, on the continent, European nations influenced by Hugo Grotius and other proponents of mitigating the destruction of war limited the influence of churches. As a result, modern secular states developed, and people scarred by war began to doubt the doctrines of churches that sanctioned its barbarity. This led to the rise of the Enlightenment, classic liberalism, and humanism, but in the new United States Protestant Christianity remained deeply ingrained in culture and politics.

German military theorist Carl von Clausewitz, a veteran of the Napoleonic Wars, understood the effects of the moral and spiritual concerns inherent in policy, writing "that the aim of policy is to unify and reconcile all aspects of internal administration as well as of spiritual values, and whatever else the moral philosopher may care to add."[4] He comprehended that when politics become extreme ideology can evoke primal hatred between people, and a war can come dangerously close to the abstract concept of total war. Clausewitz writes: "The more powerful and inspiring the motives for war, the more they affect the belligerent nations and the fiercer the tensions that precede the outbreak, the closer will war approach its abstract concept, the more important will be the destruction of the enemy, the more closely will the military and the political objects of war coincide, and the more military and less political will war appear to be."[5]

Religious Awakening, Prosperity, and Sectional Conflict

The American Civil War was the first modern war, a revolution in military affairs, and more. It tapped the primal urges of humanity, including deep-rooted expressions of religiously based justifications for violence leveled at Blacks before, during, and after. Many Americans accepted racism and white supremacy backed by pseudoscience and buttressed by the Bible, which allowed people, even opponents of slavery, to believe that whites were racially superior to Blacks.

Protestant Christianity had a major influence on developing American nationalism, and "secular and religious motifs were woven into the belief that America had a unique role in bringing the Kingdom of God to this world."[6] This was pervasive throughout the country. Northerners tended to apply it to the nation, but for Southerners it became an article of faith in themselves. The South was the New Israel, with the North, corrupted by foreigners, industrialists, and abolitionists—apostates who had abandoned the faith.

The Second Great Awakening: The Protestant Bible Belt

The Second Great Awakening was of great importance in the years leading up to the Civil War, and it would not have been possible had the Framers of the Constitution not included the establishment and free exercise of religion clauses in the First Amendment. Prior to the revolution, barely 10 percent of Americans regularly attended church, mainly because of the established state churches in many of the colonies. The end of state churches gave previously oppressed denominations such as the Baptists, Presbysterians, and Methodists the chance to worship in peace and expand, especially in the South and the West. During this period American Protestantism shifted from educated New England to less educated frontier preachers. It began at Cane Ridge, Kentucky, in August 1801 and was a watershed event that forever changed Protestantism in America; revival meetings became a staple of evangelical Protestantism for nearly two hundred years. Historian Charles Reagan Wilson notes that the evangelical belief system, "accompanied by a conservative orthodoxy of doctrine," grew in influence.[7] Conservative evangelicals labeled progressive evangelicals of New England as liberals and Christian abolitionists heretics. The outcome has been described by British evangelical theologian Alistair McGrath as "the transformation of antebellum America and the emergence of the Protestant 'Bible Belt.'"[8]

I Hate Them with Perfect Hatred

Revivalist preachers like Presbyterian Charles Finney, who gave up his career as a lawyer to preach the evangelical message became one of the most effective preachers of the time. The evangelical message resonated among people of less education and fewer means, many of whom migrated west into new territories and states. Since the "conditions on the frontier were different, the awakening now became more emotional and less intellectual, to the point that it became anti-intellectual."[9]

Protestant Christianity had a major influence on the nation, but it took on different characteristics in the North and the South. In the North it brought a greater sense of social consciousness, and believers worked for causes that required political solutions, such as abolition and women's and workers' rights. In the South personal piety, rugged individualism, and the defense of slavery took precedence. Northern and Southern clergy tended to agree on doctrinal matters. At the country's founding the "major denominations in the South—Baptist, Methodist, Presbyterian and Episcopalian—differed little in their approach to such sectional issues as slavery, abolition, or the protection of Southern rights."[10] But as the North and South drifted apart over sectional issues Southern evangelicalism provided a "transcendent framework for southern nationalism."[11]

The Second Great Awakening broadly affected society. In the antebellum era "religious and social life became intertwined for many Americans" and fueled "expectations about an advancing Kingdom of God in America, a millennial optimism that became even more prominent as religion assumed a larger role in American society and culture."[12] It also helped inspire the idea of manifest destiny. "Under the Manifest Destiny banner," writes Michael Oren, "the nation's population of 17 million inexorably fanned out across the existing twenty-six states and into the vast territories west of the Mississippi and north of the Rio Grande, uprooting Native American communities and ousting the Mexicans on route."[13]

In the 1840s religion entered politics. By the time of the

1844 presidential campaign between Democrat James K. Polk and Whig Henry Clay, "both parties had gotten religion. The fissures among evangelicals, the conflicts between Protestants and Catholics, the slavery debates, and the settlement of the West placed religion at the forefront of American politics."[14] But the short-lived Liberty Party outdid both the Whigs and Democrats as "God's Party," as "America's first Christian political party. Its conventions resembled revivals." One of its leaders recalled: "The Liberty Party, unlike any other in history was founded on moral principles—on the Bible, originating a contest not only against slavery but against atheistic politics from which the Divine law was excluded."[15] The Liberty Party had a dramatic effect on the election, its vote "total reached 65,000, possibly costing Clay the electoral votes of both New York and Michigan and therewith the election."[16]

Northern evangelical Protestantism provided authoritative justification for social causes. It influenced labor safety, workplace reforms, and the establishment of women's rights organizations; alleviated suffering through voluntary medical societies; and protected exploited women who worked as prostitutes. However, there was a dark side to parts of evangelicalism in the North and South: its religious justifications for slavery, the Mexican-American War, the wars against America's First Nations,[17] and the conviction that manifest destiny "meant removing (or eliminating) those who stood in the way."[18]

As tensions grew over the institution of slavery and other sectional issues, many Americans, especially Southerners, sought biblical justification to show that God was on their side. Political economist Thomas R. Dew combined political economics with an extreme form of Calvinism that equated prosperity with the blessing of God. The conquest of Mexico and annexation of the West convinced many Americans that God approved of both, as well as for slavery's expansion in the South. In 1832 Dew "published a description of the economic and moral necessity of slavery. Other southerners saw in Dew's proslavery a confirmation of their certainty that southern slaveholders were 'sanctioned by divine authority' and 'the great law of necessity.'"[19] Southerners, especially wealthy planters, embraced Dew's theological and economic tenants as King Cotton enriched them beyond their wildest imaginations.

Southerners' claims that slavery was ordained by God "represented not just a deeply held conviction, but a sound ideological strategy for an evangelical age, a posture designed to win support both at home and abroad."[20] Proslavery clergymen bestowed "divine sanction on the South's peculiar institution," using the Bible and natural law to marry slavery to Christianity. Southern intransigence regarding its slave-based economy encompassed government, economics, and human rights.[21] It brought the South into conflict with Northern ideas of free labor and capitalism. But the conflicts were based on a common religion, the same God, Bible, and understanding of America's role in the world, being chosen by God to spread the Christian faith:

> Whatever their differences over such matters as slavery and political preaching, both sides read their Bibles in remarkably similar ways. Ministers had long seen the American republic as a new Israel, and Confederate preachers viewed the southern nation in roughly the same light. The relentless, often careless application of biblical typologies to national problems, the ransacking of scripture for parallels between ancient and modern events produced a nationalistic theology at once bizarre, inspiring and dangerous. Favorite scripture passages offered meaning and hope to a people in the darkest hours and, at the same time, justified remorseless bloodshed.[22]

Both sides appealed to the Puritan concept of a city set on a hill, one of America's most ingrained beliefs of the antebellum era: "Before the war citizens on both sides had proclaimed America to be God's vehicle for the redemption of mankind, glorifying the tale of biblical Israel and the post-independence United States as strikingly similar and analogous."[23] Both sides claimed to be legitimate heirs of the Puritan mantle, which contributed to their inflexibility.

During the Civil War, racism, religion and ideology combined with differing conceptions of humanity and human rights created a perfect maelstrom for the terror of total war. British military historian and strategist J. F. C. Fuller might have described it the best: "Like the total wars of the twentieth century, it was preceded by years of violent propaganda, which, long before the war, had obliterated all sense of moderation and awakened in the contending parties the primitive spirit of tribal fanaticism."[24] Thus, when war came, "soldiers from both North and South marched off to fight sure that their cause was God's cause."[25]

Far from being irrational, the actions and behaviors of politicians in the North and the South were completely rational, based on their beliefs and the opinions of their opponents. The "South's fears of territorial and economic strangulation and the North's fears of a slave power conspiracy are anything but irrational, and only someone who refuses to think through the evidence available to Americans in the 1850s would find either of them at all illogical."[26]

How Religion Influences Policy, Politics, and War

Religiously based political ideology is powerful, an "often intractable force that can be quite unresponsive to all the instrumentalities of state power, let alone the instrumentalities of foreign policy."[27] Fear motivated the political intransigence over slavery and economics in both the North and the South. The politics of fear eschewed compromise and defied the efforts of men who fought for it. By the 1850s violent and bloody battles were raging in Kansas regarding its admission to the Union.

Religious beliefs were instrumental in forming a distinctive Southern sectional identity in the decades preceding the war. This "invested the political conflict between the North and South with a profound religious significance, helping create a culture that made secession possible. It established a moral consensus on slavery that could encompass differing political views and unite a disharmonious South behind the ban-

I Hate Them with Perfect Hatred

ner of disunion."[28] Slavery was an intractable moral cause for both abolitionists and proslavery partisans. To many people these positions became as much of an unalterable article of faith as the godhead; thus "religious faith itself became a key part of the war's unfolding story for countless Americans."[29] As Fuller writes of the war's religious undergirding, "As a moral issue, the dispute acquired a religious significance, state rights becoming wrapped up in a politico-mysticism, which defying definition, could be argued for ever without any hope of a final conclusion being reached."[30]

Therefore, one cannot separate the military campaigns and battles of the Civil War from the religious beliefs and ideology that informed the politics of both sides and why the foundational ideological and theological presuppositions of both cannot be ignored. Their competing worldviews, saturated by Christian nationalism, helped to cause the war and to make it so destructive.

The Civil War transformed the nation more than any other event in American history. In the words of James McPherson, "Five generations have passed, and we are still trying to measure that influence. The long shadow of the Civil War continues to affect us today. More Americans died in that conflict than all the other wars this country has fought combined, right through the latest casualty reports from Afghanistan."[31] For men and women entrusted with planning national defense and conducting military campaigns today, understanding why wars are fought—particularly their religious and ideological contexts—is important in ways they and their political leaders often fail to appreciate. Colin Gray writes, "Wars are not free floating events, sufficient unto themselves as objects for study and understanding. Instead, they are entirely the product of their contexts."[32] As Gray notes, the context of conflict matter far more than most people and leaders want to admit.

The American Civil War illuminates other civil wars as well, which have commonalities that transcend race, culture, and geography. Studying our Civil War provides a perspective on our history from which we can gain insight both into other nation's civil wars and the current divisions in America. It shows how people who share a common language, culture, religion, and history can wage war against each other in the most brutal manner: "Policy and strategy will be influenced by the cultural preferences bequeathed by a community's interpretation of its history as well as by its geopolitical-geostrategic context."[33]

For political leaders and military and law enforcement planners, these contexts are particularly important. Understanding history can show us how racially based religious or political ideology can result in wars whose atrocities beggar the imagination. Racial beliefs were central components of Nazi campaigns in Eastern Europe and the Soviet Union, permeating German military campaigns and their administration of conquered lands. No branch of the German military, police, or civil administration in occupied Poland or Russia was exempt from guilt in the crimes committed by the Nazi regime. Likewise, Stalin used the imagery of Mother Russia nationalism and recruited Orthodox clergy to support his war.

This issues a chilling warning of the consequences awaiting Americans caught up in hate-filled ideologies that dehumanize their opponents, foreign or domestic, and the tragedy that awaits. In Germany the internal and external checks that governed the moral behavior of individuals and nation failed. Caught up in the Nazi system, Germans abandoned the norms of law and decency and committed hitherto unimaginable crimes with effects still visible today. Nazi propagandists pointed out American hypocrisy in condemning Nazi actions and beliefs while Americans "presided over a society where blacks were subjected to demeaning Jim Crow laws segregation was imposed even in the military establishment, racial discrimination extended to the defense industries, and immigration policy was severely biased against all nonwhites": a warning to leaders that their nation's history can be used against them.[34]

Studying the racial, political, and ideological aspects of our

I Hate Them with Perfect Hatred

Civil War—especially slavery—helps us not only understand it but other conflicts where primal passions and hatreds overcome rational policy. This will remain the case: "As more and more people become urbanized, educated, and politicized, they will search more consciously and systematically for identity and ideology. Prescribed means and customs increasingly will come into question, and religion will be enhanced as an answer to problems. In many Third World countries, disappointment with the post-independence course of events and the discrediting of radical and Marxist philosophies may result in religiously based or influenced political views filling the vacuum."[35] Americans often try to separate the economic, strategic, military and geopolitical factors of conflicts from religious or ideological factors, as if each exists in some sort of hermetically sealed environment. For "decades, the prevailing school of thought underlying U.S. foreign policy has assumed religion would be a declining factor in the life of states and international affairs."[36] But considering the past three decades, our experience fighting Muslim radicals proves this to be a fallacy of the greatest magnitude. Political leaders, policy makers, and religious extremists are often last to see their error. In an address to the Foreign Service Association in 1973, Barbara Tuchman noted that "policy is formed by preconceptions, by long standing biases. When information is relayed to policymakers they respond in terms of what is already inside their heads and consequently make policy less to fit the facts than to fit the notions and intentions formed out of the mental baggage that has accumulated in their minds since childhood."[37]

The results of this failure are alarming. Governments and world bodies have had a tremendously hard time dealing with opponents for whom political boundaries are irrelevant when compared to the ethnic and religious loyalties that transcend them. Some may have learned this lesson, but it may be too late to save the Middle East, Eastern Europe, and maybe even ourselves from our collective blindness to history.

4

They Shall Be Your Bond-Men Forever

Human Beings as Property

J ust after the Confederate victory at the First Battle of Bull Run, Rev. John T. Wightman, a Methodist from South Carolina, drew the conclusion that God was on the side of the South because it upheld His command regarding slaves:

> The hand of God has severed this nation to perpetuate this institution, and is inflicting judicial punishment on a people who have attempted to violate his decree: "Ham shall be a bondsman." The war is the servant of slavery. As the atmosphere may become so loaded with pestilence that nothing but lightening can disinfect it, so the sword seems necessary to draw off the bloated lust of the North, restore political vigor, and impart a serener aspect to her policy.[1]

The theological and ideological clash between Northern Abolitionists and Southern proponents of slavery is key, due to the effects of slavery on much of American economic and social life.

Slavery replaced indentured servanthood by 1690, and Africans who arrived as slaves were considered property for life. By the mid-1600s the colonies enacted laws concerning indentured servitude and slavery: "Initially, most laws passed concerned indentured servants but around the middle of the seventeenth century, colonial laws began to reflect differences between indentured servants and slaves. More important, the laws began to differentiate between races: the association of

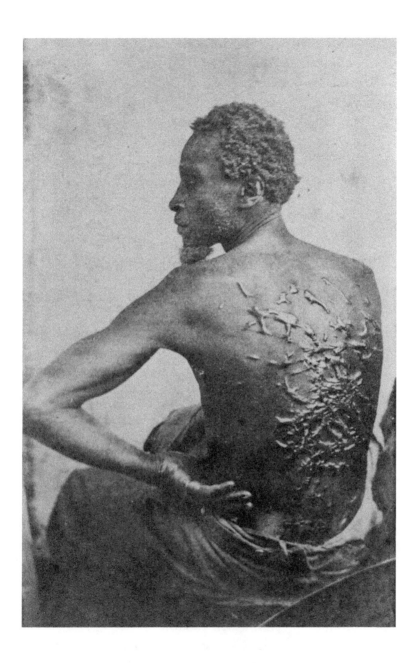

FIG. 3. An escaped slave named Peter Gordon showing his scarred back
at a medical examination in Baton Rouge, Louisiana. 1863. Courtesy of
the Library of Congress, Civil War Collection, LC-DIG-ppmsca-54375.

"servitude for natural life" with people of African descent became common."[2]

African slavery arose to meet the economic need of planters for laborers on their vast plantations as "the number of arriving whites, whether free or indentured servants (under four to seven year contracts) was not enough to meet the demand of the plantations."[3] Thus began the mass importation of African slaves "from the fifteenth through the eighteenth century, fully six of seven people who arrived in the Americas were African slaves."[4]

The lot of slaves at the hands of their European masters was significantly worse than in Africa, where slavery was one of a number of forms of labor, and where slaves usually "worked within the households of their owners and had well-defined rights, such as possessing property and marrying free persons. It was not uncommon for slaves in Africa to acquire their freedom."[5] This was not the case in European colonies because the ancient practices of slavery were now wedded to "the large scale, profit oriented production of commodities for a capitalist world market."[6]

American slavery differed radically from that practiced in Europe during antiquity—the kind described in the New Testament that was so critical to its Christian defenders. In those cultures slaves were more like the serfs of Europe and had certain protections. John Newton, the English slave trader who became an abolitionist and composed the hymn "Amazing Grace," wrote, "The state of slavery among these barbarous peoples we esteem them, is much milder than in our own colonies. For as, they have no land in high cultivation, like our West India plantations, and therefore no call for that excessive, unremitted labor, which exhausts our slaves: so. On the other hand, no man is permitted to draw blood from a slave."[7]

American slavery was characterized by massive greed and desire for profit at a terrible human cost, "the frenzy for limitless profit that comes from capitalistic agriculture; the reduction of the slave to less than human status by the use of race hatred, with that relentless clarity based on color, where white was master, black was slave."[8] The South Carolina Constitution of 1669 deemed that such a relationship between white masters and their African slaves was "necessary for society to function satisfactorily." In all dealings with "Negro slaves," it provided, "every Freeman of Carolina shall have absolute power and authority."[9] Slavery took a particularly evil form in the Americas, on the plantation. European colonial plantations produced commodities for the worldwide market, and owners viewed their slaves as commodities to be bought and sold in order to increase profits.

Most slaves were subjected to exceptionally cruel treatment: scant clothing, poor food, long hours laboring in all types of weather, from the miserable heat and humidity of the summer, to the often-freezing conditions of winter. Slaves suffered from terrible diseases including mosquito-borne viruses and fevers. Many died from want of medical care. Punishments were meted out by overseers for the smallest infractions, real or perceived. Methodist pastor Horace Moulton testified about his five years in Georgia from 1817 to 1824. What he saw horrified him. He recounted the punishments slaves received at the hands of their masters or overseers:

> The ordinary mode of punishing the slaves is both cruel and barbarous. Master seldom, if ever, try to govern their slaves by moral influence, but by whipping, kicking, beating, starving, branding, cat-hauling, loading with irons, imprisoning, or by some other mode of torturing. They often boast of having invented some new form of torture, by which they have "tamed the rascals." What passes for a moderate flogging in the south is horribly cruel. . . . The masters say that what we call ordinary flogging will not subdue the slaves; hence the most cruel and barbarous scourings ever with messed by man are daily and hourly inflicted on those naked bodies of these miserable bondmen, not by masters and negro-drivers only, but by the constables in the common markets and jailers in their yards.[10]

The British colonies in North America had a higher birth rate than other English colonies, ensuring it was not completely dependent on the importation of new slaves. Other colonies had to import slaves because they worked them to death. The higher birth rates meant the "600,000 to 650,000 Africans some 6 percent of brought from Africa to the new world" experienced almost normal population growth.[11] By 1810 there were 1.1 million slaves in the United States, which, even with the ban on the slave trade, grew to over 4 million by 1863.

The plantation system allowed owners to amass "large concentrations of laborers under the control of a single owner produced goods—sugar, tobacco, rice and cotton—for the free market."[12] The African slave trade was a major part of the world economy, and "slave labor played an indispensable part in its rapid growth."[13] In the case of the United States, this was paradoxical, as the country was founded and supposedly dedicated to the proposition that all men are created equal. Thus, by the 1820s, slavery became a source of conflict. Northern businesses prospered from slavery, and "New York merchants, working with their representatives in Southern ports and smaller towns purchased and shipped most of the cotton crop."[14] Economic gain prompted the growth in slavery, and slaves were essential for profit. As such, "[the] first mass consumer goods in international trade were produced by slaves—sugar, rice, coffee, and tobacco. The profits from slavery stimulated the rise of British ports such as Liverpool and Bristol, and the growth of banking, shipbuilding, and insurance, and helped to finance the early industrial revolution. The centrality of slavery to the British empire encouraged an ever-closer identification of freedom with whites and slavery with blacks."[15]

The Constitution, Slavery, and Disunion

The founders of the new nation had to deal with the existing institution of slavery and threat to the Union that the slavery posed: disunion. The founders feared it more than anything.

Slavery was an institution that powerful slave-owning politicians were uncomfortable maintaining; Patrick Henry wrote a powerful letter condemning the practice of slavery, even while admitting his complicity in it, on January 13, 1773:

> Is it not amazing that at a time when the rights of humanity are defined and understood with precision, in a country, above all others, fond of liberty—that in such an age and such a country we find men professing a religion the most humane, mild, meek, gentle and generous, adopting a principle as repugnant to humanity as it is inconsistent with the Bible and destructive to liberty? Every thinking, honest man rejects it in speculation. How few, in practice, from conscientious motives![16]

George Washington wrote in 1786 that "there is not a man living . . . who wishes more sincerely than I do, to see a plan for the gradual abolition of it."[17]

Slavery divided state representatives as they gathered for the Constitutional Convention in 1787. Washington confided to a friend that "he could 'foresee no greater evil than disunion,'" and now the "mere discussion of slavery was poisoning the atmosphere."[18] James Madison recognized this and noted that states differed "primarily from the effects of their having or not having slaves."[19]

The issue came to a head around the issue of how states would be represented in the federal government and how to balance the power between federal and state governments. To achieve such balance, they divided Congress into two houses: the House of Representatives, whose members were directly elected by voters, with the state's population determining the number of representatives, and the Senate, whose members were elected by state legislatures. Each state had two senators, regardless of population. The division of the legislature "enabled the individual states to retain a large measure of their jealously guarded autonomy."[20] Eligible voters in each state elected the president by electing "electors" to the Electoral College, where each state was given a number of electors equal to its representation in the Senate and the House of Representatives.

The question was about which people would be counted as citizens. Northerners wanted to base the number on the white population, while Southerners wanted to "swell their power by counting both white citizens and black non-citizens."[21] Such a ploy would have given Southerners much more power in the House of Representatives, which gave them disproportionately more power when coupled with the fact that every state had two senators, regardless of their population.

Gouverneur Morris believed if slaves "were human enough to boost the representation of the Southern States . . . they should be treated as persons and not property in the South."[22] To bridge the sectional divide the convention passed the three-fifths compromise, which permitted slaves to be counted as three-fifths of a person in slave states, allowing them more House members and electors than they would have if only free men were counted.

The compromise stipulated that a state's congressional delegation, its electors in the Electoral College, and its tax burden was determined by population. Free persons counted as a full person, and the three-fifths of all other persons were slaves, who were considered property and not people. The avoidance of the use of the words "slaves" or "slavery" was crafted to make the document acceptable to Northern delegations.

This was the first compromise Northerners made to appease the South in maintaining national unity, and the effect was devastating. Southerners got less than they wanted, but enough to ensure their power in the Electoral College. In 1790 "southern states, possessing around 40% of the nations' white population, controlled around 47% of the House and Electoral College."[23] Governor Morris knew the compromise would exaggerate Southern power and predicted that "the three-fifths clause's real legacy would be to give slaveholders majority control over electoral politics."[24] His warning went unheeded. When Northern leaders realized the damage the compromise

　　　　　　　　　They Shall Be Your Bond-Men

had wrought, they could not change it without amending the Constitution, which, with Southerners controlling the House and the courts, was impossible.

During the election of 1802, in the Electoral College the "three-fifths clause gave the Southerners 14 extra electors, the Republicans' Thomas Jefferson defeated the Federalists' John Adams 73–65. Jefferson swept the South's extra electors 12–2. If no three-fifths clause had existed and House apportionment been based strictly on white numbers, Adams would have likely squeaked by, 63–61."[25] The compromise ensured Southern dominance of the Electoral College. In the first thirty-six years of the Republic, there was only one Northern President: John Adams. The rest—Washington, Jefferson, Madison and Monroe—were all slave-owning Virginians. Apart from John Quincy Adams, every other president until Abraham Lincoln was either a Southern slaveholder or a Northern supporter of slavery.

Southerners dominated all branches of the federal government from 1789 to 1861, often with the cooperation of Northern political and business interests. James McPherson writes, "A Southern slaveholder had been president of the United States two-thirds of the years between 1789 and 1861, and two-thirds of the Speakers of the House and president pro-tem of the Senate Southerners. Twenty of the thirty-five Supreme Court justices during that period had been from slave states, which always had a majority on the court before 1861."[26] The believers in the moral, religious, and cultural supremacy of the South over the North often used the Southern domination of American politics as proof of their superiority.

The convention's delegates passed two further compromises. The first dealt with ending the African slave trade. John Rutledge and Charles Pinckney of South Carolina insisted that their state "could not join the proposed Union if the slave trade was prohibited."[27] Northerners compromised again and allowed the trade to remain legal until 1808. Northerners ceded a final compromise, requiring states to "extradite and deliver any fugitive from service to his or her master and state of origin."[28] The wording was left deliberately vague to include indentured servants, but the target was escaped slaves.

These compromises set the stage for others, as politicians feared that "failure to compromise would bring disunion" and, with it, disaster.[29] The convention approved the compromises, and Northern states that had abolished or were on the way to abolishing slavery ratified the Constitution.

Slavery in the Early Years of the United States

Slavery continued to expand after independence, despite the fact that prominent slaveholders including George Washington voluntarily emancipated their slaves in the 1780s and 1790s. But such benevolence was not the norm. This was due to the fact that United States "purposely built a weak central state, dispersing power to govern from the center to the constituent (some would have said still sovereign) parts."[30] However, the federal government created by the Constitution was far stronger than the one attempted in the confederation of states. The new Constitution, as crafted, ensured that the landowners of the South and Northern merchants held the bulk of economic, political and social power, and the central government very little. Significantly, "most of the makers of the Constitution had some direct interest in establishing a strong federal government: the manufacturers needed protective tariffs; the moneylenders wanted to stop the use of paper money to pay off debts; the land speculators wanted protection as they invaded Indian lands; slave-owners needed federal security against slave revolts and runaways; bondholders wanted a government able to raise money by nationwide taxation, to pay off those bonds."[31] The Constitution ensured that the federal government was strong enough to protect those interests, but not strong enough to encroach on powers granted to the states, especially slave states.

In the early years many Southerners were in favor of the gradual abolition of slavery. Over time the consensus began to

They Shall Be Your Bond-Men

shift as "Methodists and Baptists sought to attract slaveholding whites by moderating their opposition to slavery. By 1843 over a thousand Methodist ministers and preachers owned slaves."[32] The change of position helped to "solidify the position of clergymen and their flocks in the southern social order. Patriarchy, hierarchy, and subordination to household, congregation, and community exalted the authority of Christian masters and not coincidentally their clerical allies."[33]

All of this happened after Eli Whitney invented the cotton gin: the revolutionary machine that Jefferson and others predicted would end slavery. Instead the cotton gin required more slaves to meet expanding demand. Before the cotton gin, a single slave averaged ten hours to separate a single pound of fiber from the seeds. After the gin a team of two to three slaves using the machine could produce fifty pounds a day, thereby destroying the hopes that cotton's unprofitability would lead to slavery's end.

Thomas Jefferson wrote of slavery in 1805: "Interest is really going over to the side of morality. The value of the slave is every day lessening; his burden on his master dayly increasing. Interest is therefore preparing for the disposition to be just."[34] But Jefferson was wrong. Because of the cotton gin, slavery became more profitable. In spite of his misgivings, which he expressed in his first draft of the Declaration of Independence, Jefferson never took a public stand on abolition at any time in his life.

The effect of the cotton gin was exponential. It enabled greater production and simultaneously increased the need for slaves. When the legal African slave trade expired in 1808, the price of slaves already in the United States went up, making the interstate trafficking of slaves much more profitable. In 1790 "a thousand tons of cotton were being produced every year in the South. By 1860, it was a million tons. In the same period, 500,000 slaves grew to 4 million."[35] The increased demand for slaves pushed up their price. Prices varied depending on the location, age, sex, and condition of slaves, but they always went up. In 1835 an unskilled male field hand could be purchased for about $450. But by the 1850s, a field hand, especially a strong healthy one, could fetch up to $1600 at auction.

Cotton's profitability fed the need for more land on which to grow it, which in turn required more slaves. In 1834 Joseph Ingraham wrote that "to sell cotton in order to buy negroes—to make more cotton to buy more negroes, 'ad infinitum,' is the aim and direct tendency of all the operations of the thorough going cotton planter; his whole soul is wrapped up in the pursuit."[36] Wealthy slave owners did not lead as leisurely a life as often portrayed. They were engaged in an unending quest for more land to plant cotton and more slaves to harvest it. To buy land slave owners often used slaves as collateral, and, if their gamble failed, they lost their land and slaves. One bad crop caused by boll weevils or bad weather could ruin a man. And land was becoming increasingly expensive. What could be purchased for $600 an acre in 1835 rose to $100,000 by 1860.

Cotton also enriched Northerners: "Northern ships carried cotton to New York and Europe, northern bankers and merchants financed the cotton crop, northern companies insured it, and northern factories turned cotton into textiles. The 'free states' had abolished slavery, but they remained intimately linked to the peculiar institution."[37] Slavery's tentacles reached across America, where Americans wore clothing made of cotton produced by slaves. Likewise, since slave rebellions impacted the economy, the nation "developed a network of controls in the southern states, backed by laws courts, armed forces, and race prejudice of the nation's political leaders."[38]

Elsewhere in the world, slavery was on the decline. The Spanish, Portuguese, and French lost most of their possessions and their former colonies abolished slavery, beginning in Haiti. From there emancipation spread to central and South America. The Russians ended serfdom, which had much in common with slavery in 1861. The British emancipated all slaves in 1834.

These events increased the call for abolition. English abolitionists gave lectures in the United States and encouraged

They Shall Be Your Bond-Men

American abolitionists. Former slaves and free Blacks joined with whites to help slaves escape their bonds. The small but vocal abolitionist movement provoked an opposing response, particularly in Southern religious circles: to justify and expand slavery.

Abolition versus Slave Power

Abolitionists believed Blacks were fully human and had the same rights as whites. Southern leaders argued that Blacks were not fully human, and thus property, and that slavery was a positive good. These diverging attitudes were at the heart of the "conflict of values, rather than a conflict of interests or a conflict of cultures, lay at the root of the sectional schism."[39]

Christian supporters and opponents of slavery were prominent in political affairs. One leading Southern clergyman linked political proslavery arguments directly to the Christian faith:

> It is not the narrow question of abolitionism or slavery—not simply whether we shall emancipate our negroes or not; the real question is the relations of man to society. . . . The parties in this conflict are not only abolitionists and slaveholders—they are atheists, socialists, communists, red republicans, Jacobins, on the one side, and friends of order and regulated freedom on the other. In one word, the world is the battleground— Christianity and Atheism the combatants.[40]

Slavery permeated every aspect of American life. As historian David M. Potter sums up the connection between the ideological, cultural and economic aspects of the conflict and how slavery connected all three realms in the during the Civil War era:

> These three explanations—cultural, economic and ideological— have long been the standard formulas for explaining the sectional conflict. Each has been defended as though it were necessarily incompatible with the other two. . . . Diversity of culture may produce both diversity of interests and diversity of values. Further, the differences between a slaveholding and

non-slaveholding society would be reflected in all three aspects. Slavery represented an inescapable ethical question which precipitated a sharp conflict of values.[41]

But those who study the Civil War from a purely military perspective tend to miss or gloss over slavery. Many people are more comfortable not dealing with it and with white supremacy and "blur the reality that slavery was at the heart of the matter, ignore the baser realities of the brutal fighting, romanticize our own home-grown terrorist organization, like the Ku Klux Klan that still intrude on our national life."[42] Thus, for many Americans, it is far easier to ignore the harsh reality that slavery and racism were at the heart of the Civil War.

The war grew out of the cultural, economic, ideological and religious differences between the North and South. However, slavery linked them all, producing the conflict between slaveholders and their opponents. Slavery was "basic to the cultural divergence of the North and South, because it was inextricably fused into the key elements of southern life—the staple crop of the plantation system, the social and political ascendency of the planter class, the authoritarian system of social control."[43] Without its commitment to the slave economy, the South would have most likely undergone a similar economic transformation as the North; thus, the economic divergence between North and South would "been less clear cut and would have not met in such head-on collision."[44]

But slavery was more than economics: it was central to the racist worldview of whites, especially slave owners. "White Supremacy was a key tenet of the Southern Way of Life, and Southern ministers used the Lost Cause to reinforce it" in the century following the war.[45] The South's leading overseas propagandist Henry Hotze wrote during the war that "the negro's place in nature is in subordination to the white race," which he noted was due to the "intellectual inferiority" of Blacks.[46]

Slavery divided the United States regarding the meaning of freedom and liberty. Southerners reserved freedom for whites, who occupied positions of economic power and to whom slavery was key to their economy and social philosophy. By these Americans human equality, the heart of the Declaration of Independence, was scorned. George Fitzhugh stated that equality was "practically impossible, and directly conflicts with all government, all separate property, and all social existence."[47] He despised the founder's views of liberty and human equality:

> We must combat the doctrines of natural liberty and human equality, and the social contract as taught by Locke and the American sages of 1776. Under the spell of Locke and the Enlightenment Jefferson and other misguided patriots ruined the splendid political edifice they erected by espousing dangerous abstractions—the crazy notions of liberty and equality that they wrote into the Declaration of Independence and the Virginia Bill of Rights. No wonder the abolitionists loved to quote the Declaration of Independence! Its precepts are wholly at war with slavery and equally at war with all government, all subordination, all order. It is full if mendacity and error. Consider its verbose, newborn, false and unmeaning preamble. . . . There is . . . no such thing as inalienable rights. Life and liberty are not inalienable. . . . Jefferson . . . was the architect of ruin, the inaugurator of anarchy. As his Declaration of Independence Stands . . . it is "exuberantly false, and absurdly fallacious."[48]

Fitzhugh's political philosophy was buttressed by the belief that the South's God-ordained mission was to maintain and expand slavery. According to one Methodist preacher, "God as he is infinitely wise, just and holy never could authorize the practice of moral evil. But God has authorized the practice of slavery, not only by bare permission of his providence, but by the express permission of his word."[49]

Southern Christians felt that they were true believers and that Northern abolitionists and proponents of human equality were heretics. As such, the "South's ideological isolation within an increasingly antislavery world was not a stigma or a source of guilt but a badge of righteousness and a foundation for national identity and pride."[50] Fitzhugh believed that human beings were not equal based on race and gender, "but in relations of strict domination and subordination. Successful societies were those whose members acknowledged their places within that hierarchy."[51] He was caustic when he discussed the implications of his beliefs: "We conclude that about nineteen out of twenty individuals have 'a natural and inalienable right' to be taken care of and protected, to have guardians, trustees, husbands or masters; in other words they have a natural and inalienable right to be slaves. The one in twenty are clearly born or educated in some way fitted for command and liberty."[52] Fitzhugh summarized his chilling beliefs as "liberty for the few—slavery in every form, for the mass."[53]

Most non-slave-owning Southerners did not understand that the institution of slavery restricted their rights; most saw it as the guarantee of their social status. As John C. Calhoun said to the Senate in 1848, "With us, the two great divisions of society are not the rich and poor, but white and black; and all of the former, the poor as well as the rich, belong to the upper class, and are respected and treated as equals."[54] Calhoun's distinction is an important one if we are to understand why poor whites then and now fight for policies of no benefit to them. Abraham Lincoln cut to the heart of the matter: "'We all declare for liberty but in using the same word we do not all mean the same thing. With some the word liberty may mean for each man to do as he pleases with himself and the product of his labor; while with others the same word may mean for some men to do as they please with other men and the product of other men's labor.'"[55]

The chasm between North and South widened as the issue focused more about slavery's expansion. This led to an increased use of stereotypes, which had the "effect of changing men's attitudes toward the disagreements which are always certain to arise in politics: ordinary, resolvable disputes were converted into questions of principle, involving rigid, unne-

They Shall Be Your Bond-Men

gotiable dogma."[56] In 1858 the *Charleston Mercury* noted that "on the subject of slavery . . . the North and the South . . . are not only two peoples, but they are rival, hostile peoples."[57] Southern leaders insisted on maintaining slavery where it was legal and expanding it into new territories. But by doing so they ended up fighting a much more powerful enemy than the abolitionists: Northern industrialists, who were more concerned with "economic policy designed to secure Northern domination of Western lands than the initial step in a broad plan to end slavery."[58]

A growing culture of victimhood arose in the South. Sen. Robert Toombs offered a prime example: "For twenty years past, the Abolitionists and their allies in the Northern states, have been engaged in constant efforts to subvert our institutions, and to excite insurrection and servile war among us . . . whose 'avowed purpose is to subject our society, subject us, not only to the loss of our property but the destruction of ourselves, our wives and our children, and the dissolution of our homes, our altars, and our firesides.'"[59] As their differences with the North widened, Southerners became more closed off. David Potter writes, "More than other Americans, Southerners developed a sectional identity outside the national mainstream. The Southern lifestyle tended to contradict the national norm in ways that lifestyles of other sections did not."[60] Southern leaders inhabited a world where "social, economic, intellectual, and political were decidedly commingled."[61] They embraced slavery, even though it did not benefit poor Southern whites, yet the "system of subordination . . . required a certain kind of society, one in which certain questions were not publicly discussed . . . It must commit non slaveholders to the unquestioning support of racial subordination. . . . In short, the South became increasingly a closed society, distrustful of isms from outside and unsympathetic to dissenters. Such were the pervasive consequences of giving top priority to the maintenance of a system of racial subordination."[62]

Several slave revolts in the early 1800s heightened the fear and paranoia of Southerners living in the Black Belts, where slaves outnumbered whites by great margins: "In thickly enslaved areas, fancied dangers united white classes and sexes. Whites in black belts shared horror images about freed blacks as rioters, rapists, arsonists, and cannibals. The whites characteristically thought that using slavery to control alleged barbarians meant saving civilization."[63]

Even before abolition, Southern planters, "with an intensity that escalated through the Civil War declared war on all open criticism of the peculiar institution."[64] Thus, when William Lloyd Garrison 's the *Liberator* began to appear in the South, Southern elected officials "suppressed antislavery books, newspapers, lectures, and sermons and strove generally to deny critics of bondage access to any public forum."[65] Despite resistance abolitionists used the U.S. mail to send their literature to the South, provoking drastic actions from Southern legislators.

Yet Garrison and other abolitionists had only a small following in the North. Northerners who leaned toward abolition were supporters of gradual, not immediate, emancipation. David Goldfeld writes that Garrison and his followers were "a small and often despised group."[66] Garrison understood this all too well, which caused him to be uncompromising.[67] He despised Northern collaborators more than slave owners, viewing their "contempt more bitter, opposition more active, detraction more relentless, prejudice more stubborn, and apathy more frozen, than among slave owners themselves."[68] Opponents broke up Garrison's meetings and once paraded him "through the streets of Boston with a rope around his neck."[69]

Southerners were outraged by Garrison's "almost pornographic diatribes," which assaulted their "self-respect and sense of honor."[70] In response to the proliferation of abolitionist literature sent through the mail, John Calhoun proposed a law to prosecute "any postmaster who would knowingly receive or put into the mail any pamphlet, newspaper, handbill, or any printed, written, or pictorial representation touching the subject of slavery."[71]

Other federal and state legislators worked to block what they considered subversive literature. The condescending attitude of radical abolitionists toward slavery provoked an "emotional wildfire" in the South, uniting slave owners and poor whites in the Black Belts and increasing their fear and loathing of Yankees.[72] Had Garrison and his supporters understood how little support abolition had in the North they might not have pushed so hard for their more extreme positions. But with fears of real and imagined slave revolts, the polemics of abolitionists, especially Garrison, brought new conflict. Because of this Southerners tried to crush free speech in the North and blot out any mention of slavery in the House of Representatives. In 1836 the House passed a "gag rule" for its members that "banned all petitions, memorials, resolutions, propositions, or papers related in any way or to any extent whatever to the subject of slavery."[73] Representative and former president John Quincy Adams continually challenged it, , and eventually the House voted to rescind it in 1844.

But by "1840, support for Garrison extremism peaked at around 2 percent of the northern voting population. The other 98 percent of northern citizens considered immediate abolition to be too extreme to be American, too pro-black to be tolerable, too keen on seizing property to be capitalistic, and too anti-southern to be safe for the Union."[74] The combination of Northern racism, concern for property over people, and the delicate feelings of Southerners trumped being truthful about slavery.

Unhappy Southern politicians spouted "demands that the federal government and the Northern states issue assurances that the abolitionists would never be allowed to tamper with . . . the South's 'peculiar domestic institution.'"[75] John Calhoun defended the gag rule in the Senate:

I do not belong to the school, as Mr. C.,[76] to the school which holds that aggression is to be met by concession. Mine is the opposite creed, which teaches that encroachments must be met at the beginning. . . . If we yield, it will be followed by another; and we would thus proceed, step by step, to the final consummation of the object of these petitions. . . . .he asserted that the matter went "beyond the jurisdiction of Congress they have no right to touch it in any form, or to make it the subject of deliberation or discussion."[77]

Southern demands shaped the legislative debate, adding to existing tensions. As tensions grew in Congress, the issue of slavery, more than any other, "transformed political action from a process of accommodation to a mode of combat."[78]

About the time the gag rule played out in Congress, the Supreme Court ruled that the federal government alone "had jurisdiction where escaped slaves were concerned." This led to several states enacting personal liberty laws to "forbid their own elected officials from those pursuing fugitives." Southern politicians vigorously resisted these moves, which they saw as an assault on slavery and their rights to their human property. Virginia legislators claimed such laws were a "disgusting and revolting exhibition of faithless and unconstitutional legislation."[79]

Slavery shaped political debate and "structured and polarized many random, unoriented points of conflict on which sectional interest diverged."[80] As the divide grew, leaders and citizens reacted to a proliferation of the most distorted images imaginable: in "the North to an image of a southern world of lascivious and sadistic slave drivers; the South to the image of a northern world of cunning Yankee traders and radical abolitionists plotting slave insurrections."[81]

Edmund Ruffin and the Fire-Eaters

In order to understand the causes of secession, we need to understand the people involved. Two of these men stand out: Edmund Ruffin and Robert Barnwell Rhett. Ruffin might be the most interesting man who supported slavery, white supremacy, and secession in the antebellum South. He became the

FIG. 4. Virginia planter, secessionist, and firebrand Edmund Ruffin. n.d. Courtesy U.S. National Archives.

face of slaveholding ideology, but he was not always proslavery or prosecession. As a young man, he had been a Jeffersonian Republican, concerned about growing federal power, but his writings were scholarly and moderate. That changed, however, as the country lurched from one sectional crisis to the next.

Ruffin was an agricultural reformer who pioneered the use of lime to enhance the effectiveness of other fertilizers. He edited a successful newspaper for farmers and ran a highly successful planation outside of Hopewell, Virginia. But in 1845 Ruffin began to write about the probability of fighting the North: "We shall have to defend our rights by the strong hand against Northern abolitionists and perhaps the tariffites."[82] The Compromise of 1850 turned him into a hardline secessionist, and "he promptly threw himself into the new cause, replacing his formerly scholarly approach to issues with a fire-eater's polemical and emotional style. 'I will not pretend,' he now announced, 'to restrain my pen, nor attempt to be correct in plan or expression—as is more or less usually the case in my writing.'"[83] As a young man, Ruffin believed that slavery was an evil. But, after studying the works of Thomas Dew, he was convinced of slavery's importance and justification. In his tract *The Political Economy of Slavery*, Ruffin wrote,

> Slavery . . . would be frequently . . . attended with circumstances of great hardship, injustice, and sometimes atrocious cruelty. Still, the consequences and general results were highly beneficial . . . By this aid only could leisure be afforded to the master class to cultivate mental improvement and refinement of manners; and artificial wants be created and indulged, which would stimulate the desire and produce the effect, to accumulate the products of labor, which alone constitute private and public wealth . . . the first results of domestic slavery were due the gradual civilization and general improvement of manners and of arts among all originally barbarous peoples, who, of themselves . . . have subsequently emerged from barbarism and dark ignorance.[84]

Ruffin argued for secession and Southern independence for fifteen years. He "perceived the planter civilization of the South in peril; the source of the peril was 'Yankee' and union with 'Yankees.' Thus, he preached revolution, Ruffin was a rebel with a cause, a secular prophet."[85]

By 1850 Ruffin recognized that, for slavery to survive, the South had to secede from the Union, for there could be no compromise. In 1850 he and James Hammond attempted to use a meeting in Nashville to "secure Cooperative State Secession." He wrote Hammond: "If the Convention does not open the way to dissolution . . . I hope it shall never meet."[86]

Ruffin spread his views "with letters, articles, speeches, and travels, Ruffin widened his circle of secessionist acquaintances."[87] His arguments help to illuminate how most slave owners felt about slavery's economic and social benefits. Although many Southerners wrote about the importance of slavery, Ruffin was perhaps its most eloquent defender:

> Still, even this worst and least profitable kind of slavery (the subjection of equals and men of the same race with their masters) served as the foundation and the essential first cause of all the civilization and refinement, and improvement of arts and learning, that distinguished the oldest nations. Except where the special Providence and care of God may have interposed to guard a particular family and its descendants, there was nothing but the existence of slavery to prevent any race or society in a state of nature from sinking into the rudest barbarism. And no people could ever have been raised from that low condition without the aid and operation of slavery, either by some individuals of the community being enslaved, by conquest and subjugation, in some form, to a foreign and more enlightened people.[88]

In 1861 Ruffin, then sixty-seven, went to Charleston and joined the Palmetto Guards, where, according to legend unsupported by fact, he allegedly fired the first shot at Fort Sumter, from a battery opposite Fort Moultrie, even though other batteries had already opened fire.[89] For Ruffin Fort Sumter was a seminal event: he finally got what he wanted.

Other fire-eaters advocated for secession in the 1840s, including James De Bow, publisher of *De Bow's Review,* South Carolina representative Lawrence Keitt, who was forced out of the House for his part attacking Sen. Charles Sumner; South Carolina's James Hammond, and Beverley Tucker, chair of the William and Mary College of Law, who rejected Jefferson's views on human rights. Tucker "indoctrinated his students in the belief that the inherent racial inferiority of blacks made them suitable subjects for slavery, an institution he regarded as essential to republican government" and urged that abolitionists be silenced.[90]

But the "father" of Southern secession was Robert Barnwell Rhett. Rhett was a lawyer who was born in 1800 under the name of Robert Barnwell Smith and later adopted the surname of a famous ancestor to gain acceptance by the South Carolina aristocracy. In a twist of irony, Rhett studied law under Thomas Grimke, the brother of the two famous abolitionist sisters, and "a leader of South Carolina's anti-slavery American Colonization Society."[91] Rhett was a talented attorney with excellent oratorical skills. He was elected to the South Carolina legislature in 1826 as the nullification crisis began, Rhett, like John Calhoun and opponents of a federal tariff, urged secession as early as 1830: "Aye—disunion rather, into a thousand fragments. And why, gentlemen! would I prefer disunion to such a Government? Because under such a Government I would be a slave—a fearful slave, ruled despotically by those who do not represent me . . . with every base and destructive passion of man bearing upon my shieldless destiny."[92]

Due to Pres. Andrew Jackson's political strength and congressional opposition led by Henry Clay, South Carolina dropped nullification, angering Rhett. He told his colleagues that "your northern brethren, aye, the entire world are in arms against your institutions. . . . Until this Government is made a limited Government . . . there is no liberty—no security for the

They Shall Be Your Bond-Men

South."[93] He described disunion as the only way the South could survive and escape "unconstitutional legislation" and described a "Confederacy of the Southern States . . . [as] a happy termination—happy beyond expectation, of our long struggle for our rights against oppression."[94]

Rhett fought compromise at every opportunity. Completely convinced of his cause, he distrusted politicians who favored it and had no faith in the existing political parties. From 1833 onward he supported slavery, disunion, and secession. He dreamed for "all Southerners—to unite across party lines and unyieldingly defend slavery and Southern interests as he defined them."[95] During the secession debate in the Compromise of 1850 crisis, Rhett resigned his Senate seat rather than accept his state convention's ruling that secession was not justified. He became the editor and later the owner of the *Charleston Mercury*, where he advocated for disunion in the most outrageous ways:

> The more outrageous the Mercury's charges, the more they were picked up and reprinted by other papers. Rhett's propaganda technique was part of a larger secessionist strategy. "Men having both nerve and self-sacrificing patriotism," he wrote, "must lead the movement and shape its course, controlling and compelling their inferior contemporaries." He worked to push those without sufficient patriotic nerve—that is, moderate leaders—out of the political arena, believing correctly that without a solid middle ground to stand on, Southern voters would rally increasingly to the fire-eaters' standard.[96]

In 1860 Rhett "joined a drive to either rule or ruin the 1860 Democratic convention scheduled for Charleston."[97] He succeeded and devised a strategy to destroy the Union by destroying the Democratic Party. In January 1860 he wrote that "the destruction of the Union must . . . begin with the demolition of the party. So long as the Democratic Party, as a 'National' organization exists in power in the South . . . our public men will trim their sails."[98] Rhett drafted South Carolina's Secession Ordinance, which claimed that South Carolina was not "perpetrating a treasonous revolution, but . . . simply taking back . . . the same powers it had temporarily surrendered . . . when South Carolina ratified the federal Constitution."[99]

Rhett's inability to compromise and his intemperate behavior alienated him from Jefferson Davis and other Confederate leaders. He became one of Davis's most bitter critics during the 1864/65 debate to enlist slaves as soldiers and granting limited emancipation. Rhett opposed any compromise on slavery to the end.

5

The Privilege of Belonging to the Superior Race

Slavery and National Expansion

The South was an agrarian society whose economy depended on slavery. Southern oligarchs offered slaves no freedom, discriminated against Black freedmen, and did little to improve the lives of poor and middle-class whites. Despite this, poor whites supported the system. Southern farmers tolerated their second-class status because they "feared the fall from independent producer to dependent proletarian, a status he equated with enslavement" more than subservience to plantation owners.[1] Slavery alone kept them above Blacks.

In 1861 Dr. J. H. Van Evrie borrowed from the scientific yet deeply flawed racism of ichthyologist Louis Agassiz in a pseudoscientific pamphlet entitled *Negroes and Negro Slavery; The First an Inferior Race—The Latter, Its Normal Condition.* He described how Southerners felt about Blacks, enslaved or free. Jefferson Davis hoped that Van Evrie's arguments would persuade people to adopt the view that racial equality was a fallacy not to be tolerated. Van Evrie wrote:

> He is not a black white man, or merely a man with a black skin, but a DIFFERENT AND INFERIOR SPECIES OF MAN;—that this difference is radical and total . . . that so called slavery is neither a "wrong" nor an "evil," but a natural relation based upon the "higher law," in harmony with the order, progress, and general well-being of the superior one, and absolutely in keeping with the existence of the inferior race.[2]

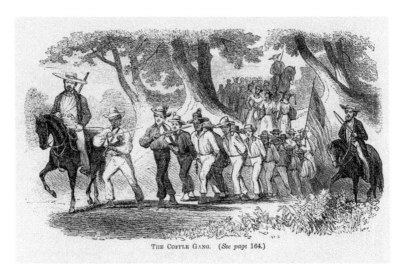

THE COFFLE GANG. (*See page* 164.)

FIG. 5. Woodcut, "The Coffle Gang," Edward Stone marching his slaves
to the Ohio River. As described by Rev. James H. Dickey in an 1822 letter.
University of Kentucky Archives.

All Northern states abolished slavery or were in the process
of gradual abolition after independence. By the Civil War,
they had transitioned to the economic concept of free labor,
while the South chained itself to slavery. In 1846 members of
an Alabama agricultural society noted that "our condition is
quite different from that of the non-slaveholding section of
the United States. Their laborers are merely hirelings, while
with us our laborers are our property."[3]

Samuel Cartwright wove the pseudoscience of the day into
the narrative of the Bible:

> I have thus hastily and imperfectly noticed some of the more
> striking anatomical and physiological peculiarities of the Negro
> race. The question may be asked, Does he belong to the same
> race as the white man? Is he a son of Adam? Does his partic-
> ular physical confirmation stand in opposition to the Bible,
> or does it prove its truth? . . . Anatomy and physiology have
> been interrogated, and the response is, that the Ethiopian, or
> Canaanite, is unfitted for the duties of a free man.[4]

He further stated that the phrase "that all men are by nature free and equal" was only intended to apply to white men.[5] Northerners, even in states where slavery held on, almost universally believed that there was dignity to free labor, and that it was essential if people were to have a better lives; it supported their belief in human dignity and in "labor [as] the source of all value."[6] This notion of the intrinsic value of free labor was found in the Calvinist theology that predominated in most Protestant Northern churches.[7] Because labor was considered integral to one's calling as a Christian and a human being, slave labor undercut that idea.

Success in one's calling glorified God and provided earthly evidence that a person was among the elect. For many Northern Christians, "the pursuit of wealth thus became a way of serving God on earth, and labor, which had been imposed on fallen man as a curse, was transmuted into a religious value, a Christian calling."[8] This idea found its way into Republican political thought, even when not related to religion. In 1856 William Evarts said, "Labor gentlemen, we of the free States acknowledge to be the source of all of our wealth, of all our progress, of all our dignity and value."[9] Lincoln noted that "the free labor system . . . opens the way for all, and energy and progress, and improvement in condition for all."[10] Lincoln also appealed to the economic theory of Adam Smith that "labor is prior to, and independent of capital . . . in fact, capital is the fruit of labor."[11]

Southern advocates deplored the free-labor movement as wage slavery while they extolled the virtue of slavery. James H. Hammond condemned it in his "King Cotton" speech of 1858:

> In all social systems there must be a class to do the menial duties, to perform the drudgery of life. . . . It constitutes the very mudsill of society. . . . Such a class you must have, or you would not have that other that leads to progress, civilization and refinement. . . . Your whole hireling class of manual laborers . . . are essentially slaves. The difference between us is, that

our slaves are hired for life and well compensated . . . yours are hired by the day, not cared for, and scantily compensated.[12]

The fact that Southern politicians "were forced at every election to solicit the votes of ignorant, slovenly, white trash in the country with frequent treats that disgrace our elections" rankled many members of the Southern aristocracy.[13] As a result Southern politics was a marriage of two widely disparate socioeconomic groups linked solely by their race; thus slavery in the South remained unchallenged by those who gained nothing from its existence.

Lincoln lauded the virtues of free labor, citing his own experiences: "I am not ashamed to confess that twenty five years ago I was a hired laborer, mauling rails, at work on a flat boat—just what might happen to any poor man's son."[14] Northerners praised it as the basis of upward mobility. The *New York Times* noted that "our paupers to-day, thanks to free labor, are our yeomen and merchants of tomorrow."[15]

Most Southern whites held labor in contempt because of slavery. Thomas Ewing wrote that labor "is held honorable by all on one side of the line because it is the vocation of freedmen—degrading in the eyes of some on the other side because it is the task of slaves."[16] Since slavery was the centerpiece of their economy, Southerners' views were influenced by race, and "if slavery was wrong, its wrongs were cancelled out for non-slave owners by the more monstrous specter of racial equity."[17]

Georgia's governor, Joseph E. Brown, emphasized the threat to whites if Blacks became social equals. Being part of the superior race assured poor Southern whites that they were superior to Blacks. An Alabama lawyer wrote that "the privilege of belonging to the superior race and being free was a bond that tied all Southern whites together."[18] But poor white workers "repeatedly complained about having to compete with slaves as well as poorly paid free blacks."[19] Thus, many moved to free states or new territories to escape the Southern system.

Southern politicians and slaveholders believed the expansion of slavery, where it was legal, was vital to its survival. Due to their political need "to maintain a balance in the Senate, check unruly slaves, and cultivate fertile soils, many planters and small plantation owners—particularly those living in the southern districts of the cotton states—asserted that their survival depended on new territory."[20] The slave owners acted on that belief, and in the following decades "a huge involuntary migration took place. Between 800,000 and 1 million slaves were moved westward."[21]

The need for slaves caused prices to soar and made the interregional slave trade much more important. It turned the slave states and new slave-holding territories into "a regionwide slave market that tied together all of the various slave-owning interests into a common economic concern."[22] In Virginia, where fewer slaves were needed, exporting slaves became a major industry:

> Male slaves were marched in coffles of forty or fifty, handcuffed to each other in pairs, with a long chain through the handcuffs passing down the column to keep it together, closely guarded by mounted slave traders followed by an equal number of female slaves and their children. Most of them were taken to Wheeling, Virginia the "busiest slave port" in the United States and from there they were transported by steamboat to New Orleans, Natchez, and Memphis.[23]

The Rev. James H. Dickey wrote in a letter about a slave coffle he witnessed in Kentucky in 1822, led by Edward Stone:

> Having passed through Paris, in Bourbon County, Kentucky, the sound of music, (beyond a little rising of ground) attracted my attention; I looked forward and saw the flag of my country waving. Supposing I was about to meet a military parade, I drove hastily to the side of the road; and, having gained the top of the ascent, I discovered, I suppose, about forty black men, all chained together after the following manner: Each of them was handcuffed, and they were arranged in rank and file.

A chain perhaps forty feet long, the size of a fifth-horse chain, was stretched between the two ranks, to which short chains were joined which connected with the handcuffs. Behind them were about thirty women, in double rank, the couples tied hand to hand. A solemn sadness sat on every countenance, and the dismal silence of this march of despair was interrupted only by the sound of two violins; yes, as if to add insult to injury, the foremost couple were furnished with a violin apiece; the second couple were ornamented with cockades, while neat the center waved the republican flag, carried by a hand literally in chains.[24]

Stone was killed in 1826 when the slaves he was marching to the Ohio River rebelled and killed him and most of his guards.

Economic Effects of the Compromise of 1850

The interregional slave trade guaranteed a source of slaves to slave owners, who "hitched their future to slavery a single cash crop and fresh land" and refused to take an interest in manufacturing or diversifying agricultural production.[25] The price of slaves tripled between 1800 and 1860, making human property the most lucrative investment. The price of a "prime male field hand in New Orleans began at around $500 in 1800 and rose as high as $1,800 by the time of the Civil War."[26] The result was that slave owners and investors who benefited from the interregional slave trade had a vested interest in its expansion.

This resulted in slave owners growing significantly richer as the value of slaves increased. Using the conservative number of $750 dollars as the value of a slave in 1860, the investment in human property was significantly more than almost any other in the nation. Steven Deyle writes:

> It was roughly three times greater than the total amount of all capital invested in manufacturing in the North and in the South combined, three times the amount invested in railroads, and seven times the amount invested in banks. It was about equal to about seven times the value of all currency in circulation in

The Privilege of Belonging

the country three times the value of the entire livestock population, twelve times the value of the entire U.S. cotton crop, and forty-eight times the expenditures of the federal government that year.[27]

The rise in the value of slaves and the growing wealth of slave owners had a depreciating effect on poor Southern whites by destroying the middle class, which "blocked any hope of social advancement for the mass of poor whites, for it was all but impossible for a non-slaveholder to rise in the southern aristocracy."[28] The impoverishment of Southern whites created some worry for those astute enough to take an interest in it:

> In 1850, about 40 percent of the South's white farmers owned real estate at all. . . . Thus, worried the Southern Cultivator in 1856, "a large number in the South who have no legal right or interest in the soil [and] no homes of their own." The editor of a South Carolina newspaper that year framed the matter in less sympathetic terms: "There is in this State," he wrote, "as impoverished and ignorant as white population as can be found in any other in the Union."[29]

Some Southerners recognized that slavery was the reason they were falling behind the North in terms of economic advancement. North Carolinian Hinton Helper owned no slaves and made his fortune in the California Gold Rush. He returned home disillusioned and wrote a book, *The Impending Crisis of the South: How to Meet It* (1857), which had a major impact in the North but was either banned or restricted in the South. It dealt with "the debilitating impact of slavery on the South in general and on southern whites in particular."[30] Helper's attack on slavery was more devastating than that of any abolitionist. As a Southerner his words furthered anti-slavery sentiments in the North. Republicans printed and distributed an abridged edition as a campaign tool during the buildup to the 1860 election. Helper wrote, "Slavery lies at the root of all the shame, poverty, tyranny and imbecility of the

South." Echoing the free-soil argument, Helper maintained that slavery degraded all labor to the level of bond labor. Planters looked down their noses at poor whites and refused to tax themselves to provide a decent school system. "Slavery is hostile to general education,' he contended. 'Its very life, is in the ignorance and stolidity of the masses.'"[31]

Southern leaders saw the danger in Helper's book and worried that if he spoke freely for long enough "'that they will have an Abolition party in the South, of Southern men.' When that happened, 'the contest for slavery will no longer be one between the North and the South. It will be in the South between the people of the South.'"[32] That was something slave owners could never tolerate. If non-slaveholding whites rejected slavery, the institution would die. Thus Helper, who held many violent racist attitudes, was denounced "as a traitor, a renegade, an apostate, a dishonest, degraded and disgraced man."[33] Helper, though, was an anomaly. More were like Jefferson Davis, who urged the creation of a "Southern system, internal improvements, building factories, even reforming education to eliminate all textbooks at odds with his notion of the blessings of slavery."[34]

Northerners embraced the Industrial Revolution long before the war, leading to technological and engineering advances that gave the region a marked economic advantage over the South. Southerners' "commitment to the use of slave labor inhibited economic diversification and industrialization and strengthened the tyranny of King Cotton."[35] The Northern population swelled as European immigrants moved there for the opportunity and not to the South.

The growing divide was not helped by compromises between Northern and Southern legislators. After the Missouri Compromise, Thomas Jefferson wrote these words of warning: "But this momentous question, like a fire bell in the night, awakened and filled me with terror. I considered it at once as the knell of the Union."[36]

The War with Mexico lit the fuse that ultimately ignited the

The Privilege of Belonging

Civil War. Proslavery expansionists saw the territories gained as fresh and fertile ground. In his memoirs Ulysses Grant wrote about the effects of the war:

> In taking military possession of Texas after annexation, the army of occupation, under General [Zachary] Taylor, was directed to occupy the disputed territory. The army did not stop at the Nueces and offer to negotiate for a settlement of the boundary question, but went beyond, apparently in order to force Mexico to initiate war. . . . To us it was an empire and of incalculable value; but it might have been obtained by other means. The Southern rebellion was largely the outgrowth of the Mexican war.[37]

Sen. Robert Toombs of Georgia demanded that slavery expand in all territories. He warned his colleagues: "In the presence of the living God, that if you by your legislation you seek to drive us from the territories of California and New Mexico, purchased by the common blood and treasure of the whole people . . . thereby attempting to fix a national degradation upon half the states of this Confederacy I am for disunion."[38]

Tensions escalated regarding the question of how slavery should be managed in the new territories, which led to the Compromise of 1850. Senators Henry Clay and Daniel Webster supported by Pres. Millard Fillmore used it to solve issues related to California's admission to the Union as well as to boundary disputes involving Texas and the new territories. Among the bills passed was the Fugitive Slave Act of 1850, which Clay devised to sweeten the deal for Southerners, but it proved toxic. It gave "slaveholders broader powers to stop the flow of runaway slaves northward to the free states, and offered a final resolution denying that Congress had any authority to regulate the interstate slave trade."[39]

The Fugitive Slave Act ordered all citizens to assist law enforcement in apprehending fugitive slaves. It voided state laws in Massachusetts, Vermont, Ohio, Connecticut, Pennsylvania, and Rhode Island, which barred state officials from aiding in the capture, arrest, or imprisonment of fugitive slaves. In the Fugitive Slave Act, Congress "nationalized slavery. No black person was safe on American soil. The old division of free state/slave state had vanished."[40] If there was any question of whose states' rights Southern leaders supported, it was certainly not those of free states.

Federal law enforcement officials, even in free states, were required to arrest fugitive slaves and anyone who assisted them and threatened with punishment if they failed to enforce the measure: "Any marshal or deputy marshal refuse to receive such warrant, or other process, when tendered, or to use all proper means diligently to execute the same, he shall, on conviction thereof, be fined in the sum of one thousand dollars."[41] The act nullified state laws and forced citizens and local officials to apprehend escaped slaves regardless of their convictions, religious views, or state or local laws and compelled citizens in free states to "aid and assist in the prompt and efficient execution of this law, whenever their services may be required."[42] Penalties were harsh and the financial incentives for compliance attractive. "Anyone caught providing food and shelter to an escaped slave, assuming northern whites could discern who was a runaway, would be subject to a fine of one thousand dollars and six months in prison. The law also suspended habeas corpus and the right to trial by jury for captured blacks."[43]

The law stripped protections from free Blacks, who were often seized and enslaved, and created an extrajudicial office of a federal commissioner to decide the fate of Blacks and circumvent federal courts. It was designed to favorably adjudicate the claims of slaveholders, as many federal courts located in free states denied them. Slave owners or their agents needed little in the way of proof; all that was required to return a Black to slavery was a sworn statement by a slave owner with an "affidavit from a slave-state court or by the testimony of white witnesses," even if it was false.[44]

The law was an extrajudicial exercise of tyranny. Blacks were

The Privilege of Belonging

denied legal counsel and could not testify on their own behalf. Commissioners had financial incentives to send Blacks back to slavery, as they received a direct financial reward: "If the commissioner decided against the claimant, he would receive a fee of five dollars; if in favor ten. This provision, supposedly justified by the paperwork needed to remand a fugitive to the South, became notorious among abolitionists as a bribe to commissioners."[45] The law was rigged to reenslave Blacks and imposed obligations considered evil by free state citizens. Frederick Douglass wrote about it in forceful terms: "By an act of the American Congress . . . slavery has been nationalized in its most horrible and revolting form. By that act, Mason & Dixon's line has been obliterated; . . . and the power to hold, hunt, and sell men, women, and children remains no longer a mere state institution, but is now an institution of the whole United States."[46]

Douglass was correct. In 1854 Anthony Burns, a former slave who had purchased his freedom, was arrested in Boston under the Fugitive Slave Act. His arrest prompted a protest in which "an urban mob—variously composed of free Negro laborers, radical Unitarian ministers, and others—gathered to free him. They stormed the Federal courthouse, which was surrounded by police and wrapped in protective chains. . . . Amid the melee, one protestor shot and killed a police deputy."[47] The opposition provoked thousands of Bostonians to join the protests, which caused the governor of Massachusetts to deploy two batteries of artillery outside the courthouse to deter any attacks. After the Federal Fugitive Slave Law commissioner consigned Burns to his Southern "owner," Burns was placed in shackles and marched down State Street. With tensions running extremely high, a "brigade of Massachusetts militia and local police were required to run Burns through a gauntlet and deposit him on the ship that would remand him to Virginia."[48]

Bostonians saw their city as one that resisted tyranny, as it had in the American Revolution. They did not forget Burns, but raised the money to purchase his freedom. As William Lloyd Garrison writes, "The deed of infamy . . . demonstrated as nothing else that only the military power of the United States could sustain slavery."[49] Boston's "mercantile elite had vindicated law and order," but in doing so they motivated pacifist abolitionists to physically resist bounty-hunting Southerners.[50] "Across the North, prisons were broken into, possies were disrupted, and juries refused to convict."[51]

Sometimes violence ensued. In 1851 "a Maryland slave owner named Edward Gorsuch crossed into Pennsylvania in pursuit of four runaways."[52] Gorsuch and his armed posse found them in the Quaker town of Christiana, where they were sheltered by a free Black named William Parker. Parker and about two dozen Black men, armed with farm implements and a few muskets, vowed to resist. Several unarmed Quakers recommended that Gorsuch and his posse leave, but Gorsuch told them, "I will have my property, or go to hell."[53] In the ensuing skirmish Gorsuch was killed and his son Tommy seriously wounded. The fugitives escaped through the Underground Railroad to Canada.

The Christiana Riot became a national story. It was celebrated as an act of resistance in the North and decried in the South. President Fillmore sent in troops and arrested a number of Quakers and over thirty Black men. According to Edward Steers Jr., "The trial turned into a test between two cultures: Southern versus Northern, slave versus free."[54] The men were charged with treason, but the trial became a farce as the government's case came apart. Steers wrote that after deliberating for just fifteen minutes, "the jury acquitted the first defendant, one of the Quakers, the government dropped the remaining indictments and decided not to press other charges."[55] Southerners were outraged, and one teenager, forever linked, with infamy never forgot: John Wilkes Booth, who was a childhood friend of Tommy Gorsuch. The unforgivable death of his friend Tommy's father would lead to tragedy for the nation fourteen years later. While Booth

The Privilege of Belonging

"would move on with his life, he would not forget what happened in Christiana."[56]

The authors of the compromise never expected such resistance. On his deathbed Henry Clay, who worked his entire career to preserve the Union, praised it: "The new fugitive slave law, I believe, kept the South in the Union in 'fifty and 'fifty-one." Clay depreciated Northern opposition and condemned the attempt to free Anthony Burns, noting, "Yes, since the passage of the compromise, the abolitionists and free coloreds of the North have howled in protest and viciously assailed me, and twice in Boston there has been a failure to execute the law, which shocks and astounds me. . . . But such people belong to the lunatic fringe."[57]

While the compromise "averted a showdown over who would control the new western territories," it only delayed disunion.[58] Sen. John C. Calhoun realized that it did not do enough to protect slavery and would inspire abolitionists to redouble their efforts to abolish it. Thus, Calhoun argued for the permanent protection of the institution, because it was the heart of Southern society and, without protection, its dissolution would destroy the union. He said, "I fix its probable [breakup] within twelve years or three presidential terms. . . . The probability is it will explode in a presidential election."[59]

Calhoun proved to be correct. The leap into the abyss of disunion and civil war had only been temporarily avoided. However, no supporters anticipated what would occur only six years later when a "train of unexpected consequences would throw an entirely new light on the popular sovereignty doctrine, and both it and the Compromise of 1850 would be wrecked with the stroke of a single judicial pen."[60]

6

A Gross Violation of a Sacred Pledge

Collapse of the Whig Party

Congress followed the Compromise of 1850 by tackling the status of the Kansas and Nebraska territories. Both lay north of the line barring slavery set by the Missouri Compromise. While that law was gutted by the Compromise of 1850, it still remained on the books and applied to the establishment of new territories.

Democratic senator Stephen Douglas of Illinois masterminded the legislation. Douglas saw the need to organize the territories and knew that he needed Southern support. Responding to pressure from Democratic senators James Mason and Robert M. T. Hunter of Virginia, Andrew Butler of South Carolina, and David Aitchison of Missouri, Douglas crafted the measure and included an "explicit repeal of the ban on slavery north of 36° 30'."[1]

The repeal of the ban on slavery in new territories created a firestorm. Northern opponents, including Salmon Chase, condemned it as "an atrocious plot" of slave power to "convert free territory" into a "dreary region of despotism, inhabited by masters and slaves."[2] Chase and his allies published the "Appeal of the Independent Democrats" who "condemned this 'gross violation of a sacred pledge'" and promised to "call the people to come to the rescue of the country from the domination of slavery."[3] Chase closed by warning that "the dearest interests of freedom and the Union are in imminent peril and called for religious and political organization to defeat the bill."[4]

Horace Greeley, publisher of the *New York Tribune*, fought against the act. Greeley charged that Southern slave owners and politicians were "not content within its own proper limits . . . it now proposed to invade and overrun the soil of freedom, and to unroll the pall of its darkness over virgin territory whereon slave has never stood. Freedom is to be elbowed out of its own home to make room for the leprous intruder. The free laborer is to be expelled that the slave may be brought in."[5]

The bill was passed after months of wrangling. Historian William Freehling describes it as "the latest and most notorious pro-southern law."[6] The only hope was a veto by Pres. Franklin Pierce. But Pierce buckled to pressure from Northern Democrats who supported businesses, banks, and industries that benefited from slavery. Southern delegations of both parties were nearly unanimous in their support, but it only passed in the House of Representatives, with the support of forty-two Northern Democrats. They antagonized their constituents and did not have majority support in any Northern delegation other than Illinois.

Southern Senators responded by humiliating their Northern colleagues: blocking a measure passed in the House that would have provided 160 acres of land from public property to new settlers in the territories. Southerners believed that its passage "would prove a most efficient ally for Abolition by encouraging and stimulating the settlement of free farms with Yankees and foreigners pre-committed to resist the participancy of slave owners in the public domain."[7] In other words, they wanted every incentive for slaveholders to move to the new territories while making it harder for slavery opponents.

Frederick Douglass condemned the measure and said the "shame of slavery was not just the South's, that the whole nation was complicit in it."[8] In his 1852 Independence Day address, Douglass thundered at the hypocrisy of the new laws that bolstered the spread of slavery, condemning them in the words of the Declaration of Independence:

> Fellow citizens: Pardon me, and allow me to ask, why I am called upon to speak here today? What have I or those I represent to do with your national independence? Are the great principles of political freedom and natural justice, embodied in that Declaration of Independence, extended to us? And am I, therefore, called upon to bring our humble offering to the national altar, and to confess the benefits, and express devout gratitude for the blessing resulting from independence to us? . . . What to the American slave is your Fourth of July? I answer, a day that reveals him to be more than all the days of the year, the gross injustice and cruelty to which he is the constant victim. To him your celebration is a sham; your boasted liberty an unholy license; your national greatness, swelling vanity; your sounds of rejoicing are empty and heartless; your denunciation of tyrants, brass-fronted impudence; your shouts of liberty and equality, hollow mockery; your prayers and hymns, your sermons and thanksgivings, with all your religious parade and solemnity, are to him mere bombast, fraud, deception, impiety, and hypocrisy—a thin veil to cover up the crimes which would disgrace a nation of savages. There is not a nation on earth guilty of practices more shocking and bloodier than the people of these United States at this very hour. Go where you may, search out where you will . . . and you will say with me that, for revolting barbarity and shameless hypocrisy, America reigns without a rival.[9]

As slavery proponents grew more extreme, the Whigs and Democrats began to crack. The political parties and alliances that for decades had worked for compromise in the interest of preserving the Union began to implode. The outrage in the North over the Kansas-Nebraska Act, combined with the previous Compromise of 1850, provoked a political and social firestorm.

Both parties broke along sectional lines. The Whigs collapsed in 1854 and were gone by 1856. The 1854 election shattered their precarious unity as bitter division destroyed the party. Sen. Truman Smith resigned in disgust, grousing, "The Whig party has been killed off by that miserable Nebraska business."[10] As a result many Northern Whigs gravitated to the nascent Republican Party. One of them was an obscure former House member named Abraham Lincoln.

Although Democrats fractured into hostile Northern and Southern factions, they maintained their outward unity until 1858. The Democrats were a nominal national party, but their losses in 64 of 88 Northern districts in the 1854 elections made them a regional party dominated by their proslavery Southern wing. The election cost the Democrats 74 of their 157 seats in the House. In New England only 1 of 13 Democrats survived. Many prominent Northern Democrats found a home in the Republican Party, including William Seward, Salmon Chase, Thaddeus Stevens, and Schuyler Colfax.[11]

As the parties that had dominated American politics for decades fell apart, the Union's fabric began to fray. The Whigs and Democrats were an important part of the bond that held the Union together. In them Northern and Southern leaders mingled, became friends, and worked together, but slavery destroyed that relationship. The Whig collapse and Democratic split boded ill for the entire country.

7

I Will Be Heard!

Religion, Ideology, and the Abolitionist Movement

In the North a small but strident abolitionist campaign took root. Every failed compromise and infringement on the rights of free states by Congress, the courts, and the executive branch to appease slaveholders helped them gain support. Abolitionism began in New England as a fringe movement, supported by religious and secular liberal elites. One wing was dominated by progressive Christians, who "arose from evangelical ranks and framed its critique of bound labor in religious terms."[1] Religious abolitionists made a major social impact, and more Northern states abolished slavery as increasing numbers of influential "former slave owners such as Benjamin Franklin changed their views on the matter."[2]

One cannot underestimate the importance that faith played in the development of abolitionist movement, which was fueled by the Second Great Awakening. Many abolitionists were inspired by the preaching of Charles Finney, who "demanded a religious conversion with a political potential more radical than the preacher first intended."[3] But the "most important child of the Awakening, however, was the abolitionist movement, which in the 1830s took on new life, placed the slavery issue squarely on the national agenda, and for the next quarter century aroused and mobilized people in the cause of emancipation."[4]

Evangelical proponents of abolition understood this in terms of the concept of "free will." They repeatedly pointed

FIG. 6. Frederick Douglass and William Lloyd Garrison, publisher of the *Liberator*, n.d. National Park Service photo.

out that slavery "denied one group of human beings the free-dom of action necessary to free will—and therefore moral responsibility for their behavior. Meanwhile, it assigned to other human beings a degree of temporal power that virtu-ally guaranteed their moral corruption. Both master and slave were thus trapped in a relationship that inevitably led both down the path of sin and depravity."[5] They identified the theo-logical contradiction between free will and slavery that denied human beings to choose how they lived—a condition that not only trapped slaves, but also their masters.

Finney's preaching was expanded by William Lloyd Garrison and the American Anti-Slavery Society. Garrison's mother was a fiery, devout woman, and his alcoholic father abandoned the family because of a series of business failures, personal trage-dies, and his wife's uncompromising religion. When Garrison was thirteen, an uncle found him a job at the offices of the *Newburyport Herald* newspaper. He learned about printing and eventually began to write, an occupation his mother detested as the devil's work. Those years set his course. Garrison "would pursue printing, and guided by his religious faith, he would speak out against injustice, including the intemperance that led his father to ruin. He would also be a scrapper, not cowed by seemingly invincible foes."[6] It appeared that Garrison's task was like that of the legendary *Don Quixote.*

Eventually Garrison founded his own paper, the *Free Press.* In 1823, soured by politics, he sold the paper and moved to Boston, where he met the Beecher family and, in 1828, took over a temperance newspaper called the *National Philanthropist.* Frustrated by the inaction of these "philanthropists," Garrison moved to Bennington, Vermont, where he began the *Journal of the Times* and started writing about politics. In the paper he "promised to contend—temperance, pacifism, practical edu-cation, and 'the gradual emancipation of every slave in the republic'—antislavery inspired his most persistent efforts."[7]

But he left that paper to focus on abolition. He traveled to Baltimore, where he became the editor of a small abolitionist paper, the *Genius of Universal Emancipation,* published by the Quaker Benjamin Lundy. As editor of the *Genius* he grew into a literary crusader and fervent opponent of slavery: "'We call things by their right names, in plain language,' he said with pride, and 'no man's power shall awe us into submission.'" He grew more proficient at extracting material from the main-stream press and public record that offered opportunities to expiate on his themes, and he spared no one, harassing gov-ernors and senators with the sharp repartee he had honed in years of combat with rival small-town editors. Eventually he and Lundy were taken to court, convicted of libel, and jailed for two and a half months. Though he lost his editorial posi-tion, he continued to write. His time in jail convinced him of the righteousness of emancipation, which became his lifetime commitment, and he was soon publishing again.[8]

Garrison returned to Boston and founded the *Liberator*, a paper devoted to overthrowing slavery. In the first issue he demanded the immediate and unconditional end to slavery: "I will be as harsh as truth and as justice. . . . I will not equivocate—I will not excuse—I will not retreat a single inch—AND I WILL BE HEARD." He was true to that promise, and for the next three decades the *Liberator* was the premier voice of militant abolitionists. As such Garrison used the *Liberator* to "pledge an all-out attack on U.S. slavery."[9]

Garrison founded a movement that "launched a campaign to change minds, North and South, with three initiatives, public speeches, mass mailings and petitions."[10] Many speakers were students or graduates of Cincinnati's Lane Seminary who became known as "the Seventy." After training they "fanned out across the North campaigning in New England, Pennsylvania, New York Ohio, Indiana and Michigan."[11] Many met with hostility and violence.[12]

Many of the articles in the *Liberator*, like other religiously based abolitionist publications, "based their call for the immediate abolition of slavery on their belief that it was a sin."[13] Likewise, churches founded new educational institutions like Oberlin College in Ohio, which "was founded as an abolitionist institution."[14] Unitarian pastor and Transcendentalist thinker Theodore Parker enunciated a very important theological-political analogy for Christians in the abolitionist movement. He concentrated less on using chapter and verse and appealed more to "the spirit of the Gospel," using the analogy "as Jesus is to the Bible, so is the Declaration to the Constitution":[15]

By Christianity, I mean that form of religion which consists of piety—the love of God, and morality—the keeping of His laws. That Christianity is not the Christianity of the Christian church, nor of any sect. It is the ideal religion which the human race has been groping for. . . . By Democracy, I mean government over all the people, by all the people and for the sake of all. . . . This is not a democracy of the parties, but it is an ideal government, the reign of righteousness, the kingdom of justice, which all noble hearts long for, and labor to produce, the ideal whereunto mankind slowly draws near.[16]

Christian abolitionists "declared slavery a sin against God and man that demanded immediate action."[17] To Garrison abolition was a matter of faith in which compromise of any kind, including gradual abolition, was unacceptable. In the words of George Rable, "William Lloyd Garrison and his fellow abolitionists believed the nation faced a clear choice between damnation and salvation."[18] Garrison wrote, "Our program of immediate emancipation and assimilation, I maintained, was the only panacea, the only Christian solution, to an unbearable program."[19] Abolitionists like Garrison identified "their cause with the cause of freedom, and with the interests of large and relatively unorganized special groups such as laborers and immigrants, the abolitionists considered themselves to be, and convinced many others that they were, the sole remaining protectors of civil rights."[20]

Their arguments were eloquently rooted in profoundly Christian terms common to evangelical Christianity and the Second Great Awakening. Henry Wilson of Massachusetts, a Radical Republican and abolitionist who served as a U.S. senator and as vice president in Ulysses Grant's second term, serves as a good example. Wilson wrote of the events leading to war explaining religiously based abolitionist thought:

> American slavery reduced man, created in the Divine image, to property. . . . It made him a beast of burden in the field of toil, an outcast in social life, a cipher in courts of law, and a pariah in the house of God. To claim for himself, or to use himself for his own benefit or benefit of wife and child, was deemed a crime. His master could dispose of his person at will, and of everything acquired by his enforced and unrequited toil.

I Will Be Heard!

This complete subversion of the natural rights of millions . . . constituted a system antagonistic to the doctrines of reason and the monitions of conscience and developed and gratified the most intense spirit of personal pride, a love of class distinctions, and the lust of dominion. Hence a commanding power, ever sensitive, jealous, proscriptive, dominating, and aggressive, which was recognized and fitly characterized as the Slave Power.[21]

Christian abolitionists focused on Southern church leaders, who they believed "had become pawns of wealthy slaveholders and southern theologians' apologists for oppression."[22] The abolitionist movement spread through Northern churches and, for "Evangelical northerners, the belief in individual spiritual and personal rights and personal religious activism made such involvement necessary."[23]Abolition divided Baptists; Northern Baptists mobilized around the abolitionist principles of English Baptists, who were at the forefront of the abolitionism in England. Rev. William Knibb "became an impassioned defender of the human rights of blacks [whose] flamboyant speeches aroused the people against slavery."[24] The English Baptist Union sent a lengthy letter to the Baptist Triennial Convention in the United States on December 31, 1833, in which they condemned "the slave system . . . as a sin to be abandoned, and not an evil to be mitigated." They urged American Baptists to do all in their power to "effect its speedy overthrow."[25]

In 1835 English Baptists Francis Cox and James Hoby, who had worked with William Wilberforce to abolish slavery in the British Empire, came to the United States "to urge Baptists to abandon slavery. This visit and subsequent correspondence tended to polarize Baptists."[26] They encouraged Christian activism in Northern abolitionist groups. In 1849 the American Baptist Anti-Slavery Convention was formed in New York and launched a polemic attack on the institution of slavery, calling Southern Baptists to repent in the strongest terms. They urged that Baptist mission agencies be cleansed of "any taint of slavery and condemned slavery in militant terms," and they called on Southern Baptists to "confess before heaven and earth the sinfulness of holding slaves; admit it to be not only a misfortune, but a crime." warning that "if Baptists in the South ignored such warnings and persisted in the practice of slavery, 'we cannot and dare not recognize you as consistent brethren in Christ.'"[27] These divisions rose to crisis proportions in every denomination, provoking Sen. Henry Clay to wonder, "If our religious men cannot live together in peace, what can be expected of us politicians, very few of whom profess to be governed by the great principles of love?"[28]

While abolitionists aimed to do away with slavery entirely, most Northerners were indifferent to or opposed complete abolition. For most Northerners abolition only became an issue after the passage of the Fugitive Slave Act of 1850. So long as slavery was confined to the South and out of sight, the majority of Northerners showed little concern for the issue, while profiting from or reaping its benefits. Though Northerners wore clothes made of cotton harvested by slaves and corporations that supported the slave economy paid the wages of Northern workers and shareholders, few considered the moral issues until their state laws were overturned by Congress and Supreme Court.

The Power of the Pen: Popularization of Abolitionism

It was only after the Compromise of 1850 that the abolitionist movement gained traction. Angelina Grimke Weld confronted the indifference of Northerners in her 1838 book *American Slavery as It Is*, which sold over one hundred thousand copies. In her harsh criticism of Northern hypocrisy and indifference, Grimke told readers that to deny that "man's capacity for cruelty is to betray a shameful ignorance of human history and, in particular, of America's past."[29] She cited the Salem witch trials, the persecution of Quakers and Baptists, the transatlantic slave trade, and the violent attacks on abolitionists in Northern cities. Garrison's diatribes found little resonance among

Northerners, but the abolitionist movement was given a large boost by Harriet Beecher Stowe's 1852 novel *Uncle Tom's Cabin*: "A vivid, highly imaginative, best-selling, and altogether damning indictment of slavery."[30]

Stowe was a gifted writer and the daughter of Lyman Beecher, president of Lane Seminary and wife of Prof. Calvin Ellis Stowe. The Beechers were abolitionists who supported the Underground Railroad, even taking fugitive slaves into their home. Stowe's relationships with escaped slaves made a profound personal impact on her life. She received a letter from her sister, distraught over the passage of the Fugitive Slave Law, exhorting challenged Stowe to write about the issue: "How, Hattie, if I could use a pen as you can, I would write something that would make this whole nation feel what an accursed thing slavery is."[31] One communion Sunday, Beecher would later write, as she

> sat at the communion table of Brunswick's First Parish Church, a vision began playing before my eyes that left me in tears. I saw an old slave clad in rags, a gentle, Christian man like the slave I had read about in American Slavery as It Is. A cruel white man, a man with a hardened fist, was flogging the old slave. Now a cruel master ordered two other slaves two other slaves to finish the task. As they laid on the whips, the old black man prayed for God to forgive them.
>
> After church I rushed home in a trance and wrote down what I had seen. Since Calvin was away, I read the sketch to my ten- and twelve-year-old sons. They wept too, and one cried, "Oh! Mamma, slavery is the most cursed thing in the world!" I named the old slave Uncle Tom and his evil tormenter Simon Legree.
>
> Having recorded the climax of my story, I then commenced at the beginning.[32]

Many of Stowe's characters were fictional versions of people that she knew or had heard about. Her powerful writing made the work a bestseller in the United States and Britain. Through it the abolitionist movement gained momentum;

the book and its success—as well as that of the play adapted from it—"raised a counter indignation among Southerners because they thought Mrs. Stowe's portrait untrue and because the North was so willing to believe it."[33]

Despite Southern furor the book influenced a generation of young Northerners, creating a stereotype of slaveholders that caused people "to think more deeply and more personally about the implications of slavery for family, society and Christianity."[34] The book drew many ambivalent people to read abolitionist publications and the accounts of escaped slaves. Stowe's images "were irredeemably hostile: from now on the Southern stereotype was something akin to Simon Legree."[35] But those images transformed the issue in the minds of many Northerners as they "touched on all these chords of feeling, faith, and experience. . . . The genius of *Uncle Tom's Cabin* was that it made the personal universal, and it made the personal political as well. For millions of readers, blacks became people."[36] One reader said, "What truth could not accomplish, fiction did,"[37] as it "put a face on slavery and a soul on black people."[38]

The book had a transatlantic impact as well. Over a half million British women "signed a massive petition advocating emancipation in the United States this, in turn, encouraged American women to step up their petitioning."[39] The book touched the conscience of many readers, prompting them to "think more deeply and more personally about implications of slavery for family, society, and Christianity."[40] Even George Fitzhugh noted Stowe's book "was 'right' concerning the bitter treatment of slaves. . . . Law, Religion and Public Opinion should be invoked to punish and correct those abuses."[41] However, such thoughts could not be spoken too openly because other slaveholders "could not calmly debate internal correction . . . while outside agitators advertised their supposed monstrosities."[42]

The inability of Southerners to openly debate the issue made their visceral response to *Uncle Tom's Cabin* appear petty

I Will Be Heard!

and impotent. Though Stowe steered clear of more radical abolitionist groups, she was denounced by Southerners as a threat to the established order; they saw "her as the embodiment of radicalism, as an emissary of both abolitionism and women's rights."[43]

American Blacks and the Northern Abolitionist Movement

Black abolitionists played a significant role in the debate. Black abolitionists joined with white abolitionists "in order to improve their lives and to attack slavery."[44] Even before "Garrison published his famous *Liberator* in Boston in 1831, the first national convention of Negroes had been held, David Walker had already written his 'appeal,' and a black abolitionist magazine named *Freedom's Journal* had appeared."[45]

Initially most free Blacks espoused the self-improvement doctrine, which focused on improving their lot and helping others do the same. But continued discrimination in the North and in places where slavery's "philosophical and political defenders became ever more in intransigent, and where racism became an increasingly rigid barrier even to the most highly talented blacks, the self-improvement doctrine lost viability."[46]

Former slaves like Frederick Douglass, Sojourner Truth, and Harriet Tubman added their voices to the debate. Unlike white abolitionists these leaders' "formative years and antislavery educations were spent on southern plantations, and not in organizations dedicated to moral suasion."[47] Douglass was critical of the complicity of churches, especially Southern churches, in the continuation of slavery. His polemics against churches in his autobiography read like the preaching of an Old Testament prophet railing against the corruption of religion in their day:

> Indeed, I can see no reason, but the most deceitful one, for calling the religion of this land Christianity I look upon it as the climax of all misnomers, the boldest of all frauds, and the grossest of all libels. Never was there a clearer case of "stealing

the livery of the court of heaven to serve the devil in." . . . We have men-stealers for ministers, women-whippers for missionaries, and cradle-plunderers for church members. The man who wields the blood-clotted cowskin during the week fill the pulpit on Sunday, and claims to be a minister of the meek and lowly Jesus. The man who robs me of my earnings at the end of each week meets me as a class-leader on Sunday morning, to show me the way of life, and the path of salvation. He who sells my sister, for purposes of prostitution, stands forth as the pious advocate of purity. He who proclaims it a religious duty to read the Bible denies me the right of learning to read the name of the God who made me. He who is the religious advocate of marriage robs whole millions of its sacred influence, and leaves them to the ravages of wholesale pollution. The warm defender of the sacredness of the family relation is the same that scatters whole families,—sundering husbands and wives, parents and children, sisters and brothers,—leaving the hut vacant and the heart desolate. We see the thief preaching against theft, and the adulterer against adultery. We have men sold to build churches, women sold to support the gospel, and babes sold to purchase Bibles for the poor heathen! All for the glory of God and the good of souls.[48]

Douglass and Black abolitionists understood that many Northern abolitionists were unconscious of their own racism. Black abolitionists were characterized by their "racial independence and pragmatism" while the movement's white leaders, though "committed to antislavery principles, increasingly divided over doctrines such as political action or evangelical reform."[49]

Douglass realized that Blacks had to take control of their destiny by taking an active role in the movement. In 1854 Douglass declared that "it is emphatically our battle; no one else can fight it for us. . . . Our relations to the Anti-Slavery movement must be and are changed. Instead of depending on it we must lead it."[50] Douglass found this necessary because many white abolitionists were unable to "comprehend the world in other than moral absolutes, as well as their unwillingness to confront issues of racial prejudice and poverty."[51] Thus, Douglass and other Black abolitionist leaders went into the decade before the Civil War understanding that the fight would be much more difficult than their white allies imagined.

Harriet Tubman did not just speak; she acted to help other slaves escape. She escaped slavery herself on September 17, 1849, and through her faith and visions of freedom became one of the most influential "conductors" of the Underground Railroad that, along with Frederick Douglass, was instrumental in helping hundreds of escaped slaves gain freedom in the North or Canada:

> The stories of her success are whispered from one cabin and the next . . . none of her passengers have been caught or injured and none tossed off her Underground Railroad car. . . . "The slaves call her Moses" is a phrase often repeated about Tubman. . . . All slaves know the song "Go Down Moses." When Harriett goes to the South, she often announces her presences by up and down the hidden paths between cabins . . . singing "Go down Moses, way down to Egypt's Land. Tell old Pharaoh, let my people go."[52]

The Expansion of Abolitionism

Walt Whitman was radicalized by the passage of the Compromise of 1850. In his poem "Blood Money," he "used the common evangelical technique of applying biblical parables to contemporary events, echoing in literary form William H. Seward's 'higher law' speech":[53]

> Of olden time, when it came to pass
> That the Beautiful God, Jesus, should finish his work on
> earth,
> Then went Judas, and sold the Divine youth,
> And took pay for his body.

Cursed was the deed, even before the sweat of the clutching
hand grew dry. . . .

Since those ancient days; many a pouch enwrapping mean-
Its fee, like that paid for the Son of Mary.
Again goes one, saying,
What will ye give me, and I will deliver this man unto you?
And they make the covenant and pay the pieces of silver. . . .

The meanest spit in thy face—they smite thee with their
Bruised, bloody, and pinioned is thy body,
More sorrowful than death is thy soul.
Witness of Anguish—Brother of Slaves,
Not with thy price closed the price of thine image;
And still Iscariot plies his trade.[54]

Abolitionist leaders who fought against the Fugitive Slave
Act, the Kansas-Nebraska Act, and the *Dred Scott* decision were
now joined by other Northerners less tolerant of the status
quo. For abolitionists "who had lost their youthful spiritual
fervor, the crusade became a substitute for religion. And in
the calls for immediate emancipation, one could hear echoes
of perfectionism and millennialism."[55] But Charles B. Hodge,
the president of Princeton Theological Seminary, along with
other Northern conservative pastors, resisted abolitionism.
In the 1840s Hodge rejected the biblical defense of slavery,
though he "denied that slavery was a sin in itself."[56]

In the Republican Party, which was founded on opposition
to slavery's expansion, and the concepts of free labor and free
land, the abolitionist movement found a formidable political
voice. There they were part of a broad coalition whose aspirations had been blocked by proslavery Democrats. These
groups included "agrarians demanding free-homestead legislation, Western merchants desiring river and harbor improvements at federal expense, Pennsylvania iron masters and New
England textile merchants in quest of higher tariffs."[57]

However, abolitionists had to face political reality. The

Republican Party was a coalition that had to balance competing interests. In order to win the 1860 election, Republicans had to become more moderate; thus "the radicals' influence in the Republican leadership did undergo a decline in the aftermath of the election of 1856, when it became clear that victory in 1860 depended on carrying the doubtful states." Even so most Republican voters "responded more favorably to radical speeches and policies than to conservative ones."[58]

In 1858 Sen. William H. Seward warned of civil war. He understood what a growing population and expanding railroad and communications networks entailed for the nation, and why slavery and free labor were incompatible:

> Indeed, so incompatible are the two systems, that every new state which is organized within our ever existing domain makes its first political act a choice of the one and the exclusion of the other, even at the cost of civil war if necessary. . . . Hitherto, the two systems have existed in different states, side by side within the American Union. This happened because the Union is a confederation of states. But in another aspect the United States constitutes only one nation. Increase in population, which is filling the states out to their very borders, together with a new and extended net-work of railroads and other avenues, and an internal commerce which daily becomes more intimate, is rapidly bringing the states into a higher and more perfect unity or consolidation. Thus, these antagonistic systems are continually coming into closer contact, and collision results. Shall I tell you what this means? . . . It is an irrepressible conflict between opposing and enduring forces, and it means that the United States must and will, sooner or later, become either entirely a slaveholding nation, or entirely a free labor nation.[59]

Seward and other abolitionist senators were opposed by Southern and Northern Democrats, including Stephen Douglas, who defended the status quo due to their fear of disunion. Thus they supported a "complete defense of the South's position in the Union on questions of representation, the fugitive slave law, on taxes, on Southern exports, and on the slave trade itself."[60] Northern Democrats felt that abolitionists deepened the divide by speaking honestly about the impending conflict. Referring to John Brown's raid on Harper's Ferry, Dan Sickles claimed that the Republicans "encouraged fanatics and traitors to invade homes and communities in our sister States; led to scenes of such excitement as we have witnessed on the floor of the House; led to Southern citizens having no security at home; led to Virginia—the mother of states—standing at her frontiers to protect herself from the uplifted blade."[61]

Abolitionists made headway by gaining the support of newly arrived immigrants, "especially among the liberal, vocal, fiercely anti-slavery Germans who had recently fled the Revolution of 1848."[62] One of those immigrants, the German Carl Schurz, observed that "the slavery question" was "not a mere occasional quarrel between two sections of the country, divided by a geographic line," but "a great struggle between two antagonistic systems of social organization."[63] Many Germans, as well as Irish and other immigrants, felt similarly. It came to pass that immigrants, though ill-disposed to the plight of Blacks, despised the Southern system, which they believed was representative of the tyranny of the Old World.

I Will Be Heard!

8

An Institution Sanctioned by God

Southern Religious Support of Slavery

S outherners used Christianity to justify slavery. As Baptist Richard Furman declared, "The right of holding slaves is clearly established by the Holy Scriptures, both by precept and example."[1] In earlier times Catholic and Protestant churches throughout Europe provided their blessing to slavery in their colonies. When a Portuguese Catholic priest wrote his superiors asking if the slave trade was legal according to canon law, he received this answer:

> Your Reverence writes me that you would like to know whether the Negroes who are sent to your parts have been legally captured. To this I reply that I think your Reverence should have no scruples on this point. . . . We have been here ourselves for forty years and there have been among us very learned Fathers . . . never did they consider the trade as illicit. Therefore we and the Fathers of Brazil buy these slaves for our service without any scruple.[2]

The Church of England accommodated itself to the plantation system in English colonies. To escape ancient Christian prohibitions against believers owning other believers, most plantation owners refused their slaves baptism. However, in 1667 a law was passed that allowed slaves to be baptized, "declaring that baptism did not change a slave's condition—another indication of the degree to which established religion was willing to bend to the interests of the powerful."[3]

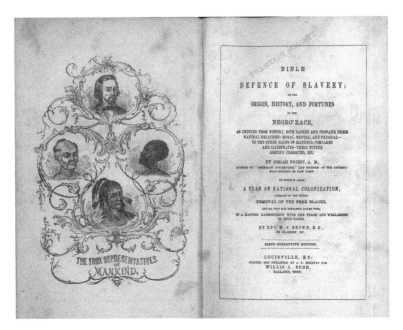

FIG. 7. Frontispiece of *Bible Defence of Slavery* or *The Origin, History, and Fortunes of the Negro Race* by Josiah Priest, 1851.

With the rise of abolition, slaveholders shifted their defense of slavery as a necessary evil to that of a positive good. Thus slavery became "in both secular and religious discourse, the central component of the mission God had designed for the South."[4] As in the North, where many abolitionist arguments were backed by Christian theology, religion was used to defend slavery in the South. British Evangelical-Anglican theologian Alister McGrath has written that "the arguments used by the pro-slavery lobby represent a fascinating illustration and condemnation of how the Bible may be used to support a notion by reading the text within a rigid interpretive framework that forces predetermined conclusions to the text."[5]

Southern Christianity was far more important to defenders of slavery than Christianity to most Northerners. John Daly writes, "Between 1801 when the Great Revival swept the region and 1831 when the slavery debate began, southern evangelicals achieved cultural dominance in the region. Looking back over

An Institution Sanctioned by God

the first thirty years of the century, they concluded that God had converted and blessed their region."[6] Southern preachers enshrined slavery as the racial key to all areas of life, a complete worldview: "It was the result of the secular transubstantiation in which the common elements of Southern life became sanctified in the Southern mind. The South's ideological cause was more than the sum of its parts, more than the material circumstances and conditions from which it sprang. . . . Questions about the Southern way of life became moral questions, and compromises of Southern life style would become concession of virtue and righteousness."[7]

Though some dissented the "dominant position in the South was strongly pro-slavery and the Bible was used to defend this entrenched position."[8] One dissenter was John Leland, the Virginia Baptist champion of religious liberty. Leland, who had helped Jefferson craft the Virginia Statute on Religious Liberty, and with James Madison, the Free Exercise and Establishment Clauses of the First Amendment. When he left Virginia for New England in 1791, he wrote his letter of valediction to his Virginia Baptist friends and colleagues: "I can never be reconciled to the keeping of them [slaves]; nor can I endure to see one man strip and whip another, as free by nature as himself. . . . Slavery, in its best appearance, is a violent deprivation of the rights of nature, inconsistent with republican government, destructive of every humane and benevolent passion of the soul, and subversive to that liberty absolutely necessary to ennoble the human mind."[9]

Southern Protestants saw slavery as an article of faith. Many Southern ministers believed the "spread of evangelical religion and slave labor in the South was a sign of God's divine favor. Ministers did not focus on defending slavery in the abstract but rather championed Christian slaveholding as it was practiced in the American South. Though conceding that some forms of slavery might be evil, Southern slavery was not."[10] John Hammond led Christian arguments for slavery, alleging biblical justifications that Blacks were biologically inferior to whites, and Scriptural support for slavery because "Christ never denounced servitude":[11] "Without white masters' paternalistic protection, biologically inferior blacks, loving sleep above all and 'sensual excitements of all kinds when awake' would first snooze, then wander, then plunder, then murder, then be exterminated and reenslaved."[12]

Southern preachers argued "that slavery was an institution sanctioned by God, and that even blacks profited from it, for they had been snatched out of pagan and uncivilized Africa and been given the advantages of the gospel."[13] Theological arguments for slavery were often based on divine punishment. "Many Southern clergymen found divine sanction for racial subordination in the 'truth' that blacks were cursed as 'Sons of Ham' and justified bondage by citing Biblical examples."[14] Their use of scripture to validate the system from which they reaped the benefits is only part of the story: the theology that justified slavery also justified what abolitionists considered "the hedonistic aspects of the Southern life style."[15]

Abolitionist preachers hammered away at the greed, sloth, and lust inherent in the culture of plantation life. Southern slaveholders took umbrage, for they believed they had divine sanction to own slaves. Proslavery theology expressed a hyper-individualistic faith that gave "new life to the claim that good men could hold slaves. Slaveholding was a traditional mark of success, and a moral defense of slavery was implicit wherever Americans who considered themselves good Christians held slaves."[16]

Slave owners were hostile to Black churches and committed acts of violence against them. The "attacks on clandestine prayer meetings were not arbitrary. They reflected the assumption (as one Mississippi slave put it) 'that when colored people were praying [by themselves] it was against them.'"[17] Yet some Southern Blacks accepted the Christian slave owner mentality. As Frederick Douglass wrote, "Many good, religious colored people who were under the delusion that God required

An Institution Sanctioned by God

them to submit to slavery and wear their chains with weakness and humility."[18]

As the rift split denominations, the heart of the matter was the way churches interpreted scripture, or hermeneutics. American Protestantism was grounded on the premise of the Protestant Reformation: sola scriptura. Southerners believed that they held a "special fidelity to the Bible and relationship with God. Southerners thought abolitionists either did not understand the Bible or did not know God's will, and suspected them of perverting both."[19] Americans

> favored a commonsense understanding of the Bible that ripped passages out of context and applied them to all people at all times. Sola scriptura both set and limited terms for discussing slavery and gave apologists for the institution great advantages. The patriarchs of the Old Testament had owned slaves, Mosaic Law upheld slavery, Jesus had not condemned slavery, and the apostles had advised slaves to obey their masters—these points summed up and closed the case for many southerners and no small number of northerners.[20]

Most denominations maintained a confusing ambivalence around slavery in the early 1800s. The Presbyterians exemplified this in 1818 when the "General Assembly of the Presbyterian Church, while opposing slavery against the law of God, also went on record as opposing abolition and deposed a minister for advocating abolition."[21] Other Christians offered alternative ways of "interpreting and applying scripture to the slavery question, but none were convincing or influential enough to force debate" with literalists.[22]

The schism between Northern and Southern branches of the largest denominations continued to widen, leading to the breakups of the 1840s. The Methodists split first in 1844, when "the Methodist General Conference condemned the bishop of Georgia for holding slaves, the church split and the following year saw the birth of the Methodist Episcopal Church."[23] Not all Southern Methodists agreed, and some Methodist abolitionists in the South "broke away from mainline Methodism to form the Free Methodist Church."[24]

The Baptists were next, when the Foreign Mission Board "refused to commission a candidate who had been recommended by the Georgia Baptist Convention, on the ground that he owned slaves," resulting in the formation of the Southern Baptist Convention.[25] The Baptist split is especially interesting, in that in 1790 the General Committee of Virginia "adopted a statement calling slavery 'a violent deprivation of the rights of nature, and inconsistent with a republican government; and therefore [we] recommend it to our brethren to make use of every legal measure, to extirpate the horrid evil from the land.'" In the early 1800s a robust antislavery contingent existed among Kentucky Baptists.[26]

But Baptists in the Deep South were strongly proslavery. In South Carolina noted Baptist preachers including "Richard Furman, Peter Bainbridge, and Edmund Botsford were among the larger slaveholders."[27] Furman wrote a defense of slavery in 1822 where he argued that "the right of holding slaves is clearly established in the Holy Scriptures by precept and example."[28] After the Nat Turner revolt in Virginia, proslavery voices "tended to silence any remaining antislavery voices in the South."[29] These voices grew more strident, and in 1835 the Charleston Association "adopted a militant defense of slavery sternly chastising abolitionists as 'mistaken philanthropists, and denuded and mischievous fanatics.'"[30]

Southern churches forced the split by trying to compel the Triennial Convention and Foreign Mission Board to accept slave owners as missionaries. The board refused, and Southern churches met to establish the Southern Baptist Convention. They claimed "the division was 'painful' but necessary because our brethren have pressed upon every inch of our privileges and our sacred rights."[31] Since the Foreign Mission Board refused to appoint slaveholders as missionaries, they justified the schism in theological terms: "Our objects, then, are the extension of the Messiah's kingdom, and the glory of

An Institution Sanctioned by God

God. Not disunion with any of his people; not the upholding of any form of civil rights . . . in the promotion of which, we find no necessity for relinquishing any of our civil rights. We will never interfere with what is Caesar's."[32] Of course, to them, "what was Caesar's" was the institution of slavery.

Presbyterians maintained outward unity before they split in 1861: "Reflecting the division of the nation, the Southern presbyteries withdrew from the Presbyterian Church and founded their own denomination."[33] Princeton's Charles Hodge warned of the dangers of disunion, writing, "If we are to be plunged into the horrors of civil war and servile insurrections, no tongue can tell how the cause of the Redeemer must suffer throughout our whole land."[34]

But Hodge was a Northern conservative who thought moderation and sentimental attachment to the Union would prevent secession and war. Southern pastors like James Henley Thornwell presented the conflict between slavery's defenders and abolitionists in Manichean terms: a battle between Christianity and atheism where the abolitionists occupied the second position. Rev. Robert Lewis Dabney, who served as Stonewall Jackson's chief of staff in the Valley Campaign and Battle of Seven Pines wrote,

> We must go before the nation with the Bible as the text and "Thus saith the Lord" as the answer. . . . We know that on the Bible argument the abolition party will be driven to reveal their true infidel tendencies. The Bible being bound to stand on our side, they have to come out and array themselves against the Bible. And then the whole body of sincere believers at the North will have to array themselves, though unwillingly, on our side. They will prefer the Bible to abolitionism.[35]

Southern church leaders were among the loudest voices for disunion. They labeled Northern critics—even fellow evangelicals—as "atheists, infidels, communists, free-lovers, Bible-haters, and anti-Christian levelers."[36] The preachers who had torn their denominations asunder now "summoned their congregations to leave the foul Union and then to cleanse their world."[37] Thomas R. R. Cobb, an outspoken advocate of slavery and secession, wrote proudly that secession "has been accomplished mainly by the churches."[38] Rev. William Leacock of Christ Church, New Orleans, declared in his Thanksgiving sermon of 1860:

> Our enemies . . . have "defamed" our characters, "lacerated" our feelings, "invaded" our rights, "stolen" our property, and let "murderers . . . loose upon us, stimulated by weak or designing or infidel preachers." With "the deepest and blackest malice," they have "proscribed" us "as unworthy members . . . of the society of men and accursed before God." Unless we sink to "craven" beginning that they "not disturb us . . . nothing is now left us but secession."[39]

The fact that Northern Protestant ministers, intellectuals, and theologians like Charles B. Hodge "supported the institution of slavery on biblical grounds, often dismissing abolitionists as liberal progressives who did not take the Bible seriously" leaves a troubling question about those who oppose issues on purely "biblical" grounds. Many Northerners opposed Christian abolitionists "in order to protect and promote interests concomitant to slavery, namely biblical traditionalism, and social and theological authority."[40] The Northern clerical defenders of slavery considered abolitionist preaching as a threat, not just to slavery, "but also to the very principle of social and ecclesiastical hierarchy."[41] Alistair McGrath asked an important question of modern Christians: "Might not the same mistakes be made all over again, this time over another issue?"[42]

9

The Triumphs of Christianity Rest on Slavery

Holy Warriors at the Forefront

The Protestant denominational breakup boded ill for the country. The churches were institutions that helped bind the country together. But their true believers—strident abolitionists and militant slavery supporters—were among the worst political partisans of their day. As David Goldfield notes, "For people of faith these internecine schisms were very troubling. If citizens could not get along in the fellowship of Christ, what did the future hold for the nation?"[1] In the 1840s the Democrats and Whigs found themselves led by militant Christians as the "fissures among evangelicals, the conflicts between Protestants and Catholics, the slavery debates, and the settlement of the West placed religion at the forefront of American politics."[2] However, slavery became the overriding issue as divisions among the faithful deepened. Kentucky senator Henry Clay asked in despair, "If our religious men cannot live together in peace, what can be expected of us politicians, very few of whom profess to be governed by the great principle of love?"[3]

A Cincinnati minister preached against secession, "citing Absalom, Jeroboam, and Judas" as examples. He argued that the "'cause of the United States and the Cause of Jehovah' were identical . . . and insisted that 'a just defensive war' against southern secessionists is 'one of the prominent ways by which the Lord will introduce the millennial day.'"[4] Southern ministers became political and military leaders. Men once considered moderates began to speak "the language of cultural warfare. Mississippi Episcopal Bishop William Mercer Green denounced the 'restless, insubordinate, and overbearing spirit of Puritanism' that was destroying the nation."[5]

John Wightman preached that Confederate victory was certain:

> The eminence of the South is the result of her domestic slavery the feature which gives character to her history, and which marshals the mighty events now at work for her defense and perpetuity. Following the guidance of Providence she was led to the lively oracles, whence she received her laws and institutions from the hand of God. . . . Her government was built on the Bible. . . . God is here. . . . The pillar of fire is police and pilot. . . . No work of God can be accomplished without resistance, revolution and blood. If we turn to Moses, Luther or Washington, we see that hardened superstitions, obdurate vices, and oppressive tyranny only could be revolutionized by the blood of martyrs. . . . Well might the South spring to arms, indignant that the foot of the tyrant should be put on her neck. Her cause is holy. . . . Need we further proof of God's providence? That our cause is just? That the South shall triumph? I see . . . a nation springing into being. . . . The triumphs of Christianity rest, this very hour, on slavery; and slavery depends on the triumph of the South.[6]

Sen. John Calhoun, who crafted so many compromises, was very concerned about the churches. He observed that church unity was important to the country's unity, noting that "the evangelical denominations once contributed greatly to strengthen the bond of the Union." If the bonds were broken, he worried, "nothing will be left to hold the Union together except force."[7]

Calhoun recognized a fact about American religious and political polity that many today do not comprehend: that America's religious denominations were essential to preserve the Union. As long as they remained together, they helped ensure the Union's existence. When they fractured, so did the Union. Calhoun's concerns are timeless. One can ask today what the fractured religious climate in the United States bodes for us.[8]

Jefferson Davis and Abraham Lincoln came to sharply different philosophical and theological understandings of slavery. In 1848 Davis defended the institution as "a common law right to property in the services of man; its origin is in Divine decree—the curse on the graceless sons of Noah." The theological belief in Black racial inferiority allowed Southern political leaders to dehumanize Blacks and define them as property. Davis believed that Southern children needed to be indoctrinated in this view: he wanted children learning from proper books that "would indoctrinate their minds to see opposing viewpoints that might corrupt their minds. Schoolteachers must be trained in the South, which for too long had relied on itinerant Yankee educators who brought concealed antislavery convictions with them."[9]

Democratic senator Stephen A. Douglas of Illinois was perhaps the most influential politician of the day. "Only five feet tall, when he spoke in the Senate, he became a verbal tornado with a voice that seemed to belong to a man ten times his size. Often, he worked himself into a near frenzy, stripping off his coat, his vest, his shirt, and finally his undershirt, as he made his thunderous points. Before long he had earned the nickname 'the Little Giant.'"[10] Douglas had many supporters in the North and the South and aspirations to the presidency. He understood the concept of white rule and proclaimed, "I care more for the great principle of self-government, the right of the people to rule, than I do for all the negroes in Christendom."[11] During his first debate with Lincoln in the 1858 Illinois senate campaign at Ottawa, Illinois, Douglas bluntly stated:

> I believe that this government was made on the white basis. I believe it was made by white men for the benefit of white men and their posterity forever, and I am in favor of confining citizenship to white me—men of European birth and European

descent, instead of conferring it upon Negroes and Indians, and other inferior races. But Mr. Lincoln, following the lead of the Abolition orators that came here and lectured in the basements of your churches and school houses, reads the Declaration of Independence that all me are created free and equal, and then says: How can you deprive the negro of that equality which God and the Declaration of Independence awards to him? He and they maintain that negro equality is guaranteed by the laws of God, and re-asserted in the Declaration of Independence. If they think so, ought thus to say and thus to vote. I do not question Mr. Lincoln's conscientious belief that the negro was made his equal, and hence his brother. But for my own part, I do not regard the negro as my equal, and I positively deny that he is my brother, or any kin of me whatever.[12]

Lincoln's Practicality: Declaration, Faith, and Emancipation

Lincoln, who was not a believer in the sense of traditional Christian orthodoxy, condemned the expansion of slavery in decidedly theological terms, noting that "slavery is founded in the selfishness of man's nature . . . opposition to it is in his love of justice. . . . Repeal all past human history, you cannot repeal human nature. It will still be the abundance of man's heart, that slavery extension is wrong."[13] During his debates with Douglas, Lincoln tied that theological understanding to his belief in the founding principle of the Declaration of Independence: that "all men are created equal." Lincoln's understanding was remarkable both then and now:

> Slavery was a violation of the Declaration's "majestic interpretation of the economy of the Universe," allowed by the founders because it is already among us, but placed by them in the course of ultimate extinction. Although unfulfilled in the present, the declaration's promise of equality was "a beacon to guide" not only "the whole race of man then living" but "their children and their children's children, and the countless myriads of generations who should inhabit the earth in other ages."[14]

The Triumphs Rest on Slavery

During their debates Lincoln attacked Douglas's position as well as the Supreme Court's decision in *Dred Scott*: "There is no reason in the world why the negro is not entitled to all the natural rights enumerated in the Declaration of Independence."[15]

Abraham Lincoln comprehended slavery as a moral and ethical issue. He believed the institution encroached on the basic human rights of Blacks, who he believed were human. While he did not believe that Blacks were equal yet in society or education, they were certainly endowed with the unalienable rights of all people. He regarded slavery as a moral, social, and political evil: "If slavery is not wrong, then nothing is wrong. I cannot remember when I did not so think, and feel."[16] Although Lincoln believed this, he was conflicted, because he also believed in an indivisible Union. Throughout his political journey Lincoln attempted to balance both, probably better than any man before or since.

Lincoln was unique: alone among Northern politicians, he had the ability to recognize the various political and economic forces at play in the battle over slavery. While some politicians staked all on free labor or abolitionism, Lincoln "combined perfectly the needs of business, the political ambition of the new Republican party, and the rhetoric of humanitarianism. He would keep the abolition of slavery not at the top of his list of priorities, but close enough to the top so that it could be pushed there by abolitionist pressures and by practical political advantage."[17]

The passage of the Kansas-Nebraska Act disillusioned Lincoln, causing him to remark to a friend that "this nation cannot exist half-slave and half-free."[18] In his debates with Douglas, he condemned slavery because it "forced the American people into an open war with the Declaration of Independence depriving 'our republican example of its just influence in the world.'"[19] But Lincoln maintained a balance and sought compromise with Southerners by not demonizing them in his pursuit of abolition.

Today some are critical of Lincoln's pragmatism regarding

abolition, but their criticism is misplaced. Frederick Douglass was often disappointed with and critical of Lincoln's compromises as president, noting that Lincoln was "the first great man that I talked with in the United States freely, who in no single instance reminded me of the differences between himself and myself, of the difference of color."[20] Lincoln "skillfully blended the interests of the very rich and the interest of the black at a moment in history when those interests met."[21] Such interests seldom meet, but only he was able to blend them into a political coalition that brought about the emancipation so long sought by men like Douglass and Garrison, and women like Stowe, the Grimkes, and Sojourner Truth.

10

With God as Our Champion

The Confederate Union of Church and State

Perhaps more than anything, the denominational splits prepared Southern citizens and clergy for secession and war. The churches set the precedent by which Southerners left other national organizations. When secession came "the majority of young Protestant preachers were already primed by their respective church traditions to regard the possibilities of political separation from the United States without undue anxiety."[1]

One of the most powerful ideological tools since ancient times is the link between religion and state. As Rev. William Seat preached in 1862, "Lo! Suddenly, to the amazement of the world a mighty kingdom arose. . . . of strictly providential Divine origin. . . . The One like the Son of Man has appeared in the ride of the Confederate States."[2]

Christianity has been a driving force in American life from the days of the Calvinist Puritans, especially the idea of being God's chosen people. But it was in the South where the Puritan beliefs took their firmest root. As God's chosen people, the Puritans' culture, society, and ideology, which justified slavery and the racial inferiority of Blacks and promoted Southern nationalism. "Confederate independence, explained a Methodist tract quoting Puritan John Winthrop, was intended to enable the South, 'like a city set on a hill' [to] fulfill her God given mission to exalt in civilization and Christianity the nations of the earth."[3]

Those beliefs "supplied the overarching framework for southern nationalism. As Confederates cast themselves as God's chosen people."[4] Ministers had to balance their most important beliefs—evangelicalism and republicanism—to justify the racial superiority of whites and Black slavery. Because these beliefs could mean different things to different people, Southern clergy and politicians had to find a way to combine them, for "republicanism and evangelicalism could be reactionary or progressive in implication, elitist or democratic."[5]

This was evident in the schisms between churches. A group of 154 clergymen calling themselves "the Clergy of the South warned the world's Christians that the North was perpetuating a plot of 'interference with the plans of Divine Providence.'"[6] A Tennessee pastor stated that "in all contests between nations God espouses the cause of the Righteous and makes it his own. . . . The institution of slavery according to the Bible is right. Therefore, in the contest between the North and the South, He will espouse the cause of the South and make it his own."[7] The denominational rifts lasted far longer than the war. The "regional isolation, war bitterness, and differing emphasis in theology created chasms by the end of the century which leaders of an earlier generation could not have contemplated."[8]

The claims of Southern preachers that Southerners were God's people were "key to their success as the foundation of a hegemonic ideology lay in making."[9] They had to convince the "Southern people to acknowledge God's authority was bound up with a legitimization of both clerical and civil rulers. Christian humility became identified with social and political deference as the clergy urged submission to both God and Jefferson Davis."[10] As a result, "sacred and secular history, like religion and politics, had become all but indistinguishable. . . . The analogy between the Confederacy and the chosen Hebrew nation was invoked so often as to be transformed into a figure of everyday speech. Like the United States before it, the Confederacy became a redeemer nation, the new Israel."[11]

Confederate Christian Nationalist ideology called for uncompromising hardness. Stonewall Jackson's brutal Old Testament concept of war allowed him to say, "No quarter to the violators of our homes and firesides," and when someone deplored the necessity of destroying so many brave men, he exclaimed, "No, shoot them all, I do not wish them to be brave."[12] Jackson told Gen. Richard Ewell, after Ewell ordered his men not to fire on a Union officer riding a white horse during the Valley campaign, "Never do such a thing again, General Ewell. This is no ordinary war. The brave Federal officers are the very kind that must be killed. Shoot the brave officers and the cowards will run away with their men with them."[13]

For Southern clergy and laymen, "slavery became in secular and religious discourse . . . the central component of the mission God had designed for the South. . . . The Confederates were fighting a just war not only because they were . . . defending themselves against invasion, they were struggling to carry out God's designs for a heathen race."[14] As William Seat wrote, "Surely since the Wars of God's ancient people has there been such a remarkable and uniform success against tremendous odds. The explanation is found in the fact that the Lord goes forth to fight against the coercion by foes of his particular people."[15]

Confederates combined the authority of church and state and became the most theocratic government to exist in North America. Thus Jefferson Davis repeatedly appealed to God as a Confederate ally: "In his repeated calls for God's aid and in his declaration of national days of fasting, humiliation, and prayer on nine occasions throughout the war, Jefferson Davis similarly acknowledged the need for a larger scope of legitimization. Nationhood had to be tied to higher ends. The South, it seemed, could not just be politically independent; it wanted to believe it was divinely chosen."[16] Davis's actions increased clergy support for the war. A clergyman told his congregation that the people of the South needed to relearn "the virtue of reverence—and the lesson of respecting, obeying, and honoring authority, for authority's sake."[17]

Confederate clergymen not only supported slavery and

preached disunion, but many also shed their clerical robes for Confederate Gray. Some were chaplains, but others served as soldiers, officers, and even generals. Bishop Leonidas Polk, a classmate of Jefferson Davis at West Point, was commissioned as a major general even as he retained his ecclesiastical office. "Northerners expressed horror at such sacrilege, but Southerners were delighted with this transfer from the Army of the Lord."[18] Lee's chief of artillery, Brig. Gen. Nelson Pendleton was an academy graduate, Episcopal priest, and unabashed racist and key proponent of the Lost Cause. Southern churches in general wholeheartedly supported the war effort; they contributed donations of "everything from pew cushions to brass bells, Southern churches gave direct material aid to the cause. Among all the institutions in Southern life, perhaps the church most faithfully served the Confederate Army and nation."[19]

Southern Christianity was a bedrock of slavery and Confederate nationalism. The Great Seal of the Confederacy used the Latin words *deo vindice*, which can be translated as "with God as our champion," or "under God [our] vindicator." Thus, Confederate nationalism was intensely theological. Secession "became an act of purification, a separation from the pollutions of decaying northern society, that 'monstrous mass of moral disease,' as the *Mobile Evening News* so vividly described it."[20] Confederate textbooks were used to indoctrinate children: "The First Reader for Southern Schools assured its young pupils that 'God wills that some men should be slaves, and some masters.' For older children Mrs. Miranda Moore's bestselling *Geographic Reader* included a detailed proslavery history of the United States that explained how northerners had gone 'mad' on the subject of abolitionism."[21]

The seeds of future white supremacy in America were planted in the hearts of white Southern children by radical religious ideologues. Theological debates fueled the fires that ignited the war. For Southerners their cause was righteous, and as it reinforced the ideology of true believers, other very real-world events further inflamed their passions.

II

They Have Closed the Heavy Doors

The Dred Scott *Decision*

The divisions over slavery deepened in the 1850s as moderate voices faded away. Southerners considered the Underground Railroad, a loose organization that helped runaway slaves find refuge, "an affront to the slaveholders pride" and claimed that "anyone who helped a man or woman escape bondage was simply a thief" who had robbed them of their property and livelihood, as an "adult field hand could cost as much as $2000, the equivalent of a substantial house."[1]

In 1856 the Supreme Court, headed by Chief Justice Roger Taney and dominated by Southern Democrats, launched a frontal attack on Congress by ruling in favor of slave owners in the *Dred Scott* decision, with profound effects on Northern politics. Taney, who wrote the majority opinion, saturated his ruling in white supremacist language: "Neither the Declaration of Independence nor the Constitution had been intended to apply to blacks, he said. Blacks were 'so far inferior that they had no rights which the white man was bound to respect.'" Taney also declared that the Missouri Compromise was unconstitutional: "Congress had exceeded its authority when it forbade slavery in the territories by such legislation as the Missouri Compromise, for slaves were private property protected by the Constitution."[2] The ruling was momentous, but the judicial fiat of the Taney court was a disaster for the American people: "In the South . . . it encouraged southern rights advocates to believe that their utmost demands were legitimatized by constitutional

FIG. 8. *Visit to Dred Scott—His Family—Incidents of His Life—Decision of the Supreme Court.* From *Frank Leslie's Illustrated Newspaper,* June 27, 1857. Courtesy of the Library of Congress, LC-DIG-ds-12470.

sanction and, therefore, to stiffen their insistence upon their 'rights.' In the North . . . it strengthened a conviction that an aggressive slavocracy was conspiring to impose slavery upon the nation, and that any effort to reach an accommodation with such aggressors was futile. While strengthening the extremists, it cut the ground from under the moderates."[3] Taney's open racism, which made Blacks property in perpetuity, was chilling:

Can a negro, whose ancestors were imported into this country, sold as slaves, become a member of the political community formed and brought into existence by the Constitution of the United States and as such become entitled to all the rights, and privileges, and immunities, guaranteed by that instrument to the citizen? . . . It is absolutely certain that the African race were not included under the name of citizens of a state . . . and were not intended to be included, under the word "citizens" in the Constitution, and therefore claim none of the rights and privileges which that instrument provides for and secures to citizens of the United States. On the contrary, they were at that time considered as a subordinate and inferior class of beings, who had been subjugated by the dominant race, and, whether emancipated or not, yet remain subject to their authority, and had no rights or privileges but those who held the power and the Government might choose to grant them.[4]

In addition, the ruling had a far reach: "No territorial government in any federally administered territory had the authority to alter the status of a white citizen's property, much less to take that property out of a citizen's hands, without due process of law or as punishment for some crime."[5] In free states Blacks were more at risk of being returned to slavery because of their status as property, not people. Free Blacks in the South were effectively stripped of citizenship and could be expelled or reenslaved. The decision "cast doubt on the free status of every African American regardless of residence."[6]

Taney's decision was deeply rooted in the prevailing white supremacism that grew in the South as justification for expanding slavery. Southerners and even many Northerners considered Blacks as "subhuman," a term coined by an American, Lothrop Stoddard. While Taney did not use "subhuman" in his ruling, he called Blacks a "subordinate class of beings." The effects of his ruling would echo in the United States and Europe long after *Dred Scott* was overturned by the Thirteenth Amendment, and the word "subhuman" found its way into the Nazi lexicon of race hate (translated Untermenschen), especially regarding Jews, Slavs, Gypsies, and the disabled, who were considered unworthy of life. Nazi propagandist Julius Rosenberg used it and introduced it to Hitler.

Taney declared that Congress "never had the right to limit slavery's expansion, and that the Missouri Compromise had been null and void on the day of its formulation."[7] With a stroke of his pen, he fulfilled Jefferson's warning that the Missouri Compromise was merely a reprieve from the broader issues involving slavery. The ruling said "that a free negro was not a citizen and the decision that Congress could not exclude slavery from the territories were intensely repugnant to many people in the free states."[8]

President-elect James Buchanan had secretly intervened in the court's deliberations, hoping it would do his dirty work by appeasing slave owners and catering to their agenda. He "wanted to know not only when, but if the Court would save the new administration and the Union from the issue of slavery in the territories. Would the judges thankfully declare the explosive subject out of bounds, for everyone who exerted federal power? The shattering question need never bother President Buchanan."[9] But Buchanan's attempt blew up in his face. *Dred Scott* ignited opposition in the North, where Republicans now led by Abraham Lincoln decried the decision, and impaired "the power of Congress—a power which had remained intact to this time—to occupy the middle ground."[10]

In 1854 Lincoln proposed that the Declaration of Independence was "the standard maxim of free society . . . constantly spreading and deepening its influence," ultimately applicable "to peoples of all colors everywhere."[11] After *Dred Scott* Lincoln warned that the Declaration had been assaulted: "Our Declaration of Independence was held sacred by all, and thought to include all" he declared, "but now, to aid in making the bondage of the Negro universal and eternal, it is assaulted, and sneered at, and construed, and hawked at, and torn, till, its framers could rise from their graves, they could not recognize it at all."[12]

In his attack on the decision, Lincoln noted that Taney "insists at great length that negroes were no part of the people who made, or for whom made, the Declaration of Independence or the Constitution." According to Doris Kearns Goodwin,

> In at least five states, black voters acted on the ratification of the Constitution and were among the "We the People" by whom the Constitution was ordained and established. Lincoln acknowledged that the founders "did not declare all men equal in all respects. They did not mean to say that all were equal in color, size, intellect, moral developments, or social capacity." But they did declare all men "equal in 'certain inalienable rights, among which are life, liberty, and the pursuit of happiness." . . . They meant simply to declare the right, so the enforcement of it might follow as circumstances permit.[13]

Lincoln's question regarding Taney's judicial activism was logical; he and other Republican leaders observed "that all slavery needed was one more *Dred Scott* decision that a state could not bar slavery and the objective of Slave Power to nationalize slavery would be accomplished."[14] Lincoln wondered how long it would be before the Court ruled that the "Constitution of the United States does not permit a state to exclude slavery from its limits?" How far off was the day when "we shall lie down pleasantly thinking that the people of Missouri are on the verge of making their State free; and shall awake to the reality, instead, that the Supreme Court has made Illinois a slave State?"[15] Lincoln identified the ramifications for Blacks, both enslaved and free:

All the powers of the earth seem rapidly combining against him. Mammon is after him; ambition follows, and philosophy follows, and the theology of the day is fast joining the cry. They have him in his prison house; . . . One after another they have closed the heavy doors upon him . . . and they stand musing as to what invention, in all the dominions of mind and matter, can be produced the impossibility of his escape more complete than it is.[16]

In the words of Frederick Douglass, "Judge Taney can do many things . . . but he cannot . . . change the essential nature of things—making evil good, and good, evil."[17]

Southerners were exultant. The *Richmond Enquirer* wrote that the court had destroyed "the foundation of the theory upon which their warfare has been waged against the institutions of the South."[18] Northerners now rightly feared that Taney's activist court would deny their states the right to forbid slavery.

Lincoln's assessment of *Dred Scott* was correct. In free states courts used it in decisions against Blacks, thus encouraging slave owners. The Supreme Court of California ominously "upheld a slaveowner's right to retain his property contrary to the state's constitution."[19] After *Dred Scott*, in 1852, Virginia assisted in a similar case meant for the New York Supreme Court, where in 1857 an appellate court "upheld the freedom of eight slaves who had left their Virginia owner while in New York City on their way to Texas."[20] Hoping for a reversal in the case of *Lemon v. The People*, "Virginia decided to take the case to the highest New York court (which upheld the law in 1860) and would have undoubtedly appealed it to Taney's Supreme Court had not secession intervened."[21]

Even the Democrats could see the writing on the wall. The national publication of the Democratic Party, the *Washington Union*, "announced that the clear implication of the *Dred Scott* decision was that all state laws prohibiting a citizen from another state, either permanently or temporarily, were unconstitutional."[22]

12

Portents Hang on All the Arches of the Horizon

The Bloody Battle for Kansas

As more settlers from free and slave states poured in, the struggle for Kansas intensified. By the fall of 1855, free-state citizens far outnumbered supporters of slavery. But Pres. Franklin Pierce "gave official recognition to a territorial government dominated by proslavery forces—a government that decreed the laws of Missouri in force in Kansas as well."[1] The proslavery government decreed: "Public office and jury service were restricted to those with demonstrably proslavery options. Publicly to deny the right to hold slaves became punishable by five year's imprisonment. To assist fugitive slaves risked a ten-year sentence. The penalty for inciting slave rebellion was death."[2]

Kansas became the front line of militant abolitionists and slave power forces. Southern leaders banked their political capital on winning the battle for Kansas: "[They] poured political, human and economic capital into the struggle for the imposition of slavery on the Kansas Territory following the passage of the Kansas-Nebraska Act. For the South, a pro-slavery victory in Kansas meant 'two new U.S. Senators for the South. If a free labor Kansas triumphed, however, the North would gain four senators: Kansas's immediately and Missouri's soon.'"[3]

Rich Southerners persuaded poor whites to fight their battles. Jefferson Buford of Alabama recruited hundreds of men, claiming to defend "the supremacy of the white race," calling Kansas "our great outpost," and warning that "a people

SOUTHERN CHIVALRY — ARGUMENT versus CLUB'S.

FIG. 9. *The Caning of Senator Charles Sumner by Representative Preston Brooks.* 1856. Created by John L. Magee, Library Company of Philadelphia.

who would not defend their outposts had already succumbed to the invader."[4]

To achieve this Buford and 415 volunteers went to Kansas, where they gained infamy as Buford's Cavalry. "When they left Montgomery each man received a Bible, and the 'holy soldiers' elected Buford as their general. Then they paraded onto the steamship Messenger, waving banners conveying Buford's twin messages: 'The Supremacy of the White Race' and 'Kansas the Outpost.'"[5] Though their campaign in Kansas failed, they proved that "Southern poor men would kill Yankees to keep blacks ground under."[6]

In late 1855 free-state settlers established a government that provoked proslavery settlers to mass violence: "Bolstered by additional reinforcements from Missouri invaded the free-state settlement of Lawrence, destroyed its two newspapers, and demolished or looted nearby homes and businesses."[7] Federal troops in Lawrence "stood idly by because they had received no orders from the inert Pierce administration."[8]

Sen. Charles Sumner of Massachusetts began a two-day

Portents Hang on All the Arches

speech known as "The Crime against Kansas." He condemned the assault on Lawrence, describing it as "the anteroom to civil war."[9] His speech burst like a bombshell in the hallowed halls of the Senate and served as a clarion call for war to both sides. Sumner proclaimed that "murderous robbers from Missouri . . . hirelings picked from the drunken spew and vomit of an uneasy civilization."[10] He continued: "The rape of a virgin Territory, compelling it to the hateful embrace of Slavery; and it may clearly be traced to a depraved longing for a new slave State, the hideous offspring of such a crime, in the hope of adding to the power of Slavery in the National Government."[11] Sumner painted a bleak picture of what was to come, stating that the "rape" of Lawrence was evidence that "'the horrors of intestine feud' were being planned 'not only in this distant Territory, but everywhere throughout the country. Already the muster has begun. The strife is no longer local, but national. Even now while I speak, portents hang on all the arches of the horizon, threatening to darken the land, which already yawns with, the mutterings of civil war."[12]

Later Sumner would be beaten with a cane by South Carolina representative Preston Brooks while sitting at his desk in the Senate. Brooks was related to Sen. Andrew P. Butler, whom Sumner had insulted in his speech. Other Southern congressmen were involved as well, and a fight broke out on the Senate floor. Sumner's injuries were so severe that they kept him from his duties for nearly two years.

Northern extremists also committed acts of violence in Kansas. John Brown carried on a holy war against slavery supporters:

> I rode into Kansas territory in eighteen and fifty-five in a one-horse wagon filled with revolvers, rifles, powder, and two-edged artillery broadswords. I expected war to break out between the free-state forces and the Border Ruffians, and I was ready to buckle on my armor and give battle . . . I heard the thundering voice of Jehovah exhorting me to slaughter the Border Ruffians as He's called Gideon to slay the Midianites. Yes, my great-

est or principal object—eternal war against slavery—was to be carried out in Kansas Territory. Praise be God![13]

Following the attack on Lawrence, Brown and his men attacked a proslavery family in their cabin at the Pottawatomie Creek settlement: they "dragged three men outside, shot the father through the head, and hacked his two sons with broadswords. Ritual murders."[14] They hacked two more victims to death with broadswords. Brown later wrote: "On the way back to camp, I was transfixed. The proslavery Philistines had murdered five or six free-state men in the great struggle for the soul of Kansas. Now we had got five of them. God alone is my judge. His will be done."[15]

David Potter has described the battle between the violent militias and mobs with great clarity: "Kansas remained bloody and full of political intrigue. Free and proslavery elements battled to control the territory. Throughout the summer and early fall of 1856, armies marched and counter-marched, threatening one another with blood-curdling threats, terrorizing peaceably inclined settlers, committing depredations upon those who could not defend themselves, and killing with enough frequency to give validity to the term 'Bleeding Kansas.'"[16] Kansas was the precursor of a far great conflict. In just under five years, armies of tens of thousands of soldiers would be marching and countermarching across northern Virginia and Tennessee, killing each other by the thousands in a war often fought without mercy, just like Bleeding Kansas.

13

General Jackson Is Dead

The Lecompton Constitution Controversy

ansas's population was overwhelmingly antislavery. Slaveholders and their supporters were a tiny minority, but
they were loud and used violence and intimidation to
gain power. Many Kansans felt disenfranchised when Franklin Pierce recognized the Lecompton legislature, which they
viewed as "a pro-slavery body elected by fraud in 1855."[1] In 1857
the Lecompton leadership, sensing the opportunity to have
Kansas admitted as a slave state over the will of the majority,
held an election for delegates to a convention to write a constitution for statehood.

Free state settlers boycotted the election, fearing that that
if they participated their votes would be "gerrymandered, and
simply counted out by stuffed ballots." The result was "a quiet
election, with many proslavery candidates unopposed and only
2,200 out of 9,000 registered voters going to the polls, a large
majority of extreme proslavery men won election as delegates
to the constitutional convention in September."[2] But the election's result was untenable; just "two thousand voters in a territory with 24,000 eligible for the franchise had elected a body
of delegates whom no one seriously regarded as representative of the majority opinion in Kansas."[3]

The Lecompton-backed constitutional convention passed a
proslavery constitution, which was vetoed by outgoing governor John W. Geary. Geary accused "the pro-slavery legislature
of attempting to stampede a rush to statehood on pro-slavery

FIG. 10. Pres. James Buchanan and Sen. Stephen A. Douglas.
Daguerrotype by Matthew Brady. Courtesy of the Library of Congress,
LC-BH82101–6628, LC-USZ62–1754.

terms," but they overrode his veto. Most Kansans opposed
the provisions that protected the owners of "the 200 slaves in
Kansas, banned free blacks from the state, and prohibited any
amendments to the constitution for seven years."[4] The free
state legislature in Topeka conducted a referendum where the
people voted 10,226 votes to 162 votes against Lecompton.[5]
The new governor, Robert J. Walker, who wanted a free and
fair referndum in what all took part, denounced Lecompton
"as a vile fraud, a bare counterfeit."[6] Southerners in Congress
responded by "threaten[ing] to secede unless the administration fired Walker and backed down on the referendum issue."[7]
The perception of danger of secession by Southern supporters of Lecompton led to chaos in the Democratic Party.

Pres. James Buchanan, a Pennsylvania Democrat, owed his
office to Southern support. Southern legislators and his cabinet, which was heavily Southern, pressured him to support Kansas's admission as a slave state. Buchanan, who had opposed

FIG. 11. *The Midnight Brawl of 5–6 February 1858 over the Lecompton Constitutional and Admission of Kansas as a Slave Stat.* From *Frank Leslie's Illustrated Newspaper*, February 20, 1858. U.S. House of Representatives Collection.

it, reversed his stance and endorsed the bill, "call[ing] on Congress to admit Kansas as a slave state with a constitution (drafted by the proslavery territorial government at Lecompton) that was never approved by Kansas voters and obviously opposed by a majority of them."[8]

Buchanan tossed aside the doctrine of popular sovereignty, which was key to earlier compromises. His move to placate slave states and overturn restrictions on slavery's expansion contained in the Missouri Compromise, the Compromise of 1850, and the Kansas-Nebraska Act provoked an outcry from Northern Democrats. Most were willing to accept slavery where it existed, but not its expansion, and Buchanan's flip-flop on Lecompton and Southern secession threats infuriated many. Buchanan's action

touched off a twelve-hour donnybrook in February 1858 [and] about 50 congressmen in various states of inebriation tangled with each other on the House floor. . . . The rumble subsided only when Mississippi congressman William Barksdale tackled an unidentified assailant as the latter snatched his toupee and waved it about like a captured flag. Barksdale finally retrieved his scalp and plopped it on his head wrong side out, the absurdity of the scene giving the combatant's pause.[9]

Many Northern Democrats rose up in opposition to the bill, but Buchanan, a "skilled political infighter, swung a remarkable percentage of Northern Democratic members of the House of Representatives, fully 60 percent, behind the Lecompton Constitution."[10] He failed, however, to reckon with Sen. Stephen Douglas.

Nicknamed "the Little Giant," Douglas skillfully crafted the Kansas-Nebraska Act of 1850 using the principle of popular sovereignty. He now led Democrats against Buchanan's acceptance of Lecompton. Douglas's previous actions supporting slave states had made him a hero in much of the South, and his stature nationwide made him the frontrunner to win the Democratic presidential nomination in 1860.

Douglas worked hard to hold the Union together and despised the tactics of the Southern Democrats. A political realist and not an ideologue, he was a racist, sympathetic to slaveholders and no supporter of emancipation. He was convinced "of the inferiority of the Negro, and he had a habit of stating it with brutal bluntness, 'I do not believe that the Negro is any kin of mine at all. . . . I believe that this government of ours was founded, and wisely founded upon white basis. It was made by white men, for the benefit of white men and their posterity, to be executed and managed by white men.'"[11] Despite his racist beliefs, Douglas understood the danger that the proslavery extremists supporting Lecompton posed to the Democratic Party and the nation. He knew that if the Lecompton Bill was passed it would destroy the Democratic Party, and quite possibly the Union.

Douglas found out about Buchanan's flip-flop when he read

General Jackson Is Dead

about it in the *Washington Union*. His fury was visible when he wrote with characteristic honesty: "This left no doubt were the old bastard stood. 'Can you believe his Goddamned arrogance?' I told a friend. 'I run the Committee on Territories. He should have consulted me before approving the Lecompton fraud. He'll pay for that. By God, sir, I made Mr. James Buchanan, and by God, sir, I'll unmake him.'"[12]

Douglas threw caution to the wind and stormed to the White House "to confront Buchanan on the 'trickery and juggling of the Lecompton constitution.'" He warned Buchanan that his actions would "destroy the Democratic party in the North," and that "if Buchanan insisted on going through with it, Douglas swore to oppose him in Congress."[13]

It was an epic confrontation. Douglas recalled:

The Lecompton constitution, I told Buchanan bluntly, was a blatant fraud on the people of Kansas and the process of democracy, I warned him not to recommend acceptance of it. With his head titled forward in that bizarre habit of his, he said that he intended to endorse the constitution and send it to Congress. "If you do," I thundered, "I'll denounce it the moment that it is read." His face turned red with anger. "I'll make Lecompton a party test," he said. "I expect every democratic Senator to support it." I will not, sir![14]

Angry and offended, Buchanan cut him off and issued his own threat to Douglas: "'I desire you to remember that no Democrat ever yet differed from an administration of his own choice without being crushed. . . . Beware of the fate of Tallmadge and Rives'—two senators who had gone into political oblivion after crossing Andrew Jackson." The redoubtable Little Giant was undeterred. "[He] riposted: 'Mr. President, I wish to remind you that General Jackson is dead, sir.'"[15] It was unprecedented for a senator to confront a president of his own party by opposing him in Congress, and Douglas was doing it to the president's face. The consequences for him, his party, and the country would be immense.

Following the confrontation Douglas was even more determined to defeat the bid to admit Kansas over the will of the majority. Douglas did what, in our day, few politicians would consider doing, and in a display of righteous anger he "took his political life into his own hands and assailed the Lecompton Constitution on the floor of the Senate as a mockery of the popular sovereignty principle."[16] Buchanan's congressional allies fought back viciously, and the two sides sometimes came into physical confrontation in the chambers of Congress.

When Buchanan's supporters pushed for Kansas's admission as a slave state, Douglas fired back:

> "You do," I said, "and it will lead directly to civil war!" I warned the anti-Lecompton Democrats of the North that the President intended to put the knife to the throat of every man who dared to think for himself on this question and carry out principles in good faith. "God forbid," I said, "that I ever surrender my right to differ from a President of the United States for my own choice. I am not a tool of any President!"[17]

At this point Douglas and the Northern Democrats joined with Republicans for the first time to defeat the measure. Douglas recollected the battle:

> After the Christmas recess, the Administration unleashed its heavy horsemen: Davis, Slidell, Hunter, Toombs, and Hammond, all southerners. They damned me as a traitor and demanded that I be stripped of my chairmanship of the Committee on Territories and read out of the Democratic party. Let the fucking bastards threaten, proscribe, and do their worst, I told my followers; it would not cause any honest man to falter. If my course divided the Democratic party, it would not be my fault. We were engaged in a great struggle for principle, I said, and we would defy the Administration to the bitter end.[18]

Southern Democrats resisted furiously. Their acrimony toward Douglas swelled to apoplectic proportions as their rhetoric against him became more heated. His opponents claimed Douglas was "at the head of the Black column . . . stained with the dishonor of treachery without parallel . . . patent double dealing . . . detestable heresies . . . filth of his defiant recreancy . . . a Dead Cock in the Pit . . . away with him to the tomb which he is digging for his political corpse."[19]

Southern newspapers joined the attacks on Douglas. Elizabeth Varon notes "how newspapers called out the traitors with the lament, 'How the mighty are fallen.' The *Texas State Gazette*, for example, observed of Douglas that 'once the favorite of the South for the Presidency,' he was now 'branded as a traitor from Washington to New Orleans. The false god was destroyed by his own worshippers.'"[20]

Despite the threats Douglas stood his ground. He believed that he was in the right, and though he thought that slavery should be protected in the South, he realized that appeasement was not an option in regard to Lecompton, for it undermined the entire concept of popular sovereignty and law:

> My forces in the House fought a brilliant delaying action while I worked to win over wavering Democrats. When we introduced a substitute bill, Buchanan called a dozen congressmen to the White House and exhorted them not to forsake the administration. He was cursing and in tears. He had reason to be: on April first, a coalition of ninety-two Republicans, twenty-two anti-Lecompton Democrats, and six Know-Nothings sent Lecompton down to defeat by passing the substitute bill. This bill provided for a popular vote on the Lecompton constitution and for a new convention if the people rejected that document, as they surely would.[21]

Douglas's bill passed the Senate and sent the Lecompton Constitution back to Kansas for a popular vote. When it was resubmitted, the results were devastating to the proslave faction, and "to the hideous embarrassment of Buchanan the voters of Kansas turned on August 30th and rejected Lecompton by a vote of 11,812 to 1,926."[22] The ever-colorful and blunt Little Giant wrote: "'The agony is over,' cried one of my aides, 'and thank God that the right has triumphed.' Poor old Buck! Poor old Buck had just had his face rubbed in shit. By our 'indomitable courage,' as another aide put it, we'd whipped this 'powerful and proscriptive' Administration and forced the Black Republicans to support a substitute measure which fully embodied the great principles of the Kansas-Nebraska Act."[23] Douglas's victory over Buchanan and his Southern Democrat allies "ended a political battle which had convulsed the country and virtually destroyed two administrations, but the full consequences of the prolonged struggle had yet to become evident."[24]

Proslavery Democrats were outraged. Buchanan had used every measure that he could to crush the anti-Lecompton Democrats but lost "one of the most vicious struggles in the history of Congress Southern Democrats had seriously damaged the patience of their Northern counterparts, and Buchanan loyalists in the North were unseated wholesale by upstart Republicans in the 1858 congressional elections."[25] Buchanan's presidency was discredited, his party divided and its congressional majority lost, and the South was hurtling toward secession. Southerners considered Douglas a traitor. "A South Carolinian lamented that 'this defection of Douglas has done more than all else to shake my confidence in Northern men on the slavery issue, for I have long regarded him as one of our safest and most reliable friends.'"[26]

The Implosion of the Democratic Party

The writers of Constitution never imagined a crisis like Lecompton and what followed. The deeply partisan fight illuminated how easily "'minuscule' minorities' initial concerns ballooned into unmanageable majoritarian crises. The tiny fraction of Missouri slaveholders who lived near the Kansas border, comprising a tinier fraction of the South and a still tinier fraction of the Union, had demanded their chance to protect the southern hinterlands."[27]

The tiny faction provoked a national crisis that galvanized

the North and demolished the national unity of Democrats. The Democrats split into hostile Northern and Southern factions. Following Lecompton, the intraparty Democrat divide widened as "pro-Douglas and pro-Buchanan Democrats openly warred on one another for the next two years; an unacknowledged but real split had taken place."[28]

Lecompton marked the first time Northern Democrats sided with antislavery forces to defeat proslavery legislation in Congress. According to William Freehling, "Republicans and anti-Lecompton Douglas Democrats, Congress had barely turned back a gigantic Slave Power Conspiracy to bend white men's majoritarianism to slavemaster's dictatorial needs, first in Kansas, then in Congress."[29] Lecompton was an unmitigated disaster for Democrats. They suffered a major defeat in the 1858 midterm elections, lost their House majority, and barely maintained a slim Senate majority. Republicans won the House but gained little legislative headway, since Democrats controlled the Senate, and Buchanan remained president.

Democrats fulfilled what Lincoln had said about the country years before, when the Democratic Party "became increasingly a house divided against itself."[30] In a sense

> there were two Democratic parties: one northern, one southern (but with patronage allies in the north); one having its center of power in the northern electorate and in the quadrennial party convention . . . the other with its center of power in Congress; one intent on broadening the basis of support to attract moderate Republicans, the other more concerned to preserve a doctrinal defense of slavery even if it meant driving heretics out of the party.[31]

Southern Democrats turned on the man who had once been their standard bearer for his courageous opposition to Lecompton. The 1860 National Democratic Convention was their chance for revenge. In the account of James McPherson, "Most southern Democrats went to Charleston with one overriding goal: to destroy Douglas."[32] When the convention met in April, it rapidly descended into a nightmare, as "Southern delegates were much more intent on making a point than on nominating a presidential candidate."[33] The "Southern delegates demanded a promise of federal protection of slavery in all the territories and a de facto veto in the selection of the party's presidential candidate."[34] To defeat Douglas, Southern radicals "led by William Lowndes Yancey of Alabama stood for seven days agitating for a pro-slavery platform."[35]

Ohio Democrat George A. Pugh responded to Southern fire-eaters by saying that "Northern Democrats had worn themselves out defending Southern interests—and he declared that the Northern Democrats like himself were now being ordered to hide their faces and eat dirt."[36] Georgia senator Alexander Stephens, who supported Douglas, wrote that the radicals' "strategy was to 'rule or ruin.'"[37] Southerners' attempts to place proslavery measures in the party platform were defeated by Northern delegates, prompting "a walkout by delegates from Alabama, South Carolina, Georgia, Florida, Mississippi, Louisiana, and Texas."[38] This deprived Douglas of the two-thirds majority needed for nomination, and "the shattered convention adjourned, to reconvene in Baltimore on June 18."[39] But the "incendiary rhetoric left the Democratic Party in ashes."[40] A friend of Stephens suggested that the party might patch things up in Baltimore, but, as Stephens told his friend, "the party is split forever. The only hope was in Charleston."[41]

Former Whigs led by Kentucky senator John J. Crittenden formed the Constitutional Union Party and declared a pox on the Buchanan and Douglas factions. They nominated John Bell, a cold and uninspiring moderate slave owner from Tennessee as their presidential candidate and, paradoxically, "chose a man who overshadowed him, Edward Everett of Massachusetts, aged sixty-seven, as the vice-presidential nominee."[42] But they had no chance of success; Bell "stood for moderation and the middle road in a country that just now was not listening to moderates, and the professional operators were not with him."[43]

When the Democrats reconvened, the results were as Stephens predicted, resulting in a final split: "Rival delegations from the Lower South States arrived in Baltimore, one side pledged to Douglas and the other to obstruction. When the convention voted for the Douglas delegations, the spurned delegates walked out, this time joined by colleagues from the Upper South."[44] Douglas did not have the two-thirds majority, but the convention "adopted a resolution declaring Douglas unanimously nominated."[45] A day later the radicalized Southern delegates nominated Vice President John C. Breckinridge as their candidate "for president on a slave-code platform."[46]

There were now four presidential tickets, three for Democrats and former Whigs, "each supported by men who felt that they were following the only possible path to salvation. A Republican victory was almost certain, and the Democrats, who had the most to lose from such a victory, were blindly and with a fated stubbornness doing everything they could to bring that victory to pass."[47] A Democratic Party implosion doomed their candidates. The *Augusta Daily Chronicle* and *Sentinel* editorialized: "It is an utterly futile and hopeless task to re-organize, re-unite and harmonize the disintegrated Democratic party unless this is to be done by a total abandonment of principle. . . . No, sensible people might as well make up their minds to the fact that the Democratic party is dissolved forever, that new organizations must take its place."[48]

14

Cuba Must Be Ours

Fire-Eaters and Filibusters Spread Slavery

Following the *Dred Scott* decision, Jefferson Davis and others crafted legislation to ensure Congress could not exclude slavery but protect it in all places and at all times. They wanted to guarantee "that slave owners and their property would be unmolested in all Federal territories." Called the Doctrine of Positive Protection, it was designed to "prevent a free-soil majority in a territory from taking hostile action against a slave holding minority in their midst."[1]

Slavery supporters likewise envisioned turning the United States into a slave empire. They demanded slavery's expansion in all federal territories, and "in their most exotic fantasy, proslavery expansionists would land several dozen or several hundred American freedom fighters on Central or South American shores."[2] Their targets included Panama, Nicaragua, and Cuba. In 1857 Jefferson Davis provoked Northern ire when he insisted that "African Slavery as it exists in the United States is a moral, a social, and a political blessing."[3]

Others clamored to reopen the African slave trade. A delegate at the 1856 commercial convention insisted, "We are entitled to demand the opening of this trade from an industrial, political, and constitutional consideration. . . . With cheap negroes we could set hostile legislation at defiance. The slave population after supplying the states would overflow to the territories, and nothing could control its natural expansion."[4] In 1858 the Southern Commercial Convention declared that "all laws State and Federal, prohibiting the African slave trade, ought to be repealed."[5]

The debate over the African slave trade was resumed in 1858 when the schooner *Wanderer*, owned by Charles Lamar, delivered a cargo of four hundred slaves to Jekyll Island, earning him "a large profit."[6] The USS *Dolphin*, on antislavery patrol in the Caribbean, captured "the slaver Echo off Cuba and brought 314 Africans to the Charleston federal jail."[7] A federal grand jury in Charleston indicted Lamar, but its members were so vilified in the press that "they published a bizarre recantation of their action and advocated the repeal of the 1807 law prohibiting the slave trade. Longer to yield to a sickly sentiment of pretended philanthropy and diseased mental aberration of 'higher law' fanatics."[8] The judges and juries involved refused to indict or convict any of those responsible.

Southerners tried to expand slavery into Central America and Cuba, which was central to their plans; Americans had eyed it for annexation even prior to 1850. "Jefferson Davis declared in 1848 'Cuba must be ours' in order to 'increase the number of slaveholding constituencies.'" Davis was not alone; Pres. James K. Polk, having conquering Mexico, authorized "his minister to Spain to offer $100 million for the island."[9] The effort was bungled, and the highly insulted Spaniards rejected it.

Others launched armed invasions. Southerners and Cuban expatriates made several attempts between 1849 and 1851 to spur revolution and drive the Spanish out. Cuban revolutionary Francisco Lopez and William Crittenden, nephew of the attorney general, led the most infamous attempt: they commanded a "'regiment' of southern volunteers in the invasion force of 420 men."[10] Their actions prefigured the Bay of Pigs fiasco. The invaders landed in Cuba, but local supporters failed to mobilize. Spanish soldiers knew that they were coming and surprised them, killing 200 and capturing 160, who were taken to Spain as prisoners. Fifty, including Crittenden, were executed by firing squad in Havana, and Lopez was garroted there in a public execution. President Fillmore's political future was destroyed when he refused to denounce the executions. The *Washington Union* concluded, "Cuba has killed Fillmore."[11]

Undeterred by failure other filibustering expeditions were planned, but Franklin Pierce, having expended his political capital during the Kansas-Nebraska battle, refused to sanction them. Pierce, however, authorized James Buchanan, minister to England, to acquire Cuba through negotiation. Buchanan met with James Mason, ambassador to France, and Pierre Soule, ambassador to Spain, to draft "a statement on the future of Cuba and the proposed role of the United States."[12] Soule dominated the meeting, and the statement drafted by Soule and Buchanan's deputy Dan Sickles was highly inflammatory. They ignored orders to maintain secrecy and released it to the press, resulting in a diplomatic disaster. Known as the Ostend Manifesto, it "was one of the most truly American, and at the same time most undiplomatic, documents every devised."[13]

Soul and Sickles wrote: "Cuba is as necessary to the North American Republic as any of its present members, and that it belongs naturally to the great family of states of which the Union is the Providential Nursery."[14] They threatened Spain, should it not to comply with American demands, and declared that the United States "decided its sovereignty depended on acquiring Cuba and if Spain would not pass on sovereignty in the island to the United States by peaceful means, including sale, then, 'by every law, human and Divine, we shall be justified in wresting it from Spain.'"[15]

The manifesto "sent shivers through the chancelleries of Europe, provoked hurried conversations between the heads of the French and British admiralties."[16] European diplomats and leaders reacted harshly. Secretary of State William Marcy supported the manifesto, he quickly distanced himself and American foreign policy from it.

Pierce's administration was condemned as the advocate of a policy of "shame and dishonor," the supporter of a "buccaneering document," a "highwayman's plea." American diplomacy, said the *London Times*, was given to "the habitual pursuit of dishonorable object by clandestine means."[17] The incident ended American attempts to obtain Cuba until the USS *Maine* was destroyed in 1898, and the United States acquired it in the Spanish-American War.

Others attempted to expand slavery by invading Nicaragua and Honduras. William Walker led the expeditions. In 1853 he failed to seize Baja California and in 1855 "led an army of two thousand American filibusters into Nicaragua, where in alliance with local rebels he gained control of the government in 1856, named himself president and reinstituted slavery."[18]

While Pierce recognized Walker's government, Walker offended Cornelius Vanderbilt by revoking "the franchise for a Vanderbilt-controlled steamship company . . . and this proved his undoing. Vanderbilt was able to cut off his support, and within a year."[19] A military alliance of Central American countries deposed Walker's regime. Walker, now a Southern hero, led expedition in 1860 to seize Honduras. It failed, and Walker surrendered to a British naval captain assuming, he would be returned to the United States. Instead, the British gave Walker to the Hondurans, who executed him.

15

The Final Kingdom Has Arisen

Hubris and Fanaticism Bring On the War

Despite the efforts of politicians on both sides to compromise, secession loomed. Southern Christian nationalism helped to drive the debate, and manifest destiny led Americans to violate nearly every warning of the founders as they embarked on a policy of conquest, imperialism, and genocide. Evangelical Protestants not only failed to prevent war; their leaders were as responsible as fire-eating politicians for bringing it on, as they "fueled the passions for a dramatic solution to transcendent moral questions. Evangelical religion did not prepare either side for the carnage, and its explanations seemed less relevant as the war continued. The Civil War destroyed the Old South civilization resting on slavery it also discredited evangelical Protestantism as the ultimate arbiter of public policy."[1]

When Edmund Ruffin and fellow secessionists lit the powder keg by firing on Fort Sumter, evangelical Protestants on the opposing side raced to frame their cause in the light of their theology. Some saw war as a prelude to Christ's return and the beginning of the millennium. As American Tract Society agent Hollis Read proclaimed:

A few more such strides, a few more such terrific struggles and travail-pains among the nations; a few more such convulsions and revolutions, that shall break to pieces and destroy what remains of the inveterate and time-honored systems and confederations of sin and Satan and the friends of freedom may then lift up their heads and rejoice, for their redemption draweth nigh. The Day of Vengeance Has Always Preceded and Been preparatory to the Year of the Redeemed.[2]

Similar theological bombast burst forth in the Confederacy, which some saw as the embodiment of Christ: "The One like the Son of Man has appeared in the rise of the Confederate States."[3] William Seat wrote that the Confederacy would take its place among the nations, and through it "liberty and pure Christianity would go abroad on earth," and soon the "peaceful millennial reign would dawn," and the stone cut from the mountain—the South—would be glorified: "There shall be no more curse nor death nor sorrow nor crying. There shall be fullness of joy and pleasures forevermore. We solemnly believe that the great prophetic periods have closed: the mystery is finished, and the vision of prophecy unsealed. The Final Kingdom has arisen, and the Divine Redeemer has come to reign."[4] When their short, glorious war became one of protracted bloodletting, these ministers and theologians saw their presuppositions dashed upon the cruel shoals of reality, which William Tecumseh Sherman understood all too well: "War is hell."

As the war turned against the Confederacy, Southern ministers reframed their cause and the reasons for their defeat. Instead of slavery they blamed Southern character flaws and economic policies. Likewise, the terrible costs of the war shattered the faith of many Northern Christians. As one of Charles Finney's correspondents wrote in 1864, "So many are skeptical, doubtful, so many good people are cutting loose from creeds & forms. . . . I am sometimes tempted to ask whether prayer can make any difference."[5]

American Protestantism, which helped sow the seeds of war, reaped the benefits after it. Many Northern Protestants shifted their emphasis from justice to economic power. Ministers preached a gospel of wealth to align themselves with the rising tide of the newly rich. Russell Conwell, a former Union soldier turned Baptist preacher, whose church later formed Temple University, delivered his "acres of diamonds" sermon, in which he proclaimed: "Money is power, money is force. . . . I say to you to get rich, and it is your duty to get rich."[6] The sermon became popular throughout the country, and people did not tire of it.

The theology of wealth fit in well in the age of the robber barons. It was apolitical, preached no moral crusades, called for no sacrifice, and did not consider any understanding of justice traditionally associated with Christianity. Instead it appealed to people's basest instincts. It gave no thought to the poor, war-wounded, oppressed Blacks, or immigrants. Walt Whitman wrote of American Christianity, "Genuine belief seems to have left us. . . . The spectacle is appalling. We live in an atmosphere of hypocrisy throughout. . . . A lot of churches, sects, etc., the most dismal phantasm I know, usurp the name of religion."[7]

Southern Evangelicals retreated into skepticism and denial of human progress. After the war they "expected little from the corrupted world and expected even less from the knowledge of corrupted men, especially men of science and power. The war brought to the South a theology, as well as a politics and economics of diminished expectations," where faith was personal and rooted in unscientific fundamentalism still tied to racism.[8]

Evangelical Christianity never played as dominant cultural role as it did in the years leading to and in the early days of the war: "From the 1860s onward, American Protestantism was increasingly marked by the quiet erosion of faith, and religious experience became plagued more and more decaying faith, and in an increasing appeal to feeling and imagination over confessional reason or evangelical conversion."[9]

This trend continues today, despite the unswerving allegiance of most conservative Christians to former president Trump and his racist and blatant use of white nationalism, racism, and an armed insurrection to overthrow the Constitution and democracy in a manner unseen since the Civil War. Mark Twain's criticism of the "gospel of money" prefigured the critics of the contemporary prosperity gospel: "What is the chief end of man?—to get rich. In what way?—dishonestly if we can; honestly if we must. Who is God, the one only and true? Money is God. Gold and Greenbacks and Stock—father, son, and the ghost of same—three persons in one, these are the true and only God, mighty and supreme."[10]

The Battle Lines Solidify: A House Divided

Lincoln was moderate, but in his "House Divided" speech of June, 16, 1858, he threw out caution to explain the danger slavery posed. Lincoln understood that the divide over slavery was deep, and that the country could not survive divided as it was. He favored a moderate gradual emancipation policy. However, following *Dred Scott* and the Lecompton fight, the mood of the country was inflamed. Though moderate, Lincoln allowed his "language to take on an uncompromising quality," as any compromise would be "a retreat from his particular position, as surrender—hence there could be no retreat at all."[11]

The Union that Lincoln "would fight to preserve was not a bundle of compromises that secured the vital interests of both slave states and free . . . but rather, the nation—the single, united, free people—Jefferson and his fellow Revolutionaries supposedly had conceived and whose fundamental principles were now being compromised."[12] He spoke with a clarity few American politicians had used before or since. His language was so stark, in fact, that even some Republicans felt it too divisive:

> We are now far into the fifth year since a policy was initiated with the avowed object and confident promise of putting an end to slavery agitation. Under the operation of that policy, that agitation has not only not ceased but has con-

stantly augmented. In my opinion, it will not cease until a crisis shall have been reached and passed. "A house divided against itself cannot stand." I believe this government cannot endure, permanently, half slave and half free. I do not expect the Union to be dissolved; I do not expect the house to fall; but I do expect it will cease to be divided. It will become all one thing, or all the other. Either the opponents of slavery will arrest the further spread of it and place it where the public mind shall rest in the belief that it is in the course of ultimate extinction, or its advocates will push it forward till it shall become alike lawful in all the states, old as well as new, North as well as South.[13]

The divide lay in how each side understood the Constitution and the Union. Southern leaders believed the Constitution established a Union that was "only a league of quasi-independent states that could be terminated at will."[14] Their interpretation of states' rights was that slavery's continuance and expansion was essential, and that the right of Northern states to make slavery illegal were unconstitutional, because they denied the existence and expansion of slavery.

Southerners valued their right to expand slavery even more than that of Northern states to outlaw it. Southern leaders challenged the right of Northerners to speak freely against the institution, feeling that that free speech was a threat. Thus, "so long as Southerners continued to believe that northern anti-slavery attacks constituted a real and present danger to Southern life and property, then disunion could not be ruled out as an ugly last resort."[15]

Northern Unionists saw it differently: "For devout Unionists, the Constitution had been framed by the people rather than created as a compact among the states. It formed a government, as President Andrew Jackson insisted of the early 1830s, 'in which all the people are represented, which operates directly on the people individually, not upon the States.'"[16] Lincoln, like many Northerners, believed that the Union "had a transcendent, mystical quality as the object of their patriotic devotion and civil religion."[17]

Lincoln's beliefs about the Union were on display in the Gettysburg Address, where he began with the words "Four score and seven years ago our fathers brought forth on this continent, a new nation, conceived in Liberty, and dedicated to the proposition that all men are created equal." To Lincoln disunion "evoked a chilling scenario within which the Founders' carefully constructed representative government failed, triggering 'a nightmare, a tragic cataclysm' that would subject Americans to the kind of fear and misery that seemed to pervade the rest of the world."[18]

Theodore Parker also understood the intent of Southerners in Congress and on the Supreme Court: "The first [step] is to establish Slavery in all of the Northern States—the *Dred Scott* decision has already put it in all the territories. . . . I have no doubt The Supreme Court will make the [subsequent] decisions."[19] Abolitionists saw slavery as disastrous to the moral and spiritual foundation of the country.

Some Southerners wanted to preserve the Union. One of those was Lt. Col. Robert E. Lee. Lee was the son of Revolutionary War hero Harry "Lighthorse" Lee, and his wife, Mary Custis, was a descendant of George Washington. Lee, a West Point graduate who had served as an officer for over thirty years, wrote his son Custis in January 1861, "I can anticipate no greater calamity for the country than the dissolution of the Union. It would be an accumulation of all the evils we complain of and I am willing to sacrifice everything but honor for its preservation. I hope, therefore, that all Constitutional means before there is a resort to force. Secession is nothing but revolution." But, he added, "a Union that can only be maintained by swords and bayonets has no charms for me."[20] Lee valued the Union, but only to a point, whereas for Lincoln the Union was the foundation of liberty for all. Lee ended up resigning his commission, even saying that he would sit out the war. But as Lee's most recent biographer, Allen Guelzo, notes, in his resignation and his decision to accept command of Virginia's military forces, Lee "irrevokably, finally, publically turned his back on his service, his flag, and ultimately, his country. All of this was done for a political regime whose acknowledged purpose was the preservation of a system of chattel slavery that he knew to be evil and for which he had little affection and whose constitutional basis he dismissed as fiction."[21] As Ty Seidule, the retired chair of the history department at the U.S. Military Academy, writes of Lee's acceptance of a commission in the Virginia armed forces, "Lee couldn't even wait until his resignation was processed—three days—before he took a train to Richmond to accept a wartime commission from a rebellious state."[22]

Sen. Alexander Stephens, for his part, stood against disunion. He believed in the doctrine of states' rights and that the long-term interest of the South was best served by remaining in the Union. He told a friend "that the men who were working for secession were driven by envy, hate jealousy, spite—'these made war in heaven, which made devils of angels, and of the same passions will make devils of men. Patriotism in my opinion, had no more to do with it than love of God had to do with the other revolt.'"[23] Stephens did not oppose slavery or its expansion, but he believed that the institution was best maintained within the Union. However, like Lee and many other Unionist Southerners, he resigned his office and joined the Confederate government, as vice president.

John Brown: The Fanatical Idealist

While "the restraining hand of churches, political parties and familial concerns bounded other antislavery warriors," some religious fanatics were willing to light the fuse that would cause the powder keg of raw emotion to explode.[24] Most prominent of these was John Brown: a "Connecticut-born abolitionist [and] a man with the selfless benevolence of the evangelicals wrought into a fiery determination to crush slavery."[25] Brown's father was an early abolitionist who helped found

Oberlin College. In his youth Brown "formulated a certitude about divine intervention against sinners, starring himself as God's warrior against slaveholders."[26] As early as 1834, Brown was "an ardent sympathizer the Negroes," desiring to raise a Black child in his own home and to offer "guidance to a colony of Negroes on the farm of the wealthy abolitionist Gerrit Smith at North Elba New York."[27] Brown, who despised moderates, was a fanatical Christian who knew no church, "only his conception of God's unbounded command."[28]

Brown "ridiculed Republican's mainstream tactics. He disparaged even Yankee extremists for deploying too non-violent a strategy."[29] After several failed business ventures, he moved to Kansas to use terror to change the equation. After the sack of Lawrence, a vengeful Brown slaughtered a family of pro-slavery settlers at Pottawatomie Creek.[30] Two years later, in Missouri, Brown "murdered a slaveholder, seized eleven slaves, and led the new freedmen 1100 miles to Canadian sanctuary."[31]

Brown's violence provides a useful case for understanding violent religious extremism. *The Army and Marine Counterinsurgency Field Manual* provides a description as applicable to Brown as well as to religiously motivated terrorists today: "Religious extremist insurgents. . . . frequently hold an all-encompassing worldview; they are ideologically rigid and uncompromising. . . . believing themselves to be ideologically pure, violent religious extremists' brand those they consider insufficiently orthodox as enemies."[32]

Brown was "a religious zealot . . . but was nevertheless every much the product of his time and place."[33] In Kansas he earned the nickname "the apostle of the sword of Gideon," possessed as he was by a zealous belief that God appointed him as his warrior against slaveholders. Brown despised peaceful abolitionists and demanded action: "Brave, unshaken by doubt, willing to shed blood unflinchingly and to die for his cause if necessary, Brown was the perfect man to light the tinder of civil war in America, which was what he intended to do."[34]

In 1859 Brown tried to persuade wealthy abolitionists Virginia to fund his revolt, but they rejected his idea. After listening to William Lloyd Garrison and other abolitionist leaders plead for peaceful abolition, he remarked, "'We've reached a point . . . where nothing but war can get rid of slavery in this guilty nation. It's better that a whole generation of men, women, and children should pass away by a violent death than that slavery should continue to exist.' I meant that literally, every word of it."[35]

Frederick Douglass also rejected Brown's plan. Despite the lack of support, Brown collected recruits and set off to seize ten thousand muskets to ignite a slave revolt. Brown and twenty-one motley followers—sixteen whites and five Blacks—attacked the arsenal. Reflecting later the event, Brown wrote, "We would probably fail. . . . But I believed that all we had to do was make the attempt, and Jehovah would do the rest: the Heavens would turn black, the thunder would rend the sky, and a mighty storm would uproot this guilty land, washing its sins away with blood. With God's help, I, John Brown, would effect a mighty conquest even though it was like the last victory of Samson."[36]

Brown's men captured the arsenal, only to be crushed by the quick federal response of U.S. Marines, led by Col. Robert E. Lee. Brown was captured, and several of his men were killed, but his raid "effectively severed the country into two opposing parts, making it clear to moderates there who were searching for compromise that northerners' tolerance for slavery was wearing thin."[37] Brown's capture, trial, conviction, and execution made no difference to Southerners, though he was "a half-pathetic, half-mad failure, his raid a crazy, senseless exploit to which only his quiet eloquence during trial and execution lent dignity."[38] Neither side recovered from Brown's raid, for all had gone too far down the road to disunion to turn back.

New England elites supported Brown, with the "names of Howe, Parker, Emerson and Thoreau among his supporters."[39] To many Brown became a martyr, "but to Frederick Douglass and the negroes of Chatham, Ontario, nearly every one of whom had learned something from personal experience on how to gain freedom, Brown was a man of words trying to be a man of deeds, and they would not follow him. They understood him, as Thoreau and Emerson and Parker never did."[40]

Brown represented an existential threat to Southern life, and the "spectacle of devout Yankee women actually praying for John Brown, not as a sinner but as saint, of respectable thinkers like Thoreau and Emerson and Longfellow glorifying his martyrdom in Biblical language" horrified Southerners and drove pro-Union Southern moderates into the secession camp.[41] In an editorial the *Richmond Enquirer* wrote, "The Harper's Ferry invasion has advanced the cause of Disunion, more than any other event that has happened since the foundation of the Government; it has rallied to that standard men who formerly looked on it with horror; it has revived, with ten fold strength the desire of a Southern Confederacy."[42]

Brown penned his final missive the day he was hanged. He portrayed himself as a Christ figure going to his cross on the behalf of a guilty people, but people for whom his blood could not atone:

> It's now December second—the day of my hanging, the day the gallows become my cross. I'm approaching those gallows while sitting on my coffin in the bed of a military wagon. O dear God, my eyes see the glory in every step of the divine journey that brought me here, to stand on that platform. . . . I am ready to join thee now in Paradise. . . . They can put the halter around my neck, pull the hood over my head. Hanging me won't save them from God's wrath! I warned the entire country: I, John Brown, am now quite certain that the crimes of this guilty land will never be purged away, but with blood.[43]

Brown's composure during his trial had impressed Gov. Henry Wise, who signed Brown's death warrant. Edmund Ruffin was similarly impressed, and in his diary he praised Brown's "animal courage" and "complete fearlessness & insensibility to danger and death."[44]

The death of Brown, who was considered a martyr, was mourned throughout the North. Henry David Thoreau pronounced him "a crucified hero."[45] William Lloyd Garrison, who condemned violence to further the cause of emancipation, now praised Brown's actions, while across the North "church bells tolled, black bunting was hung out, minute guns were fired, prayer meetings assembled, and memorial resolutions adopted. In the weeks following, the emotional outpouring continued: lithographs of Brown circulated in vast numbers, subscriptions were organized for the support of his family, immense memorial meetings took place in New York, Boston, and Philadelphia."[46]

Future Confederate general Lafayette McLaws spoke for many Southern army officers when he wrote in his diary on February 27, 1860: "Debates in congress show no mitigation of sec. feeling. . . . I think it would be better not to be so fanatical on any subject, the extreme pro-slavery man is as bad as that type as that type of anti-slavery, John Brown. I do not consider slavery an evil by any means, but I certainly do not think it the greatest blessing."[47]

Southerners saw Brown's raid as a foretaste of what was to come. Despite Lincoln's denunciations of him, Southern newspapermen, ministers, and politicians proclaimed their distrust of the North. Northern praise "was seized upon as argument-clinching proof that the North was only awaiting its opportunity to destroy the South by force."[48]

16

The South Will Never Submit

Lincoln and the Choice for Secession and War

The crisis continued to build, and when Lincoln was elected in November 1860, the simmering volcano finally erupted. The crisis of the 1850s had brought emotions to a fever pitch. The 1860 election included a dramatic rise in the overtly racist invective of proslavery Democrats and "marked the crystallization of two fully sectionalized parties."[1] No compromise could save the Union. A Mississippian observed: "The minds of the people are aroused to a pitch of excitement probably unparalleled in the history of our country."[2]

Like now, where the internet, social media, and other platforms allow people the unparalleled opportunity to spew hatred and conspiracy theories, the changing nature of communications technology made the 1860 campaign one of the most merciless in American history. Adam Goodheart writes, "Cheap printing and the telegraph made it easier and easier for the shrillest of ideologues to find audiences, even national ones."[3] In this sense the 1860 campaign prefigured the elections of today. Newspapers and ideologues did not change the minds of the many voters who were hardened in their positions, but "they likely helped spur a gigantic voter turnout—some 80 percent of eligible white males nationwide—which was deemed crucial to Republican success in swing states like Indiana and Pennsylvania."[4]

Lincoln ran a masterful campaign. Due to his debates with Douglas during the 1858 Illinois Senate campaign, he went from

FIG. 12. Political cartoon, *The National Game. Three "Outs" and One "Run."* Louis Mauer, 1860. Currier and Ives. Courtesy of the Library of Congress, Cartoon Prints Collection, LC-DIG-ppmsca-33122.

a virtual unknown to a national figure. His Republican Party was a "coalition of old Democrats, former Whigs, and members of the nativist American Party."[5] Lincoln defeated party favorites— New York senator William Seward, Sen. Salmon Chase of Ohio, and Missouri's elder statesman Edward Bates—to become the Republican nominee. Lincoln took the nomination on the third ballot and then cemented a coalition with his rivals to defeat a fractured opposition.

The Democrat split ensured Lincoln's victory, but that was what Southern fire-eaters wanted. Southern Democrats envisioned "the destruction of the national Democratic Party—and its powerful contingent of moderates in the state—as a visible vehicle for protecting slavery in the Union."[6] They hated Douglas, whom they once revered, because he opposed Lecompton and the expansion of slavery. Their hatred of Douglas resulted in "an open party rupture" that destroyed any chance of defeating Lincoln.[7] Alexander Stephens, "who stood with Douglas to the last, despaired, not only for his party but for his coun-

The South Will Never Submit

try: 'There is a tendency everywhere, not only in the North, but the South, to strife, dissension, disorder, and anarchy.'"[8]

Lincoln's opponents turned the election into a referendum on race. The influential *New York Herald* was typical of papers that expressed criticism of Lincoln, serving up "a patented blend of sarcasm and sensationalism. The *Herald*'s editorial page cracked wise almost every day about 'the Eternal nigger,' the 'Almighty nigger,' the 'Irrepressible nigger' and the 'nigger-loving black republicans.'"[9] Northern and Southern opponents of Lincoln and the Republicans conjured up the fear of a future Black president to further stoke the flames of racial hatred and division.[10]

During the campaign Lincoln was careful to not to go beyond the printed words of his published speeches and refused to mollify the conspiracy theory hysteria that had engulfed the South. "What is it I should say to quiet alarm?" he asked in October. "Is it that no interference by the government, with slaves or slavery within the states, is intended? I have said this so often already, that a repetition of it is but mockery, bearing an appearance of weakness."[11]

But Lincoln and other Republicans misread the Southerners and "considered the movement South as sort of a political game of bluff, gotten up by politicians, and meant solely to frighten the North. He believed that when the leaders saw their efforts in that direction unavailing, the tumult would subside."[12] William Seward equated the Southern threats to cries of "wolf" that had little meaning. The editor of a Tennessee paper admitted that "the cry of disunion had been raised so often that few had taken it seriously in the campaign. Evidently, the 'Northern sectionalists' had believed it to be 'all talk' . . . while most intelligent Southerners had assumed that it was 'an idle menace, made to sway Northern sentiment.'"[13]

The Republican Party was a coalition where factions held opposing views, and Lincoln understood that the election was about more than one issue. Abolition was important to the party, but other interests had to be considered: for example, protective tariffs, infrastructure, railroads, and homestead legislation. Lincoln could not go too far in any direction that deviated from the party platform without risking a party fracture. "It would be both impudent," he noted, "and contrary to the reasonable expectation of friends for me to write or speak anything upon doctrinal points right now. Besides this my published speeches contain nearly all I could willingly say."[14]

The unique presidential campaign of 1860 unfolded into "three distinct campaigns: Douglas against Lincoln in the North; Breckinridge versus Bell in the South; and Douglas contesting Bell in the border states, with Lincoln and Breckinridge hoping for some support there as well."[15] But Breckinridge had no hope of winning the North, and Lincoln no chance of winning in the South.

Southerners were so convinced that no matter what Lincoln said, no matter how many times he stated that he would not interfere with slavery where it existed—that no matter what he did—Lincoln was their enemy. The fire-eaters and other rabid secessionists' warnings of a Lincoln presidency bordered on paranoid hysteria. In a sense they engaged in a propaganda campaign of what we now call "fake news." Conspiracy theories and outright lies about supposed atrocities committed by Blacks were presented as truth without any factual basis, whipping up passions and stoking fear:

> R.S. Holt, a wealthy Mississippi planter and brother of the U.S. postmaster general, reported that "we have constantly a foretaste of what Northern-brotherhood means, in almost daily conflagrations & in discovery of poison, knives & pistols distributed among our slaves by the emissaries sent out for that purpose. . . . There cannot be found in all the planting States a territory ten miles square in which the footprints of these miscreants have not been discovered."[16]

Edmund Ruffin, always one of most consistent defenders of secession, wrote to Yancey that "a Republican victory was obviously coming and that it would be 'a clear and unmistakable indication of future & fixed domination of the Northern section & its abolition party over the Southern states & their institutions, & the speedy progress to the extermination of Negro slavery & and the consequent ruin of the South.'"[17] A Georgia newspaper warned: "Let the consequences be what they may—whether the Potomac is crimsoned in human gore, and Pennsylvania Avenue is paved ten fathoms deep with mangled bodies . . . the South will never submit to such humiliation and degradation as the inauguration of Abraham Lincoln."[18]

Prominent Southern ministers, though more cautious than newspapermen and politicians, also sounded the alarm. Evangelical "proslavery had popularized the South's unique approach to the Bible and the founding of the nation. The Bible supported slaveholding; God supported the South. The formula was clear. Right made might. The South had to triumph."[19] A Presbyterian editor urged prayer but added, "An agitation that perpetually sends dread and disturbance into every hamlet, and to every home and fireside in the land is intolerable. No people can abide it long."[20] A Southern journal remarked: "In religious sentiment the South stands as a unit. Its pure doctrines are linked insuperably, though not by legal constraint, with the laws of the land. No isms and schism rankle our hearts. Christ is acknowledged as the common bond of union."[21] Church leaders demanded secession if Lincoln won. As always, religious extremism fueled the fire of war.

The Democrats' only hope was "fusion" of the opposition in key Northern states to deny Lincoln their electoral votes and throw the election into the House.[22] But Buchanan's Breckinridge-headed faction, vitriolic hatred of Douglas, and distrust of Bell prevented it. Davis went to Douglas to convince him to drop out of the race in favor of a fusion ticket. Douglas would later recall Davis's words: "'If the Democrats run two candidates,' he said, 'the Black Republicans will win the election. In that event the slave states will secede.'"[23] Davis asked Douglas to drop out, saying that Breckinridge and Bell had already agreed to the deal. Douglas wrote:

This was strange talk from Davis, and I was damned suspicious that it might be a trap. It was all I could do to control my hatred for the Goddamned bastard. "The plan is impractical I said coldly. If I withdraw, my friends in the North will go over to Lincoln. I'm in the hands of my friends and they won't accept this proposition." "Then I've done all that I can," he said, rose and walked out.

Why the Goddamned hell should I withdraw? I asked my aides. I was a matter of honor with me. I had won my nomination fairly, on the basis of the party's time honored principles. I refused to unite with a bunch of traitors and disunionists. Maybe Breckinridge himself and some of his followers were not for disunion; but every southern disunionists was a Breckinridge man.

Others pressed me to unite with the "vandals," as we called the Breckinridge party, but I answered with a thundering no. "I'm utterly opposed to fusing with any man or party who'll not enforce the laws maintain the Constitution, and preserve the Union in all contingencies," I said. I wish to God Old Hickory was still alive, so that he could hang northern and southern traitors from the same gallows.[24]

The Democratic Party split was irrevocable. All factions had some measure of responsibility for the party's implosion, but the Southern faction doomed it. Bruce Catton contends that

primary responsibility for the Democratic split in 1860—the act that ensured a Republican triumph and left the South no cohesive national institution through which it could hope to share or regain power—belongs to those respected Southern leaders whose threats of party rupture and secession as political tactics, in the vain hope that a majority in the party and nation would fall in behind them before the tactic got out of hand. Because they would not adjust to circumstances, they were engulfed by them—all without understanding that they were the leading architects of their disaster.[25]

The election of 1860 enthralled the nation as candidates and their surrogates made their cases: "Americans everywhere—North and South, men and women, slave and free—took an active part in the four-way campaign of 1860. Issues, platforms, speeches, and candidates were reviewed and debated in corn fields and cotton fields, workshops and markets, family gatherings, churches, picnics, races, sewing circles, family gathering, schoolhouses, slave quarters, taverns and beer gardens."[26] Unlike today the 1860 election consisted of state votes conducted over a two-month period. When Lincoln won early contests in Northern states, Douglas took his campaign south. He did not mince words in his campaign speeches and defied secessionists to urge preserving the Union. He told his secretary, "Lincoln is the next President. We must try to preserve the Union. I'll go to the Deep South where the secession spirit is strongest."[27] But he was greeted with hostility and scorn.

In the end "some 4,700,000 Americans—well over two thirds of the electorate—marched to the polls and cast their ballots. By the early hours of November 7th, it was clear that Lincoln had won, and when the final results were tallied it was clear that he had won rather decisively" in the Electoral College; Douglas received 29 percent of the national vote, Breckinridge 18 percent, and Bell just 13 percent.[28] "Lincoln carried seventeen free states and no slave states; Breckinridge, eleven slave states and no free states, Bell three slave states and no free states."[29] Douglas only won Missouri. Lincoln captured 40 percent of the popular vote and won 180 electoral votes, far more than the 152 needed. Lincoln's gains among former Whigs who voted for his economic versus antislavery policies allowed Lincoln to sweep the North and secure the electoral majority. When Douglas heard the final results, he told his friend John Forsyth, "Well, John, I am beaten. . . . Lincoln will win by a big margin in the Electoral College Even if Breckinridge, Bell, and I had withdrawn and united behind a single Democratic candidate, Lincoln would still have won a majority of electoral votes."[30]

For decades "Southerners had shown how minorities dominate majoritarian processes. The overwhelmingly anti-Slave Power North had now shown how an awakened majority routs a minority."[31] By November Lincoln realized that the South was not bluffing about secession. Bruce Catton writes, "The election had clarified nothing. It simply meant that a nation which had spent a long generation arguing about slavery had grown tired of talk and wanted something done—without specifying what that something might be."[32] The process "of sectional polarization was almost complete, and it remained to see what the response would come from the section that was at the losing end of the axis."[33] The answer was not long in coming, as secessionist leaders met to plan their exit from the Union.

17

Whom the Gods Intend to Destroy

The Madness of Southern Extremists

Incoln attempted to reassure Southerners that he would abide by his campaign promise not to interfere with slavery where it already existed, but he refused to give in to threats of secession. Lincoln believed that anything he said would be twisted into its exact opposite by Southerners, but he still released a statement:

> The states will be left in complete control of their affairs and property within their respective limits as they have under any administration. . . . Disunionists per se, are now in hot haste to get out of the Union, precisely because they perceive they cannot, much longer, maintain apprehension among the southern people that in their homes, and firesides, and lives, are to be endangered by the action of the Federal Government.[1]

En route to Washington DC, Lincoln stopped in New York and gave a speech promising that he would never of his own volition "consent to the destruction of this Union." He qualified this promise with "unless it were that to be that thing for which the Union itself was made."[2] Two days later Lincoln spoke at Philadelphia's Independence Hall, where he referred to the premise of the Declaration of Independence:

> He asserted that he "never had a feeling politically that did not spring from the sentiments embodied in the Declaration. . . .
> It was not the mere matter of separation of the colonies from

THE "SECESSION MOVEMENT".

FIG. 13. Political cartoon, *The "Secession Movement,"* 1861. Currier and Ives. Courtesy of the Library of Congress, Cartoon Prints Collection, LC-DIG-pga-05004.

the mother land; but rather something in that Declaration" that provided "hope for the world for all future time. It was that which gave promise that in due time the weights should be lifted from the shoulders of all men, and that all should have an equal chance."[3]

Lincoln continued to refine the idea in the Emancipation Proclamation, the Gettysburg Address, the Thirteenth Amendment, and in his second inaugural address.

Douglas tried to reassure Southerners and argued against secession. He reminded them how he fought against Lincoln and the platform of the Republican Party. He stated "that the mere election of any man to the Presidency does not furnish just cause for dissolving the Union."[4] Douglas reminded Southerners that the answer lay in the Constitution and in the ballot box:

It is apprehended that the policy of Mr. Lincoln and the principles of his party endanger the peace of the slaveholding states. Is that apprehension founded? No, it is not. Mr. Lincoln and his party lack the power, even if they had the disposition, to disturb or impair the rights and institutions of the South. . . . they will be a minority in both houses of Congress, with the Supreme Court against them. Hence no bill can pass either house of Congress impairing or disturbing these rights or institutions of the southern people in any manner whatever, unless a portion of southern senators and representatives absent themselves so as to give an abolition majority in consequence of their actions.

In short, the President will be utterly powerless to do evil. . . . Four years shall soon pass, when the ballot box will furnish a peaceful, legal, and constitutional remedy for the evils and grievances with which the country might be afflicted.[5]

James Buchanan and Senator Crittenden attempted a compromise, and a senate committee convened to entertain propositions. But most favored Southern interests and failed.

A frustrated Lincoln wrote, "I'll tell you now what bothered me: the compromises measures introduced in Congress required the Republicans to make all the concessions."[6] Lincoln warned Crittenden that such proposals were not acceptable: "Entertain no proposition for a compromise in regard to the extension of slavery. . . . The instant you do they have us under again. . . . The tug has to come & better now than later."[7]

Throughout the 1850s Lincoln had seen how Southerners had pushed for compromises that only benefited them, at the expense of Northern rights. He would not let it happen again.

The Crittenden plan, I feared, would put the country back on the high road to a slave empire. . . . "Let neither be done," I warned Republicans in Washington, "and immediately filibustering and extending slavery recommences. Within a year, we shall have to take Cuba as a condition on which the South will stay in the Union. Next it will be Mexico, then Central American. On the territorial question, I am inflexible. On that point hold firm as a chain of steel."[8]

Secession was revolutionary. The pleas of Southern Unionists like Alexander Stephens to discourage secession were ignored. Stephens had faith in the Constitution's checks and balances; he pleaded with his fellow Georgians, saying that they would render Lincoln "powerless to do any great mischief," and he warned that "the dissolution of the Union would endanger this 'Eden of the world,'" and that, "instead of becoming gods, we shall become demons, and no distant day commence cutting one another's throats."[9] Stephens's speech was met with little enthusiasm.

Southern preachers fanned the flames of secession. James Furman expressed outrage and paranoia by warning, "If you are tame enough to submit, Abolition preachers will be at hand to consummate the marriage of your daughters to black husbands."[10] Southern denominations endorsed secession; Southern Methodists railed

> about a Union dominated by abolitionists as they called on the Lord for deliverance from the northern "Egypt." The division of Israel and Judah . . . became typologies for the American crisis. Just as southern Methodists had once "seceded from a corrupt church," a Mississippi politician declared, "We must secede from a corrupt nation." To drive the point home, Georgia Methodists ministers endorsed disunion by an overwhelming 87–9 vote.[11]

As Lincoln, Douglas, and Stephens tried to strike a conciliatory tone, Southern states seceded. The sectional nature of Lincoln's victory "emboldened many Southern politicians and journalists to insist that they would not be bound by the result."[12]

Senators who became prominent leaders of the Confederacy made speeches as they resigned, some tinged with regret, others with fury. Robert Toombs lambasted the "black Republicans" and abolitionists: "We want no negro equality, no negro citizenship, we want no negro race to degrade our own; and as one man [we] would meet you upon the border with the sword in one hand and the torch in the other."[13] Stephen Mallory, the future Confederate secretary of the navy, delivered a fiery broadside against his Northern colleagues: "You cannot conquer us. Imbue your hands in our blood and the rains of a century will not wipe away from them stain, while the coming generation will weep for your wickedness and folly."[14]

Alexander Stephens lamented the election even as he prepared to leave the Senate and warned that "revolutions are much easier started than controlled, and the men who begin them [often] . . . themselves become the victims."[15] But, he said, "if the policy of Mr. Lincoln and his Republican associates be carried out . . . no man in Georgia will be more willing or ready than myself to defend our rights, interest, and honor at every hazard and to the last extremity."[16] To a friend's question "Why must we have civil war?," Stephens replied, "Because there are not virtue and patriotism and sense enough left in the country to avoid it. Mark me, when I repeat that in less than twelve months we shall be in the midst of a bloody war. What will become of us then God only knows?"[17]

Passionate secessionist "commissioners" spread their message of fear throughout the South. "Thus fanned," Bruce Catton writes, "mob spirit ran close enough to the surface to intimidate many moderates—the very temperament that inclines men toward moderation is apt to respond timidly when threatened or abused—and to push others closer to the extremist position."[18] Southern Unionists found themselves swept up in the tumult as their states seceded. Sen. Judah P. Benjamin of Louisiana wrote, "The prudent and conservative men South . . . were not able to stem the wild torrent of passion which is carrying everything before it. . . . It is a revolution . . . of the most intense character . . . and it can no more be checked by human effort, for the time, than a prairie fire by a gardener's watering pot."[19]

South Carolina was the first to secede. Its senior senator, James Chesnut, launched a fusillade against the North, arguing that the South could not wait for another election:

Because of the Yankee puritans' invasive mentality, incendiary documents would flood our region, Southern Republicans would fill our offices. Enemies would control our mails. The resulting upheaval would make "Lincoln's election . . . a decree for emancipation. Slavery cannot survive the four years of an administration whose overwhelming influences" will be "brought to bear against it . . . we must slay the Negro, or ourselves be slain."[20]

William Tecumseh Sherman was president of the Louisiana State Seminary of Learning and Military Academy. Sherman had thought little about the slavery issue, but he was concerned with preserving the Union. He thought secession made no sense, especially for Southerners. When he read the news of South Carolina's secession, it "cut to the depths of his nationalistic soul." The future general wept. He told his friend David Boyd:

> Boyd, you people of the South don't know what you are doing! You think you can tear to pieces this great union without war. . . . The North can make a steam-engine, locomotive, or railway car; hardly a yard of cloth or shoes can you make. You are rushing into war with one of the most powerful, ingeniously mechanical and determined people on earth. . . . You are bound to fail. Only in spirit and determination are you prepared for war.[21]

Sherman, who later proclaimed, "War is hell," proved a remarkably accurate seer regarding the rebellion's fate.

In seceding from the Union, South Carolina was followed by Mississippi, Florida, Alabama, Georgia, Louisiana, and Texas. Catton observes that "a belt of seven states . . . embracing nearly one-sixth of the country's population and nearly one-fifth of the national domain, had proclaimed independence and severed its ties with the Union."[22] All of the declarations for secession made it clear that slavery was the primary reason for seceding. South Carolina's declaration was typical:

> All the States north of that line have united in the election of a man to the high office of President of the United States

whose opinions and purposes are hostile to slavery. He is to be entrusted with the administration of the common Government, because he has declared that that "Government cannot endure permanently half slave, half free," and that the public mind must rest in the belief that slavery is in the course of ultimate extinction.[23]

While slavery was the cause of secession, even now some Northerners were "content to tolerate slavery's indefinite survival in the South so long as it did not impinge on their own rights and aspirations at home."[24]

The transgressions of slavery supporters energized Northerners as never before. The legislative compromises that extended slavery to the territories and the use of the courts—especially the Supreme Court in *Dred Scott*, which allowed slaveholders to recover their slaves, even in free states—provoked no end of indignation. Southern actions demonstrated "just how fundamental and intractable the differences with Southern political leaders were. Thus educated, most northern voters had decided by 1860 that only an explicitly anti-slavery party could protect their interests."[25]

In a rather astute analysis of Southern leaders' behavior after 1860 election, William Lloyd Garrison used biblical imagery to describe the Southern response:

Never had the truth of the ancient proverb "Whom the gods intend to destroy, they first make mad" been more signally illustrated than in the condition of southern slaveholders following Lincoln's election. They were insane from their fears, their guilty forebodings, their lust for power and rule, hatred of free institutions, their merited consciousness of merited judgments; so that they may be properly classed as the inmates of a lunatic asylum. Their dread of Mr. Lincoln, of his Administration, of the Republican Party demonstrated their insanity. In vain did Mr. Lincoln tell them, "I do not stand pledged to the abolition of slavery where it already exists." They raved just as fiercely as though he were another John Brown, armed for southern invasion and universal emancipation In vain did the Republican party present one point of antagonism to slavery—to wit, no more territorial expansion. In vain did that party exhibit the utmost caution not to give offense to any other direction—and make itself hoarse in uttering professions of loyalty to the Constitution and the Union. The South protested that its designs were infernal, and for them was "sleep no more!" Were these not the signs of a demented people?[26]

Both sides miscalculated the effects of the election. Few Northerners appreciated that Lincoln's election would result in secession, while Southerners "were not able to see that secession would finally mean war."[27] Southerners "believed that the Yankees were cowards and would not fight. . . . Senator James Chesnut of South Carolina offered to drink all the blood that was spilled as a consequence of secession. It became a common saying in the South during the secession winter that 'a lady's thimble will hold all the blood that will be shed.'"[28]

Following secession the five states of the lower South "appointed commissioners to the other slave states, and instructed them to spread the secessionist message across the entire region. . . . From December 1860 to April 1861, they carried the gospel of disunion to the far corners of the South."[29] The editors of the *Philadelphia Press* accused secessionists of being enemies of democracy:

Should the Cotton States go out in a body, we shall witness the beginning of an experiment to establish, on this continent, a great slaveholding monarchy. With few exceptions, the leaders of the Disunion cabal are men of the most aristocratic pretensions—men who . . . easily adopt the habits and titles of the European nobility. South Carolina which is the head of Secession, is almost a monarchy herself. Her representatives . . . have acted upon the idea that the people of the free states are servile, and Mr. Hammond, the most candid and straightforward of the set, denounced the laboring white masses of the free States as the mudsills of society.[30]

By the end of 1860 the South was "fearful, uncertain, impatient and volatile, eager to adopt the course that best offered hope of deliverance—which was ideally suited for the immediacy and urgency of the radical secessionists."[31] Using the political machinery of the Democratic Party, the proponents of secession were far better organized than Southern Unionists, who were unable to put up a united from against the radicals.

Slavery and white supremacy were at the heart of the message brought by the commissioners to the undecided states. Former congressman John McQueen of South Carolina told the Texas Convention, "Lincoln was elected by a sectional vote, whose platform was that of the Black Republican part and whose policy was to be the abolition of slavery upon this continent and the elevation of our own slaves to an equality with ourselves and our children."[32]

Southern secessionists knew what Lincoln's election meant in terms of slavery in the United States: emancipation was coming. It might take a decade, but they knew that it was coming. Secession was the only action left "consistent with their ideology."[33] Southern states did not even wait for Lincoln to be inaugurated before they seceded and seized federal installations, As this was happening, Lincoln left Springfield to travel to Washington to take the oath of office, fully understanding the gravity of the situation. He addressed his friends and neighbors as he boarded the train that would take him and his family to Washington:

> Today I leave you. I go to assume a task far more difficult than that which devolved on General Washington. Unless the great God who assisted him shall be with and aid me, I must fail; but if the same Omniscient Mind and Almighty Arm that directed and protected him shall guide me and support me, I shall not fail—I shall succeed. Let us all pray that the God of our fathers may not forsake us now. To Him I commend you all. Permit me to ask that with equal sincerity and faith you will invoke His wisdom and guidance for me.[34]

Lincoln cut to the heart of the country's division in his first inaugural address: "One section of our country believes slavery is right and ought to be extended, while the other believes it is wrong and ought not to be extended. This is the only substantial dispute."[35] He was right, of course, and his Southern opponents agreed, though they viewed Lincoln's opposition to slavery's expansion as an existential threat. Jefferson Davis wrote: "The great northern party . . . succeeded in electing to the office of the Presidency a man who openly proclaimed his hatred of slavery, who declared that the government could not endure 'half slave and half free.'"[36]

Before the first shot was fired, Southerners railed against the hated Yankee. With the Orwellian slogan "'Freedom is not possible without slavery' ringing in their ears, they went to war against the Yankees alongside their slave-owning neighbors to 'perpetuate and diffuse the very liberty for which Washington bled, and which the heroes of the Revolution achieved.'"[37]

Alexander Stephens, the longtime friend of Lincoln who supported Stephen Douglas until the bitter end, was now the vice president of the Confederacy. Elected by the Confederate Congress the same day as Jefferson Davis as President, he traveled across the South speaking about the new government. Stephens gave his Cornerstone Speech of March, 21, 1861, in Charleston, South Carolina. In it he defined Confederacy's nature. The speech echoed the racist nationalism Southerners held to for years—that Blacks were a lesser order of humanity, and slavery was their natural condition: "Our new government is founded upon exactly the opposite idea; its foundations are laid, its corner-stone rests upon the great truth, that the negro is not equal to the white man; that slavery—subordination to the superior race—is his natural and normal condition. [Applause.] This, our new government, is the first, in the history of the world, based upon this great physical, philosophical, and moral truth."[38]

When he read the speech, Davis was furious, since he issued instructions to cabinet members to downplay slavery to gain foreign recognition. He agreed with Stephens, but he believed the speech a personal attack: "That speech infuriated me, Oh, what Stephens had said was true, perfectly true, but could anything hurt us more abroad than such impolitic remarks? It was the beginning of a fatal falling out between me and that rebellious and vindictive dwarf, who was hell-bent on forming his own policies and disputing mine with niggardly deviousness."[39]

The Northern press mocked Southerner's of definition of slavery as necessary for liberty. Likewise, claims of Confederate leaders that they were comparable to the founding fathers was condemned throughout the North. The editors of the *New York Evening Post* wrote:

> The founders fought to "establish the rights of man . . . and principles of universal liberty." The South was rebelling "not in the interest of general humanity, but of a domestic despotism. . . . Their motto is not liberty, but slavery." Thomas Jefferson's Declaration of Independence spoke for "Natural Rights against Established Institutions," added the New York Tribune, while "Mr. Jeff. Davis's caricature thereof is made in the interest of an unjust, outgrown, decaying institution against the apprehended encroachments of human rights." It was, in short, not a revolution for liberty but a counterrevolution "reversing the wheels of progress. . . . to hurl everything backward into deepest darkness . . . despotism and oppression."[40]

Commissioners from seven Confederate states traveled to undecided Slave states to urge secession. Henry Benning of Georgia spoke to the secession convention of Virginia, a state that the Confederacy deemed all-important, which had to be on its side in the coming war. The Georgia Supreme Court justice used the time-honored method of racial fearmongering to sway the men of the Virginia House of Delegates. He thundered: "If things are allowed to go on as they are, it is certain that slavery is be abolished except in Georgia and the other cotton States, and . . . ultimately in these States also. . . . By the time the North shall have attained the power, the black race will be a large majority, and we will have black governors, black legislatures, black juries, black everything."[41] Charles Dew portrayed Benning's apocalyptic vision of the outcome of a Northern invasion of the South; he told his audience, "We will be overpowered and our men compelled to wander like vagabonds all over the earth, and for our women, the horrors of their state cannot contemplate in imagination." This then, was "the fate that Abolition will bring upon the white race. . . . We will be exterminated."[42]

Virginia's governor, John Letcher, was a foe of slavery who advocated abolition before becoming governor. But once elected governor during the secession crisis he sold his soul to disunion. Jubal Early was a Unionist delegate to the convention. In his account of the proceedings,

> The scenes witnessed within the wall of that room . . . have no parallel in the annals of ancient or modern times. On the morning of the 17th, Mr. Wise rose from his seat and drawing a large Virginia horse-pistol from his bosom laid it before him and proceeded to harangue the body in the most violent and denunciatory manner. He concluded by taking his watch from his pocket and, with glaring eyes and bated breath, declared that events were now transpiring which caused a hush to come over his soul.[43]

Wise was referring to the seizure of federal facilities, including the Harpers Ferry Arsenal and Portsmouth Naval Yard. But not all Virginians were convinced. The Unionist western counties, where few owned slaves, and where those who did held very few, voted against secession. They withstood the initial shock of secession and gave little support to the Confederacy. These counties would "in a wholly extra-legal way, abetted by Washington—perform its own act of secession, breaking away from Virginia and clinging to the Union as a bob-tailed but finally acceptable new state."[44] Thus West Virginia was born.

Former president John Tyler joined the rebellion and "personally drafted a document placing the state's military force under Jefferson Davis's direct command." Tyler was "elected to the Confederate Congress—becoming the only former President to win office in a foreign country."[45] Tyler, now an intractable enemy of the Union, died in Richmond before he could take office. His portrait was removed from its place of honor in the White House.

Tennessee was problematic. The eastern part of the state was strongly Unionist, and the counties "held a convention, denounced the governor and legislature for making the alliance with the Confederacy and sent a memorial asking that the eastern counties be allowed to form a new state."[46] The request was rejected, but the area would prove a problem for Davis and Confederate military leaders. Although Lincoln wanted to help, he had no military means of doing so until Union forces gained control in 1864.

Kentucky and Missouri remained in the Union, but became highly partisan battlegrounds between secessionists and Unionists throughout the war in which insurgents used terrorist methods. Kentucky's pro-secession governor, Beriah Magoffin, called on the legislature to decide secession, "but the legislature, by a vote of 54 to 36 in the lower house, refused to call one and adjourned on February 11 without taking any decisive action."[47] After losing that vote, Magoffin issued a declaration of neutrality that caused Lincoln and Davis to move with caution.

Lincoln understood Kentucky's strategic importance and said, "I think to lose Kentucky is nearly the same as to lose the whole game. . . . Kentucky gone, we cannot hold Missouri, nor, as I think, Maryland. These all against us, and the job on our hands is too large for us. We may as well consent to separation at once, including the surrender of this capital."[48] Lincoln's use of caution, diplomacy, and, when needed, the force of the law, courts, and the military paid strategic and economic dividends, as the Ohio River remained under Union control.

Maryland remained in the Union as Gov. Thomas H. Hicks, with the help of federal troops, resisted the legislature's secession vote. When Union volunteers marched through Baltimore, some regiments were attacked. The Sixth Massachusetts Volunteer Infantry was attacked when a "crowd of southern sympathizers threw bricks and stones and fired into their ranks as they changed trains. They returned the fire, killing twelve citizens and wounding many more, then packed their four dead on ice for shipment north, and came on to Washington, bearing their seventeen wounded on stretchers."[49]

To Lincoln secession was "never just about politics. To him it spoke about the nation, even if primarily as a symbol. In his mind the nation must be about freedom, never slavery."[50] For him the Union was sacred and could not be dissolved for any reason, especially slavery. In contrast to secessionists who claimed the right to dissolve it, Lincoln used the argument of Daniel Webster in his inaugural address that the Union predated the Constitution:

> Descending from these general principles, we find the propositions that, in legal contemplation, the Union is perpetual, confirmed by the history of the Union itself. The Union is much older than the Constitution. It was formed, in fact, by the Articles of Association in 1774. It was matured and continued by the Declaration of Independence in 1776. It was further matured, and the faith of all the then thirteen States expressly plighted and engaged that it should be perpetual, by the Articles of Confederation in 1778. And final, in 1787, one of the declared objects for ordaining and establishing the Constitution, was "to form a more perfect Union."[51]

Before the attack on Fort Sumter, a *New York Times* editorial unveiled the reality of the situation confronting the nation: "If two sections can no longer live together, they can no longer live apart in quiet until it is determined which is master. No two civilizations ever did, or can, come into contact as the North and South threaten to do, without a trial of strength, in which the weaker goes to the wall. . . . We must remain master of the occasion and the dominant power on this continent."[52]

America's religious-ideological war erupted following decades of political conflicts, frustrated compromises, and doomed attempts to save the Union. Slavery was the cause. Nothing could or would change so long as "one section of the country regarded it as a blessing, the other as a curse."[53] As Frederick Douglass wrote, "Whatever was done or attempted with a view to the support and security of slavery only served to fuel the fire and heated the furnace of [antislavery] agitation to a higher degree than had any before attained."[54]

18

The Heather Is On Fire

Politics, Religion, and War

No middle ground remained, and Americans embraced war. Once conciliatory leaders became pro-war demagogues almost overnight. While Northerners reacted furiously to the seizure of federal installations by Confederates, Southern Unionists joined the secession movement. Bruce Levine writes, "Northerners greeted secession as a deadly assault upon their own rights, welfare and security. Secession leaders sought not to nullify a single law, but the results of an entire presidential election. Far worse, they intended to shatter a nation that was liberty's last, best hope. That could not be tolerated."[1]

Only four installations in the Confederacy remained in federal hands, "two far away in the Florida Keys; Fort Pickens at Pensacola, Florida; and the most visible, Fort Sumter."[2] Sumter sat in the eye of the brewing hurricane as war threatened the nation. Southern Church leaders offered up "ministerial hosannahs to the providential nature of secession, such as Benjamin Palmer's, contributed vital ideological work to the creation of the Confederacy. Such sermonizing language provided the appearance of a seamless bridge between pro-slavery and the revolution creating an independent nation."[3]

Southerners and Northerners alike used the events of any given day to interpret God's will. All were subject to massive shifts as the God of battles seemed at times to favor the Confederacy and then the Union. Tennessee Presbyterian pastor William H. Vernor was blunt in his opinion: "In all contests

FIG. 14. Wood engraving, *Bombardment of Fort Sumter by the Batteries
of the Confederate States, April 13, 1861.* From *Harper's Weekly,*
April 27, 1861. Courtesy of the Library of Congress,
Civil War Collection, LC-DIG-ppmsca-35361.

between nations God espouses the cause of the Righteous and
makes it his own. . . . The institution of slavery according to
the Bible is right. Therefore, in the contest between North
and South, he will espouse the cause of the South and make
it his own."[4]

On November 29, 1860, Thanksgiving, Benjamin Morgan
Palmer, one of the most influential Southern preachers, gave
one of the most polemic proslavery secession sermons ever,
which became one a Confederate propaganda tools: "Some
50,000 copies of that sermon were printed in pamphlet form
and circulated throughout the South. That pamphlet became
a most powerful part of Southern propaganda."[5] Palmer thundered against abolitionists, particularly Northern ministers,
equating them to atheists and French Revolution radicals:

> Last of all, in this great struggle, we defend the cause of God
> and religion. The abolition spirit is undeniably atheistic. The
> demon which erected its throne upon the guillotine in the

days of Robespierre and Marat, which abolished the Sabbath and worshipped reason in the person of a harlot, yet survives to work other horrors, of which those of the French Revolution are but the type. Among a people so generally religious as the American, a disguise must be worn; but it is the same old threadbare disguise of the advocacy of human rights. . . . These self-constituted reformers must quicken the activity of Jehovah or compel his abdication. . . . This spirit of atheism, which knows no God who tolerates evil, no Bible which sanctions law, and no conscience that can be bound by oaths and covenants, has selected us for its victims, and slavery for its issue. Its banner-cry rings out already upon the air—"liberty, equality, fraternity," which simply interpreted mean bondage, confiscation and massacre. . . . To the South the high position is assigned of defending, before all nations, the cause of all religion and of all truth.[6]

As fires of war engulfed the nation, Palmer pointed to divine providence as justification for secession. Southerners doubtful or in opposition to secession were overcome by events when Fort Sumter was attacked. Edmund Ruffin spoke for many when he proclaimed, "The shedding of blood . . . will serve to change many voters in the hesitating states, from submission or procrastinating ranks, to the zealous for immediate secession."[7]

But very few radical secessionists joined the army. Many took the exemptions granted to them as slave owners or by joining state militias. Gen. Jubal Early saw the sour irony in this. A strong Unionist, Early argued against secession during Virginia's secession debate. When he accepted secession's reality, he went to war and never looked back, becoming an intractable enemy of the Union. During the war he was one of the most uncompromising rebels and, afterward, one of the primary proponents of Lost Cause. Early took a perverse pleasure in taunting "the identifiable secessionists in gray uniform who came his way, especially when the circumstances were less

The Heather Is On Fire

than amusing."[8] After the defeat at the Third Battle of Winchester in 1864, Early looked at Maj. Gen. John C. Breckinridge, Buchanan's vice president, as they retreated amid the "chaos and horror of his army's rout. Early took the occasion to mock his celebrated subordinate: 'Well, General', he crowed, 'what do you think of the "rights of the South" in the territories now?'"[9]

Some prominent ministers believed slavery would not survive war. Prof. James P. Boyce expressed his apprehension about secession to his brother-in-law, who was serving as a chaplain in a Georgia regiment:

> Alas, my country! . . . I know I am cautious about taking any step without arranging for the consequences. . . . Moreover, I believe I see in all this the end of slavery I believe we are cutting its throat, curtailing its domain. And I have been, and am, an ultra pro-slavery man. . . . I feel our sins as to this institution have cursed us,—that the negroes have not been cared for in their marital and religious relations as they should be; and I fear that God is going to sweep it away.[10]

Northerners' sentiments were very different. One Pennsylvania volunteer wrote:

> I cannot believe . . . that "Providence intends to destroy this Nation, the great asylum for all the oppressed of all other nations and build a slave Oligarchy on the ruins thereof." An Ohio volunteer mused: "Admit the right of the seceding states to break up the Union at pleasure . . . and how long before the new confederacies created by the first disruption shall be resolved into smaller fragments and the continent become a vast theater of civil war, military license, anarchy and despotism? Better to settle it at whatever cost and settle it forever."[11]

When mobilization began clergymen proclaimed a holy war to support their side's cause. Palmer provided Confederate soldiers a religious basis for their fight: "He insisted that the Louisiana Washington Artillery resist the Northern invasion in order to protect the right of self-government. To them he advocated the pursuit of a holy war, a war of true Christian faith against fanaticism."[12] The religious character of the war was evidenced as "clergymen and their congregations became caught up in the patriotic fervor. . . . It would not be entirely fair to say that politics rode roughshod over religion, but Americans exhibited more spiritual hubris than spiritual reflection."[13] The depth of religious devotion was readily seen in the hymn most commonly associated with the war: In her epic song "The Battle Hymn of the Republic," lyricist Julia Ward Howe penned the lines "As he died to make men holy, let us live to make men free! / While God is marching on."[14]

Evangelical churches and tract societies on both sides actively conducted revival meetings to convert soldiers. As "early as 1862, large-scale 'conversion seasons' swept through both Union and Confederate troops: the Army of the Cumberland and the Army of Northern Virginia both experienced large-scale religious revivals during the winter and spring of 1864."[15] The 1864 revivals were last as the war entered a new and more brutal phase, which tested and shattered the faith of many soldiers. An Illinois surgeon named John Hostetter remarked, "There is no God in war. It is merciless, cruel, vindictive, unchristian, savage, relentless. It is all that devils could wish for."[16]

Some Northern evangelicals wanted to make Christianity the state religion. They believed the war was God's judgment because the founders left God out of the Constitution. The group, the National Reform Association, proposed a so-called Bible amendment in 1863 in order to unite evangelical Protestantism to the Republic and proclaim a Christian nation. They met with Lincoln to propose changing the Constitution to read, "We the people of the United States humbly acknowledging Almighty God as the source of all authority and power and civil government, the Lord Jesus Christ as the Ruler among the nations, His revealed will as the supreme law of the land, in order to form a more perfect union."[17]

Lincoln brushed them off, however, and never referred to

the United States as a Christian nation, as the framers refused to do in the Constitution, as well as Adams, who crafted the Treaty of Algiers which specifically stated that the United States did not have a Christian government. Yet the Confederacy "proudly invoked the name of God in their Constitution. Even late in the war, a South Carolina editor pointed to what he saw as a revealing fact: the Federal Constitution—with no reference to the Almighty—'could have been passed and adopted by Atheists or Hindoes or Mahometans.'"[18]

The First Flash of Gunpowder: Fort Sumter and War

The forts remaining in federal control were a thorn in the side of Jefferson Davis. Davis attempted negotiations for them, but was rejected by Buchanan and Lincoln, so he began military preparations instead. This was complicated when Maj. Robert Anderson withdrew his garrison from Charleston to Fort Sumter in Charleston harbor due to Buchanan's dithering on their status.

Anderson used the cover of darkness to withdraw his men from Fort Moultrie to Fort Sumter. In doing so he was met with adulation in the North and condemnation in the South. Buchanan wanted to abandon Sumter, but "when it appeared that Northern public opinion was solidly behind Anderson, Buchanan changed his mind and attempted to persuade the South Carolinians to accept Anderson's occupation of Fort Sumter as a legitimate exercise of federal authority."[19] Jefferson Davis, yet to resign from the Senate, awaiting Mississippi's secession, "pleaded with Buchanan to give up Sumter and avert impending calamity. Once again the old imbecile refused, after his fashion, which is to say that he muttered to himself, nodded and tilted his head as if in agreement. . . . Had this lame-duck President withdrawn the troops from Sumter, he might have turned away the threatening of civil war."[20]

Jefferson Davis was blind to the political anger and hostility that secession and the seizure of other federal installations provoked. A Northern Democrat wrote that "Anderson's course of action is universally approved and that if he is recalled or if Sumter is surrendered. . . . Northern sentiment will be unanimous in favor of hanging Buchanan I am not joking— Never have I known the entire people more unanimous on any question. We are ruined if Anderson is disgraced or Sumter given up."[21]

Rep. Dan Sickles, a friend of the South for many years who even backed peaceful secession, spoke out against the seizure of federal installations, stating that secessionists had committed "a fatal error." He charged: "It will never do, sir, for them to protest against coercion, and, at the same moment seize all the arms and arsenals and forts and navy yards, and ships that may, through our forbearance, fall within their power. This is not peaceful secession. These acts, whensoever or whomsoever done, are overt acts of war."[22]

On January 9, 1861, Buchanan made a belated attempt to reinforce and resupply Sumter using an unarmed merchantman, the *Star of the West*. But South Carolinians knew the ship was coming, and Anderson did not receive permission to fire if it was attacked. As a result, when Confederate gunners opened fire, Anderson did nothing to intervene. "If he opened fire, the United States and South Carolina would be at war. . . . Major Anderson hesitated, plainly uncertain, an immense weight of responsibility resting on him."[23]

The *Star of the West* retreated, leaving the garrison unreinforced. But the secessionists "had overplayed their hand. The South Carolina gunners who fired on the *Star of the West* had, in effect, invited the Federal government to start the war then and there if it wanted a war."[24] The attack on the ship further infuriated Northerners. Dan Sickles thundered in the House: "The authorities of South Carolina, through their military forces, opened fire upon that defenseless ship, and compelled her to retire and abandon the peaceful and legitimate mission in which she was engaged. Now, sir, that was an act of war, unqualified war."[25]

The stalemate continued as both sides maneuvered for strategic advantage. Buchanan did not want to drive undecided slave states toward secession by using overt military means to relieve Sumter, and Davis did not want South Carolina to attack prematurely. As they waited the balance of power shifted, "as local troops day by day strengthened the ring of batteries confronting Sumter's garrison."[26] The incoming Lincoln administration debated what to do. Lincoln thought about abandoning Sumter, but knew that if he ordered evacuation, "the credibility of his presidency and the Republican administration would be in pieces before either had scarcely begun."[27]

Lincoln sought more information and sent three men "down to Charleston to observe the situation and report on what they saw. The first two, both southern-born, were Illinois law associates, both reported reconciliation impossible. . . . The third, a high-ranking naval observer who secured and interview with Anderson at the fort, returned to declare a relief expedition was feasible."[28] Lincoln continued to meet with cabinet members to decide how to meet the challenge. "He met with Francis Blair who, like his son, Monty, believed passionately that the surrender of Sumter 'was virtually a surrender of the Union unless under irresistible force—that compounding with treason was treason to the Govt.'"[29] On March 29 Lincoln and the cabinet met again, having weighed all options, and decided to resupply Sumter, "but not rearm, it. And he would announce the plan in advance so the South could not regard the effort as an act of hostility by an enemy."[30] If successful it would avoid violence, but if Confederates opened fire, the fault would lay with them.

Confederates moved more troops and guns into position around Sumter. But impatient and influential Southerners feared that, if the attack met further delays, some states might return to the Union. Davis was under pressure to act. A Mobile Alabama newspaper editorialized: "If something is not done pretty soon . . . the whole country will be so disgusted with the sham of independence that the first chance the people get at a popular election the y will turn the whole movement topsy-turvy."[31]

Southern sympathizers in Washington sent word that a relief expedition was coming. Gen. P. T. G. Beauregard "had already cut off Major Anderson's purchases in the Charleston market the day before Governor Pickens received Lincoln's message about the intention to provision Sumter."[32] Pickens forwarded it to Davis, which forced to fire the first shot or back down. From a messaging standpoint, opening fire was worse, for "that first shot would be for the immediate purpose of keeping food from hungry men."[33]

Davis was livid when he conferred with his cabinet on April 9, after hearing of the relief expedition. The debate "ran long and heated. Davis favored proceeding with the bombardment. Charleston's batteries were ready, and the South Carolinians were more than anxious."[34] With exception of Robert Toombs, all concurred. Davis later wrote:

> I summoned the Cabinet and told them that negotiation was now at an end, and that it was time to bombard the fort. Yes, I said, we would now be firing the first shot, but that was not our fault. It was Lincoln who intended war. He and that lying Seward had drawn the sword, and we were responding to them. We were defending our honor.
>
> Toombs, my Secretary of State disagreed. "Sir," he said to me, "firing at the fort is suicide. It's unnecessary, it puts us in the wrong, it's fatal."
>
> "Sir," I said, "you are wrong."
>
> On April tenth, I ordered General Beauregard to demand the evacuation of Fort Sumter, and if refused, to reduce it with his guns.[35]

Beauregard delivered the ultimatum to Anderson, who rejected it: "His sense of honor and obligations to his government prevented his complying."[36]

Confederate fears that the relief force might arrive prompted them to open fire at 4:30 a.m. on April 12. Anderson's troops resisted, but could not man all of their guns and were short on ammunition and powder. Following a thirty-three-hour bombardment, the fort damaged by over four thousand hits and with a fire threatening the powder magazines, Anderson gave the order to surrender.

Beauregard allowed the garrison to evacuate on navy ships, and as a parting gesture he allowed Anderson's troops to fire a last salute to Old Glory. They hauled down the torn, smoke-stained flag and marched to the ship with their drums beating the tune "Yankee Doodle Dandy." Lincoln realized the importance all too well. He noted, "They attacked Sumter. It fell and thus did more service than it otherwise would."[37]

Only Two Parties

When Sumter surrendered on April 14, 1861, the North was galvanized as never before, as "the clash at Fort Sumter brought forth an outpouring of support for the Union and President Lincoln."[38] In the words of Abner Doubleday, "With the first shot fired against Fort Sumter the whole North became united."[39]

Another observer wrote: "The heather is on fire. . . . I never knew what popular excitement can be. . . . The whole population, men, women, and children, seem to be in the streets with Union favors and flags."[40] The attack on Fort Sumter unified the North in ways that Southern leaders never expected. They did not believe that Northerners had the will to go to war, but they were wrong; the bombardment had the opposite effect. For Northerners, even abolition opponents, an attack on a federal garrison by massed artillery meant war. Sen. Stephen Douglas went to the White House to visit Lincoln and make a call to national unity. Returning to Chicago just a month before his untimely death, he told a huge crowd, "There are only two sides to the question. Every man must be for the United States or against it. There can be no neutrals in this war, only patriots—or traitors."[41]

For Frederick Douglass the shots marked a new phase in abolition:

The first flash of rebel gunpowder and shell upon the starving handful of men at Sumter instantly changed the nation's whole policy. Until then, the ever hopeful North was dreaming of compromise. . . .

I wrote in my newspaper; "On behalf of our enslaved and bleeding brothers and sisters, thank God! The slaveholders themselves have saved the abolition cause from ruin! The government is aroused, the dead North is alive, and its divided people united. Never was a change so sudden, so universal, and so portentous. The whole North from East to West is in arms. . . ."[42]

Douglas died less than a month later, but his impact on Northern Democrats was immense: for a year or more his war spirit lived among most Democrats. "Let our enemies perish by the sword," was the theme of democratic editorials in the spring of 1861. "All squeamish sentimentality should be discarded, and bloody vengeance wreaked upon the heads of the contemptible traitors who have provoked it by their dastardly impertinence and rebellious acts."[43]

One Democrat was Rep. Dan Sickles. He had defended Southerners just months before, but when Fort Sumter was attacked, he took the actions of his former friends personally. He became one of the first Union Democrats and wholeheartedly followed Lincoln. Despite his notoriety he remained true to the Union during and after the war.[44]

Sickles, who in 1859 said that no troops would cross through New York to invade the South, now proclaimed "the men of New York would go in untold thousands anywhere to protect the flag of their country and to maintain its legitimate authority."[45] In one of his last speeches in Congress, Sickles lambasted the South for seizing U.S. funds in the subtreasuries and mints and sending envoys to England and France. He condemned the Confederacy's actions, which, despite Northern compromises, had "been followed by insults to our flag; by the expulsion of the United States troops and authorities from navy yards and forts and arsenals; by measures to control the vast commerce of the Mississippi and its tributaries."[46]

Sickles recruited the legendary Excelsior Brigade, became a general, and while commanding III Corps at the Battle of Gettysburg lost his leg. He oversaw early Reconstruction in North Carolina and ordered the end to the public whippings of Blacks by state officials. President Andrew Johnson relieved him for supporting voting rights for Blacks. Congress reinstated him, but Sickles, who had earnestly supported the South as late as 1860, could no longer stomach Democrats who were once friends and political allies. During the 1876 elections, Sickles, a lifelong Democrat, labeled his party as "the party of treason."[47] He joined forces with Republicans to prevent the election of New York Democrat Samuel Tilden through shrewd political electioneering in key battleground states, but he was betrayed when Republican Rutherford B. Hayes ended Reconstruction.

For Stephen Douglas the attack on Fort Sumter brought an end to his efforts to bring about reconciliation. When the Little Giant heard about the attack and the statements of Confederate leaders, he rushed to Lincoln to offer his support. Douglas wrote of the meeting:

> "I heartily approve of your proclamation calling up 75,000 militia," I told him. "Except that I would make it 200,000. You don't know the dishonest purposes of these southern men as well as I do." After a review of the strategic situation with the President Douglas continued, "Mr. President," I said. "Let me speak plainly. I remain unalterably opposed to your Administration on purely its political issues. Yet I'm prepared to sustain you in the exercise of all your constitutional functions to preserve the Union, maintain the government, and defend the capital. A firm policy and prompt action are necessary. The capital of our country is in danger, and must be defended at all hazards, and at any expense of men and money. I speak of the present and future without reference to the past."

He shook my hand, hard. "We need more patriots like you, Douglas," he said as he walked me to the door. "I depreciate war," I said in parting, "but if it must come, I'm with my country and for my country, under all circumstances and in every contingency."[48]

Douglas went to his fellow Democrats in Washington and told them, "We must fight for our country and forget all differences. There can be only two parties now—the party of patriots and the party of traitors. We belong to the first."[49]

Most Southern officers were conflicted by their commitment to the army, to the flag they fought under, to long-standing friendships versus loyalty to home and family. Richard Ewell described the feelings of many: "Officers generally are very much adverse to any thing like civil war, though some of the younger ones are a bit warlike. The truth is in the army there are no sectional feelings and many from extreme ends of the Union are the most intimate friends."[50]

Three officers bade tearful farewells as they parted ways in California: Brig. Gen. Albert Sidney Johnston, Capt. Winfield Scott Hancock, and Capt. Lewis Armistead. Hancock had sympathy for his Southern friends, but had previously said, "I shall fight not upon the principle of state-rights, but for the Union, whole and undivided."[51] Johnston, his commander, and his best friend, Armistead, were departing to serve the Confederacy. Almira Hancock wrote of that final night: "The most crushed was Major Armistead, who with tears, which were contagious, streaming down his face, put his hands upon Mr. Hancock's shoulders, while looking him steadily in the eye, said, 'Hancock, good-bye; you can never know what this has cost me; and I hope God will strike me dead if I am ever induced to leave my native soil, should worse come to worst.'"[52]

Col. Robert E. Lee of Virginia opposed secession but valued the Union less than loyalty to Virginia. As he left his command in Texas, he told a friend, "If Virginia stands by the old Union, so will I. But if she secedes (though I do not believe in secession as a constitutional right, nor that there is sufficient cause for revolution), then I will follow my native State with my sword, and if need be, with my life."[53] Yet, on his return to Washington, he accepted a promotion to Colonel in the regular army just before Lincoln asked him to lead the Union armies. Lee refused the offer. In his final interview with Gen. Winfield Scott, Lee admitted that "the struggle had been hard. He did not believe in secession, he said, and if he owned every slave in the South, he would free them all to bring peace; but to fight against Virginia was not in him."[54] When Virginia seceded, Lee submitted his resignation: "With all my devotion to the Union and feeling of loyalty and duty of an American citizen, I have not been able to make up my mind to raise my hand against my relatives, my children, my home. I have therefore, resigned my commission in the Army, and save in the defense of my native State. . . . I hope I may never be called upon to draw my sword."[55]

Within days Lee was appointed a general and commander of Virginia's military forces. Lee arrived at the State House, and, "before he had much time to ruminate, he found himself being presented with George Washington's sword, and hailed as a hero in a powerful tribute by the president of the convention."[56] He was assailed by much of his Unionist family, many of whom served the Union with distinction during the war. One relative wrote of Lee's decision: "I feel no exalted respect for a man who takes part in a movement in which he says he can see nothing but 'anarchy and ruin' . . . and yet very utterance scarce passed Robt Lees lips . . . when he starts off with delegates to treat traitors."[57]

Lee's future lieutenant Thomas Jackson was a professor at the Virginia Military Institute. The grim Jackson saw secession as he did all his life, through the prism of his Calvinistic faith. For Jackson disunion was a matter of divine providence. When secession came Jackson heard a minister in Lexington lamenting the troubles and said, "Why should Christians be at all disturbed about the dissolution of the Union? It can only come by God's permission, and only will be permitted, if it is for his people's good, for does he not say that all things shall work together for the good to them that love God?"[58]

In San Francisco Lt. James McPherson attempted to dissuade Lt. Porter Alexander from joining the Confederacy. To the future Confederate artillery general, McPherson bluntly spoke of what would happen to the South in the war:

> The population of the seceding states is only eight million while the North has twenty million. Of your 8 million over 3 million are slaves & may pose a dangerous element. You have no army, no navy, no treasury, no organization & practically none of the manufacturers—the machine shops, coal & iron mines & such things—which are necessary for the support of armies & carrying on war on a large scale. You are but scattered agricultural communities & will be isolated from the world by blockades. It is not possible for your cause to succeed in the end.[59]

But Alexander, like so many Southern officers, realized "that a crisis in my life was at hand. But I felt helpless to avert it or even debate the question what I should do. I could not doubt or controvert one of McPherson's statements or arguments."[60] George Pickett felt much as Lee and wrote his fiancée, Sallie Corbel, "While I love my neighbor, i.e., my country, I love my household, i.e., my state, more, and I could not be an infidel and lift my sword against my own kith and kin, even though I do believe . . . that the measure of American greatness can be achieved only under one flag."[61]

However, many Southern-born army and navy officers did not leave. Close to half of the "Southern West Point graduates on active duty in 1860 held to their posts and remained loyal to the Union."[62] One was Kentucky's Capt. John Buford, who gained immortal fame at the Battle of Gettysburg. Buford's family were Democrats, and Kentucky's pro-secession governor, Beriah Magoffin, offered him a commission in the state militia. Kentucky was an "undeclared border slave state," and Buford refused the offer. He told his comrades that "I sent

[Magoffin] word that I was a Captain in the United States Army and I intend to remain one."[63] Around the same time, the Confederate government "offered Buford a general officer's commission, which reached him by mail at Fort Crittenden."[64] According to Buford's biographer, "a well-known anecdote has him wadding up the letter while angrily announcing that whatever future had in store he would 'live and die under the flag of the Union.'"[65] A starker contrast could not be drawn.

Roughly 40 percent of Virginians serving on active duty remained faithful to the Union, including the commander of the army, Gen. Winfield Scott, and Robert E. Lee's friend George Thomas, both of whom were ostracized in the Old Dominion: "Thomas's family never again communicated with him except to ask him to change his name. A young Virginian just out of West Point, acknowledged that by retaining his commission he had been shunned by all of his Southern associates; yet he still derided those who would hold their obligations so lightly as to abandon the nation when it most needed them."[66] Others were less introspective. Less than a year out of West Point, young Stephen Ramseur did not wait on his state to secede before resigning to take a Confederate commission. The vast majority, however, waited to resign until their states seceded.

Most Southerners were delirious at the surrender of Fort Sumter. In Richmond "bonfires and fireworks of every description were illuminating in every direction—the whole city was a scene of joy owing to [the] surrender of Fort Sumter—and Virginia wasn't even part of the Confederacy."[67] John Gordon, a future confederate general, leading Georgia volunteers to Richmond, "found the line of march an unbroken celebration: fires lighted the hilltops; fife-and-drum corps shrilled and thumped; cannons exploded their welcome."[68]

Far to the north, in Bangor, Maine, a little-known professor at Bowdoin College named Joshua Lawrence Chamberlain read the news and "could not abide the thought of a divided nation; the Founding Fathers 'did not vote themselves into a people; they recognized and declared that they were a people' whose bonds out not to be severed by political, social, or economic grievances."[69] The professor was seized with anger that "the flag of the Nation had been insulted," and "the integrity and existence of the people of the United States had been assailed in open and bitter war."[70]

In Illinois a struggling former officer and Mexican-American War veteran whose in-laws were Southern sympathizers, Ulysses S. Grant volunteered to lead a regiment of volunteers. He wrote, "Whatever may have been my opinions before, I have but one sentiment now. That is to have a Government, and laws and a flag and they all must be sustained. . . . There are but two parties now, Traitors and Patriots and I want hereafter to be ranked with the latter."[71]

Even in Southern-leaning cities like Cincinnati, people rushed to proclaim their patriotism and support of the Union. George Ticknor told an English friend, "The whole population, men, women, and children, seem to be in the streets with Union favours and flags. . . . Civil war is freely accepted everywhere . . . by all, anarchy being the obvious, and perhaps the only alternative." Pacifists who had rejected violence, even in support of righteous causes, turned bellicose. Ralph Waldo Emerson enthused, "Sometimes gunpowder smells good."[72] The Sixth Massachusetts Volunteer Infantry, marching through New York on their way to Washington, were greeted with cheers from thousands of New Yorkers. The *New York Times* reported the event:

> Flags were displayed at all the hotels on the route and waving handkerchiefs from the balconies and windows signified the warm greetings of the fair sex to the brave Bay State soldiers. Opposite the New York Hotel a gray-haired old man mounted a stoop and addressing the soldiers and people, said that he had fought under the Stars and Stripes in the War of 1812 against a foreign power, and now that the flag was spit upon by those who should be its defenders. He closed his remarks by a "God

bless our flag," and left the crowd with tears streaming down his wrinkled cheeks.[73]

A rubicon had been crossed, and there was no going back. Poet Walt Whitman wrote: "War! An arm'd race is advancing! The welcome for battle, no turning away; War! Be it weeks, months, or years, an arm'd race is advancing to welcome it."[74]

19

Sound the Loud Timbrel

The Emancipation Proclamation

From the beginning many Northerners, especially abolitionists, believed that, "as the 'cornerstone' of the confederacy
(the oft-cited description by the South's vice-president, Alexander H. Stephens) slavery must become a military target."[1]
But when some Union generals issued emancipation orders,
Lincoln countermanded them for exceeding their authority.

Lincoln resisted early calls of abolitionists to make emancipation a primary war goal for practical reasons. He had to
ensure that the border slave states did not secede, for if they
did the Union would be destroyed. So, for the first year of the
war, Lincoln "maneuvered to hold Border South neutrals in the
Union and to lure Union supporters from the Confederacy's
Middle South white belts. He succeeded on both scores. His
double success with southern whites gave the Union greater
manpower, a stronger economy, and a larger domain. These
slave state resources boosted free labor states' capacity to shoulder the Union's heavier Civil War burden."[2]

His success enabled him to turn to emancipation in 1862.
Twenty months after Fort Sumter, and after nearly two years
of unrelenting slaughter, culminating in the bloody Battle of
Antietam, Lincoln signed the preliminary Emancipation Proclamation. Emancipation was a tricky legal issue for Lincoln,
as "an executive order of emancipation would be beyond the
powers of the president, but not, Lincoln concluded, if such
an order were issued as furtherance of the executive's war pow-

FIG. 15. Abraham Lincoln, president of the United States, signing the Emancipation Proclamation. 1866. Paintied by W. E. Winner; engraved by J. Serz. Courtesy of the Library of Congress, LC-DIG-pga-08284.

ers."[3] Lincoln desired to issue the order during the summer of 1862 and sought counsel from elected officials and soldiers.

For example, Lincoln discussed emancipation with Gen. George McClellan during a visit to McClellan's headquarters at Harrison's Landing on July 7, 1862. McClellan stated his opposition to Lincoln's war aims and emancipation in writing that night. McClellan's letter took the form of a lecture that covered the whole of the conduct of the war. In it he wrote that the rebellion had "assumed the character of war." He not only criticized its conduct; he also wrote, "Neither confiscation of property, political executions of persons, territorial organization of States, or forcible abolition of slavery should be contemplated for a moment." He called abolition "a declaration of radical views"—a statement that he used as part of the Copperhead mantra against slavery's opponents and an attack on Lincoln himself, warning that such a policy would "rapidly disintegrate our present armies." Lincoln, who read it with McClellan present and when he was finished put it in his pocket, said, "Very well."[4] McClellan wrote his wife two days later: "His Excellency . . . really seems quite incapable of rising to the heights and merits of the question & magnitude of the crisis."[5]

McClellan did not admire slavery, but he was an unrepentant racist and a Democrat who despised abolitionists and Republicans and had designs on the presidency. He wrote a political backer, "Help me to dodge the nigger—we want nothing to do with him. I am fighting for the Union. . . . To gain that end we cannot afford to mix up the negro question."[6]

Then, on July 12, Lincoln met with border state congressmen to sound them out on the subject, only to be met with opposition. This caused Lincoln "to give up trying to conciliate conservatives. From then on the president tilted toward the radical position, though this would not become publicly apparent for more than two months."[7]

Lincoln's cabinet met to discuss the proclamation on July 22, and after some debate he decided that it should be issued, over the opposition Postmaster General Montgomery Blair, who believed that "the Democrats would capitalize on the unpopularity of such a measure in the border states and parts of the North to gain control of the House in the fall elections."[8] Wisely, Lincoln heeded Secretary of State William H. Seward's advice to delay the announcement until military victories ensured that it was not seen as a desperate measure. Seward told Lincoln, "I approve of the proclamation, but I question the expediency of its issue at this juncture. The depression of the public mind, consequent on our repeated reverses, is so great I fear . . . it may be viewed as the last measure of an exhausted government, a cry for help . . . our last shriek on the retreat." He suggested that Lincoln wait "until the eagle of victory takes his flight," and, buoyed by military success, "hang your proclamation about his neck."[9]

When Lincoln issued the preliminary Emancipation Proclamation after the Battle of Antietam, it served as a warning to Confederate leaders, by announcing that much more was at stake in their rebellion. The document cautioned "that unless the South laid down its arms by the end of 1862, he would emancipate the slaves."[10] The Confederates could and would not acquiesce, even as their cities burned, and the Confederacy collapsed around them in 1864.

The proclamation was a military order by which Lincoln mandated the emancipation of slaves located in the rebel states, as well as in areas of those states occupied by Union troops. It did not change law, which had to wait until Congress amended the Constitution; thus "the doctrine of military necessity justified Lincoln's action."[11] The concept emanated from Boston lawyer William Whiting, who argued "the laws of war 'give the President full belligerent rights' as commander and chief to seize enemy property (in this case slaves) being used to wage war against the United States."[12] It was a legitimate military necessity, as Confederate armies used slaves as teamsters, laborers, cooks, and other noncombatant roles to free up white soldiers for combat duty. The proclamation inspired many slaves to desert to the Union cause or to labor less efficiently for their Confederate masters. A South Carolina planter wrote in 1865:

> The conduct of the Negro in the late crisis of our affairs has convinced me that we were all laboring under a delusion. . . . I believed that these people were content, happy, and attached to their masters, But events and reflection have caused me to change these positions. . . . If they were content, happy and attached to their masters, why did they desert him in the moment of need and flocked to the enemy, whom they did not know[?][13]

The proclamation authorized the army to recruit free Blacks and ensured that freed slaves would not again be surrendered into slavery. But, as Blair predicted, the Republicans suffered sharp electoral reverses as "Democrats made opposition to emancipation the centerpiece of their campaign, warning that the North would be 'Africanized'—inundated by freed slaves competing for jobs and seeking to marry white women."[14]

Lincoln issued the Emancipation Proclamation in spite of electoral reverses and political resistance. The vehemence of some Northern Democrats came close to matching that of white Southerners, whose "view of Lincoln as a despot, hell-bent on achieving some unnatural vision of 'equality,' was shared by Northern Democrats, some of whom thought the president was now possessed by a 'religious fanaticism.'"[15] But Lincoln was undeterred and understood "that he was sending the war and the country down a very different road than people thought they would go."[16] In December 1862 he stated, "Fellow citizens, we cannot escape history. . . . This fiery trial through which we pass, will light us down, in honor or dishonor, to the latest generation. . . . In giving freedom to the slave, we assure freedom to the free—honorable alike in what we give, and what we preserve."[17]

Lincoln believed that he had to issue the Emancipation Proclamation, that it might be the only thing that he did in his life that would be remembered. He was long convinced of its necessity, but timing mattered. Six months earlier it might have created a backlash that would have destroyed support for the war effort, but now the time was right, for it had military, political, diplomatic as well as moral implications.

The military purposes were twofold. First, Lincoln hoped the proclamation would encourage former slaves, and free Blacks in the North, to enlist to serve in the federal army. Emancipation vested Blacks to the Union's cause as little else could, and almost immediately it began to choke off the slave labor that was the Confederate economy's lifeline. Speaking in Philadelphia in July 1863, Frederick Douglass made the case for Blacks to serve:

> Do not flatter yourself, my friends, that you are more important to the Government than the Government is to you. You stand but as a plank to the ship. This rebellion can be put down without your help. Slavery can be abolished by white men: but Liberty so won for the black man, while it may leave him an object of pity, can never make him an object of respect. . . . Young men of Philadelphia you are without excuse. The hour has arrived, and your place is in the Union army. Remember that the musket—the United States musket with its bayonet of steel—is better than all the parchment guarantees of Liberty. In your hands the musket means Liberty.[18]

The diplomatic effects isolated the Confederacy from Europe. After the proclamation Europe's working classes turned solidly against the Confederacy, tying the hands of English and French proslavery elites. From it sprang the Thirteenth Amendment, which Lincoln needed to abolish slavery legally as the government's irrevocable pledge of freedom for Blacks.

Lincoln signed the proclamation on January 1, 1863. As he prepared to sign it, he paused and put down the pen and told Seward, "I never, in my life, felt more certain that I was doing right, than I do now in signing this paper. . . . If my name ever goes down in history it will be for signing this act, and my whole soul is in it."[19] The opening paragraph read:

That on the first day of January, in the year of our Lord one thousand eight hundred and sixty-three, all persons held as slaves within any State or designated part of a State, the people whereof shall then be in rebellion against the United States shall be then, thenceforward, and forever free; and the Executive Government of the United States, including the military and naval authority thereof, will recognize and maintain the freedom of such persons, and will do no act or acts to repress such persons, or any of them, in any efforts they may make for their actual freedom.[20]

Lincoln added words suggested by his devoutly Christian secretary of the treasury Salmon Chase: "And upon this act, sincerely believed to be an act of justice, warranted by the Constitution, upon military necessity, I invoke the considerate judgment of mankind, and the gracious favor of Almighty God."[21]

Celebrations occurred throughout the North. In some cities one-hundred-gun salutes were fired. At Boston's Tremont Temple, people broke out singing: "Sound the loud timbrel o'er Egypt's dark sea / Jehovah hath triumphed, his people are free."[22] The *Boston Daily Evening Telegraph* predicted, "Slavery from this hour ceases to be a political power in this country . . . such a righteous revolution as it inaugurates never goes backward."[23] As Frederick Douglass described his reaction when he heard the proclamation:

The fourth of July was great, but the first of January, when we consider it in all of its relations and bearings in incomparably greater. The one we respect to the mere political birth to a nation, the last concerns national life and character, and is to determine whether that life and character shall be radiantly and glorious with all high and noble virtues, or infamously blackened, forevermore, with all the hell-darkened crimes and horrors which we attach to Slavery.[24]

The Emancipation Proclamation evoked anger in the South and among some Northern Democrats. Southerners accused

Lincoln of inciting racial warfare. Jefferson Davis roared: "The day is not so distant when the old Union will be restored with slavery nationally declared to be the proper condition of all of African descent."[25] But the proclamation also did something that many politicians and lawyers could not comprehend: "The details of the emancipation decree were less significant than the fact that there was an emancipation decree, and while the proclamation read like a dull legal brief . . . It was its existence, its title, its arrival into this world, its challenge to the accepted order, and from that there was no turning back. In this sense it was a revolutionary statement, like the Declaration itself, and nearly as significant."[26]

The proclamation meant that there was no stepping back. "It irrevocably committed the government of the United States to the termination of slavery. It was an act of political courage, take at the right time, in the right way."[27]

It took two more years, with the Confederacy crumbling before the armies of Grant and Sherman, before the Thirteenth Amendment was passed, in January 1865. It abolished slavery and involuntary servitude throughout the country, as well as nullified the Fugitive Slave Act and the Three-Fifths Compromise.

Despite its limited scope, the Emancipation Proclamation had military, social and political effects. It ensured that Britain and France would not intervene on behalf of the Confederacy; covert private British support for the rebels withdrew, including the impounding of powerful warships contracted for by Confederate agents then building in British yards.

The Proclamation's Effect on Military Law

The Emancipation Proclamation changed the Union War effort in terms of military law. It eventually became a part of international law as nations began to adapt to the changing character of war. Slavery's illegality was now included in the laws of war through the propagation of General Orders No. 100, often known as the Lieber Code. The code was meant to govern tne armies of the United States in the field and included numerous sections that now appear in military laws of other nations and international law. Since the Emancipation Proclamation was a military order and not a legislative action, it relied on military law to ensure that it could be enforced. The man to do this was Francis Lieber.

Lieber was born in Berlin in 1798 and spent his young life fighting for Prussia during the Napoleonic Wars. As a child he fought the French in occupied Germany, and the age of seventen he served in a Prussian infantry regiment at Waterloo and, during the pursuit of Napoleon's army, was severely wounded. In 1820 he joined an international brigade to fight for Greek independence against the Ottoman Empire. However, in the reactionary period following the Napoleonic wars, young freedom fighters and revolutionaries were not welcome. He earned his PhD at the University of Jena and, with few prospects in Europe, emigrated to the United States and settled first in Boston, where he published the extremely popular *Encyclopedia Americana*, and made friends with numerous influential Americans. However, he could never be one of Boston's elites, so he took a professorship in economics and history at South Carolina College 1835, but his time in South Carolina engendered in him no love or appreciation of slavery.

Lieber had a great interest in the conduct of war, and he learned through study and experience that current military law, designed for the limited wars of the eighteenth century, of little value in modern war. The revolutionary wars of the Napoleonic era involved armies of hundreds of thousands of men fighting battles that dwarfed those of recorded history. Lieber studied war, particularly the theory of Carl Von Clausewitz, which were radically different than that being taught in the United States by Denis Hart Mahan, who adapted the ideas of French military theorist Henri Jomini, and focused on a war between armies rather than a clash of peoples and ideologies. Previous European laws of war did not concern themselves with the justice or morality of a soldier's actions in war.

Clausewitz's theory, which Lieber applied to the laws of war, "asked the statesman, the general, and the soldier to take the objectives of their conduct into account at all times. Ends, in Lieber's view, could not be separated from means; to the contrary they helped determine the scope and character of conduct appropriate to the situation."[28] Appointed to the faculty of Columbia College in New York in 1857 he would become acquainted with Abraham Lincoln.

He presented a lecture course "at Columbia's new law school in the fall of 1861 titled 'The Laws and Usages of War."[29] These lectures would become the basis for later laws that he helped draft for the Lincoln administration during the war. Lieber's overriding concern was justice, and the rules he established involving combatants, noncombatants, and irregular insurgents and guerillas remains a part of international law today, in the Third Geneva Convention of 1949. He also condemned the use of torture for any reason. Lieber became a key advisor to Gen. of the Armies Henry Halleck, and Halleck had Lincoln's ear. "Like Lieber's lectures, Emancipation pressed humanitarian limits and justice back together by measuring the conduct by the justice of its ends."[30]

Lincoln understood the legal and moral complexities of emancipation. He knew that if he included the slave states that remained in the Union, since they had not seceded, the proclamation would reach the proslavery Supreme Court of Roger Taney. Since the Confederate states had seceded from the Union and removed themselves from civil jurisdiction, "the Confederate states were now under the jurisdiction of the president as commander in chief of the Army and Navy of the United States."[31] Since under Articles 1 and 3 of the Constitution only Congress, not the Supreme Court, has the power to adjudicate military law, the proclamation as a military order directing the military's actions in rebellious states was outside of Taney's jurisdiction. But as a "measure based in military necessity, the Emancipation Proclamation condensed a millennium of moral and legal reasoning into the short text.

It contained an entire world of moral considerations between means and ends."[32]

Lieber drafted the "Instructions for the Government of Armies of the United States in the Field, General Orders No. 100 by President Lincoln, April 24, 1863. Article 42" of that code stated:

> Slavery, complicating and confounding the ideas of property, (that is of a thing,) and of personality, (that is of humanity,) exists according to municipal or local law only. The law of nature and nations has never acknowledged it. The digest of the Roman law enacts the early dictum of the pagan jurist, that "so far as the law of nature is concerned, all men are equal." Fugitives escaping from a country in which they were slaves, villains, or serfs into another country, have, for centuries past, been held free and acknowledged free by judicial decisions of European countries, even though the municipal law of the country in which the slave had taken refuge acknowledged slavery within its own dominions.[33]

It continued in Article 43:

> Therefore, in a war between the United States and a belligerent which admits of slavery if a person held in bondage by that belligerent be captured by or come as a fugitive under the protection of the military forces of the United States, such person is immediately entitled to the rights and privileges of a freeman to return such person into slavery would amount to enslaving a free person, and neither the United States nor any officer under their authority can enslave any human being. Moreover, a person so made free by the law of war is under the shield of the law of nations, and the former owner or State can have, by the law of postliminy, no belligerent lien or claim of service.[34]

Lieber's code owed little to past military codes. It was not designed to reinforce the laws of the ancien regimes of the eighteenth Century: "Lieber aimed to write a distillation of the laws of war for the age of democratic nations and mass

Sound the Loud Timbrel

armies."[35] This was a major break with the past for all military and international laws of war developed since its inception. In addition to its immediate importance in the crafting of the Emancipation Proclamation, it was, as Anthony Hartle writes, "innovative in that it was the first example of a detailed manual for combatants concerning the conduct of war that attempted to codify existing law and standards applying to all nations."[36]

The fact that Lincoln, Halleck, Lieber, and other advisors deftly used this means to begin the process of emancipation, as a military order applying only to the states in revolt to avoid giving Roger Taney, the author of the *Dred Scott* decision, the opportunity to overturn it, was one of the most momentous and courageous decisions ever made by a president. Thankfully, it was just a beginning that allowed Lincoln and his allies in Congress to craft and pass the Thirteenth Amendment, which is something that its modern critics often fail to recognize. Be they critics from the political Right or Left, they do not understand its context.

The Fight for Emancipation

There was concern that slavery might survive. Lincoln knew that by issuing the Emancipation Proclamation he raised the stakes of the war. He wrote, "We shall nobly save, or meanly lose, the last best hope on earth."[37] The threat of disunion, the continuance of slavery in any state, or the continuance of the Union without emancipation were fates too great for Lincoln to contemplate.

Following the Wilderness Campaign in the summer of 1864, Grant's armies were stalled outside Richmond. As a result, the Copperheads and the Peace Party gained influence and threatened to defeat Lincoln and allow Confederate independence and the continuance of slavery. Secretary of War Edwin Stanton wrote in the spring of 1864:

> In such a state of feeling, under such a state of things, can we doubt the inevitable results? Shall we escape border raids after

fleeing fugitives? No man will expect it. Are we to suffer these? We are disgraced! Are we to repel them? It is a renewal of hostilities! . . . In the case of a foreign war . . . can we suppose that they will refrain from seeking their own advantage by an alliance with the enemy?[38]

However, by capturing Atlanta, Gen. William Tecumseh Sherman's armies dealt a fatal blow to Lincoln's opponents. His march to the sea, coupled with Adm. David Farragut's victory at the Battle of Mobile Bay, broke the back of the Confederacy and broke the Copperhead stranglehold over Northern politics. These victories secured Lincoln's reelection by a large margin over Copperhead, and Peace Democrat nominee George McClellan could not endorse their platform.

In his second inaugural address, Lincoln said that slavery was the chief cause of the war and noted the complicity of Christians, many of whom "believed weighty political issues could be parsed into good or evil. Lincoln's words offered a complexity that many found difficult to accept."[39] The war devastated the playground of evangelical politics and "'thrashed the certitude of evangelical Protestantism' as much as World War I shattered European Protestant liberalism."[40] Lincoln's contention that Christians played a role in causing the war offers an illuminating and devastating critique of the way toxic religious attitudes stoke fires of hatred. His realism in confronting facts was both masterful and badly needed. Lincoln spoke of "'American slavery' as a single offense ascribed to the whole nation."[41]

One-eighth of the whole population were colored slaves, not distributed generally over the Union, but localized in the southern part of it. These slaves constituted a peculiar and powerful interest. All knew that this interest was somehow the cause of the war. To strengthen, perpetuate, and extend this interest was the object for which the insurgents would rend the Union even by war, while the Government claimed no right to do more than to restrict the territorial enlargement of it. . . . Both read the same Bible and pray to the same God, and each invokes His aid against the other. It may seem strange that any men should dare to ask a just God's assistance in wringing their bread from the sweat of other men's faces. . . . The prayers of both could not be answered. That of neither has been answered fully. The Almighty has His own purposes. . . . If we shall suppose that American slavery is one of those offenses which, in the providence of God, must needs come, but which, having continued through His appointed time, He now wills to remove, and that He gives to both North and South this terrible war as the woe due to those by whom the offense came, shall we discern therein any departure from those divine attributes which the believers in a living God always ascribe to Him? Fondly do we hope, fervently do we pray, that this mighty scourge of war may speedily pass away. Yet, if God wills that it continue until all the wealth piled by the bondsman's two hundred and fifty years of unrequited toil shall be sunk, and until every drop of blood drawn with the lash shall be paid by another drawn with the sword, as was said three thousand years ago, so still it must be said "the judgments of the Lord are true and righteous altogether."[42]

It is interesting that Lincoln, who was for the most part a skeptic in terms of religion and certainly not a Christian in any sense of orthodoxy, was also knowledgeable enough about Christian theology that he included it in this, his second inaugural address. His remarks were remarkable in their understanding of the faith and doctrines of Christians, Southern and Northern, and they are immensely important for us today in understanding just how much religious beliefs—be they Christian, Jewish, or Muslim—still influence political and foreign policy decisions. Lincoln's decision to proclaim emancipation with a military order that could not be countermanded by a hostile Supreme Court was masterful. His understanding of the way the deeply embedded beliefs of Christians in the South and the North brought about the war were among

the most insightful words spoken about the war made by anyone before or after. The Emancipation Proclamation and the
Lieber Code were and remain revolutionary. They both regard
the importance of justice as the most important part of law
and freedom. To paraphrase a civil rights leader, without justice, there can be no peace.

20

I Knew What I Was Fighting For

Black Soldiers in the Civil War and After

The Emancipation Proclamation was a seismic event that profoundly shaped American history, life, and culture. It gave Blacks the opportunity to serve in the Union Army: a revolutionary, controversial change that had strategic implications for the war effort.

Prior to the proclamation, a few Union commanders in occupied Confederate territory "had unofficially recruited black soldiers in Kansas and in occupied portions of South Carolina and Louisiana in 1862."[1] But their actions were unsanctioned. Therefore, from 1861 to mid-1862, Lincoln, who needed to keep border slave states in Union, countermanded their orders—not because he disagreed with them, but because they overstepped their authority.

Although he was sympathetic, Lincoln insisted that such decisions were not for local commanders to make, and any such proclamation had to come from him, as commander in chief. He told U.S. treasury secretary Salmon Chase, "No commanding general shall do such a thing, upon my responsibility, without consulting me."[2] Lincoln's decision infuriated some in his cabinet and in Congress, but he remained firm, knowing he needed the cooperation of the border states, without which victory and emancipation would be impossible.

Gen. Benjamin Butler commanded federal forces at Fort Monroe in Hampton Roads and learned that the Confederates were using slaves to construct fortifications to support

FIG. 16. Lithograph, *The Storming of Fort Wagner by the 54th Massachusetts Infantry, 18 July 1863*, 1890, Kurz and Allison. Courtesy of the Library of Congress, LC-DIG-pga-01949.

their army on the peninsula. In May 1862 twenty-three slaves escaped to his lines, and their owner, a Confederate colonel, "demanded the return of his property under the Fugitive Slave Law! With as deadpan expression as possible (given his cocked eye), Butler informed him that since Virginia claimed to have left the Union, the Fugitive Slave Law no longer applied."[3]

Butler declared that since the escaped slaves worked for the Confederate Army, they were "contraband of war—enemy property subject to seizure."[4] He used against them the Southern argument that slaves were property. Lincoln and his secretary of war, Simon Cameron, approved of Butler's action, and "Congress passed a confiscation law ending the rights of masters over fugitive slaves used to support Confederate troops."[5] Salmon Chase and other abolitionists vehemently opposed Lincoln, but soon afterward he decided for full emancipation through the proclamation and the Thirteenth Amendment.

Lincoln wanted to announce emancipation in the spring of 1862, but, following McClellan's humiliating defeat and with-

I Knew What I Was Fighting For

drawal from Richmond, he was forced to postpone it. McClellan opposed emancipation; when Lincoln visited him after he withdrew from the peninsula, the defeated but arrogant general handed Lincoln a memorandum on the "proper conduct of the war." McClellan told Lincoln that the war "should not be a war looking to the subjugation of any State in any event . . . but against armed forces and political organizations. Neither confiscation of property, political executions of persons, the territorial organization of States, or the forcible abolition of slavery should be contemplated for a moment."[6]

Lincoln had had enough of McClellan and did not want his advice. He put the letter in his pocket. A few months earlier, Lincoln had agreed with McClellan's views on a limited war. But experience taught him that the Confederacy was fully committed to independence and the expansion of slavery. Lincoln now understood the foolishness of fighting a limited war with limited aims. A few days later, he told a Unionist Democrat that the war could not be fought "with elder-stalk squirts, charged with rose water. . . . This government cannot much longer play a game in which it stakes all, and its enemies stake nothing. Those enemies must understand that they cannot experiment for ten years trying to destroy this government, and if they fail still come back into the Union unhurt."[7]

From Slavery to Soldiering

After eighteen months of war, Lincoln and the closest members of his Cabinet realized that the "North could not win the war without mobilizing all of its resources and striking against Southern resources used to sustain the Confederate war effort."[8] Slaves were essential to the Confederate war effort, as they still worked the plantations or were impressed into war industries and as laborers for the Confederate Army.

Lt. Col. Arthur Freemantle, a British observer with Lee's army at Gettysburg, noted that "in the rear of each regiment were from twenty to thirty negro slaves."[9] The Blacks who accompanied the army were slaves, not the mythical Black soldiers who rallied to the Confederacy, as Lost Cause proponents allege: "Tens of thousands of slaves accompanied their owners to army camps as servants or were impressed into service to construct fortifications and do other work for the Confederate army."[10]

Col. William Allan, of Stonewall Jackson's staff, recorded that "there were no employees in the Confederate army."[11] Slaves were needed to free white soldiers for combat duties and used for "driving wagons to unloading trains and other conveyances. In hospitals they could perform work as nurses and laborers to ease the burdens of patients."[12] As an English-born artilleryman in Lee's army in 1863 wrote: "In our whole army there must be at least thirty thousand colored servants."[13] When Lee marched to Gettysburg, he used between ten thousand and thirty thousand slaves in support roles. During the campaign Confederate troops rounded up and reenslaved as many Blacks as possible.

Edwin Stanton, a passionate believer in the justice of emancipation, who was among the first to realize the importance of slave labor to Confederate armies, "instantly grasped the military value of the proclamation. Having spent more time than any of his colleagues contemplating the logistical problems facing the army, he understood the tremendous advantage to be gained if the massive workforce of slaves could be transferred from the Confederacy to the Union."[14] Lincoln emphasized the "military necessity" of emancipation and "justified the step as a 'fit and necessary war measure for suppressing the rebellion.'"[15] Emancipation was now a central part of national strategy. Lincoln "calculated that making slavery a target of the war would counteract the rising clamor in Britain for recognition of the Confederacy."[16]

Lincoln wrote his future vice president, Andrew Johnson, military governor of occupied Tennessee, that "the colored population is the great available and yet unavailed of force for restoration of the Union."[17] As Lincoln stopped coddling border states, policy changed to "depriv[e] the Confederacy

I Knew What I Was Fighting For

of slave labor. Mobilizing that manpower for the Union—as soldiers as well as laborers—was a natural corollary."[18]

Gen. Henry Halleck wrote to Ulysses Grant, "The character of the war has very much changed within the past year. There is now no possibility of reconciliation with the rebels. . . . We must conquer the rebels or be conquered by them. . . . Every slave withdrawn from the enemy is the equivalent of a white man put hors de combat."[19] Grant concurred with Lincoln and wrote him following the Fifty-Fourth Massachusetts Volunteer Infantry attack on Battery Wagner: "By arming the negro we have added a powerful ally. They will make good soldiers and taking them from the enemy weakens him in the same proportion as it strengthens us."[20]

William Tecumseh Sherman was supportive, but a realist, concerned with winning the war and protecting Blacks. "The first step in the liberation of the Negro from bondage," he wrote, "will be to get him and his family to a place of safety . . . then to afford him the means of providing for his family . . . then gradually use a proportion—greater and greater each year—as sailors and soldiers."[21] Lincoln stated that "the emancipation policy, and the use of colored troops, constitute the heaviest blow yet dealt to the rebellion."[22]

In conjunction with the Emancipation Proclamation, Sec. of War Edwin Stanton, who had replaced the notoriously corrupt and ineffective Cameron in January 1862, "authorized General Rufus Saxton to 'arm, uniform, equip, and receive into the service of the United States such number of volunteers of African descent as you may deem expedient, not exceeding 5,000, and [you] may detail officers to instruct them in military drill, discipline, and duty, and to command them.'"[23]

Black regiments formed in liberated areas of Louisiana and South Carolina were comprised mostly of newly freed slaves. Others, like the Fifty-Fourth and Fifty-Fifth Massachusetts Volunteer Infantry regiments, were composed of free Blacks in Massachusetts and adjoining states. The Enrollment Act of March of 1863, which established the draft, also allowed more

Blacks to serve. In March Stanton urged state governors to enlist more Black regiments, which became the U.S. Colored Troops (USCT). The USCT units, which were commanded by white officers and organized into infantry, cavalry and artillery regiments, "grew to include seven regiments of cavalry, more than a dozen of artillery, and well over one hundred of infantry."[24]

Some Union soldiers and officers opposed enlisting Blacks, alleging "that making soldiers of blacks would be a threat to white supremacy and hundreds of Billy Yanks wrote home that they would no serve alongside blacks."[25] But most soldiers accepted emancipation, especially those who had shed blood or who saw the misery slaves endured. As one Illinois soldier wrote, "The necessity of emancipation is forced upon us by the inevitable events of the war . . . and the only road out of this war is by blows aimed at the heart of the Rebellion. . . . If slavery should be left undisturbed the war would be protracted until the loss of life and national bankruptcy would make peace desirable on any terms."[26]

Cpl. Chauncey B. Welton of Ohio's letters show his conversion after the Emancipation Proclamation: "Father I want you to write and tell me what you think of Lincoln's proclamation of setting all the negroes free. I can tell you we don't think much of it hear in the army for we did not enlist to fight for the negro and I can tell you that we never shall or many of us any how[.] no never." After two years of service with Sherman's army he became a critic of Copperheads and wrote in February 1865: "Dear parents let us trust in Him that never forsakes the faithful, and never cease to pray . . . that soon we may look upon an undivided Country and that Country free free free yes free from that blighting curs[e] Slavery the cause of four years of Bloody warfare."[27]

Union Soldiers came to praise the soldierly abilities and bravery of Black soldiers. An officer who refused a commission to serve with a USCT regiment watched as Black troops attacked the defenses of Richmond in September 1864:

I Knew What I Was Fighting For

The darkies rushed across the open space fronting the work, under a fire which caused them loss, into the abatis . . . down into the ditch with ladders, up and over the parapet with flying flags, and down among, and on top of, the astonished enemy, who left in utmost haste. . . . Then and there I decided that "the black man could fight" for his freedom, and that I had made a mistake in not commanding them.[28]

Likewise, "once the Lincoln administration broke the color barrier of the army, blacks stepped forward in large numbers. Service in the army offered to blacks the opportunity to strike a decisive blow for freedom."[29]

The USCT formations dwarfed state-raised Black regiments. The inspiration provided by the first state regiments raised in Louisiana and Massachusetts, based on reports in Northern newspapers of their heroic actions at Fort Wagner, Miliken's Bend. Likewise, the gratuitous violence committed against Blacks by whites during the 1863 New York draft riots provoked "many northerners into a backlash against the consequences of violent racism."[30]

Despite the prejudice Black soldiers urged others to enlist, as risking their lives for freedom mattered more than self-preservation. Henry Gooding, a sergeant from Massachusetts, wrote the *New Bedford Mercury* urging fellow Blacks to enlist: "As one of the race, I beseech you not to trust a fancied security, laying in your minds, that our condition will be bettered because slavery must die. . . . [If we] allow that slavery will die without the aid of our race to kill it—language cannot depict the indignity, the scorn, and perhaps the violence that will be heaped upon us."[31] The valor of the state and USCT regiments was remarkable as they faced discrimination in the North, and the threat of death if captured by Confederates. The Confederate Congress branded Union officers and Black troops as war criminals; Black soldiers who were captured were to be executed or returned to slavery.

In late 1862 Maj. Gen. Nathaniel Banks was in desperate

need of soldiers and received permission to form Black regiments. The First, Second, and Third Regiments of Louisiana Native Guards were composed of mulattos who were children of prominent whites and escaped slaves. During an inspection the white colonel of the guards told another officer:

> Sir, the best blood of Louisiana is in that regiment! Do you see that tall, slim fellow, third file from the right of the second company? One of the ex-governors of the state is his father. That orderly sergeant in the next company is the son of a man who has been six years in the United States Senate. Just beyond him is the grandson of Judge—— . . . ; and through all the ranks you will find the same state of facts. . . . Their fathers are disloyal; [but] these black Ishmaels will more than compensate for their treason by fighting in the field.[32]

In May 1863 Banks ordered two "Louisiana Native Home Guard regiments on a series of attacks on Confederate positions at Port Hudson Louisiana," where they underwent their baptism by fire.[33] They suffered heavy losses: "Of the 1080 men in the ranks, 271 were hit, or one out of every four."[34] A white Wisconsin soldier said the Black soldiers "fought like devils," and a soldier in the 156th New York regiment recounted, "They charged and re-charged and they didn't know what retreat meant. They lost in their two regiments some four hundred men as near as I can learn. This settles the question about niggers not fighting well. They on the contrary make splendid soldiers and are as good fighting men as we have."[35] In his action report Banks stated, "They answered every expectation. . . . In many respects their conduct was heroic. . . . The severe test to which they were subjected, and the determined manner in which they encountered the enemy, leave upon my mind no doubt of their ultimate success."[36]

The Fifty-Fourth Massachusetts Regiment, commanded by Col. Robert Gould Shaw, was the "North's showcase black regiment."[37] Convened in Boston and officered by the sons of Boston's blue blood abolitionist elite, the regiment was authorized

I Knew What I Was Fighting For

FIG. 17. *Men of Company 4th Regiment of U.S. Colored Troops,* ca. 1863–65. Courtesy of the Library of Congress, Civil War Collection, LC-DIG-cwpb-04294.

in March 1863 by Gov. John Andrew, under the command of white officers, as Blacks were not allowed to serve in that capacity. But Gov. Andrew was determined to ensure that the officers of the Fifty-Fourth were men of "firm antislavery principles . . . superior to a vulgar contempt for color."[38]

The Fifty-Fourth saw action in early June 1863, and at Shaw's urging they led an attack against Fort Wagner on July 18, 1863. The Fifty-Fourth lost nearly half its men, "including Colonel Shaw with a bullet through his heart. Black soldiers gained Wagner's parapet and held it for an hour before falling back."[39] Despite their gallantry they were unable to hold their position. "Sergeant William H. Carney staggered back from the fort with wounds in his chest and right arm, but with the regiment's Stars and Stripes securely in his grasp. 'The old flag never touched the ground, boys,' Carney gasped as he collapsed at the first field hospital he could find."[40]

Shaw was buried in a mass grave with his men. When Union commanders asked for the return of Shaw's remains they were told, "We have buried him with his niggers." Shaw's father quelled a Northern effort to recover his son's body with these words: "We hold that a soldier's most appropriate burial-place is on the field where he has fallen."[41] But, like most frontal attacks on prepared positions, valor could not overcome a well-dug-in enemy. "Negro troops proved that they could stop bullets and shell fragments as good as white men, but that was about all."[42]

Under Col. Edwin Hallowell, the regiment distinguished itself in many battles. Northern press coverage helped change how many Northerners saw Blacks. *Atlantic Monthly* editors wrote: "Through the cannon smoke of that dark night, the manhood of the colored race shines before many eyes that would not see."[43]

In the Fifty-Fifth Massachusetts Regiment, twenty-one-year-old Sgt. Isaiah Welch wrote a letter from Folly Island, South Carolina, published by the *Philadelphia Christian Recorder.*

> I will mention a little about the 55th Massachusetts Regiment. They seem to be in good health at the present and are desirous of making a bold dash upon the enemy. I pray God the time will soon come when we, as soldiers of God, and of our race and country, may face the enemy with boldness. For my part I feel willing to suffer all privations incidental to a Christian and a soldier. . . . In conclusion, let me say, if I fall in the battle anticipated, remember, I fall in defense of my race and country. Some of my friends thought it very wrong of me in setting aside the work of the Lord to take up arms against the enemy. . . . I am fully able to answer all questions pertaining to rebels. If taking lives will restore the country to what it once was, then God help me to slay them on every hand.[44]

Like the Fifty-Fourth Massachusetts, the Fifty-Fifth saw much action. After a sharp engagement in July 1864, in which numerous soldiers demonstrated exceptional valor under fire, their commander, Col. Alfred S. Hartwell, "recommended that three of the black sergeants of the 55th be promoted to the rank of 2nd Lieutenant." Hartwell's request was rejected. As one sol-

I Knew What I Was Fighting For

FIG. 18. Sgt. William Carney, 54th Massachusetts Infantry 1864, with colors of 54th that he saved at Fort Wagner. Awarded Medal of Honor in 1900. Collection of the Smithsonian National Museum of African American History and Culture, Gift of the Garrison Family in memory of George Thompson Garrison.

dier complained, "But the U.S. government has refused so far to trust them because God did not make them White. . . . No other objection is, or can be offered."[45]

Frederick Douglass, who had two sons serving in the Fifty-Fourth, understood the importance of Blacks taking up arms in order to win their freedom: "Once let a black man get upon his person the brass letters U.S . . . let him get an eagle on his button, and a musket on his shoulder and bullets in his pockets, and there is no power on earth which can deny he has won the right to citizenship in the United States." Douglass urged Black men to enlist while addressing the inequities they suffered in the military; Black soldiers were paid less than whites and could not be officers. Douglass appealed to duty, reminding Blacks them that the purpose of the Confederacy was "nothing more than to make the slavery of the African race universal and perpetual on this continent . . . based upon the idea that colored men are an inferior race, who may be enslaved and plundered forever."[46]

Douglass did not stop there. He understood that winning the war was more important than continuing to address the government's failures before emancipation:

> Now, what is the attitude of the Washington government towards the colored race? What reasons have we to desire its triumph in the present contest? Mind, I do not ask what was its attitude towards us before the war. . . . I do not ask you about the dead past. I bring you to the living present . . . Do not flatter yourselves, my friends, that you are more important to the Government than the Government to you. You stand but as the plank to the ship. This rebellion can be put down without your help. Slavery can be abolished by white men: but liberty so won for the black man, while it may leave him an object of pity, can never make him an object of respect. . . . Young men of Philadelphia you are without excuse. The hour has arrived, and your place is in the Union army. Remember that the musket—the United States musket with its bayonet of steel—is better than all the mere parchment guarantees of liberty. In your hands that musket means liberty.[47]

Other Black regiments distinguished themselves in battle. Two newly recruited regiments were encamped at Milliken's Bend, Louisiana, when a Texas Division, attempting to relieve Vicksburg, attacked. Though untrained and ill-armed, they beat back the Texans:

> Most of the black troops nevertheless fought desperately. With the aid of two gunboats they finally drove off the enemy. For raw troops, wrote Grant, the freedmen "behaved well." Assistant Secretary of War Dana, still with Grant's army, spoke with more enthusiasm. "The bravery of the blacks," he declared, "completely revolutionized the sentiment in the army with regard to the employment of negro troops. I heard prominent

officers who had formerly in private had sneered at the idea of negroes fighting express after that as heartily in favor of it."[48]

The bravery of the Black regiments attracted the attention of Ulysses Grant, who wrote a cover letter to the after-action report: "In this battle most of the troops engaged were Africans who had little experience in the use of fire-arms. Their conduct is said, however, to have been most gallant, and I doubt not but with good officers that they will make good troops."[49]

The Battle of Millikan's Bend

The press cheered them. Harpers published an illustrated account of the battle with a "double-page woodcut of the action placed a black color bearer in the foreground, flanked by comrades fighting hand-to-hand with Confederates. The article called 'the sharp fight at Milliken's bend where a small body of black troops with a few whites were attacked by a large force of rebels.'"[50]

The battle shocked Southerners. One woman commented, "It is hard to believe that Southern soldiers—and Texans at that—have been whipped by a mongrel crew of white and black Yankees. . . . There must be some mistake." As a Louisiana woman confided to her diary, "It is terrible to think of such a battle as this, white men and freemen fighting with their slaves, and to be killed by such a hand, the very soul revolts from it, O, may this be the last."[51]

Over 179,000 Black soldiers, commanded by 7,000 white officers, served in Union armies. But many regiments were employed in logistic support and rear area duties. The relegation of numerous USCT regiments to noncombat roles "frustrated many African American soldiers who wanted a chance to prove themselves in battle."[52] Black soldiers and their white officers argued for combat assignments, for they felt that "only by proving themselves in combat could blacks overcome stereotypes of inferiority and prove their 'manhood.'"[53] In some Union armies, USCT and Black state regiments were scorned:

A young officer who left his place in a white regiment to become colonel of a colored regiment was frankly told by a staff officer that "we don't want any nigger soldiers in the Army of the Potomac," and his general took him aside to say: "I'm sorry to have you leave my command, and am still more sorry that you are going to serve with Negroes. I think that it is a disgrace to the army to make soldiers of them." The general added that he felt this way because he was sure that colored soldiers just would not fight.[54]

The general was wrong, for "nothing eradicated the prejudices of white soldiers as effectively as black soldiers performing well under fire. And nothing inspired black soldiers to fight as desperately as the fear that capture meant certain death."[55]

When USCT units were allowed to fight, they did so with varying degrees of success. Like white regiments, regiments who were well led and well trained performed better than those that were not. However, when given the chance, Blacks always fought well, even when badly commanded and thrown into hopeless situations. One such fight was the Battle of the Crater at Petersburg, when "that battle lost beyond all recall."[56] The troops advanced sharply, singing as they went, while their commander, General Ferrero, took cover in a dugout and began drinking. The Confederate defenders, who had recovered from their initial shock, were ready. According to a witness, the division "unsupported, subjected to a galling fire from batteries on the flanks, and from infantry fire in front and partly on the flank . . . broke up in disorder and fell back into the crater."[57] Pressed into the carnage of the crater, where three broken divisions of white troops had taken cover, the "black troops fought with desperation, uncertain of their fate if captured."[58] The division lost 1,327 of the approximately 4,000 men that attacked.[59]

Benjamin Butler, who had commanded Black soldiers, was an eyewitness at Petersburg, and he railed against those who questioned their courage: "The man who says that the negro will not fight is a coward, his liver is white, and that is all that is truly white about him. His soul is blacker than then dead faces of these dead negroes, upturned to heaven in solemn protest against him and his prejudices."[60]

At the Battle of Saltville, the troops of the Fifth USCT Cavalry were taunted by white Union soldiers before they attacked Confederate troops defending the salt works. The regiment's commander, Colonel Wade, ordered his troops to attack. As Col. James Brisbin detailed it:

> The Negroes rushed upon the works with a yell and after a desperate struggle carried the line killing and wounding a large number of the enemy and capturing some prisoners. . . . Out of the four hundred men engaged, one hundred and fourteen men and four officers fell killed or wounded. Of this fight I can only say that men could not have behaved more bravely. I have seen white troops in twenty-seven battles and I never saw any fight better. . . . On the return of the forces those who had scoffed at the Colored Troops on the march out were silent.[61]

Confederate actions against Black Union soldiers would be considered war crimes today: In "the autumn of 1862 General Beauregard referred the question of a captured black soldier to Davis's latest Secretary of War, James A. Seddon the later replied '. . . my decision is that the negro is to be executed as an example.'"[62] In November 1862 Davis approved of summary executions of Black prisoners in South Carolina. A month later "Davis issued a general order requiring all former slaves and their officers captured in arms to be delivered up to state officials for trial."[63] Davis said, "The army would consider black soldiers as 'slaves captured in arms,' and therefore subject to execution."[64] Confederate soldiers frequently massacred captured Black soldiers. Lincoln responded to Confederate crimes by threatening reprisals against Confederate soldiers if Black soldiers suffered harm. It "was largely the threat of Union reprisals that thereafter gave African-American soldiers a modicum of humane treatment."[65] Even so, they and their white officers were always in more danger than white soldiers at the hands of Confederates,

Black soldiers and their white officers often received no quarter when captured. Gen. Edmund Kirby Smith, who commanded Confederate forces west of the Mississippi, instructed Gen. Richard Taylor to execute Black soldiers and their white officers: "I hope . . . that your subordinates who may have been in command of capturing parties may have recognized the propriety of giving no quarter to armed negroes and their officers. In this way we may be relieved from a disagreeable dilemma."[66]

Confederates targeted white officers commanding Blacks: "Any commissioned officer employed in the drilling, organizing or instructing slaves with their view to armed service in this war . . . as outlaws" would be "held in close confinement for execution as a felon."[67] Following the attack of the Fifty-Fourth Massachusetts Regiment on Fort Wagner, Confederates gave no quarter. One Georgia soldier "reported with satisfaction that the prisoners were 'literally shot down while on their knees begging for quarter and mercy.'"[68]

On April 12, 1864, Gen. Nathan Bedford Forrest's raiders massacred at least 231 mostly Black Union soldiers at Fort Pillow. While Forrest did not order the massacre, he lost control of his troops, and "the best evidence indicates that the 'massacre' . . . was a genuine massacre."[69] Forrest's soldiers fought with the fury of men possessed by hatred of an enemy they considered a "lesser race," slaughtering Union troops as they tried to surrender or flee.

Forrest was not bothered by this. His subordinate, Gen. James Chalmers, told an officer from the gunboat *Silver Cloud* that neither he or Forrest ordered the massacre, but that "the men of General Forrest's command had such a hatred toward the armed negro that they could not be restrained from killing the negroes." He added, "I was nothing better than we could expect so long as we persisted in arming the negro."[70] The massacre was a portent of what many of the same men

I Knew What I Was Fighting For

would do to defenseless Blacks and whites as members of the Ku Klux Klan and other terrorist paramilitaries after the war.

An infuriated Ulysses Grant threatened reprisals if others were massacred. In his after-action report, he wrote:

> These troops fought bravely, but were overpowered I will leave Forrest in his dispatches to tell what he did with them. "The river was dyed," he says, "with the blood of the slaughtered for up to 200 yards. The approximate loss was upward of five hundred killed; but few of the officers escaped. My loss was about twenty killed. It is hoped that these facts will demonstrate to the Northern people that negro soldiers cannot cope with Southerners." Subsequently Forrest made a report in which he left out the part that shocks humanity to read.[71]

Most of those killed were soldiers of the Sixth U.S. Colored Heavy Artillery, which composed over one-third of the garrison. Shelby Foote writes that "of the 262 Negro members of the garrison, only 58—just over 20 percent—were marched away as prisoners; while of the 295 whites, 168—just under sixty percent were taken."[72] A white survivor of the Union Thirteenth West Tennessee Cavalry recounted:

> We all threw down our arms and gave tokens of surrender, asking for quarter . . . but no quarter was given. . . . I saw 4 white men and at least 25 negroes shot while begging for mercy. . . . These were all soldiers. There were also 2 negro women and 3 little children standing within 25 steps of me, when a rebel stepped up to them and said, "Yes, God damn you, you thought you were free, did you?" and shot them all. They all fell but one child, when he knocked it in the head with the breech of his gun.[73]

A Confederate sergeant wrote home after the massacre: "The poor deluded negroes would run up to our men, fall upon their knees and with uplifted hands scream for mercy, but were ordered to their feet and shot down."[74] The Confederates allowed the *Silver Cloud* to evacuate the wounded and for the dead to be buried. The gunboat's captain was appalled at the sight:

All the buildings around the fort and the tents and huts in the fort had been burned by the rebels, and among the embers of the charred remains of numbers of our soldiers who had suffered terrible death in the flames could be seen. All the wounded who had strength enough to speak agreed that after the fort was taken an indiscriminate slaughter of our troops was carried on by the enemy. . . . Around on every side horrible testimony to the truth of this statement could be seen, Bodies with gaping wounds, . . . some with skulls beaten through, others with hideous wounds as if their bowels had been ripped open with bowie-knives, plainly told that little quarter was shown. . . . Strewn from the fort to the river bank, in the ravines and the hollows, behind logs and under the brush where they had crept for protection from the assassins who pursued them, we found bodies bayoneted, beaten, and shot to death, showing how cold-blooded and persistent was the slaughter. . . . Of course, when a work is carried by assault there will always be more or less bloodshed . . . but here there were unmistakable evidences of a massacre carried on long after any resistance could have been offered, with a cold-blooded barbarity and perseverance which nothing can palliate.[75]

The Confederate press propagandized the massacre. John R. Eakin of Arkansas's *Washington Telegraph* reported:

The Slave Soldiers.—Amongst there are stupendous wrongs against humanity, shocking to the moral sense of the world, like Herod's massacre of the Innocents, or the eve of St. Bartholomew, the crime of Lincoln in seducing our slaves into the ranks of his army will occupy a prominent position. . . .

Meanwhile, the problem has been met our soldiers in the heat of battle, where there has been no time for discussion. They have cut the Gordian knot with the sword. They did right. . . .

It follows that we cannot treat negroes in arms as prisoners of war without a destruction of the social system for which we contend. We must be firm, uncompromising and unfaltering. We must claim the full control of all negroes who may fall into our hands, to punish with death, or any other penalty, or remand them to their owners. If the enemy retaliate, we must do likewise; and if the black flag follows, the blood be upon their heads.[76]

When Black soldiers were victorious, they often treated captured Confederates mercifully. Colonel Brisbin wrote following Battle of Saltville, "Such of the Colored Soldiers who fell into the hands of the Enemy during the battle were murdered. The Negroes did not retaliate but treated the Rebel wounded with great kindness, carrying them water in their canteens and doing all they could to alleviate the sufferings of those whom the fortunes of war had placed in their hands."[77]

Black soldiers paved the way for Lincoln, Radical Republicans in Congress, and Ulysses Grant to secure for the equality, citizenship, and suffrage of all Blacks. If they could fight and die for the country, how could they be denied the right to vote, to be elected to office, to serve on juries, or to go to public schools? During the summer of 1864, under political pressure to end the war, Lincoln reacted angrily to Copperheads and wavering Republicans on the issue of emancipation, as James McPherson wrote:

"But no human power can subdue this rebellion without using the Emancipation lever as I have done." Lincoln pointed out to War Democrats that some 130,000 black soldiers were fighting for the Union: "If they stake their lives for us they must be prompted by the strongest motive—even the promise of freedom. And the promise being made, must be kept." To abandon emancipation "would ruin the Union cause itself. All recruiting of colored men would instantly cease, and all colored men in service would instantly desert us. And rightfully too. Why should they give their lives for us, with full notice of our purpose to betray them? . . . Abandon all the posts now possessed by black men, surrender these advantages to the enemy, & we would be compelled to abandon the war in 3 weeks." Besides there was the moral question: "There have been men who proposed to me to return to slavery the black warriors of Port Hudson & Ousttee [a battle in which Black soldiers fought] I should be damned in time & in eternity for so doing. The world shall know that I will keep my faith to friends & enemies, come what will."[78]

The importance of Black soldiers to the war effort cannot be minimized, for without them the conflict could have dragged on much longer, or ended in stalemate, which would have meant Confederate victory. Lincoln wrote in 1864 about the importance of the Black contribution:

> Any different policy in regard to the colored man, deprives us of his help, and this is more than we can bear. We can not spare the hundred and forty or hundred and fifty thousand now serving us as soldiers, seamen, and laborers. This is not a question of sentiment or taste, but one of physical force which may be measured and estimated as horse-power and Steam-power are measured and estimated. Keep it and you save the Union. Throw it away, and the Union goes with it.[79]

Yet Blacks faced discrimination during and after the war, sometimes even from white men that they served alongside, but most often from those who did not support the war or emancipation. Lincoln took note of this: "There will there will be some black men who can remember that, with silent tongue, the clenched teeth, the steady eye, the well poised bayonet, they have helped mankind on to this great consummation; while, I fear, there will be some white ones, unable to forget that, with malignant heart, and deceitful speech, they have strove to hinder it."[80]

The process that began in 1863 with the brave service and sacrifice of Black soldiers to achieve civil and voting rights continues today. It was not until after the war that Blacks were commissioned as army officers. When Gov. John Andrew, who had raised the Fifty-Fourth Massachusetts Regiment, attempted to "issue a state commission to Sergeant Stephen Swails of the 54th . . . the Bureau of Colored Troops obstinately refused to issue Swails a discharge from his sergeant's rank, and Swails promotion was held up until after the end of the war. 'How can we hope for success to our arms or God's blessing,' raged the white colonel of the 54th, Edward Hallowell 'while we as a people are so blind to justice?'"[81]

Jaded white Union soldiers who had opposed emancipation began to change their outlook as the armies marched into the South, and they saw firsthand the horrors of slavery. In the words of Russell Weigley, "Confronting the scarred bodies and crippled souls of African Americans as they marched into the South experienced a strong motivation to become anti-slavery men. . . . Men do not need to play a role long, furthermore, until the role grows to seem natural and customary to them. That of liberators was sufficiently fulfilling to their pride that soldiers found themselves growing more accustomed to it all the more readily."[82]

A sergeant of the Nineteenth Michigan Regiment, who had lost a stepson in the war, wrote from Georgia to his wife before being killed in action himself during the Atlanta campaign: "The more I learn of the cursed institution of Slavery, the more I feel willing to endure, for its final destruction. . . . After this war is over, this whole country will undergo a change for the better. . . . Abolishing slavery will dignify labor; that fact will revolutionize everything. . . . Let Christians use all their influence to have justice done to the black man."[83]

The sight of Black regiments marching "through the slave states wearing the uniform of the U.S. Army and carrying rifles on their shoulders was perhaps the most revolutionary event of a war turned into revolution."[84] At peak one in eight Union troops were Black, and the contribution they made to the Union victory was immense: "Black troops fought on 41 major battlefields and in 449 minor engagements. Sixteen soldiers and seven sailors received Medals of Honor for valor.

37,000 blacks in army uniform gave their lives and untold sailors did, too."[85]

The significance of the number of Black soldiers is visible when comparing it to the number of Confederate troops serving on January 1, 1865: on that day they exceeded the "aggregate present" in Confederate ranks by over 20,000 men. Of these soldiers "134,111 were recruited in states that had stars in the Confederate battle flag, and the latter figure in turn was several thousand greater than the total of 135,994 gray-clad soldiers 'present for duty' that same day."[86] When Black Soldiers faced Confederates in combat, they fought with distinction: "Deep pride was their compensation. Two black patients in an army hospital began a conversation. One of them looked at the stump of an arm he had once had and remarked: 'Oh I should like to have it, but I don't begrudge it.' His ward mate, minus a leg, replied: 'Well, 'twas [lost] in a glorious cause, and if I'd lost my life I should have been satisfied. I knew what I was fighting for.'"[87]

After the war many Black soldiers became leaders in the Black community. No less than 130 held elected office in the U.S. Congress and various state legislatures during and after Reconstruction. The liberating effects of "the black military experience radiated from black soldiers and their families into the larger black community, so it spread into white society as well."[88] Many officers who volunteered or were assigned to USCT or served with state Black regiments continued to be voices for the civil rights of Blacks after the war: "Black veterans continued to play a central role in black communities, North and South. The skills and experience black men gained during the war not only propelled many of them into positions of leaders and sustained the prominence of others, but it also shaped the expectations and aspirations of all black people. The achievements and pride engendered by military service helped to make a new world of freedom."[89]

The sacrifices of Black Soldiers who fought for freedom are too often forgotten. But the "contribution of black soldiers

FIG. 19. Integrated crew of sidewheel gunboat USS *Miami*, ca. 1864.
Navy crews had integrated crews since the Revolution. Photograph
by Matthew Brady. U.S. Naval History Center.

to Union victory remained a point of pride in black communities. 'They say,' an Alabama planter reported in 1867, 'the Yankees never could have whipped the South without the aid of the Negroes.' Well into the twentieth century, black families throughout the United States would recall with pride that their fathers and grandfathers had fought for freedom."[90]

Blacks in the Navy

Blacks had served aboard U.S. naval vessels since the American Revolution and were an important part of ship's crews all through the age of sail and during the Civil War. However, in 1798, Secretary of the Navy Benjamin Stoddert, a slaveholder, "barred 'Negroes or Mulattoes' from serving in the new navy, and the Marine Corps did the same. Given the need to fill out their crews, however, captains often took free blacks as crew members. Both free blacks and slaves had served in the Continental Navy, the state navies, and privateers during the revolution, but that precedent had been forgotten."[91]

In colonial times many free Blacks took up seafaring by serving as merchantmen or in the Royal Navy. Likewise, "life at sea during the eighteenth century was difficult and dangerous. Therefore, navies were forced to enlist practically anyone who was willing to serve."[92] Free Blacks comprised between 10 and 20 percent of U.S. Navy crews during the War of 1812. Capt. Oliver Hazard Perry initially complained about having Blacks on his ships, but came to believe in their ability. At the Battle of Lake Erie, "blacks constituted one-fourth of his 400-man force aboard the 10-vessel fleet." He was so impressed by their performance under fire that he wrote the secretary of the navy, "praising their fearlessness in the face of excessive danger."[93] As such Stoddert's ban on Blacks was lifted, and more Blacks enlisted.

The navy became a place for Blacks to serve their country, and with distinction. Blacks made up a higher percentage of navy personnel than the army. They were praised by naval officers like David Dixon Porter, who recruited them for his Mississippi Squadron as "coal heavers, firemen, and even gun crews" and who declared, "They do first rate work, and are far better behaved than their masters. What injustice to these poor people, to say they are only fit for slaves. They are far better than the white people here, who I look upon as brutes."[94]

In 1862 the navy faced a manpower shortage as federal and state governments pushed recruits into the army. The government did not provide "bounties for those who joined nor counting them in local recruiting quotas."[95] When navy commanders encountered slaves, or "contrabands," Secretary of the Navy Gideon Welles authorized their enlistment. Due to the nature of shipboard life, there were no segregated quarters, so white and Black sailors messed and lived in common spaces. Black sailors also had complete control of their pay and the same privileges as their white shipmates.

Most naval officers were not abolitionists, and some defended

I Knew What I Was Fighting For

slavery. Their wartime experiences, however, converted many officers to the abolitionist cause. Samuel Francis Du Pont would state,

> "I have never been an abolitionist . . . on the contrary most of my life a sturdy conservative on the vexed question." He explained, in 1861, that he had "defended it all over the world, argued for it for it as patriarchal in its tendencies. Oh my! What a delusion. . . . The degradation, the overwork, and ill treatment of the slaves in the cotton states is great than I deemed possible, while the capacity of the Negro for improvement is higher than I believed." He noted that no officer in his squadron had voted for Lincoln, and by April 1862, he wrote, "there is not one proslavery man among them."[96]

Opportunities for Blacks decreased after the war. They continued to serve in the military, but as the navy became more technological, recruiters sought out educated men to crew new steel and steam navy vessels. Jim Crow affected naval recruiting as well, and by 1917 only 7,500 Blacks were still in the Navy, mostly as mess stewards. After *Plessy v. Ferguson*, the navy excluded Blacks from "all but the most undesirable jobs. Moreover, whites still would not tolerate blacks in blacks in positions of authority over them. Promotion was rare, and 'to avoid friction between the two races,' commanders also segregated their eating and sleeping areas."[97] With the exception of a successful experiment to integrate crews of some auxiliary ships in 1944 and to commission 20 Black officers, this practice continued until President Truman ordered the integration of the military in 1948.

The Confederate Debate about Black Soldiers

Forty percent of the Confederate population was composed of Black slaves. The Confederacy hoped to "turn back the tide of abolition that had swept the hemisphere in the Age of Revolution. . . . Confederate founders proposed instead to perfect the slaveholder's republic and offer it to the world as the political form best suited to the modern age."[98]

The racist nature of the Confederacy meant that there was no question of recruiting Blacks to serve in the military. The leaders of the free Black and mulatto Louisiana Native Guard volunteered their unit to serve in the Confederate Army to defend their homes, but were refused. As Riccardo Herrera writes, "Such devotion aside, it would not do to have a confederacy predicated on race-based slavery. The Confederate government refused the Native Guard's generous and patriotic offer."[99] Instead these men would serve the Union after being abandoned by other Louisiana militias when New Orleans was captured in in 1862, becoming the First Regiment of Louisiana Native Guards. But after the twin disasters at Vicksburg and Gettysburg, some Southern newspapers began to broach the subject of employing slaves as soldiers, even if it meant emancipation. The editor of the *Jackson Mississippian* opined that "such a step would revolutionize our whole industrial system' and perhaps lead to universal emancipation, 'a dire calamity to both the negro and the white race.' But if we lose slavery anyway, for Yankee success is death to the institution . . . so that it is a question of necessity—a question of choice of evils. . . . We must . . . save ourselves form the rapacious north, WHATEVER THE COST."[100]

Some Confederate military leaders understood that the South could not fight for independence and slavery at the same time. The "necessity of engaging slaves' politics was starting to be faced where it mattered most: in the military."[101] Gen. Patrick Cleburne, an Irish immigrant and division commander in the Army of Tennessee, demonstrated a capacity for forward thinking in terms of race, slavery, and military-political objectives superior to that of most Confederate leaders. Cleburne argued the hypocrisy of claiming to fight for liberty while subjugating Blacks to slavery. He told his staff: "It is said [that] slavery is all we are fighting for, and if we give it up we give up all. Even if this were true, which we deny, slavery is not

I Knew What I Was Fighting For

all our enemies are fighting for. . . . We have now briefly proposed a plan which we believe will save our country. It may be imperfect, but in all probability, it would give us our independence."[102] He said that Blacks should be emancipated and allowed to serve as Confederate soldiers. James McPherson notes that "thirteen brigadier generals and other officers in his division signed the paper. But officers in other units condemned the 'monstrous proposition' as 'revolting to Southern sentiment, Southern prides, and Southern honor.'"[103]

Cleburne honestly believed that slavery was incidental to the conflict, saying, "If southerners had to choose between securing their own freedom and maintaining the system of slavery, he had no doubt that his friends and neighbors, indeed the entire South, would willingly let slavery expire in order to ensure their own political independence."[104] He soon learned how wrong he was. Cleburne argued, most significantly, that "slavery from being one of our chief sources of strength at the beginning of the war, has now become in a military point of view, one of our chief sources of weakness,"[105] and that "all along the lines . . . slavery is comparatively valueless to us for labor, but of great and increasing worth to the enemy for information," an "omnipresent spy system, pointing out our valuable men to the enemy, revealing our positions, purposes, and resources."[106] He noted that "every soldier in our army already knows and feels our numerical inferiority to the enemy. . . . If this state continues much longer, we shall surely be subjugated."[107]

Cleburne was the ultimate realist about the way slavery hurt the Confederate cause: troops had to guard against slave uprisings, which denuded frontline armies without adding economic value; slaves were increasingly pro-Union, and the "'fear of insurrection in the rear' filled troops with 'anxieties for the fate of loved ones when our armies have moved forward.' When Union armies liberated plantations, they found 'recruits waiting with open arms.' He complimented the fighting skills of Blacks 'to face and fight bravely against their former masters.'"[108] He also appealed to the high command:

> Ever since the agitation of the subject of slavery commenced the negro has been dreaming of freedom and his vivid imagination has surrounded the condition with so many gratifications that it has become the paradise of his hopes. . . . The measure we propose will strike dead all John Brown fanaticism, and will compel the enemy to draw off altogether or in the eyes of the world to swallow the Declaration of Independence without the sauce and disguise of philanthropy.[109]

Cleburne's "logic was military, the goal more men in uniform, but the political vision was radical indeed."[110] He asked more from Southerners than most could do: "To surrender the cornerstone of white racism to preserve their nation."[111]

Few Southerners could stomach Cleburne's words: "As between the loss of independence and the loss of slavery we can assume that every patriot will freely give up the latter—give up the Negro slave rather than be a slave himself."[112] He went even further: "When we make soldiers of them we must make free men of them beyond all question . . . and thus enlist their sympathies also."[113] But far too many Southerners believed "the loss of slavery as virtually synonymous with the loss of his own liberty."[114]

Cleburne's words were blasphemous to Southerners who believed slavery was mandated by God. Gen. William B. Bate proclaimed that emancipation would "contravene principles upon which I have heretofore acted," and it proposed "to discard our received theory of government [and] destroy our legal institutions and social relations."[115] Another officer declared it a "monstrous proposition . . . revolting to Southern sentiment, Southern pride, and Southern honor."[116]

Gen. W. H. T. Walker obtained a copy of Cleburne's proposal to emancipate slaves who would volunteer to fight for the South and sent it directly it to Jefferson Davis, despite Gen. Joseph Johnston's order not to forward it. Walker expressed outrage, demanding that Davis crack down on "the agitation of such sentiments and propositions," which "would ruin the

　　　　　I Knew What I Was Fighting For

efficiency of our Army and involve our cause in ruin and disgrace."[117] Cleburne's proposal was to Walker a challenge too political for an officer to make.

Davis realized slavery was doomed but saying so was "was a potential bombshell for his administration."[118] Thus he ordered Seddon to quash Cleburne's proposal and keep it from public knowledge. Davis directed "the suppression, not only of the memorial itself, but likewise all discussion and controversy respecting or growing out of it."[119] Seddon wrote the order, and Davis and Seddon were convinced that the "'propagation of such opinions' would cause 'discouragements, distraction, and dissension' in the army."[120]

The matter seemed over. James McPherson writes, "The only consequence of Cleburne's action seemed to be the denial of promotion to this ablest of the army's division commanders, who was killed ten months later at the Battle of Franklin."[121] Cleburne was "passed over for command of an army corps and promotion to lieutenant general" between the plan's suppression and his death at the Battle of Franklin. In "each case less distinguished, less controversial men received the honors."[122] Gen. Braxton Bragg, a personal foe of Cleburne, recently promoted to be Davis's chief military advisor, seems to have been behind this, calling Cleburne's supporters "agitators [who] should be watched." To ensure that his point was clear, he added ominously, "We must mark these men."[123] All known copies of Cleburne's proposal were destroyed. Sadly, the "type of radical thinking Cleburne offered would not be seen again."[124] The cover-up was so successful it would have never come to light had not a member of Cleburne's staff discovered a copy in 1890.

Cleburne was not alone in his thinking. Richard Ewell suggested the idea of arming slaves and emancipation as early as 1861, volunteering to "command a brigade of Negroes."[125] Eventually Robert E. Lee became a proponent. After the war Lee said that he told Davis "often and early in the war that the slaves should be emancipated, that it was the only way to remove a weakness at home and to get sympathy abroad, and divide our enemies, but Davis would not hear of it."[126]

Ten months after killing Cleburne's proposal, Davis suggesting arming slaves, due to military necessity. Stephanie McCurry writes, "In mid-September Davis acknowledged that two-thirds of the army was absent, most without leave."[127] The manpower crisis deepened every day, and Davis reluctantly admitted that to survive the Confederacy had to tap the vast manpower pool of Black slaves, even if it meant emancipation.

Davis realized that Confederate nationalism meant more than slavery. "Preserving slavery had become secondary to preserving his new nation."[128] On November 7, 1864, Davis shocked Congress by announcing his support for enlisting Blacks and limited emancipation: "The slave . . . can no longer be 'viewed as mere property' but must be recognized instead in his other 'relation to the state—that of a person.' As property, Davis explained, slaves were useless to the state, because without the 'loyalty' of the men could be gained from their labor.'"[129]

Lack of foreign recognition and manpower shortages forced Davis to ask Congress for "consideration . . . of a radical modification in the theory of law of slavery." He noted that the Confederacy might have to hold out "his emancipation . . . as a reward for faithful service."[130] Davis angered supporters and influential publications, who would rather lose the war that win it with Black help. Black soldiers meant equality, and equality meant emancipation. Some North Carolina newspapers attacked Davis's proposal as "farcical": "All this done for the preservation and perpetuation of slavery and if 'sober men . . . are ready to enquire if the South is willing to abolish slavery as a condition of carrying on the war, why may it not be done as a condition of ending the war?'"[131]

Robert E. Lee lent his formidable voice to the debate. In a letter to Andrew T. Hunter he argued,

It is certain that the surest foundation upon the fidelity of an army can rest, especially in a service which imposes peculiar

I Knew What I Was Fighting For

hardships and privations, is the personal interests of the soldier in the issue of the contest. Such an interest we can give our negroes by giving immediate freedom to all who enlist, and freedom at the end of the war to the families of those who discharge their duties faithfully (whether they survive or not,) together with the privilege of residing in the South. To this might be added a bounty for faithful service.[132]

Likewise, Lee also wrote to a member of the Virginia legislature:

We must decide whether slavery shall be extinguished by our enemies and the slaves used against us or use them ourselves at the risk of the effects which may be produced on our social institutions. . . . any act for the enrolling of slaves as soldiers must contain a "well digested plan of gradual and general emancipation the slaves could not be expected to fight well if their service was not rewarded with freedom."[133]

Lee's previous letters were private and not public, and, as James McPherson notes, "on February 18 he broke his public silence with a letter to the congressional sponsor of a negro soldier bill. 'The measure was not only expedient but necessary. . . . The negroes, under proper circumstances will make effective soldiers. I think we could do as well with them as the enemy. . . . Those employed should be freed. It would be neither just nor wise . . . to require them to serve as slaves.'"[134]

Some slave owners supported Davis. One who had lost two sons in the war said, "We should do away with pride of opinion—away with false pride. . . . The enemy fights us with the negro—and they will do well to fight the Yankees. . . . We are reduced to the last resort."[135] Others reacted in horror. When Howell Cobb heard of it, he told Secretary of War James Seddon, "I think that the proposition to make soldiers of our slaves is the most pernicious idea that has ever been suggested since the war began. It is to me a source of deep mortification and regret to see the name of that good and great man and soldier, General R. E. Lee, given as authority for such policy."[136]

A South Carolina planter's wife wrote that "slaveholders on principle, & those who hope one day to become slaveholders in time, will not tacitly allow their property & their hopes & allow a degraded race to be placed on a level with them."[137]

The debate revealed the divide between realists and true believers. Judah Benjamin and a few governors "generally supported arming the slaves."[138] But limited emancipation was opposed by governors Joe Brown and Zebulon Vance and by Senate president pro tempore R. M. T. Hunter, who forcibly opposed it. Sen. David Yulee of Florida told Davis, "This is a White Man's government. To associate colors in camp is to unsettle castes; and when thereby the distinction of color and caste is so far obliterated that the relation of fellow soldier is accepted, the mixture of races and toleration of equality is commenced."[139]

The Southern press supported the opposition. Robert Rhett's *Charleston Mercury* called it apostasy and proclaimed: "Assert the right in the Confederate government to emancipate slaves, and it is stone dead."[140] Others were more realistic. J. H. Stringfellow, who led the sack of Lawrence, wrote to Davis in support of Black soldiers but not emancipation:

> We allege that slaves will not fight in our armies. Escaped slaves fight and fight bravely for our enemies; therefore, a freed slave will fight. If at the beginning of this war all our negroes had been free does anyone believe that the Yankees would have been able to recruit an army amongst them? Does anyone know of a solitary free negro escaping to them and joining their army?
> . . . Would not our freed negroes make us as good of soldiers as they do for our enemies?[141]

The Confederate Congress passed a watered-down bill to recruit slaves by one vote in March 1865, stipulating that "the recruits must all be volunteers,"[142] and that they had to have "the approbation of his master by a written instrument conferring, as far as he may, the rights of a freed man."[143]

But, even staring defeat in the face, slave owners were will-

I Knew What I Was Fighting For

ing to sacrifice their property for the country. During the November debate, the *Richmond Sentinel* noted, "If the emancipation of a part is the means of saving the rest, this partial emancipation is eminently a pro-slavery measure."[144] The law made "no mention of emancipation as a reward of military service,"[145] and in deference to "state's rights, the bill did not mandate freedom for slave soldiers."[146]

Lee's prestige helped the measure pass, but now Lee's patriotism was questioned by people who cared nothing for all he sacrificed in the war. The *Richmond Examiner* expressed doubt if Lee was "a 'good Southerner': that is, whether he is thoroughly satisfied of the justice and beneficence of negro slavery."[147] Robert Toombs stated, "The worst calamity that could befall us would be to gain our independence by the valor of our slaves."[148] A Mississippi congressman exclaimed, "Victory itself would be robbed of its glory if shared with slaves."[149] Though the bill was inadequate, "and fell short of General Lee's preferred plan of general gradual emancipation,"[150] the debate finally forced Southerners "to realign their understanding of what they were protecting and to recognize the contradictions in their carefully honed rationalization. Some would still staunchly defend it; others would adopt the ostrich's honored posture. But many understood only too well what they had already surrendered."[151]

The War Office issued General Order No. 14 on March 23, 1865, authorized the military recruitment of slaves, but not their emancipation. It concluded "that nothing in this act shall be construed to authorize a change in the relation which the said slaves shall bear to their owners, except by the consent of the owners and of the States which they may reside."[152] Despite the fact that the measure failed emancipate volunteers, Davis insisted that the army would "enroll no slaves, only freemen, by their own consent."[153]

Whatever anyone else thought, Davis realized that consent and emancipation were the only just and reasonable terms on which to enlist Black soldiers. It was earth-shattering: the man who labored to build the perfect slave republic decided on emancipation. "Davis ordered the War Department to issue regulations that 'ensured them the rights of a freedman. The president tried to jump-start the recruitment of black regiments. But the effort was too little and too late.'"[154]

Twelve days later two companies of Blacks formed for drill in Richmond's Capitol Square. Commanded by Maj. J. W. Pegram and Maj. Thomas P. Turner, the recruits assembled to the sounds of fifes and drums and "proudly marched down the street for the first time in their Southern uniforms, whites lining the sidewalks threw mud at them."[155] They were met with derision and violence; even "small boys jeered and threw rocks."[156] It was fitting that they never saw action, because they were still hated by the people they volunteered to defend. Davis proclaimed while fleeing: "Again and again we shall return, until the baffled and exhausted enemy shall abandon in despair his endless and impossible task of making slaves of a people resolved to be free."[157]

Within a week Lee surrendered at Appomattox and within the month Davis was in federal prison. After Davis fled Richmond's provost marshal set fire to the arsenal and destroyed much of Richmond. The fires "roared out of hand and rioters and looters too to the streets until the last Federal soldiers, their bands savagely blaring 'Dixie,' marched into the humiliated capital and raised the Stars and Stripes over the old Capitol building."[158] Davis went south, hoping to continue resistance. He reached Joseph Johnston's remnant of an army in North Carolina, but Johnston told the hopelessly deluded Davis, "My views are, sir, that our people are tired of the war, feel themselves whipped and will not fight. . . . My men are daily deserting in large numbers. Since Lee's defeat they regard the war as at an end."[159] Johnston recited to Davis a litany of the Confederacy's shortcomings and added: "The effect of keeping our forces in the field would be, not to harm the enemy, but to complete the devastation of our country and the ruin of its people," and resistance would constitute

FIG. 20. *Troops of the 29th U.S. Colored Troops lead the Union XXV Corps into Richmond, April 3, 1865.* From *Frank Leslie's Illustrated Newspaper,* April 25, 1865.

"the greatest of human crimes."[160] Beauregard, an old foe of Davis, concurred with Johnston. A Confederate soldier noted, "Poor President. . . . He is unwilling to see what all around him see. He cannot bring himself to believe that after four years of glorious struggle we are to be crushed into submission."[161] Davis dissolved his cabinet, and he and his wife, Varina, and others were captured by a Union cavalry patrol near Irwinville, Georgia.

The USCT soldiers of Gen. Godfrey Weitzel's Twenty-Fifth Corps liberated Richmond. Every Black regiment the Army of the James was consolidated in Weitzel's corps, including Ferrero's former division. Bruce Catton writes that, "two years earlier in New Orleans, Weitzel had protested that he did not believe in colored troops and did not want to command them, and now he sat at the gates of Richmond in command of many thousands of them, and when the citadel fell he would lead them in and share with them the glory of occupying the Rebel capital."[162] Weitzel's units included regiments of Black "cavalrymen and infantrymen. Many were former slaves; their presence showed their resolve to be free."[163]

Abraham Lincoln entered Richmond to the cheers of former slaves who remained in the city on April 4. For them the president's appearance was like that of the Messiah. The historian of the Twelfth New Hampshire Volunteer Infantry wrote,

> His reception in a city which, only a day or two before, had been the headquarters and centre of the Rebellion, was most remarkable; and more resembled a triumphant return from, than an entry into the enemy's capital. Instead of the streets being silent and vacated, they were filled with men, women, and children shouting and cheering wherever he went.
>
> "I'd rather see him than Jesus," excitedly exclaims one woman, as she runs ahead of the crowd to get a view of his benign countenance. "De kingdom's come, and de Lord is wid us," chants another. "Hallelujah!" shouts a third; and so on through a whole volume of prayers, praises, blessings, and benedictions showed down upon his, the great emancipator of a race, and the savior of his country, thus redeemed, as he walked slowly forward with smiling and uncovered head.[164]

A journalist witnessing the event described the scene:

> They gathered around the President, ran ahead, hovered upon the flanks of the little company, and hung like a dark cloud upon the rear. Men, women, and children joined the consistently increasing throng. They came from the by-streets, running in breathless haste, shouting and hallooing and dancing with delight. The men threw up their hats, the women their bonnets and handkerchiefs, clapped their hands, and sang, Glory to God! Glory! Glory! Glory![165]

One old man rushed to Lincoln and shouted, "Bless the Lord, the great Messiah! I knowed him as soon as I seed him. He's been in my heart four long years, and he's come at last to free his children from their bondage. Glory, hallelujah!" When he threw himself at the embarrassed president's feet,

Lincoln said, "Don't kneel to me. You must kneel to God only, and thank Him for the liberty you will enjoy hereafter."[166]

U.S. Colored Troops who had rallied to the Union fought bravely even against the prejudice of their own countrymen and endured the vengeance of their enemies in emancipated Richmond. They were followed by the man who had made the decision to emancipate them and who then persevered against all opposition, risking his presidency, and ten days later losing his life for their freedom.

Truman, Desegregation, and the March for Equality

Frederick Douglass predicted to the men of Philadelphia in July 1863, "I have not the slightest doubt that, in the progress of this war, that we shall see black officers, black colonels, and generals even."[167] Full equality for Blacks in the military was still far off, but it would eventually come through the signature of Pres. Harry S. Truman. Some advances had occurred during World War II, but the result was still a modified form of segregation. Truman signed Executive Order 9981, which ended the practice of racial segregation in the armed forces.

Even after desegregation Blacks in the military still faced discrimination. Truman's executive order established a long chain of events that led to the end of segregation, but there is still much to accomplish. Racism remains entrenched in parts of the U.S. military. And yet the military has been a leader in race relations and equality and for some time has been more progressive than much of civilian society.

The confirmation of Gen. Charles Q. "C. Q." Brown as chief of staff of the air force in August 2020 was a major step in correcting racial inequality in the military. He is the first Black person to ever be appointed the head of any service. A fighter pilot and son of an army colonel, General Brown understands the loneliness of being a Black leader in a heavily white organization. After his confirmation he gave a speech that reflects the experience of many Black officers, regardless of their branch of service. Brown said: "I can't fix centuries of racism in our country, nor can I fix decades of discrimination that may have impacted members of our Air Force," he said. "I'm thinking about how I can make improvements."[168]

Things have changed, but there is still much to do. When former army lieutenant general Lloyd Austin was confirmed as the first Black secretary of defense, he almost immediately announced a stand down to deal with racism in the ranks. While Austin's and Brown's success is due in large part to their stellar service and integrity, it was was presaged by the unselfish sacrifice of Black soldiers and sailors from the USCT until today, where Black service members continue to be trailblazers in the struggle for equal rights.

A white soldier who served with the Forty-Ninth Massachusetts wrote, "All honor to our negro soldiers. They deserve citizenship. They will secure it!" There would be much suffering in what he termed "the transition state" but a "nation is not born without pangs."[169] Those birth pangs helped to bring about a new birth of freedom for the United States.

21

Reconstruction and Redemption

The Failure to Win the Peace

olin Gray wrote, "A successful exercise in peacemaking should persuade the defeated party to accept its defeat."[1] This outcome has been observed throughout history as militarily defeated nations rise up against their occupiers to regain what they lost. As British military historian B. H. Liddell-Hart writes, "History should have taught the statesman that there is no practical halfway house between a peace of complete subjection and a peace of moderation."[2]

The Confederacy was beaten. In the spring of 1865, most Southerners would have agreed to anything the North presented regarding peace and reunification. Lincoln saved the Union, and emancipation was one of the military measures with political and foreign policy ramifications that secured victory. James McPherson writes, "During the last two years of the war the abolition of slavery evolved from a means of winning the war to a war aim—from national strategy to national policy."[3]

Lincoln's reelection in 1864 ensured the unconditional surrender of the Confederacy as well as the passage of the Thirteenth Amendment. Lincoln advocated moderation in achieving the political and social goals of his war policy, as well as in the just restoration of the Southern states to the Union, but his assassination by John Wilkes Booth destroyed that goal. Lincoln had believed Southerners might be rational and acknowledge the results of defeat. When he died, his policies—which balanced his hopeful view of former Con-

FIG. 21. *The Freedmen's Bureau.* Drawing by A. R. Waud. From
Harper's Weekly, July 25, 1868. Courtesy of the Library of Congress,
LC-USZ62–105555.

federates with the reality of war and the evils of slavery and
racism—came to an end. Andrew Johnson was as racist and
unreconstructed as any Southern leader. Throughout his presidency Johnson and Radical Republicans in Congress warred
against each other, turning military victory into political defeat.

Many Union soldiers were disgusted with what they saw of
antebellum Southern society. Col. Robert Hunt Rhodes of the
Second Rhode Island Infantry wrote of an experience while
on occupation duty in Wellsville, Virginia: "This life reminds
me of *Uncle Tom's Cabin.* Many of the ex-slaves are at work, and
this gives me a chance to watch plantation life. I cannot say
that I admire it much, for it seems to be a lazy sort of living."[4]

Within a year of Appomattox, many Northerners were willing to abandon the victory their soldiers gave their lives to
achieve: the reestablishment of the Union, emancipation,
and the suffrage of Blacks. Those who felt most betrayed by
their fellow citizens were the white and Black soldiers who
had fought to restore the Union and to free Blacks from slav-

ery. Brian Jordan writes that "Union veterans looked on with genuine astonishment as northern civilians 'nourish[ed] by the spirit of rebellion into life again,' truckling to the foremost rebels at the expense of the victors."[5]

Gen. Joshua Lawrence Chamberlain, the hero of Little Round Top at Gettysburg on July 2, 1863, was filled with bitterness toward those whom he believed did not care for his comrades or their families, while saluting those who served in the Christian and Sanitary Commissions during the war, as well as their families. They were different than other Northerners, he noted, who were too willing to forgive the South, admire Confederate heroes, and demean Union soldiers and the cause for which they fought:

> Those who can see no good in the soldier of the Union who took upon his breast the blow struck at the Nation's and only look to our antagonists for examples of heroism—those over magnanimous Christians, who are so anxious to love their enemies that they are willing to hate their friends. . . . I have no patience with the prejudice or the perversity that will not accord justice to the men who have fought and fallen on behalf of us all, but must go round by the way of Fort Pillow, Andersonville and Belle Isle to find a chivalry worthy of praise.[6]

Many Union veterans shared Chamberlain's anger as the myths of the Noble South and Lost Cause swept the country. They directed their anger at Northern political and business leaders, among others who treated Union veterans with distain while venerating Confederate military leaders. Lt. Henry Church, who served in the Iron Brigade, was as incensed as Chamberlain. As he wrote to his wife: "Their tongues were very smooth and their promises fair, when they needed men to save the Union. . . . But now that the crisis has passed, and danger no longer apprehended, they think not of us. . . . It makes my blood fairly boil, when I recall the risks we have seen."[7]

Robert Rothwell noted that many Northerners did not appreciate Union soldiers or their sacrifices. He insisted that

Northern veterans were treated with hostility and discriminated against like Blacks by their neighbors and leaders. The visibly maimed soldiers were an uncomfortable reminder to Northerners, who wanted to forget the war. Rothwell himself was crippled by his wounds and unable to wear a prosthetic arm. Before he enlisted in the Seventieth Ohio Volunteer Infantry in 1861, he wrote, he "lived like a white man. . . . [but] now [I live] a little like a nigger."[8] Unable to work he viewed himself as a drain on society. His comparison of his plight with Blacks was less an example of racism than a scathing commentary on Northern hypocrisy. Many veterans understood the complicity of Northern business and political leaders in failing to complete what they won on the battlefield during Reconstruction.

Unfortunately, many Americans, including Pres. Andrew Johnson, abandoned Union veterans. Still bearing their scars, many went South to help the former slaves whom they sacrificed their bodies to set free. Even those who were not abolitionists changed when they saw the suffering that plantation owners had inflicted on Blacks and returned as part of the Freedmen's Bureau under the direction of Maj. Gen. Oliver Howard. Howard graduated from Bowdoin College before attending West Point. After a rough start, he graduated fourth in his class.[9] His high standing assured him prime assignments, during which time he married and became what we would now call a "born-again Christian." While teaching mathematics at West Point, he considered entering the ministry.

When the war came, Howard applied for command of a Maine volunteer regiment and was appointed colonel of the Third Maine and was a brigade commander at the Battle of Bull Run. The carnage of war "confirmed his determination and minimize casualties. Together with his diligence and sense of fairness, that spirit raised him rapidly to the rank of brigadier general and led to a nickname, 'the Christian General.'"[10] He lost his right arm commanding his brigade at the Battle of Fair Oaks, yet rose first to command a division, then to the command of two different corps, and finally command an army. He led the Eleventh Corps at Chancellorsville and Gettysburg, where he received much undue criticism and little credit for choosing Cemetery Hill to make a stand. He commanded the Fourth Corps under Sherman and ended the war commanding the Army of Tennessee, with a brigadier general's commission in the Regular Army. Sherman wrote of Howard: "In General Howard throughout I found a polished and Christian gentleman, exhibiting the highest and most chivalric traits of the soldier."[11] At the war's end, he was appointed to head the Freedmen's Bureau.

Sherman respected Howard's abilities, integrity, compassion, and diligence and warned him about the dangers of his new assignment. Sherman was a realist who cared about Howard, as reflected in the following letter:

> I hardly know whether to congratulate you or not, but of one thing you may rest assured, that you possess my entire confidence, and I cannot imagine that matters, that may involve the future of four millions of souls, could be put be put in more consciousness hands. So far as man can do, I believe you will, but I fear you have Hercules' task. God has limited the power of man, and though the kindness of your heart you would alleviate all the ills of humanity it is not in your power. Nor is it in your power to fulfill one-tenth part of expectations of those who framed frame the bureau for freedmen, refugees, and abandoned estates. It is simply impracticable. Yet you can and will do all the good one man may, and that is all you are called on as a man and Christian to do, and to that extent count on me as a friend and fellow soldier for counsel to do.[12]

Sherman was a wise counselor; Johnson undercut Howard at every opportunity.

The bureau's mission was to offer "relief to destitute southerners, promote education and health care among the freedmen, secure equal justice in southern courts, and in other ways oversee the transition from slavery to freedom."[13] Howard was committed to his work. His faith, experience, humanity, and sense of justice made it a priority to do everything he could for the newly freed Blacks. But his charity did not extend to the former Confederate leaders who profited from slavery and, with Johnson's help, were profiting from it again. One of Howard's aims was to reunite Black families separated by slavery:

> "All colored preachers" employed by the military as chaplains to gather information on divided families. Once data was collected, the Bureau transported refugees about the South at the government's expense. Despite his enormous workload, typical was Howard's order to procure transportation for a black family living in Gordonsville, Virginia to Annapolis, Maryland where their father had been located.[14]

Many veterans serving in the Freedmen's Bureau had seen how Black soldiers were treated and had heard of massacres at Fort Pillow and elsewhere. They recalled the inhuman conditions in which they had found slaves. Those memories changed their hearts as much as Confederate bullets and shells changed their bodies, and the rebel yell remained burned in their brains. They went south to fulfill the vision of freedom and equality.

President Johnson vetoed an extension of the Freedmen's Bureau Bill in 1868 along with the Civil Rights Act. Congress failed to override the Freedmen's Bureau veto by a single vote, but passed a similar bill in July that extended it to 1870. Johnson "insisted, he had neither the need or the authority to protect freedpeople's rights. Assistance by the Freedmen's Bureau would encourage blacks to believe that they did not need to work for a living, thereby encouraging them to lead a 'life of indolence.'"[15] But such was hardly the case, especially among "Black veterans who recollected decades of uncompensated labor hardly needed to be reminded of the importance of hard work. Nor did they believe that the opportunity to save toward purchasing a parcel of land on the estates where they had been born constituted government charity."[16]

Blacks who stepped into the political minefield of the South did so at great personal danger. Most received death threats,

FIG. 22. *A Visit from the Ku-Klux Klan.* Engraving drawn by Frank Bellew,
published in *Harper's Weekly*, February 24, 1872, 160. Courtesy of the
Library of Congress, LC-DIG-ppmsca-71959.

and at least "thirty-five Black officials were murdered by Ku
Klux Klan (KKK) or kindred terrorist organizations during
reconstruction."[17] During the 1875 campaign Alabama Republican state senator Charles Caldwell "boldly led a black militia
unit through the town of Clinton in order to bolster blacks'
courage and in order to intimidate local whites."[18] He fled for
his life, but returned to his office on Election Day. Alabama
Democrats promised a truce, but killings continued before,
during and after the election. Caldwell was lured by whites
wanting to "share a drink" on Christmas night and violently
attacked. His assailants brought the mortally wounded man
to his house. As he died, he told his killers in the presence of
his wife: "Remember when you kill me you kill a gentleman
and a brave man. Never say you killed a coward. I want you to
remember it when I am gone."[19]

During its existence the bureau and Howard came under frequent and hostile investigation from "two investigating boards

and while he was publicly exonerated on each occasion there lingered a feeling that his control of his subordinates was lax, his records sometimes incomplete, he was careless with money matters, and especially that he was too willing to take liberties with the law."[20] Regardless of criticism, limitations in funding and manpower, and Johnson's attempts to impede its operations, the bureau accomplished much. It did so "with ever changing personnel, operating over a vast area, among a hostile white population, and with only three years to accomplish its major goals (the education program excepted) performed near miracles."[21]

Despite their best efforts, however, the bureau's work was not enough. Their efforts to build schools, train teachers, and educate Blacks bore much fruit in the coming decades, especially in founding Black colleges throughout the South; primary schools had some success initially, but after Reconstruction were gutted by segregation. Impoverished Black schools had inadequate facilities, books, and school supplies; as such they remained separate and certainly not equal.

Without federal troops the bureau was at the mercy of white paramilitary groups backed by leaders who wanted to discredit and drive them from the South. When a reporter asked Adelbert Ames, "What was the sentiment of the ruling elements of the whites?," Ames answered with the hard truth:

> In one phrase—hostility to the Negro as a citizen. The South cares for no other question. Everything gives way to it. They support or oppose men, advocate or denounce policies, flatter or murder, just as such action will help them as far as possible to recover their old power over the Negro. . . . Any man who stands by the constitutional amendments—it makes no difference whether he is a Northern man or a Southerner—they are bound to get rid of, in order that the Negro may be compelled to do their bidding in politics. They care nothing for human life.[22]

In the words of Eric Hoffer, "The practice of terror serves the true believer not only to cow and crush his opponents but also

Reconstruction and Redemption

to invigorate and intensify his own faith. Every lynching in our South not only intimidates the Negro but also invigorates the fanatical conviction of white supremacy."[23]

Andrew Johnson: The Unreconstructed President

Abolition necessitated remaking Southern culture, where all life was inevitably intertwined with slavery and white supremacy. Reconstruction was "what the war was about."[24] A Northern correspondent who traveled throughout the South in May 1865 and surveyed the mood of Southerners "concluded that any conditions for reunion specified by the President, even black suffrage, would be 'promptly accepted.'"[25]

Johnson was the Anti-Lincoln. He worked with Southerners to reestablish white rule, by adopting a "minimalist process that would establish a mechanism by which former Confederate states could return to the Union with little or no change except for the abolition of slavery,[26] and 'As for freedmen, he seemed to think that the needed no further protection beyond the fact of their emancipation.'"[27] He limited the vote to those eligible in 1861, which excluded Blacks and ensured white rule. He was the worst possible man to lead the Union, and his presidency was a disaster. He destroyed the chance to rebuild the Union based on the guiding principle of the Declaration of Independence: that "all men are created equal."

Unfortunately, one of emancipation and abolition's leading voices ended his fight at the war's end. Believing that emancipation, abolition, and passage of the Thirteenth Amendment were enough, William Lloyd Garrison retired. He urged dissolving the American Anti-Slavery Society in May 1865, declaring, "My vocation, as an Abolitionist, thank God, is ended."[28] His retirement was unfortunate; while the membership rejected dissolution, it was a harbinger of things to come as other abolitionists gave up the fight.

Johnson was "a lonely stubborn man with few confidants, who seemed to develop his policies without consulting anyone, then stuck to them inflexibly in the face of any and all criticism. He lacked Lincoln's ability to conciliate his foes and his capacity for growth, which was best illustrated by Lincoln's evolving attitude to black suffrage during the Civil War."[29] Within months Johnson demonstrated that he did not understand Lincoln's political goals for the South or care about the desires of the Republican Congress.

He indicated "that his sympathies were with the Southern white population and that he believed that their interests should be cared for even at the expense of freedmen."[30] Johnson's approach to Reconstruction was to impose minimal demands on Southerners and help Northern business expand into the South. Howard's biographer John A. Carpenter writes of Johnson, "As for freedmen, he seemed to think that the needed no further protection beyond the fact of their emancipation."[31] Johnson gave individual pardons to over thirteen thousand "high-ranking Confederate civil and military officers and wealthy Southerners."[32] He attempted to sideline Southern Unionists like himself, who had not supported the Confederacy and excluded freed slaves from the political process. He gave orders "appointing interim provisional governors and urging the writing of new state constitutions based upon the voter qualifications in force at the time of secession in 1861— which meant, in large but invisible letters, no blacks."[33]

Johnson issued hundreds of pardons a day to Confederate leaders, eager to restore rebels to citizenship and political power. Between June and August 1865, "the president awarded more than five thousand pardons in three states alone—Virginia, North Carolina, and Alabama."[34] The pardons ensured that former Confederates never had to worry about being charged with treason or war crimes, and no "federal law permitted them from voting once their states had been readmitted to the Union."[35] The grim irony meant that rebels were able to vote before Blacks.

He countermanded the orders of Union Generals in the South that protected the rights of freed Blacks, emboldening former Confederates. Relieved by Johnson's mild terms, Southerners used "defiant talk of states' rights and resistance to black suffrage. By midsummer, prominent whites realized that Johnson's Reconstruction empowered them to shape the transition from slavery to freedom and to define black's civil status."[36]

Richard Henry Dana, now a federal district attorney in Boston, declared after Lee's surrender that "a war is over when its purpose is secured. It is a fatal mistake to hold that this war is over because the fighting has ceased. This war is not over."[37] As Dana noted so succinctly, and Clausewitz understood so well, the end of military operations does not mean that war is over. Southerners, though defeated, were emboldened by Johnson and used every means, including violence, to reverse their losses on the battlefield.

Frederick Douglass understood that emancipation was not enough, and that the "war and its outcome demanded racial equality."[38] He knew that failure would be disastrous: "Whether the tremendous war so heroically fought . . . shall pass into history a miserable failure . . . or whether on the other hand, we shall, as the rightful reward of victory over treason have a solid nation, entirely delivered from all contradictions and social antagonisms, must be determined one way or another."[39]

Some Northern leaders deluded themselves into believing that Southerners would change their way of life because they lost the war. Oliver Howard "believed that the Southern whites, or at least a sufficient number of them, through their humanitarian instincts and sense of fair play, or if not that, through enlightened self-interest, would deal fairly and justly with the freedmen, would aid in his education, and would give him the same civil and legal rights as the white man."[40] Howard had no idea of the depth of Southern antipathy toward Blacks, but he would find out. Likewise, Maj. Gen. Henry Slocum, who served with Howard at Gettysburg and was appointed military commander of the District of Mississippi, like many others assumed his duties and "did not fathom the depth of anger and loathing many white Southerners harbored toward blacks, and to the new system in general."[41]

Frederick Douglass led a delegation to meet Johnson in February 1866. Johnson argued that Blacks could not have political freedom. Douglass objected, and Johnson grew angry, saying, "I do not like to be arraigned by some who can get up handsomely-rounded periods and rhetoric, and talk about abstract ideas of liberty, who never periled life, liberty, or property."[42] When Douglass told a Washington newspaper of Johnson's tirade, Johnson railed against Douglass: "I know that d——d Douglass . . . he's just like any other nigger & would sooner cut a white man's throat than not."[43]

Douglass had faced reenslavement or death from of bounty hunters since escaping slavery. His sons, who fought in the war, knew danger well. Johnson's ad hominem attacks on Douglass revealed that he cared not for justice or freedom for Blacks but instead for returning Southern whites to power. Johnson encouraged Southern plantation owners to ally themselves with Northern businesses, especially railroad companies and textile manufacturers, to reenslave Blacks using the black codes.

Resistance to Reconstruction and the Black Codes

While "the Civil War settled definitively the South's continued existence as part of the United States," there was "in 1865 no strategy for cleansing the South of the economic and intellectual addiction to slavery."[44] Johnson undermined those charged with securing racial equality and emboldened opponents. His mass pardon, the "Proclamation of Amnesty, pardoning most Confederates and remitting any confiscated lands," worsened the situation.[45]

Johnson stirred the cauldron of discontent, which "grew progressively more radical as Americans reacted with anger to what they saw as the efforts of slaveholders, abetted by President Johnson, to steal from the jaws of defeat and deny true freedom to the former slaves."[46] Black and white abolitionists demonstrated against Johnson. But Radical Republicans in the House could not persuade the Republican majority to overturn Johnson's actions. It was heartbreaking to Blacks, especially

Reconstruction and Redemption

FIG. 23. *Black Code Convicts Used as Labor.* Atlanta,1895. Georgia State
Archives, Vanishing Georgia Collection.

former soldiers who fought for freedom, to find themselves at the mercy of their former owners. Johnson, Democrats, and recalcitrant Republicans ensured that former Confederates returned to power and thereby condemned the country to another century and a half of racial inequality and violence.

Pardoned Confederates enacted Black codes that "codified explicit second-class citizenship for freedpeople."[47] The laws forced newly freed Blacks into a different form of slavery. Some former Confederate states refused to ratify the Thirteenth Amendment; Mississippi did not do so until 1995. One Southerner wrote: "Johnson held up before us the hope of a 'white man's government,' and this led us to set aside negro suffrage. . . . It was natural that we should yield to our old prejudices."[48]

Others, including Alexander Stephens, were elected to high office. Stephens resumed his Senate seat while others returned to the House of Representatives. But aggrieved Republicans in Congress refused to admit them. Many veterans were incensed by Johnson's chicanery; as one New York artilleryman noted, "I would not pardon the rebels, especially the leaders, until they should kneel in the dust of humiliation and show their deeds that they sincerely repent."[49] He was not alone: other Northern veterans of the integrated Grand Army of the Republic despised Confederate leaders and maintained a patent disregard, if not hatred, for all that the South represented. They felt betrayed by President Johnson.

Johnson's unabashed racism was apparent in word and deed. He fought against every measure for the integration. He told a regiment of U.S. Colored Troops in October 1865, "There is a great problem before us . . . whether this race can be incorporated and mixed with the people of the United States. . . . If it should be that the two races cannot agree and live in peace and prosperity," then "they are to be taken to their inheritance and promise, for such is a one before them."[50] His words foretold his future actions. He restored property to former slave owners and drove tens of thousands of Blacks off lands that

Reconstruction and Redemption

they had been farming since being freed. Johnson counter-manded Gen. William Tecumseh Sherman and Secretary of War Edwin Stanton's Field Order 15 January 1865 that began a process to "divide abandoned and confiscated lands on the Sea Islands and in a portion of the Low Country coast south of Charleston into forty-acre plots for each black family."[51] The order allowed forty thousand freed Blacks to move to the Sea Islands to begin new lives. But these newly freed people were now at the mercy of their former owners. Johnson's reversal of Sherman and Stanton's field order was a travesty of justice that became the first nail in the coffin of Reconstruction.

Johnson worked stridently to frustrate the efforts of Howard's Freedmen's Bureau to help Blacks to become landowners and to protect their legal rights while Howard remained a stalwart defender of the civil and voting rights of Blacks his entire life and helped found Howard University, among other Black colleges. Johnson permitted Southern states to organize all-white police forces and state militias composed of Confederate veterans, many still wearing gray uniforms. The officers of the Freedmen's Bureau lamented the situation. One bureau officer wrote that no jury would "convict a white man for killing a freedman,' or 'fail to hang' a Black man who killed a white in self-defense. Blacks, commented another agent, 'would be just as well off with no law at all or no Government,' as with the legal system established in the South under Andrew Johnson. 'If you call this Freedom,' wrote one Black veteran, 'what do you call slavery?'"[52]

Johnson's policy of readmitting the former Confederate states into the Union and moving to bring former Confederate leaders to justice was met with anger: "Union veterans looked upon with genuine astonishment as northern civilians 'nourish[ed]' the spirit of rebellion into life again, 'truckling to the former rebels at the expense of the victors.'"[53]

When Johnson vetoed the Civil Rights Bill of 1868, Congress overrode him. Events reached a climax when Johnson was impeached when he tried to remove Secretary Stanton from office for subverting his pro-Southern policies. Johnson was acquitted by one vote in 1868. However, impeachment doomed his reelection effort. As Johnson and Congress dueled, Southern states

> passed labor laws that bound blacks to employers almost as tightly as slavery once bound them to their masters. Other codes established patterns of racial segregation that had been impossible under slavery, barred African Americans from serving on juries or offering testimony in court against whites, made "vagrancy," "insulting gestures," and "mischief" offenses by blacks punishable by fines or imprisonment, forbade black-white intermarriage, ad banned ownership by blacks of "firearms of any kind, or any ammunition, dirk or bowie-knife."[54]

Mississippi was first to enact black codes. Vagrancy laws were rewritten to target emancipated Blacks:

> That all freedmen, free Negroes, and mulattoes in this state over the age of eighteen years found on the second Monday in January, 1866, or thereafter, with no lawful employment or business, or found unlawfully assembling themselves together in the day or night time, and all white persons so assembling with freedmen, free Negroes, or mulattoes on terms of equality, or living in adultery with a freedwoman, free Negro, or mulatto, shall be deemed vagrants; and on conviction thereof shall be fined . . . and imprisoned.[55]

Johnson supported the black codes. While they recognized the bare minimal elements of Black freedom, their provisions confirmed the observations of one journalist, who wrote: "The whites seem wholly unable to comprehend that freedom for the negro means the same thing as freedom for them. They readily admit that the Government has made him free, but appear to believe that the have the right to exercise the old control."[56]

As state after state followed Mississippi's lead of Mississippi, Northern anger grew. Some newspapers took the lead: "We tell the white men of Mississippi," exploded the *Chicago Tribune* on December 1, "that the men of the North will convert the state of Mississippi into a frog pond before they allow any such laws to disgrace one foot of soil in which the bones of our soldiers sleep and over which the flag of freedom waves."[57]

Within months of the war's end, violence against Blacks broke out in the South. The unrest spread as Johnson and Congress battled each other regarding Reconstruction policy. Johnson had no intention of following Lincoln's ideals and worked to ensure the oppression of Blacks, including supporting massacres: "In Memphis, Tennessee, in May of 1866, whites on a rampage of murder killed forty-six Negroes, most of them veterans of the Union army, as well as two white sympathizers. Five Negro women were raped. Ninety homes, twelve schools and four churches were burned. In New Orleans in the summer of 1866, another riot against blacks killed thirty-five Negroes and three whites."[58]

Hatred and violence against Blacks was not limited to adult perpetrators; children also joined in. An incident in Natchez, Mississippi, indicated the depth of white hatred to Blacks when, on a Sunday afternoon, "an elderly freedman protested to a small white boy raiding his turnip patch. The boy shot him dead, and that was that. In Vicksburg the *Herald* complained that the town's children were hitting innocent bystanders when using their 'nigger shooters.'"[59]

Col. Samuel Thomas's Freedmen's Bureau saw how deeply whites hated emancipated Blacks. He wrote that whites had not progressed since the Confederacy's defeat, had not "come to the attitude in which it can conceive of the negro having any rights at all. Men, who are honorable in their dealings with their white neighbors, without feeling a single twinge of honor. . . . And however, much they confess that the President's proclamation broke up the relation of the individual slave to their owners, they still have the ingrained feeling that the black people at large belong to whites at large."[60]

A reporter asked Adelbert Ames, "How can the Negro be

protected in his rights?" Ames replied: "Only by the nation. The nation must protect this class of citizens in its rights at home just as it would protect the rights of any other class abroad. Unless this is done the will be practically defrauded of their citizenship and reduced to a state of servitude." The reporter then asked about "military interference"—a question Ames knew was loaded, as few federal troops remained, and white paramilitaries had nearly total control. Knowing what he and other Reconstruction governors and Freedmen's Bureau officials were facing, he replied: "No—national protection. 'Military interference' is a crafty phrase, invented to make odious the first and Chief duty of all Governments—the protection of the citizen. The military forces in Mississippi never interfered in any man's rights; they only prevented wrongs. If an American citizen cannot rightfully demand protection from his Government, what is the use of Government?"[61]

When the Freedmen's Bureau was disestablished, Howard continued his military career and retired as a major general in November 1894 after forty-four years of service. Years later he would write:

> My glory, if I ever have any, consists in results attained; and the results in the case of the Freedmen's Bureau are, for me, more marked than those of the war . . . It's a pleasure to know that institutions of higher learning like Howard University, Hampton Institute, Atlanta University, and others in whose incipiency I bore a part, are now constantly increasing in power and influence, and will continue their work long after I am gone.[62]

State and local governments used black codes to sell Blacks convicted under "vagrancy" statutes to a new form of slavery. They leased prisoners to corporations, railroads, mines, plantations, and even to men like Nathan Bedford Forrest of the Fort Pillow Massacre and founder of the KKK, to work his land, enriching him through cheap Black labor, which became a lucrative revenue source for states and local governments. States collected fees from the companies involved and did not have to pay for housing or feeding prisoners. Mortality rates were higher among prisoners in private custody, despite regulations stipulating that they would be adequately fed and housed.[63]

> [By 1877] every former Confederate state except Virginia had adopted the practice of leasing black prisoners into commercial hands. There were variations among the states, but all shared the same basic formula. Nearly all the penal functions of government were turned over to the companies purchasing convicts. In return for what they paid each state, the companies received absolute control of the prisoners. . . . Company guards were empowered to chain prisoners, shoot those attempting to flee, torture any who wouldn't submit, and whip the disobedient— naked or clothed—almost without limit. Over eight decades, almost never were there penalties to any acquirer of these slaves for their mistreatment or deeds.[64]

Northern investors, sensing profits, jumped in, including the owners and shareholders of U.S. Steel. Northern banks and corporations benefited as they had during the antebellum days.

The system harmed poor Southern whites who could not fairly compete in the labor market. In 1891 miners of the "Tennessee Coal Company were asked to sign an 'iron-clad contract': pledging no strikes, agreeing to get paid in scrip, and giving up the right to check the weight of the coal they mined (they were paid by weight). They refused to sign and were evicted from their houses. Convicts were brought in to replace them."[65] The miners rose to take control and freed five hundred of the convict-slaves. The leaders were primarily Union Army veterans and members of the Grand Army of the Republic. The Tennessee Coal Company backed down, but other companies learned the lesson and employed heavily armed Pinkerton agents and state militias to deal with the nation's growing labor movement.

Nonconvict Black laborers and poor white "sharecroppers were forced into servitude. Legislatures gave 'precedence to a landlord's claim to his share of the crop over that of the laborer for wages or a merchant for supplies, thus shifting the risk of farming from employer to employee.'" Likewise, "a series of court decisions defined the sharecropper not . . . as a wage laborer possessing 'only a right to go on the land to plant, work, and gather the crop.'"[66]

The system existed until Franklin Delano Roosevelt directed Attorney General Francis Biddle to order federal prosecutors to prosecute individuals and companies involved. Biddle was the first attorney general to admit that "African Americans were not free and to assertively enforce the statutes written to protect them."[67] During World War II, Biddle—who served as a justice at the Nuremberg trials—commented: "One response of this country to the challenge to the ideals of democracy made by the new ideologies of Fascism and Communism has been a deepened realization of the values of a government based on a belief in the dignity and the rights of man."[68]

Biddle ordered the Civil Rights Division of the Justice Department to shift its focus from organized crime to discrimination and racial abuse, which he denounced, writing that the "law is fixed and established to protect the weak-minded the poor, the miserable"; the contracts of states that allowed it, he said, were "null and void."[69] His action ushered in another phase where Blacks and their allies in the civil rights movement worked to bring about Lincoln's "new birth of freedom."

The Passage of the Fourteenth Amendment

The situation for emancipated Blacks deteriorated as President Johnson's pro-Confederate governors supervised elections, a practice that ensured new state governments were composed of former Confederate leaders. Blacks could not vote, and poor Southern whites retained their social status so long as Blacks were deprived of their rights.

When abolition was officially proclaimed in Texas on June 19, 1865, a day now known as Juneteenth, newly emancipated Blacks rejoiced, but they soon found their joy turned into another hundred years of discrimination, violence, and suffering. Emancipation freed them, but the question as to what freedom meant was still to be decided. James A. Garfield asked, "What is freedom? . . . Is it the bare privilege of not being chained? . . . If this is all, then freedom is a bitter mockery, a cruel delusion."[70]

Garfield was an abolitionist who served with distinction as colonel of the Forty-Second Ohio Volunteer Infantry Regiment, as a brigade commander, and as chief of staff for the Army of the Cumberland. In 1863 he was elected to Congress and left active duty. Garfield, who believed Confederate leaders had forfeited their constitutional rights, favored the confiscation of Southern plantations and the execution or exile of Confederate leaders to ensure a permanent end to slavery. He was also committed to secure justice for all loyal persons regardless of color.

Benjamin G. Humphreys, a former Confederate general pardoned by Andrew Johnson, was appointed as governor of Mississippi in October 1865. In his message to the legislature, Humphreys declared: "Under the pressure of federal bayonets, urged on by the misdirected sympathies of the world, the people of Mississippi have abolished the institution of slavery. The Negro is free, whether we like it or not; we must realize that fact now and forever. To be free does not make him a citizen or entitle him to social or political equality with the white man."[71]

Republicans passed the legislation over Johnson's veto, giving Black men the right to vote and hold office. They overturned the whites-only elections by which Johnson propelled ex-Confederates into political power. Congress took power over Reconstruction: "Constitutional amendments were passed, the laws for racial equality were passed, and the black man began to vote and to hold office."[72] In 1867 Congress mandated that new constitutions provide for "universal suffrage and for the temporary political disqualification of many ex-Confederates."[73]

These measures helped elect biracial legislatures in the

South and enacted progressive reforms, including the creation of public schools where none existed. Eric Foner writes that "the creation of tax-supported public school systems in every state of the South stood as one of Reconstruction's most enduring accomplishments."[74] By 1875 approximately half of Southern children, white and Black, were in school. Public schools were usually segregated and Blacks banned from traditionally white colleges. However, the thirst for education became a hallmark of free Blacks across the county. Since they were banned from most white colleges, the Black colleges and universities opened the doors of higher education for them.

The white Democrat majorities that returned to power after Reconstruction defunded the public primary school systems that had been created during it. Spending on public education for white and Black children dropped to abysmal levels. This was made worse by the Supreme Court's ruling in *Plessy v. Ferguson*, which codified "separate but equal" systems. Congress ratified the Thirteenth and Fourteenth Amendments, but the new Southern legislatures composed of Southern Unionists, Northern Republicans, and Blacks "elicited scorn from the former Confederates and from the South's political class in general."[75] Southerners viewed Republican governments as an alien presence and used subterfuge and armed violence to undermine them.

The Fourteenth Amendment was decisive then and has remained so. It overturned the *Dred Scott* decision, which denied citizenship to Blacks. Johnson opposed it and campaigned for men who would also oppose it during the 1866 elections. Former supporters turned on him, including the editors of the *New York Herald*, who declared that Johnson "forgets that we have passed through a fiery ordeal of a mighty revolution, and the pre-existing order of things is gone and can return no more."[76] Despite the amendment's passage, upon which it became law, Johnson never recanted his racism. In his final message to Congress, he wrote: "If a state constitution gave Negroes the right to vote, it is well-known that a large portion of the electorate in all the States, if not a majority of them, do not believe in or accept the political equality of Indians, Mongolians, or Negroes with the race to which they belong."[77]

The amendment set a constitutional precedent for future laws, among them suffrage for women, Native Americans, and the Chinese. Using the Fourteenth Amendment, the Warren court ruled in the 1954 *Brown v. Board of Education* decision that the separate but equal laws enacted after *Plessy v. Ferguson* violated the Constitution and overturned the Jim Crow laws. The ruling led to the passage of the Voting Rights Act of 1964 and Civil Rights Act of 1965. Most recently it was the basis of the Supreme Court ruling in *Obergfell v. Hodges*, which gave homosexuals the right to marry. Section 1 read:

> All persons born or naturalized in the United States, and sub-ject to the jurisdiction thereof, are citizens of the United States and of the state wherein they reside. No state shall make or enforce any law which shall abridge the privileges or immuni-ties of citizens of the United States; nor shall any state deprive any person of life, liberty, or property, without due process of law; nor deny to any person within its jurisdiction the equal protection of the laws.[78]

For Southerners in 1868, "freedom for African Americans was not the same as freedom for whites, as while whites might grant the black man freedom, they had no intention of allow-ing him the same legal rights as white men."[79] As soon as plant-ers returned to their lands, they "sought to impose on blacks their definition of freedom. In contrast to African Americans' understanding of freedom as an open ended ideal based on equality and autonomy, white southerners clung to the ante-bellum view that freedom meant mastery and hierarchy; it was a privilege, not a universal right, a judicial status, not a promise of equality."[80] They systematically ensured that Blacks remained a lesser order of citizen, enduring poverty, discrimination, seg-regation, and disenfranchisement for another century.

In the antebellum South, the power of white male property owners ensured their dominance over slaves, married women, and the remaining indigenous peoples. Likewise, non-property-owning whites had few rights, other than being a step above Blacks in the social hierarchy. The expansion of citizenship and voting rights for Blacks threatened the little influence poor whites had in Southern society, and they would join the great plantation owners and other rich whites in a campaign of violence to reestablish their dominance.

22

The Failure of Will

Reconstruction's End and Return to White Rule

The Constitutional amendments provoked Southerners to more violence. Paramilitary groups progressed from attacking sporadically to mounting a full-fledged insurgency against Reconstruction governments and Blacks. Organizations like the KKK and heavily armed "social clubs" operating under the aegis of Southern Democrat leadership led the campaign. Membership in the KKK specifically "was estimated at five hundred thousand."[1]

These shadowy organizations grew and became more aggressive in their attacks on Blacks, members of Reconstruction governments, and Southern Jews. After an investigation in 1870–71, Congress submitted a thirteen-volume report that "revealed to the country an almost incredible campaign of criminal violence by whites determined to punish black leaders, disrupt the Republican Party reestablish control over the black labor force, and restore white supremacy in every phase of southern life."[2]

Allegedly organized for self-defense against free Blacks, these groups named themselves White Leagues (Louisiana), White Liners or Rifle Clubs (Mississippi), or Red Shirts (South Carolina). They were, in fact, paramilitary organizations that functioned as armed auxiliaries of the Democratic Party in southern states in their drive "to 'redeem' the South from 'black and tan Negro-Carpetbag rule.'"[3] They "rode roughshod over the South, terrorizing newly freed slaves, their car-

"*THIS IS A WHITE MAN'S GOVERNMENT.*"

"We regard the Reconstruction Acts (so called) of Congress as usurpations, and unconstitutional, revolutionary, and void."—*Democratic Platform.*

FIG. 24. *This Is a White Man's Government.* "We regard the Reconstruction Acts (so called) of Congress as usurpations, and unconstitutional, revolutionary, and void."—Democratic platform. Drawing by Thomas Nast. From *Harper's Weekly*, September 1868. Courtesy of the Library of Congress, LC-DIG-ppmsca-71958.

petbagger allies, and anyone who dared to imagine a biracial democracy as the war's change."[4] Their fierce hatred and hostility set the stage for continued persecution and murder of Blacks and their supporters in the South over the next century. The KKK and other violent white supremacist groups offer "the most extensive example of homegrown terrorism in American history."[5]

Throughout his term in office, Johnson adopted arguments used by "critics of civil rights legislation and affirmative action. He appealed to fiscal conservatism, raised the specter of an immense federal bureaucracy trampling on citizens' rights, and insisted that self-help, not government handouts, was the path to individual advancement."[6] In 1868 Ulysses S. Grant was elected president and took office in 1869. Unlike Jonson Grant believed in freedom and equal rights: "For Grant, freedom and equal rights were matters of principle, not symbolism."[7] He ordered army commanders to enforce the Reconstruction Act, and when the KKK attempted to stop Blacks from voting, Grant persuaded Congress to pass the "Enforcement Act which made racist terrorism a federal offense."[8] He created the Justice Department to deal with crimes against federal law. In 1871 he pushed Congress to pass the Ku Klux Klan Act and sent in the army and agents from the Justice Department and Secret Service to enforce it.

Grant's efforts were successful. Thousands of Klansmen, Red Shirts, and White Leaguers were arrested. Hundreds were convicted and jailed while others were driven underground or disbanded their groups. The 1872 election was the first and last in which Blacks were nearly unencumbered in voting, until the passage of the 1964 Voting Rights Act.

But success triggered a political backlash that doomed Reconstruction. The seminal moment came in 1873, when Gen. Philip Sheridan, commanding federal forces in Louisiana, asked Grant for "'permission to arrest leaders of the White League and try them by courts-martial' for their attacks on Blacks and seizure of New Orleans's city hall."[9] Outrage erupted when Sheridan's request was leaked; even Northern papers condemned Grant and Sheridan in the harshest of terms.

Apart his from the passage of the Fifteenth Amendment and 1875 Civil Rights Act, Grant's efforts at Reconstruction failed. Much was due to the weariness or opposition of Northerners. Carl Schurz worried that the use of the military against the KKK in the South could set precedent to use it elsewhere as other Republicans embraced an understanding of social Darwinism that stood against government interference in what they called "the 'natural' workings of society, especially misguided efforts to uplift those at the bottom of the social order . . . and African Americans were consigned by nature to occupy the lowest rungs of the social ladder."[10]

Southerners knew that they were winning the political battle. They continued to apply pressure in Congress and the media to demonize supporters of Reconstruction and Blacks. They rigged elections, using terror to demoralize and drive from power anyone—Black or white—who supported Reconstruction. By 1870 every former Confederate state had been readmitted to the Union. But their Reconstruction governments were under siege by former Confederates and unsupported by Washington.

The Passage of the Fifteenth Amendment

Slavery was abolished, and Blacks were citizens, but, in many states, they still lacked the right to vote. Grant used his political capital to secure passage of the Fifteenth Amendment, which gave Black men that right. He remained proud of this throughout his life, saying, "A measure which makes at once four million people voter who were heretofore declared by the highest tribunal in the land to be not citizens of the United States nor eligible to become so . . . is indeed a measure of grander importance than any other act of the kind from the foundation of our free government to the present day."[11]

The Fifteenth Amendment gave Black men suffrage across the nation. Yet some Northern states voted against ratification.

FIG. 25. *Of Course, He Wants to Vote the Democratic Ticket.* B. Frost. From *Harper's Weekly*, October 1876. Tennessee State Library and Archives.

The old abolitionist Thaddeus Stevens favored the amendment because "it would assure every American male the right to vote. To Stevens, that would safeguard was the only way 'you and I and every other man can protect himself against ignorance and inhumanity.'"[12]

Unfortunately, Black civil and voting rights were abolished in most of the South before they had time to make a lasting change. The racist leaders of the Confederate rebellion returned to power as an indifferent Northern population along with Northern banking and industrial interests cooperated with Southerner landowners to profit at the expense of Blacks.

It is easy to blame Reconstruction's collapse on recalcitrant Southerners. But they could not have succeeded in reestablishing white man's rule without the help of the North. The economic crash of 1873 unleashed a surge of thinly veiled racism as economic considerations trumped justice, and Northerners moved away from Reconstruction to more profitable activities.

The Rollback and "Redemption"

As Southern extremism turned Reconstruction into a violent quagmire with no end, Northerners turned against efforts aiding Blacks. They lacked the political will, moral capacity, determination, or patience to continue to the political fight to complete the military victory.

Northern supporters of the civil and voting rights of Blacks failed to understand the social and political views of Southerners, most of whom believed "political equality automatically led to social equality, which in turn automatically led to race-mixing. It was inevitable and unthinkable. To a people brought up to believe that Negroes were genetically inferior—after all, that was why they were slaves—the mere hint of 'mongrelization' was appalling."[13] Most progressive Northerners could not comprehend Southern attitudes.

Rep. Thaddeus Stevens, one of the most effective leaders of Radical Republicanism and friends of Blacks, despaired that the rights of Blacks were being rolled back even as legislation was passed supporting them. According to A. J. Langguth, a few weeks before his death in 1868, a despair-filled Stevens lamented, "My life has been a failure. . . . I see little hope for the republic."[14] The old firebrand asked to be buried in a segregated cemetery for African American paupers so that "I might illustrate in death the principles which I advocated through a long life, Equality of man before his creator."[15] Stalwarts like Senator Ben Wade were not returned to office, and Edwin Stanton, Salmon Chase, and Charles Summer all died during Grant's second term.

Grant attempted to defeat the KKK by military means, but Congress was of little help. He faced increased opposition from conservative Republicans, who had little interest in fighting for rights for Blacks, and his efforts were complicated by the "financial panic which hit the stock market in 1873 [and] produced an economic downturn that soon worsened into a depression, which continued for the rest of the decade."[16] As a result, Republicans lost their House majority.

By "1870 Radical Republicanism as a coherent political movement was rapidly disintegrating."[17] During the early 1870s, many antislavery activists had either died or defected from the Republican party. Likewise, Black rights supporters "no longer felt at home in a party that catered to big business and lacked the resolve to protect black rights."[18] In 1872 some Republicans revolted against Grant and corruption in his administration. Calling themselves "Liberal Republicans," they supported Horace Greeley and united with Democrats to end Reconstruction. Their concern for the economy outweighed their support of Black rights: "Economic concerns now trumped race relations. . . . Henry Adams, who shared the views of his father, Charles Francis Adams, remarked that 'the day is at hand when corporations far greater than [the] Erie [Railroad] . . . will ultimately succeed in directing the government itself.'"[19]

Grant's best efforts to continue Reconstruction failed. Despite winning the battles to secure citizenship and suffrage for Blacks, racism remained heavily entrenched across the country. After the crash of 1873, economics trumped justice, and "racism increasingly asserted its hold on northern thought and behavior."[20] Many Northerners took the side of Southerners, condemning Blacks as lazy and slothful usurpers of white civilization.

Likewise, labor unrest in the North brought about by the economic depression made "many white northerners more sympathetic to white southern complaints about Reconstruction. Racial and class prejudices reinforced one another, as increasing numbers of middle-class northerners identified what they considered the illegitimate demands of workers and farmers in their own society with the alleged misconduct of the former slaves in the South."[21] The crash of 1873 hit Blacks in the South with a vengeance, leaving them vulnerable to former white masters who forced them into unfair and inequitable long-term employment contacts. Whites working for Reconstruction were marginalized and victimized by a campaign of propaganda and violence. Called "carpetbaggers" and "scalawags," they were accused of profiting from emancipation. However, most moved South to build schools, rebuild churches, and protect the civil rights of Blacks and poor whites or profit from their service.

Grant's support for Reconstruction was undercut by congressional Republicans and Attorney General Edwards Pierrepont, who tacitly approved of the brutalities committed by the KKK and other racist paramilitaries, as this became the primary means to further the political ends of Southern white supremacists. Violence conducted in broad daylight was "intended to demoralize black voters and fatally undermine the Republican Party. . . . [White supremacist paramilitaries] 'paraded at regular intervals through African American sections of small towns in the rural black majority areas, intimidating the residents and inciting racial confrontations."[22] After provoking racial incidents, they fanned out to find more Blacks and, in their rampages, killed hundreds of them.

In the 1876 election, white nationalist paramilitaries threatened Republican rallies. On Election Day they swarmed the polls to keep out Blacks and Republicans, even deploying cannons at poll entrances. They seized ballot boxes, either destroying them or counting the votes for Democrats, whose paramilitaries used "lawless and utterly undemocratic means . . . to secure the desired outcome, which was to win a lawful, democratic election."[23]

The pressure was too much for most Southern Republicans. They left the South or "crossed over to the Democratic fold; only a few stood by the helpless mass of Negroes."[24] Northerners did nothing to confront Confederate mythology; instead they worked against equal rights for Blacks and "embraced racism in the form of imperialism, Social Darwinism and eugenics."[25]

Adelbert Ames and the Battle for Mississippi

Mississippi's governor, Adelbert Ames, was one of the most able and honest men to hold elected office in the South. The son of a Maine sea captain, Ames graduated from West Point and fought in nearly every major engagement in the eastern theater of operations—a total of sixteen battles, including Antietam, Chancellorsville, and Gettysburg. He was promoted to brevet brigadier general of volunteers in May 1863 and awarded the Medal of Honor before he was thirty years old. He married Blanche Butler, daughter of Maj. Gen. Benjamin Butler, one of the leading proponents of emancipation.

While serving a brief tour of duty in the former Confederate states, he wrote his parents in 1866 describing how South Carolinians treated Blacks: "They think about as much as taking the life of a Freedman as I would that of a dog . . . I am in hopes that in the course of time the pious s people of this State will be convinced that it is according to our law it is, if not a sin, to kill what their term a—'nigger.'"[26]

Ames was promoted to brevet major general in 1867 to command the military district of Arkansas and Mississippi, where he battled for justice for Blacks. Under his direction during the election of 1868, Blacks were given suffrage, and in 1869 a new state constitution guaranteed Black civil rights. In 1870 Ames was elected one of Mississippi's senators. He gave a speech in which he sounded a warning that about the reality that Southerners would not give up: "Hatred to the Union, treason, cannot be whipped out of men. Defeats, disasters, and humiliations are not likely to generate love for our Government. . . . The country makes a sad and grievous mistake when it supposes that all the evils of slavery ended on that day of surrender at Appomattox Court House."[27]

The first man to appoint Blacks to state offices in Mississippi, as a senator "[Ames] combatted segregation in the U.S. Army and stood in the forefront of the campaign waged against the KKK. For his efforts on behalf of downtrodden blacks, Ames was to brave years of unremitting violence from the white power structure in the state."[28] He made a trip to observe the 1872 elections in Louisiana and was disgusted with what he saw. He wrote Blanche, "It causes two different conflicting emotions to rise up within me—the one to abandon a life of politics where such things find alone find place, and another, to buckle on my armor anew that I might better fight the battle of the poor and oppressed colored man, who is regarded by the old holder as an inferior, and not fit for the duties of citizenship."[29] He also noted the power of paramilitary groups: "The 'white liners' have gained their point—they have, by killing and wounding, so intimidated the poor Negroes that they can in all human probability prevail over them at the election. I shall try at once to get troops from the general government. Of course it will be a difficult thing to do."[30]

Elected governor in 1873, Ames requested federal troops "to restore peace and supervise the coming elections," but, due to the subterfuge of Attorney General Pierrepont, did not get them.[31] Grant told Pierrepont he must issue a proclamation for the use of federal troops if local forces could not keep order: "The proclamation must be issued; and if it is I shall instruct the commander of the forces to have no child's play."[32] But the attorney general changed Grant's words and instructed Ames, "The whole public are tired out with these autumnal outbreaks in the South . . . and the great majority are now ready to condemn any interference on the part of the government. . . . Preserve the peace by the forces in your own state."[33]

As a military commander, senator, and governor, Ames fully supported emancipation and Black suffrage. However, Pierrepont had betrayed both him and Grant. To prevent more bloodshed, he gave up the fight and negotiated peace with the White League. Ames, like Grant, realized that most of the country "had never been for Negro civil rights in the first place. Freedom, yes; but that didn't mean all the privileges of citizenship."[34] The deal resulted in Blacks being unable to vote, and Democrats returning to power. Ames wrote: "A revolution has taken place—by force of arms—and a race disenfranchised—they are to be returned to a condition of serfdom—an era of second slavery. . . . The nation should have acted but it was tired of the annual autumnal outbreaks in the South—See Grant and Pierrepont's letter to me. The political death of the Negro will forever from the weariness from such 'polit-

The Failure of Will

ical outbreaks.' You May think I exaggerate. Time will show how accurate my statements are."[35]

As the retired chief of the armies, Grant expected his orders to be obeyed, and to not be altered without his approval; he "labored mightily to force change on a resistant South." For his troubles he was abandoned by white Republicans—even the former radical abolitionist Carl Schurz, who accused Grant of "trampling on white civil liberties."[36]

The 1876 elections were a disaster for Blacks. Democrats lied that Blacks would be able to vote safely, but they were prevented from voting, and some were even murdered. The violence used by Mississippi Democrats and White Liners became the future of Southern elections. In Aberdeen Black voters were driven off by a "cannon, placed on the courthouse lawn, and a complement of more than a hundred armed and mounted soldiers, wearing makeshift uniforms under the command of a former Confederate General." The White Liners attacked just before the polls were to open, as Blacks waited in line to vote. "Several hundred colored men were knocked down with pistols and sticks, and they fled in wild disorder and confusion from the courthouse in every direction."[37]

Though Ames remained governor, when Democrats took control of the legislature, they drafted spurious articles of impeachment. Ames was threatened with assassination, and shots were fired at the governor's mansion. Finally, on March 28, a dejected Ames "made a deal with the Mississippi legislature: he would resign as governor if the impeachment charges against him were dropped."[38]

Grant told John R. Lynch, a mixed-race Black man and the only Republican to survive the Democratic election onslaught in Mississippi, "I should not have yielded. I believed at the time I was making a grave mistake. But as presented it was duty on one side, and party obligation on the other. Between the two I hesitated, but finally yielded to what I believed was my party obligation. If it was a mistake, it was one of the head and not the heart."[39]

Other states embraced Mississippi's strategy to "redeem" the South. The word choice was no accident; redemption was and is a key part of Christian theology. Southern opponents of Reconstruction used biblical language to describe themselves as "Redeemers," in a blasphemous perversion of Christianity's belief in Jesus the Christ as the redeemer of humanity.

Mississippi's plan worked to perfection and was followed throughout the South. Violence and intimidation, coupled with Northern apathy and the Republican party's abandonment of Lincoln's principles, ensured the collapse of the remaining Reconstruction governments. When Hayes "withdrew all Federal troops in 1877 . . . the Democrats had 'redeemed' the South, which remained solid for their part and for white supremacy." Grant told Lynch:

> The northern retreat from reconstruction would lead to Democrats recapturing power in the South as well as future mischief of a very serious nature. . . . It requires no prophet to foresee that the national government will soon be at a great disadvantage and that the results of the war of the rebellion will have been in large measure lost. . . . What you have passed through in the state of Mississippi is only the beginning of what will follow. I do not wish to create unnecessary alarm, nor be looked on as a prophet of evil, but it is impossible for me to close my eyes in the face things that are as plain to me as the noonday sun.[40]

After leaving Mississippi, the Ameses moved to the Midwest to supervise flour mills owned by his father-in-law, upon whose death in 1893 they inherited the Butler family homestead in Lowell, Massachusetts. However, the war was not yet over for them. E. Benjamin Andrews, the president of Brown University, published an article in *Scribner's Magazine* about Reconstruction that falsely linked Ames to financial mismanagement and fraud. A furious Ames responded with a lengthy letter:

The Failure of Will

There was a time when policy made it advisable for the white men of Mississippi to advance "corruption," "negro mobs," anything and everything but the real reason for their conduct. That time has long since passed. There is no good reason why the truth should not be stated in plain terms. It is that they are white men, Anglo-Saxons—a dominant race—educated to believe in negro slavery. To perpetuate their existing order of things they ventured everything and lost. An unjust and tyrannical power (from their standpoint) had filled their state with mourning, beggared them, freed their slaves and as a last insult and injury made the ex-slave a political equal. . . . Then they announced boldly that this is a white man's government and that the negro and ex-slave should forever form no part of it.[41]

Ames defended the Union men who went South:

The northern men in Mississippi as a class, were the brave youths who marched at your side for four years of bloody war. They were noble comrades, possessed by virtues equal to those of their associates; and were worthy sons of the fathers who founded this republic. They went to Mississippi under the same commendable impulses as had those who had populated this land from one ocean to another. They wanted to establish new homes. They took their whole capital and persuaded others to follow them. . . .

The offense of the Union soldier was in reconstruction at all—in giving the negro the ballot. Political equality for the negro meant to the white, negro supremacy. Physical resistance resulted. . . . The few Union soldiers and their allies in Mississippi soon fell before the Mississippians and their reinforcements from Louisiana and Alabama

"No negro domination"—"no force Bill"—this is the spirit of our modern Sermon on the Mount. The South is consistent.

The southern man has a motive in slandering the reconstructionists. He committed crime upon crime to prevent the political equality of the negro.[42]

Andrews admitted his mistake and corrected the article. But the incident demonstrated how false information, spread by political partisans, helped to disseminate the myths of the Noble South and the Lost Cause and glorify the Redeemers. Ames continued to set the record straight. In 1913, the fiftieth anniversary of the Battle of Gettysburg, he received a copy of John R. Lynch's memoirs, *The Facts of Reconstruction*, which were exceptionally accurate. He was happy to see it, but he wrote to Lynch, "He who was a slave is now at best a serf. His road to life, liberty, and the pursuit of happiness seems endless—thanks to the attitude of our Christian nation of this day and generation."[43]

Ames was demonized after his death at the age of 97 in 1933, the last of all of the Civil War generals. Many histories of Reconstruction depict him as a greedy carpetbagger. In 1954, in his book *Profiles in Courage,* John Fitzgerald Kennedy wrote about Mississippi senator Lucious Lamar, one of Ames's principal opponents, who "as a young congressman . . . was an avid secessionist who drafted Mississippi's ordinance of secession. Kennedy was especially critical of Senator and Governor Adelbert Ames."[44] Kennedy's words about Ames were slanderous.

> No state suffered more than Mississippi. Adelbert Ames, First Senator, then Governor, was a native of Maine, a son-in-law of the notorious "butcher of New Orleans," Ben Butler. . . . He was chosen Governor by a majority composed of freed slaves and radical Republicans sustained and nourished by Federal bayonets. . . . Vast areas of northern Mississippi lay in ruins. Taxes increased to a level fourteen times as high as normal in order to support the extravagance of the reconstruction government and heavy state and national war debts.[45]

Kennedy's depiction was a rehash of disproved allegations that achieved the status of history when Blacks had few rights and were still being lynched. Ames's daughter Blanche wrote Kennedy to correct the account and apologize, but he died without doing either.

The Day Freedom Died

The passage of the Fourteenth and Fifteenth Amendments, combined with the number of Blacks elected to office during the 1872 elections, provoked acts of terrorism. In Louisiana, following Democrat attempts to sabotage the vote by attacking polling sites and stealing ballot boxes, a federal court ruled in favor of Republican Reconstruction candidates. Following their election losses in 1872, Louisiana Democrats "established a shadow government and organized paramilitary unit known as the White League to intimidate and attack black and white Republicans."[46]

The White League was a well-funded and well trained paramilitary designed to threaten, kill, and force Blacks and Republicans out of power. In 1873 Democrats and the White League terrorists "initiated a paramilitary campaign to undermine the Republicans at the local level, within the parishes they controlled. Launching what was essentially an insurrection at the grass root, members of the state's White League attacked parish government buildings and assaulted Republican officials over the course of two years."[47] Ulysses Grant did what he could, but, due to Northern indifference, his best efforts were doomed. As a result, white supremacist violence increased, not only against individual Blacks, but against entire towns.

When the election of Republican William Pitt Kellogg was upheld by a federal judge, "the powder keg of Louisiana politics exploded in April 1873."[48] The White League executed an insurgency campaign that used race, religion, and ideology combined with violence to restore white rule. Many White Leaguers were former Confederate soldiers with combat experience who overwhelmed poorly trained and equipped Reconstruction militias and police forces. The league used the tactics of the successful insurgents who have followed them to drive more powerful opponents from power by wearing them down, using propaganda that resonated locally and in the state capitals of their opponents.

FIG. 26. *The Colfax Massacre, April 13, 1873.* From *Frank Leslie's Illustrated Newspaper*, May 5, 1873. Historic New Orleans Collection, Acc. No. 1995.10.4.

The well-organized and well-armed paramilitary terrorists of the White League were particularly brutal. Their worst massacre occurred on Easter Sunday 1873, when they attacked the village of Colfax—a nondescript hamlet about 350 miles northwest of New Orleans that sat on the grounds of a former plantation whose owner, William Calhoun, worked with the former slaves. The town, located in the newly established Grant Parish, was "composed of only a few hundred white and black voters."[49] The "parish totaled about 4,500, of whom about 2,400 were Negroes living on the lowlands along the east bank of the Red."[50] Between 1869 and 1873 it was the scene of numerous violent incidents. Following the 1872 elections, white Democrats were out for blood, and with Blacks serving in the militia they were primed to kill. In Grant Parish whites "retaliated by unleashing a reign of terror in rural districts, forcing blacks to flee to Colfax for protection."[51] Blacks fled to the courthouse—seeking protection from a white mob that murdered a Black farmer and his family on the outskirts of town—where a few armed Black militiamen and citizens deputized by the sheriff took shelter.

As the White League force assembled, one leader told his men what the day was about: "Boys, this is a struggle for white supremacy. . . . There are one hundred-sixty-five of us to go into Colfax this morning. God only knows who will come out. Those who do will probably be prosecuted for treason, and the punishment for treason is death."[52]

The force of 150 White League insurgents killed at least 71 and possibly up to 300 Blacks in Colfax, most of whom died while trying to surrender. Major Merrill of the Seventh Cavalry documented that most victims had either been shot execution-style, either in the back, the nape of the neck, or the back of the head. Others were butchered or burned alive by the terrorists. It was "the bloodiest peacetime massacre in nineteenth-century America."[53]

The perpetrators claimed, falsely, that they acted in self-defense, alleging that "armed Negroes, stirred up by white

Radical Republicans seized the courthouse, throwing out the rightful officeholders: the white judge and sheriff," and that Blacks said "their intention to kill all the white men, they boasted they would use white women to breed a new race."[54] After sending former army officers in the Secret Service to investigate, the U.S. attorney for Louisiana, J. R. Beckwith, sent an urgent telegram to the attorney general:

> The Democrats (White) of Grant Parish attempted to oust the incumbent parish officers by force and failed, the sheriff protecting the officers with a colored posse. Several days afterward recruits from other parishes, to the number of 300, came to the assistance of the assailants, when they demanded the surrender of the colored people. This was refused. An attack was made, and the Negroes were driven into the courthouse. The courthouse was fired, and the Negroes slaughtered as they left the burning building, after resistance ceased. Sixty-five Negroes terribly mutilated were found dead near the ruins of the courthouse. Thirty, known to have been taken prisoners, are said to have been shot after the surrender, and thrown into the river. Two of the assailants were wounded. The slaughter is greater than the riot of 1866 in this city. Will send report by mail.[55]

Federal marshals arrested nine white men for participating in the massacre. White-majority juries, fearing reprisal by White Leaguers, convicted only three for "violating the Enforcement Act of 1871."[56] Despite overwhelming evidence no murder charges were filed. White supremacists, enraged by the lesser convictions, employed the best lawyers, with unlimited financial backing. Assisted by Supreme Court associate justice Joseph Bradley, who had a long racist past of his own, they appealed the convictions to the Supreme Court, where the. appeal of the men convicted at Colfax was upheld, in *United States v. Cruickshank.* The ruling led to a "narrowing of Federal law enforcement authority," and its subsequent limits on federal law enforcement were "milestones on the road to a 'solid' Democratic South."[57]

Perverse in its interpretation of constitutional rights and protections, in *United States v. Cruickshank* the court ruled in favor of terrorists and declared that "the right of the black victims at Colfax to assemble hand not been guaranteed because they were neither petitioning Congress nor protesting a federal law. Assembling for any other cause was not protected."[58] The ruling endorsed violence against Blacks and made it "impossible for the federal government to prosecute crimes against blacks unless they were perpetrated by a state and unless it could prove a racial motive unequivocally."[59]

Following the *United States v. Cruickshank* ruling, Northern politicians and newspapermen who initially denounced the massacre reversed themselves and, cowardly, ran from their previously held positions. A Republican wrote: "The truth is, our people are tired out with this worn cry of 'Southern outrages.' . . . Hard times and heavy taxes make them wish the 'nigger,' the 'everlasting nigger,' were in hell or Africa."[60]

Following the court's ruling, whites in Grant Parish conducted brutal reprisals against Blacks, leading to many murders and lynchings that were not prosecuted because of fears of reprisal. Governor Kellogg wrote Attorney General Williams blaming the violence on Justice Bradley. He stated that Bradley "was regarded as establishing the principle that hereafter no white man could be punished for killing a negro, and as virtually wiping the Ku Klux laws of the statute books" and warned that if the army left the South, Reconstruction governments would fall: "If Louisiana goes . . . Mississippi will inevitably follow and, that end attained, all the results of the war so far as the colored people are concerned will be neutralized, all the reconstruction acts of Congress will be of no more value than so much waste paper and the colored people, though free in name, will be practically remitted back to servitude."[61] Governor Kellogg could not have been more correct.

White newspapers in Louisiana used Colfax as grist for the 1874 election. The *Shreveport Times* wrote:

There has been some red-handed work done in the parish that was necessary, but evidently, but evidently has been done by cool, determined, and just men, who knew just how far to go, and we have no doubt if the same kind of work is necessary it will be done.

We say again that we fully, cordially, approve what the white men of Grant Rapides did at Colfax; the white man who does not is a creature so base that he shakes the worst class of his species. We say, again, we are going to carry the elections in this State next fall.[62]

The terrorists were applauded in the South, and their leader, Christopher Columbus Nash, was reappointed to office. Blacks were reminded every day of what they had lost. On April 13, 1921, the terrorists who attacked Colfax were honored with a monument in the village cemetery calling them "heroes . . . who fell in the Colfax Riot fighting for White Supremacy. In 1951 the Louisiana Department of Commerce and Industry dedicated a marker outside the Courthouse which read: 'On the site occurred the Colfax Riot in which three White men and 150 Negroes were slain, this event on April 13, 1873 marked the end of Carpetbag misrule in the South.'"[63] That marker still stands; no other commemorates the victims.

Other massacres followed across the South. In August 1874 a White League detachment attacked Republican office holders in Coushatta, the parish seat of Red River Parish, "forced six white Republicans to resign their office on pain of death—and then brutally murdered them after they had resigned."[64] The Coushatta massacre in particular was a watershed: for the first time the White League targeted whites and only killed Blacks who witnessed the executions.

In 1875 President Grant addressed Congress to discuss the Colfax massacre and the court decisions: "Fierce denunciations ring through the country about office-holding and election matters in Louisiana . . . while every one of the Colfax miscreants goes unwhipped of justice, and no way can be found

in this boasted land of civilization and Christianity to punish the perpetrators of this bloody and monstrous crime."[65]
Grant, who wanted to help Blacks attain the full measure of
freedom, was powerless as Congress and the courts took the
side of Southern insurgents.

The Failure to Win the Peace

The Thirteenth Amendment, which made emancipation the
law and overturned the *Dred Scott* decision; the Fourteenth,
which made Blacks citizens; and the Fifteenth, which gave
Black men suffrage, were revolutionary documents. Had the
federal government used the full force of law to destroy the
white nationalist paramilitaries of the KKK, the White League,
the Red Shirts and White Liners, the results of Reconstruction might have been completely different.

By the end of Reconstruction, Black rights had been systematically rolled back, ensuring that the "resurrected South
would look a great deal like the Old South, a restored regime
of white supremacy patriarchy, and states' rights. This political and cultural principles became holy tenants, dissent from
which threatened redemption."[66] The newly installed white
governments, led by Democrats, passed legislation against
Blacks, used the rulings of federal courts to void their rights,
and condoned violence committed against them by the KKK
and paramilitaries.

By 1876 whites in the North, including most Republicans,
were weary of Reconstruction. Most Northern Democrats had
opposed it from the first, but the loss of Republican support—
even that of long-time abolitionists—meant that, once Grant
left office, Reconstruction was doomed. Grant's successor,
President Rutherford Hayes, put an end to Reconstruction in
1877 as part of a deal with Southern Democrats to elect him in
the 1876 election over New York Democratic governor Samuel Tilden. All federal troops assigned to enforce Reconstruction were withdrawn.

But some former Confederates, in their own way, fought

for the rights of Blacks, including men like former generals James Longstreet and, to a lesser extent, Wade Hampton. The two men could have not been more dissimilar. Hampton was a racist and one of the leading slaveholders in the South. Longstreet came from modest means and had been a soldier all of his adult life. Longstreet recanted his Confederate views and received a pardon by Congress, after which he took up a dangerous life fighting for Reconstruction and opposing the Lost Cause. Hampton became the Redeemer governor of South Carolina. Eventually, both were vilified by the press and Southern political opponents. The attacks on Longstreet were particularly vicious, and, in the myth of the Lost Cause, he is painted as even worse than Judas Iscariot. Despite his racism Hampton made attempts to enforce laws that provided protections and equality for Blacks. Thus, he, too, became a traitor to the Lost Cause cult.

Hampton was a complicated and often contradictory man. He was a wealthy major slaveholder and white supremacist who fought the entire war to keep the institution of slavery in place. When the war began, he used his money to finance, recruit, and lead a regiment-sized combined arms unit called the Hampton Legion. He fought well, was wounded several times, and ended up leading the Army of Northern Virginia's Cavalry Corps before surrendering at Appomattox.

After being pardoned by Johnson, Hampton returned home penniless, but to South Carolinians he represented the best of manhood and leadership and was elected as South Carolina's first post-Reconstruction governor. However, once in office he earned the ire of many supporters. He received generous assistance from the Red Shirts in rigging the election by suppressing the Black vote, when they rode into towns ahead of him to bully the opposition. Although Hampton benefited from their tactics, he did not condone their actions, criticizing them in private while remaining silent in public.

During the campaign he denigrated the Reconstruction government, carpetbaggers, and scalawags. But he also "attacked the South's imposition of so called 'black codes' and pledged to 'render to the whole people of this state equal and impartial justice."[67] But, despite his promise, "many of his supporters, inspired by the example of Mississippi, sought to neutralize the considerable black voting majority."[68] Led by Martin Gary and backed by young firebrands such as Benjamine Tillman, the Red Shirts embarked on a bloody campaign against Blacks and white Republicans.

Hampton removed Black Republicans from office and replaced them with Red Shirt leaders while enacting other discriminatory measures. But Hampton moderated his politics, angering supporters. He appointed Blacks to patronage offices and maintained a regiment of Black state militia in Charleston. The sight of Blacks serving in Charleston, the very place South Carolinians had begun the rebellion against the Union, evoked strident opposition by Hampton's former white supremacist allies.

Despite his past and racist views, Hampton saw himself as a father figure to South Carolinians, committed to the upholding the law and "promoting the political rights to which freedmen were entitled to under law, and he consistently strove to protect those rights."[69] This made him anathema to South Carolina Democrats, including Benjamine Tillman. Tillman had not served in the war and treated the former slaves working his land as remorselessly as any antebellum slave master. He raised a company of Red Shirts known as the Sweetwater Sabre Club and built his base by opposing moderate Democrats, especially Hampton.

Despite his racist views, Hampton was able to bridge gaps between some Blacks and whites. He did not openly oppose anyone who helped him into office, including Blacks. Following two terms as governor, he served two unremarkable terms in the U.S. Senate and returned to South Carolina politically isolated. Tillman refused to reappoint him to the Senate, and he was nearly destitute. President Grover Cleveland appointed him as commissioner of U.S. railroads in 1892, which saved him from disaster. He returned to Washington and served until Republican William McKinley replaced him with the now-despised James Longstreet.

When Hampton returned to Columbia, he lived in a small home, not far from his children. In 1898 it burned to the ground in a fire that consumed most of his possessions, including papers and documents that would have had much value to historians, and he moved to an outlying shanty on the property. "Touched by his plight, his neighbors pooled what funds they could spare to erect a new and larger house in the city limits"; Hampton was touched by their generosity, "but he could not bring himself to accept such a grand and costly gift. He relented only when his benefactors 'flanked him' by presenting it [to his daughter] Daisy." He died on April 11, 1902, at the age of eighty-four. His last words were a benediction to the people of his state: "God bless all my people, Black and white."[70] Hampton's legacy is a complex one. A racist and a rebel, at times he appeared remorseful and repentant, and at other times allowed his baser nature to influence his decisions.

Benjamine Tillman was a vicious political animal, ruthless and radically determined to ensure that Blacks were deprived of every right imaginable, working with the Red Shirts to murder and terrorize them. After Tillman was elected governor of South Carolina in 1890, he dismantled Hampton's reforms that allowed Blacks political patronage appointments and then set out to deprive them of their civil rights. In 1895 he led "a successful effort to rewrite the South Carolina constitution in such a way as to virtually disenfranchise every black resident of the state."[71]

Tillman used his notoriety to get elected to the South Carolina legislature, the governorship, and the U.S. Senate, where he served four terms. As governor he used his office to systematically persecute Blacks and deprive them of civil liberties, and he bragged about participating in massacres in which Blacks were killed. The first of these occurred in the town of Hamburg, just across the river from Augusta, Georgia. Hamburg was a majority-Black town on the border of Edgefield County, which also had a Black majority. However, influential former slave owners and Confederate officers promoted racist fears among whites. They helped Democrats win an election where they were outnumbered by Blacks and recruited men to serve in the Red Shirts and other paramilitary terrorist groups.

Former Confederate general Martin W. Gary, for instance, led the Edgefield Marauders. Gary refused to surrender at Appomattox, and he and two hundred soldiers escorted Jefferson Davis as he fled Richmond. Gary disrupted Republican meetings, using violence, during the 1876 election campaign. On July 4 in Hamburg, Red Shirts masquerading as planters disrupted the local militia as it drilled in the street. All of the militiamen, who were Black, realizing they were outnumbered and knowing that if they went to the courthouse they would be ambushed and slaughtered by Red Shirts who outnumbered them and occupied good ground, withdrew from the town. On July 8 they moved to their armory and barricaded themselves in. They refused the demands of "General" Matthew Butler to surrender, and Butler brought up another two companies of Red Shirts from Augusta. Just after dark the Red Shirts opened fire. The militia had only few rounds per man, so they held their fire. When they did fire they killed one of the Red Shirts. Butler sent people to Augusta to get gunpowder and a cannon.

Militiamen heard Butler's orders and evacuated the armory to save themselves. A half hour later the Red Shirts opened fire with the cannon. Realizing the militia had fled, they searched the town, pursuing and killing a militiaman named Moses Parks and the town marshal, Jim Cook. Butler was particularly pleased with this, as Cook had once fined him five dollars. He searched Cook's body for money and, finding none, took the dead man's watch.[72] One Red Shirt cut out Cook's tongue. Meanwhile, Tillman's men rounded up twenty-seven militiamen and led them to a circle of armed Red Shirts. Five were chosen for death and led away to the riverbank. Four were killed, but one, Pompey Curry, was only hit below the knee and crawled into bushes, where he feigned death. Tillman and his men also murdered South Carolina state legislator Simon Coker, who was executed as he prayed. Survivors never forgot what happened:

> What the colored people of Hamburg remembered most were the words they heard over and over from the white men as they shaft and killed and cavorted through the night.
>
> By God, we've killed a sufficient number to prevent nigger rule any longer in Aiken County.
>
> We've put a quietus on nigger rule in Aiken County for all time to come.
>
> By God, we'll carry South Carolina about the time we kill four or five hundred more, we will scare the rest.
>
> This is the beginning of the redemption of South Carolina.[73]

Tillman's company also participated in the destruction the town of Ellenton in September. The attack destroyed a fusion ticket of moderate Republicans and Democrats and returned South Carolina to Democrat control. Northerners turned their backs. It was a foretaste of worse to come throughout the South. After the election Black Republican officials, even those who won by significant majorities, were removed from office, including the attorney general. The legislature then appointed Matthew Butler, a key leader of the Hamburg massacre, as South Carolina's next senator. On June 9 it revoked Hamburg's charter, effectively ending Black rule there and throughout the state.[74]

During the 1890s Democrats throughout the South campaigned on the massacres committed to reestablish the white man's rule.

> Ben Tillman rode to the State House and later to four terms in the U.S. Senate recounting the redemption and its fragile legacy. . . . [In his campaigns he] openly detailed his participation in the violence at Hamburg in Edgefield County in July

The Failure of Will

FIG. 27. Cartoon, *Decrying the Hamburg Massacre of July 1876.*
Thomas Nast. *Harper's Weekly,* August 1873.

1876 to suppress the black and white Republican vote in state-wide elections. "The leading white men of Edgefield," Tillman related, had decided to "seize the first opportunity that the Negroes might offer them to provoke a riot and teach the Negroes a lesson" by "having the whites demonstrate their superiority by killing as many of them as was justifiable." By keeping the memory of Redemption alive, Tillman kept the state of crisis vivid for the white South.[75]

At his inauguration Tillman boasted, "I, as the exponent and leader of the revolution which brought about the change, am here to take the solemn oath of office. . . . The triumph of democracy and white supremacy over mongrelism and anarchy, of civilization over barbarism, has been most complete."[76] During his governorship he and Democrats rolled back Black rights and supported the epidemic of lynching. Tillman vilified Hampton, whose friends abandoned him to support Tillman, who abolished the few things Hampton—whom Tillman called "an elitist who scorned his lower-class constituents"—

had done to help Blacks.[77] Senator Tillman also bragged about the return of South Carolina to White rule in Senate:

> In my State there were 135,000 negro voters, or negroes of voting age, and some 90,000 or 95,000 white voters. . . . Now, I want to ask you, with a free vote and a fair count, how are you going to beat 135,000 by 95,000? How are you going to do it? You had set us an impossible task.
>
> We did not disfranchise the negroes until 1895. Then we had a constitutional convention convened which took the matter up calmly, deliberately, and avowedly with the purpose of disfranchising as many of them as we could under the fourteenth and fifteenth amendments . . . As to his "rights"—I will not discuss them now. We of the South have never recognized the right of the negro to govern white men, and we never will. . . . I would to God the last one of them was in Africa and that none of them had ever been brought to our shores.[78]

Tillman was the most influential political leader in South Carolina since John C. Calhoun. He made his mark on generations of South Carolinian politicians, including Sen. Strom Thurmond. Another Southerner, the future president Lyndon Johnson would say, "He might have been president. I'd like to sit down with him and ask how it was to throw it away for the sake of hating."[79]

As for Hamburg, it died a lingering death. Reduced to a few hundred poor Blacks, it was frequently vandalized by people from Augusta, even as a new town named North Augusta was established ten miles up the river, becoming a recreation and golfing resort for well-off Northerners as well as Southerners. "In 1929 two huge floods swept down the Savannah River, and the last physical remains were erased from the map."[80] Later a dam named the Strom Thurmond Dam put an end to the flooding, and in 1998 a golf course and a row of executive homes were built where Hamburg once stood.

But Tillman did not represent all former Confederates. John Singleton Mosby, the former commander of the famous cavalry unit Mosby's Raiders, never recanted his family's slave owning history and remained proud of his service as an officer in the Confederate Army. However, he told the truth, admitting that slavery was the cause of war. He proudly joined the Republican Party, become a friend of Ulysses Grant, supporting Reconstruction and Black rights. He was one of the most perplexing, yet maybe the most honest, of former Confederates.

The Battle of Liberty Place

The Louisiana White League got another chance to crush the rights of Blacks using terrorist methods. Prior to the 1874 elections, their forces, supported by the Democratic Party, churches, and newspapers, announced their goal, as expressed in this editorial, published in the *Franklin Enterprise*:

> We own the soil of Louisiana, by virtue of our endeavor, as a heritage of our ancestors, and it is ours, and ours alone. Science, literature, history, art, civilization, and law belong to us, and not to the negroes. They have no record but barbarism and idolatry, nothing since the war of that error, incapacity, beastliness, voudouism, and crime. Their right to vote is but the result of the war, their exercise of it a monstrous imposition upon us for that ill-advised rebellion. Therefore we are banding together in a White League army, drawn up only for defensive, exasperated by continual wrong, but acting under Christian and high-principled leaders, and determined to defeat these negroes in their infamous design of depriving us of all we hold sacred and precious on the soil of our nativity or adoption, or perish in the attempt.[81]

Robert E. Lee's "Old War Horse" James Longstreet, became a Republican, supported Reconstruction, and was appointed by President Grant to be New Orleans's surveyor of customs in 1869. The governor also made him head of the largely Black state militia. Former Confederate general Harvey Hill typified the outrage of many regarding Longstreet. As he wrote in an editorial: "Our scalawag is the local leper of the community.

Unlike the carpet bagger [a Northerner], [Longstreet] is a native, which is so much the worse."[82]

Longstreet's "chief antagonists were such diehards as Jubal Early, Nelson Pendleton, and John B. Gordon. Especially through the pages of a monthly publication, *Southern Historical Society Papers*, Longstreet was blasted as a turncoat, unfaithful to the Confederate cause, and the major factor in Lee's defeat at Gettysburg, 'the climactic struggle for independence.'"[83]

On September 24, 1873, in an attack that left him wounded, Longstreet led an integrated force of about 3,500 New Orleans police officers and militia against 8,400 White Leaguers advancing on the city's federal buildings. His men were defeated, and most of the police and militia fled or were captured. 38 were killed and 79 wounded. The White Leagues held the city hall; only the timely deployment of federal troops prevented the coup attempt from succeeding. Called "the Battle for Liberty Place," the assault energized other militant groups. Longstreet was vilified by many Southern politicians, since he "led mostly black troops against former Confederate soldiers, which to white Southerners was another indication of his betrayal of the cause."[84] To Confederate-leaning historians "the turncoat Longstreet appeared as the cause of every defeat."[85]

Renamed "Liberty Place" in 1882, New Orleans's city hall became a pilgrimage site for white supremacists. In 1891 Democrat leaders in the city erected a monument at the foot of Canal Street honoring sixteen White Leaguers killed in the attack. They referred to the monument as "the most overt monument to white supremacy in the United States."[86] An inscription was added in 1932, claiming the battle was fought for the "overthrow of carpetbag government," and that Yankees had "recognized white supremacy in the South and gave us our state." Following the Voting Rights Act of 1964, city leaders used the centennial of the event to cement over the previous words and put a countermarker next to the monument reading, "Although the 'Battle of Liberty Place' and this monument are important parts of New Orleans history, the sentiments in favor of white supremacy expressed thereon are contrary to the philosophy and beliefs of present-day New Orleans." It was moved to a less conspicuous place in 1993. In September 2015 the "Vieux Carre Commission, which controls aesthetics in the historic French Quarter, voted 5–1 to remove the obelisk." Supported by Mayor Mitch Landrieu, the City Council voted to remove it.[87]

Court Battles and Jim Crow

The Supreme Court, Congress, a series of presidents, and state governments systematically rolled back the rights of Blacks after Reconstruction, with the courts especially settng the precedent for decades of injustice. In 1883 "the Civil Rights Act of 1875, outlawing discrimination against Negroes using public facilities, was nullified by the Supreme Court, which said: 'individual invasion of individual rights is not the subject-matter of the amendment.' The Fourteenth Amendment, it said, was aimed at state action only.'"[88]

Associate Justice Joseph Bradley again acted to overturn a law that he despised on racist principle. When Grant signed it in 1875, Bradley wrote, "To deprive white people of the right of choosing their own company would be to introduce another kind of slavery. . . . It can never be endured that the white shall be compelled to lodge and eat and sit with the Negro. . . . The antipathy of race cannot be crushed and annihilated by legal enactment." In his opinion overturning it, Bradley wrote that it made Blacks a "special favorite of laws," ignoring that in most of the country Blacks faced discrimination, segregation, political disenfranchisement, systematized violence, murder and lynching.[89]

The actions of the court and the alliances between Northern corporations and Southern landowners led to even more discrimination and disenfranchisement for Blacks: "From the 1880s onward, the post-Reconstruction white governments grew unwilling to rely just on intimidation at the ballot box and themselves in power, and turned instead to systematic legal disenfranchisement."[90] After *United States v. Cruickshank* Southern Blacks attempted to vote despite intense opposition from bands of white thugs. With white Democrats in charge of local government and "in control of the state and local vote-counting apparatus, resistance to black voting increasingly took the form of fraud as well as overt violence and intimidation. Men of color who cast Republican votes often found later that they had been counted for the party of white supremacy."[91]

In 1896 the Supreme Court in *Plessy v. Ferguson* upheld the black codes and Jim Crow laws. *Plessy* established the "separate but equal" doctrine and ushered in an era of de jure segregation in almost all arenas of life, including education, transportation, entertainment, and health care. The limited privileges left to Blacks were erased by a stroke of the judicial pen. The case involved a challenge made by an organization of Blacks and Creoles to the Separate Car Act of 1890 for which they recruited Homer Plessy, who was seven-eighths white. On July 7, 1892, Plessy bought a first-class ticket and boarded a whites-only car on the Louisiana Railroad, which opposed the law. The railroad had been informed he would be on the train, and the committee that recruited Plessy placed a private detective aboard to make the arrest in order to use the case to overturn the law. After the detective ordered Plessy to move to the Blacks-only car, Plessy refused and was arrested. He was convicted in the Orleans Parish Court and ordered to pay $25, but appealed to the Louisiana Supreme Court, which denied the appeal, using a Pennsylvania ruling in a similar case as precedent: "To assert separateness is not to declare inferiority. . . . It is simply to say that following the order of Divine Providence, human authority ought not to compel these widely separated races to intermix."[92]

In their appeal to the U.S. Supreme Court, Plessy's lawyers argued that the law effectively stigmatized Blacks and made them second-class citizens, thus violating the Equal Protection Clause. In 1896 the justices rejected their arguments and ruled in a 7–1 decision that the Constitution only guaranteed people's political rights, and that in the social arena Blacks could not interact with whites, due to their racial inferiority. Justice Harley Billings Brown wrote for the majority: "We consider the underlying fallacy of the plaintiff's argument to consist in the assumption that the enforced separation of the two races stamps the colored race with a badge of inferiority. If this be so, it is not by reason of anything found in the act, but solely because the colored race chooses to put that construction on it."[93]

Not all of the justices agreed with the ruling. Associate Justice John Harlan, a former slaveholder, was the most consistent defender of the rights included in the Thirteenth, Fourteenth, and Fifteenth Amendments. Harlan was born into a prominent slave-owning Kentucky family. A Unionist Democrat, he raised a regiment of Kentucky Infantry for the Union cause and became Kentucky's attorney general in 1863, but was voted out of office in 1867, after which he became the leader of Kentucky's Republican Party. In 1877 Rutherford B. Hayes nominated him to the Supreme Court, where he proved to be a reliable voice for strong national government civil rights. He believed that the Thirteenth, Fourteenth, and Fifteenth Amendments had changed the relationship between the federal government and the states in a positive way regarding the civil rights of all citizens. He had a strong commitment to the economically disadvantaged and those discriminated against by race, social status, or religion.

Harlen dissented from the court's decision to overturn the Civil Rights Act of 1875 and 1896 in *Plessy v. Ferguson.* In the case of the Civil Rights Act, ruling in 1883 Harlan insisted "our Constitution is color blind" and wrote a strongly worded dissent:[94]

> The destinies of two races, in this country are indissolubly linked together, and the interests of both require that the common government of all should not permit the seeds of race hate to be planted under the sanction of law. What can more certainly arouse race hate, what more certainly create and perpetuate a

FIG. 28. Justice John Harlan, the "Great Dissenter." Photo by Mathew Brady or Levin Handy. Courtesy of the Library of Congress, Brady-Handy Collection, LC-BH832-1038 [P&P].

feeling of distrust between these races, than state enactments, which, in fact, proceed on the ground that colored citizens are so inferior and degraded that they cannot be allowed to sit in public coaches occupied by white citizens? That, as all will admit, is the real meaning of such legislation as was enacted in Louisiana.[95]

Although eloquent and correct, Harlan's argument regarding the Civil Rights Act was not sufficient to turn the tide as the court backed the segregation laws. Harlan "was fighting a force greater than the logic of justice; the mood of the Court reflected a new coalition of northern industrialists and southern businessmen-planters."[96] In 1896 the "separate but equal" measures approved by the court majority in *Plessy v. Ferguson* led to the widespread passage of Jim Crow laws throughout the country. The *Plessy* decision was a watershed in that it "legitimatized the contemptuous attitudes of whites. . . . Moreover, it certified that any charade of equal treatment for African Americans was not just acceptable and practical at the dawn of the twentieth century, but morally and legally legitimate in the highest venue of white society."[97]

In *Plessy v. Ferguson*, only Justice Harlan dissented. In his dissent in *Plessy* in 1896, Harlan laid waste to the strongest arguments of the White Redeemers who had taken power throughout the South, and their Northern allies:

> In respect of civil rights, common to all citizens, the constitution of the United States does not, I think, permit any public authority to know the race of those entitled to be protected in the enjoyment of such rights. Every true man has pride of race, and under appropriate circumstances, when the rights of others, his equals before the law, are not to be affected, it is his privilege to express such pride and to take such action based upon it as to him seems proper. But I deny that any legislative body or judicial tribunal may have regard to the race of citizens when the civil rights of those citizens are involved. . . .

The thirteenth amendment does not permit the withholding or the deprivation of any right necessarily inhering in freedom. It not only struck down the institution of slavery as previously existing in the United States but it prevents the imposition of any burdens or disabilities that constitute badges of slavery or servitude. It decreed universal civil freedom in this country. . . . But, that amendment having been found inadequate to the protection of the rights of those who had been in slavery, it was followed by the fourteenth amendment, which added greatly to the dignity and glory of American citizenship, and to the security of personal liberty, by declaring that "all persons born or naturalized in the United States, and subject to the jurisdiction thereof, are citizens of the United States and of the state wherein they reside," and that "no state shall make or enforce any law which shall abridge the privileges or immunities of citizens of the United States; nor shall any state deprive any person of life, liberty or property without due process of law, nor deny to any person within its jurisdiction the equal protection of the laws." These two amendments, if enforced according to their true intent and meaning, will protect all the civil rights that pertain to freedom and citizenship. Finally, and to the end that no citizen should be denied, on account of his race, the privilege of participating in the political control of his country, it was declared by the fifteenth amendment that "the right of citizens of the United States to vote shall not be denied or abridged by the United States or by any state on account of race, color or previous condition of servitude."

These notable additions to the fundamental law were welcomed by the friends of liberty throughout the world. They removed the race line from our governmental systems. They had . . . a common purpose, namely, to secure "to a race recently emancipated, a race that through many generations have been held in slavery all the civil rights that the superior race enjoy." They declared, in legal effect, this court has further said, "that the law in the states shall be the same for the black as for the white; that all persons, whether colored or white, shall stand equal before the laws of the states; and in regard to the colored race, for whose protection the amendment was primarily designed, that no discrimination shall be made against them by law because of their color." . . .

It was said in argument that the statute of Louisiana does not discriminate against either race, but prescribes a rule applicable alike to white and colored citizens . . . Every one knows that the statute in question had its origin in the purpose, not so much to exclude white persons from railroad cars occupied by blacks, as to exclude colored people from coaches occupied by or assigned to white persons . . . The fundamental objection, therefore, to the statute, is that it interferes with the personal freedom of citizens. . . .

It is one thing for railroad carriers to furnish, or to be required by law to furnish, equal accommodations for all whom they are under a legal duty to carry. It is quite another thing for government to forbid citizens of the white and black races from traveling in the same public conveyance. . . . Further, if this statute of Louisiana is consistent with the personal liberty of citizens, why may not the state require the separation in railroad coaches of native and naturalized citizens of the United States or of Protestants and Roman Catholics? . . .

The white race deems itself to be the dominant race in this country . . . But in view of the constitution, in the eye of the law, there is in this country no superior, dominant, ruling class of citizens. There is no caste here. Our constitution is color-blind, and neither knows nor tolerates classes among citizens. In respect of civil rights, all citizens are equal before the law. The humblest is the peer of the most powerful. The law regards man as man, and takes no account of his surroundings or of his color when his civil rights as guaranteed by the supreme law of the land are involved. . . .

In my opinion, the judgment this day rendered will, in time, prove to be quite as pernicious as the decision made by this tribunal in the *Dred Scott* case.[98]

The permission of government leaders and courts, explicit or implicit, has often served to unleash the worst in human behavior. In this case whites understood that anything they did to harm Blacks, from administrative actions to lynching, would receive no penalty. The *Plessy v. Ferguson* ruling came on the heels of decades of massacres, lynchings, and other discriminatory court rulings; after the decision these crimes continued without letup.

> Whites reigned supreme. Within about three decades of Lee's surrender, angry and alienated Southern whites who had lost a war had successfully used terror and political inflexibility . . . to create a postbellum world of American apartheid. . . . Lynchings, church burnings, and the denial of access to equal education and to the ballot box were the order of the decades. A succession of largely unmemorable presidents served after Grant; none successfully marshaled the power of the office to fight the Northern acquiescence to the South's imposition of Jim Crow.[99]

Jim Crow took nearly a century to reverse and "only began to disappear with *Brown v. Board of Education* in 1954 and the Civil Rights and Voting Rights Acts of 1964 and 1965."[100]

Southern state governments employed a strategy of subterfuge to suppress the Black vote and dodge the Fifteenth Amendment. Along with the intimidation of armed white supremacists, the states complicated voter registration and voting procedures; Redeemer governments used poll taxes, which required people to pay in order to vote, and literacy tests, which mandated that prospective voters "'interpret' a section of the state constitution, and enacted standards which few blacks could fulfill, such as limiting registration to those whose grandfathers had voted." Few Blacks could meet these standards, as their grandfathers were slaves and thus ineligible to vote. The laws were so devious that "when a journalist asked an Alabama lawmaker could pass his state's understanding test, the legislator replied that would depend on entirely

The Failure of Will

on which way he was going to vote."[101] These court decisions and legislation strengthened racism and discrimination, "effectively excluding blacks from public places, from the right to votes, from good public education, and so forth."[102]

After *Plessy v. Ferguson,* Southern legislators, unencumbered by federal interference, passed "state laws mandating racial segregation in every aspect of life, from schools to hospitals, waiting rooms to toilets, drinking fountains to cemeteries. . . . Segregation was part of a complex system of white domination, in which each component—disenfranchisement, unequal economic status, inferior education—reinforced the others."[103] For decades future courts cited *Plessy v. Ferguson* and *United States v. Cruickshank* as precedent to deny Blacks their rights. In 1954 the Supreme Court overturned *Plessy* and "separate but equal" Jim Crow laws in *Brown v. Board of Education,* ruling that separate schools were "inherently unequal." The reaction, especially in Mississippi, was one of shock, disbelief, and anger: "A Mississippi judge bemoaned 'black Monday' and across the South 'Citizen's Councils' sprung up to fight the ruling."[104]

Mississippi led the way in disenfranchising Black voters and purged most Blacks from voter rolls. The intent of the Mississippi Constitutional Conventions of 1889–1990 was to negate the Fifteenth Amendment and to scrap the 1869 Constitution to ensure the supremacy of the white minority. In 1895 the state legislature passed a measure that would "technically applied to everybody but actually eliminated the Negro without touching the white."[105] In 1896 the Supreme Court of Mississippi ruled accordingly in *Ratliff v. Beale.*

> It is in the highest degree improbable that there was not a consistent, controlling directing purpose governing the convention by which these schemes were elaborated and fixed in the constitution. . . . By reason of its previous condition of servitude and dependence, this race had acquired or accentuated certain peculiarities of habit, of temperament, and of character, which clearly distinguished it as a race from that of the

whites,—a patient, docile people, but careless, landless, and migratory within narrow limits, without forethought, and its criminal members given rather to furtive offenses than to the robust crimes of the whites. Restrained by the federal constitution from discriminating against the negro race, the convention discriminated against its characteristics.[106]

The law nullified the Fifteenth Amendment and tens of thousands of Black voters were dropped from voter rolls. By 1896 less than 5 percent of Black voters who had been eligible to vote in 1885 could still vote. The Supreme Court rewarded Mississippi in 1898 in *Williams v. Mississippi*:

> Though the law itself be fair on its face and impartial in appearance, yet, if it is applied and administered by public authority with an evil eye and an unequal hand, so as practically to make unjust and illegal discriminations between persons in similar circumstances, material to their rights, the denial of equal justice is still within the prohibition of the constitution. . . . This comment is not applicable to the constitution of Mississippi and its statutes. They do not on their face discriminate between the races, and it has not been shown that their actual administration was evil; only that evil was possible under them.[107]

Mississippi's open contempt for its Black population was evident in how few Blacks were allowed to vote. In *Williams v. Mississippi* the court completely disregarded the plaintiff's factual statements about the state's post-Reconstruction Constitution of 1890: "That the constitutional convention was composed of 134 members, only one of whom was a negro. That under prior laws there were 190,000 colored voters and 69,000 white voters."[108]

Yet, just two years after *Williams*, in 1900, "blacks comprised 62 percent of Mississippi, the highest percentage in the nation. Yet the state had not one black elected official."[109] It was not until 1987, when Mike Espy was elected to Mississippi's Second District, that the state elected a Black person to federal office. Espy joined the Clinton administration in 1993 and was succeeded by another Black official, Bennie Thompson, who remains in office. Apart from that Mississippi has not elected any Blacks to any statewide office.

Between 1880 and 1968, at least 3,500 Black people were lynched. It had become easier for perpetrators to commit acts of violence against Blacks, as the Supreme Court "interpreted black peoples' other constitutional rights almost out of existence."[110] Since the court had "limited the federal government's role in punishing violations of Negro rights," the duty fell to the states, which seldom acted. When "those officials refused to act, blacks were left unprotected."[111] The effects were shown in the number of Blacks in elected office. In 1869 there were two Black senators and twenty Black members of the House of Representatives. After the end of Reconstruction, the numbers dwindled until "the last black left Congress in 1901."[112]

In *United States v. Harris*, federal prosecutors indicted "twenty members of a Tennessee lynch mob for violating section two of the enforcement Act, which outlawed conspiracies to deprive anyone of equal protection of the laws. However, the Court struck down section 2 because the 'lynching was not a federal matter, the Court said, because the mob consisted only of private individuals.'"[113]

Southern states, especially Mississippi, continued to tighten Jim Crow laws throughout the first half of the twentieth century. "In 1922 a new Jim Crow law kept up with the times by segregating taxis. In 1930 another new law prohibited 'publishing, printing, or circulating any literature in favor of or urging inter-racial marriage or social equality.'"[114] Not only were physical barriers erected, but, if one supported equal rights, even free thought and free speech were illegal.

Lynching and Mob Violence, 1877–1950

Violence against Blacks ran rampant during and after Reconstruction. The Alabama-based Equal Justice Initiative reported in June 2020 that at least 2000 Blacks were lynched during

Reconstruction, in addition to roughly 4400 between 1877 and 1950.[115] The public nature of lynching made it a uniquely U.S. phenomenon; even the Nazis sought to hide the worst of their crimes against from view. However, the mass killings of Blacks, as well as the destruction of their townships, churches, and businesses, was not only public knowledge, but also hailed by white supremacists. While the Nazis concealed their deeds and swore the killers to silence, this was not the case in the United States, where prominent politicians, business and religious leaders, and newspaper editors ensured that white supremacy's message of violence was communicated far and wide.

While the previously mentioned Colfax, Hamburg, and Ellenton massacres had been among the most violent attacks against Blacks in the United States to that date, they had in fact been the tip of the iceberg. The Supreme Court in *United States v. Cruickshank* ruled that the Fourteenth Amendment only "prohibits a State from depriving any person of life, liberty, or property, without due process of law; but this adds nothing to the rights of one citizen as against another."[116] The decision allowed the KKK and others, because they were not government organizations, to kill and trample the rights of Blacks without fear.

Mass violence against Black towns escalated after President Rutherford B. Hayes officially ended Reconstruction and withdrew federal troops from the South in 1877. The Supreme Court overturned the Civil Rights Act of 1875 and affirmed racial segregation in *Plessy v. Ferguson*. By 1900 Blacks had been stripped of most civil and voting rights. Many were driven out of their homes and killed, their communities businesses, and churches destroyed by white paramilitaries often aided by police and even National Guardsmen.

Lynching, mass killings and the destruction of Black towns, churches and business districts were all too common. The most notorious were the Wilmington Massacre of 1898, in North Carolina; the Black Wall Street Massacre of 1919, in Tulsa, Oklahoma; and the Axe Handle Sunday of 1960, in Jackson-

The Failure of Will

ville, Florida. Violence against Blacks in many cities continued unabated.

The Civil Rights Movement, 1900–1968

The modern civil rights movement can be traced to the Black soldiers who fought in and returned from World War II. Army veteran W. E. B. DuBois would write about what Blacks faced in the war and confront the lies of the Lost Cause. Jackie Robinson, also a veteran, broke the color barrier in baseball, and Rosa Parks refused to go to the back of the bus. Young Emmett Till was brutally murdered by Klansmen based on a lie, his battered body bearing witness to white hatred. Rising leaders like the Rev. Dr. Martin Luther King Jr. began to blaze a trail to bring about equality for Blacks.

Once again Mississippi became the primary battleground against civil rights. In 1961 James Meredith, a veteran of the U.S. Air Force, became the first Black student ever admitted to the University of Mississippi. University officials and Mississippi politicians, including Sen. James Eastland, Gov. Ross Barnett, and numerous congressmen, state representatives, as well as an angry populace, threatened violence if the federal government or courts ordered them to comply. Governor Barnett proclaimed in a televised address: "We must either submit to the unlawful dictates of the federal government or stand up like men and tell them 'NEVER!'"[117] He said any federal officials who attempted to arrest a state official for defying federal court orders would be arrested. Backed by federal court orders and by the *Brown v. Board of Education* ruling, Attorney General Robert F. Kennedy called Barnett on September 24.

> "Governor," Kennedy observed, "you are a part of the United States."
>
> "We have been a part of the United States but I don't know whether we are or not."
>
> "Are you getting out of the Union?"

"It looks like we are being kicked around—like we don't belong to it."

Back to specifics again, Kennedy ended the talk with a typical crisp wrap-up. "My job is to enforce the laws of the United States."[118]

The situation grew violent as thousands of Mississippians, whipped into an anti-Black and anti-federal frenzy by their elected leaders, radio, television and newspaper commentators, supported by the KKK, the John Birch Society, and other militants mobilized to fight the "invasion."

On September 30 a deal was reached to admit Meredith to the university. Meredith entered the campus protected by federal marshals, border patrol officers, and the state police, which just a few hours before had been deployed to keep Meredith out. Thousands of angry whites ringed the campus, where students raised the Confederate battle flag over the campus's Civil War memorial. Rioters shouted death threats and assaulted Meredith's supporters. Members of the press and faculty were beaten; bricks, stones and bottles thrown; the tires of federal vehicles slashed. When attacked the marshals were forced them to deploy tear gas in self-defense. The state police withdrew, and federals took the lead. As Meredith enrolled U.S. Marshals escorted him.

The violence resulted in the calling up of U.S. Army MPs and National Guard units, who battled Molotov cocktails thrown by the protestors to relieve the beleaguered marshals and border patrolmen. The soldiers cleared the campus and ended the riot. Over 160 marshals were injured, including 28 wounded by bullets. The next morning, with Meredith admitted, a local clergyman saw the Confederate flag still flying, and, "with firm step, he strode out to the pole, loosened the halyard and lowered the Confederate flag."[119] But instead of thanking or supporting those who helped him, Meredith supported Ross's 1967 election. He also worked for ardent segregationists such as Sen. Jesse Helms of North Carolina. The battle to integrate Ole' Miss was over, and Meredith graduated peacefully in August 1963. But many Mississippians continued to protest the admission of Blacks to the university, in addition to the passage of the Civil Rights and Voting Rights Acts. And as the civil rights movement, now ably led by King Jr., made headway, violence intensified.

South Carolina fought integration in the courts, but outgoing governor Ernest F. Hollings realized the writing was on the wall. South Carolina was not Mississippi; its racism was the old, aristocratic type, which now valued order. Hollings told the legislature:

> As we meet, South Carolina is running out of courts. If and when every legal remedy has been exhausted, the General Assembly must make clear South Carolina's choice, a government of laws rather than a government of men. As determined as we are, we of today must realize the lesson of once hundred years ago and move on for the good of South Carolina and our United States. This should be done with dignity. It must be done with law and order.[120]

When Clemson University, founded by Benjamine Tillman, admitted its first Black student, there was no violence.

More unrest erupted across the South during the 1960s. During the 1964 Freedom Rides, students, activists, and educators came to Mississippi from around the nation to help Blacks register to vote, bringing generations of barely concealed racist hatred to the surface. Bruce Watson writes:

> In Mississippi's most remote hamlets, small "klaverns" of ruthless men met in secret to discuss the "nigger-communist invasion of Mississippi." They stockpiled kerosene, shotguns, and dynamite, then singled out targets—niggers, Jews, "niggerlovers." One warm April night, their secret burst into flames. In some sixty counties, blazing crosses lit up courthouse lawns, town squares, and open fields. The Klan was rising again in Mississippi. Like "White Knights" as their splinter group was

named, the Klan planned a holy war against the "dedicated agents of Satan . . . determined to destroy Christian civilization." The Klan would take care of your business, a recruiting poster said. "Get you Bible out and PRAY! You will hear from us."[121]

The events became the focus of national attention during a series of violent attacks on Blacks and civil rights organizers throughout the South. One of them claimed the life of Dr. Martin Luther King Jr. A bomb planted by a Klansman killed four little girls at the Sixteenth Street Baptist Church in Birmingham, Alabama. Peaceful demonstrators in Selma were attacked by local deputies and state troopers armed with tear gas, truncheons, and attack dogs. Among those injured was U.S. congressman John Lewis, then twenty-three years old and a leader of the protest. Lewis later wrote:

> Many have asked me whether I was afraid when I was standing on the Edmund Pettus Bridge, looking out at a sea of Alabama State Troopers. They seem bewildered when I tell them I was not afraid. I was at peace. It did not matter that I was looking down the barrel of a gun or an army of guns. It did not matter that troopers were on horseback ready to fire tear gas. It did not matter that citizens had been deputized and were carrying every weapon they could find. I had long before accepted that I might die in a protest, when I saw those troopers, I realized my time might have come to an end. . . . My soul was at peace with whatever the outcome might be. I had faced the truth of my circumstances. I made a choice not to abide in the deep disturbance of a silent, segregated South, but to find peace in the midst that turned things upside down to make them right side up.[122]

Those killed by lynching and acts of terrorism probably outnumber the official count by thousands. This would account for how quickly Blacks were disenfranchised throughout the South after Reconstruction ended in 1877.

Robert Smalls of South Carolina, who served as a congressman from from 1868 to 1887, told the convention bent on changing South Carolina's Constitution in 1895 that

the "negro was here to stay . . . and it was to the interests of the white man to see that he got all of his rights." He supported his argument with data: tables and figures designed to demonstrate the economic and political clout of his state's 600,000 black citizens (a slight majority of a total population of 1.1 million). In South Carolina alone, he observed, "the negroes pay tax on $12,500,000 worth of property," citing the most recent census. He argued for adopting a combined "property and educational qualification" for voting, but that was a bluff: Many white farmers had lost their property during the war, and he knew that wealthy white Democrats could never sell such a proposal to their poorer constituents.

Smalls then advanced a startling claim: "Since the reconstruction times, 53,000 negroes have been killed in the South."[123]

The number quoted by Smalls is over ten times the estimates of 4,000 killed since 1877. But those killed during Reconstruction were never tallied because the Redeemer governments had no interest in reporting them. Smalls didn't generalize; he was quite specific in his tally of 53,000 deaths. As a multiple-term congressman, he had access to reports from sources often overlooked. Douglas Egerton writes:

Too often, the central question about the postwar period is why Reconstruction failed, which implies that the process itself was flawed in ways that contributed to its own demise. But Smalls' death toll, if even close to accurate, adds substantial weight to the idea that Reconstruction was overthrown—by unremitting clandestine violence.

To evaluate his number, I combed through sources that would have been available to him. I quickly learned one thing: Those sources lack basic information, such as victims' last names, making it unlikely that anyone will be able to establish a precise number of people targeted for assassination by

Southern whites. Gradually, though, I came to another conclusion: Those sources clearly demonstrate that white Democrats an electoral minority in every Southern state after the war, engaged in racial terrorism to restore the prewar social order. Despite the imprecision in the records, I found Smalls' figure to be entirely plausible.[124]

As a congressman Smalls received hundreds if not thousands of letters from Blacks throughout the South regarding the killings. He also had access to "the extensive regional reports from officers assigned to the Freedmen's Bureau, the federal agency that helped former slaves and impoverished Southern whites obtain food, land, education and labor contracts from 1865 to 1872. In hundreds of bound volumes, innumerable letters documented attacks on black and white teachers employed by the bureau, and during election seasons the reports from the field contained almost nothing but accounts of violence."[125] He also had access to Black-owned newspapers, which reported violence committed against Blacks more reliably than other sources. Consequently, one has to take what Smalls said seriously—facts that are damning to any white supremacist.

Klan violence in Mississippi led to the killings of three voting registration organizers—Michael Schwerner, James Cheney, and Andrew Goldman—by Klansmen and members of the Neshoba County Sheriff's Department on June 21, 1964. The search for their bodies and the subsequent investigation into their deaths transfixed the nation, leading to the passage of the Civil Rights and Voting Rights Acts of 1964 and 1965. The murders are remembered in the 1988 film *Mississippi Burning*, and in Norman Rockwell's classic 1965 painting *Southern Justice*.

After he left office, Ulysses Grant gave a sober assessment of Reconstruction's failure. He concluded that what the South really needed was a benevolent dictatorship until it could be fully reintegrated into the Union. As he told an interviewer, "Military rule would have been just to all . . . [to] the Negro who wanted freedom, the white man who wanted protection, the Northern man who wanted Union. . . . The trouble about the military rule in the South was that our people did not like it. It was not in accordance with our institutions. . . . But we made our scheme, and we must do what we must with it."[126]

Grant was correct. The North's benevolent policies of 1865 were seized upon as signs of weakness in the defeated South. The Confederacy lost the war, but in the "ways that mattered most to white Southerners—socially, politically, and ideologically—the South itself did not."[127] Grant died in 1885 knowing that he had not been able to secure the freedom for which he, his friend Abraham Lincoln, and so many others had fought and died. Reconstruction's failure shows that that military victory must be accompanied by political will to ensure that the goals of victory are met.

White Southerners used political, social, economic, judicial and violent means to reverse their military defeat, "justice was sacrificed for the unjust peace ushered in by 'redemption' of the South, a peace marred by Jim Crow, poverty and lynching."[128] Most Northern leaders failed to appreciate this and, hindered by Johnson, failed to win the peace when the opportunity was greatest. They found out that, even after a military victory, "there is a need for further threats, and indeed action, because postwar disorder and even chaos will have to be addressed, and victorious allies are always likely to squabble over the spoils of victory."[129]

The Republican Party was a perfect target for Southerners to exploit. The tensions that always existed between abolitionists, business-minded Republicans, and anti-immigrant Know Nothings were fissures to be exploited. By the time of Grant's election, many Northerners were tired of Reconstruction and Blacks. But Grant was undeterred in protecting their rights under the "Fourteenth and Fifteenth Amendments and the Civil Rights Act of 1866 which been directed primarily against discriminatory action by state and local governments."[130]

In response to the pleas of Reconstruction governors, Congress passed and Grant signed the Enforcement Acts, "the most sweeping [of which] was the Ku Klux Klan Act of 1871."[131] It was one of the most far-reaching measures enacted by the federal government during Reconstruction. Grant resorted to harsh yet effective means by using federal marshalls to quell violence and enforce the laws protecting Blacks from terrorist paramilitaries. It was first time that the federal government intervened to stop crimes normally prosecuted by states. But the arrests and convictions hardened the "handful of Democrats who had never accepted defeat and now fought one, having exchanged their uniforms for hoods, [and to whom] the arrests of the Klansmen was a blatant assault on 'southern' rights."[132]

Even so most Northern leaders failed to appreciate what was happening in the South. One who "recognized that white vigilantism was combat by another name was the sixty-year-old abolitionist Wendell Phillips. 'There was still a state of war with the South,' he warned a Manhattan audience in the spring of 1871. 'Let General Grant lay his hands on the leaders of the South,' he shouted, 'and you will never hear of the Ku-Klux-Klan again.'"[133]

Phillips was right. Johnson's rush in 1865 to reintegrate the South into the nation without ensuring protections and civil rights for newly emancipated Blacks doomed Reconstruction. Former Confederate leaders regained power and passed the black codes:

> The resistance to what should have been the obvious consequences of losing the Civil War—full emancipation for the slaves and shared political control between blacks and whites—was so virulent and effective that the tangible outcome of the military struggle between the North and the South remained uncertain even twenty-five years after the issuance of President Abraham Lincoln's Emancipation Proclamation The role of the African American in society would not be clear for another one hundred years.[134]

But Northerners as a whole had given up the fight. Insurgencies are difficult to put down, and counterinsurgency campaigns, which require massive numbers of troops to succeed, can last for years. If there is no political will to support such a campaign, it will, like Reconstruction, fail.

Frederick Douglass wrote about the failure of Reconstruction in 1880:

> How stands the case with the recently emancipated millions of colored people in our own country? What is their condition today? What is their relation to those who the people who formerly held them as slaves? These are important questions, and they are such as trouble the minds of thoughtful men of all colors, at home and abroad. By law, by the Constitution of the United States slavery has no existence in our country. The legal form has been abolished. By law and the Constitution, the Negro is a man and a citizen, and has the rights and liberties granted to any other variety of the human family, residing in the United States. . . .
>
> But today, in most of the southern states, the fourteenth and fifteenth amendments are virtually nullified. The rights which they were intended to guarantee are denied and held in contempt. The citizenship granted in the fourteenth amendment is practically a mockery, and the right to vote, provided for in the fifteenth amendment, is literally stamped out in face of government. The old master class is today triumphant, and the newly-enfranchised class in a condition but little above that in which they were found before the rebellion.
>
> Do you ask me how, after all of that has been done, this state has been made possible? Our reconstruction measures were radically defective. They left the former slave completely in the power of the old master, the loyal citizen in the hand of the disloyal rebel against the government.[135]

The failure of Reconstruction ensured former Confederates of a political and social victory that took nearly another hundred years to end, if indeed it truly ended.

23

A New Religion

The Noble Confederacy and the Lost Cause

When Edmund Ruffin pulled the lanyard of the cannon that fired the first shot at Fort Sumter, it marked the end of an era. The war that he helped start destroyed it. Ruffin could not abide the Confederacy's defeat. In a carefully crafted suicide note, the hate-filled man wrote:

> I here declare my unmitigated hatred to Yankee rule—to all political, social and business connections with the Yankees and to the Yankee race. Would that I could impress these sentiments, in their full force, on every living Southerner and bequeath them to every one yet to be born! May such sentiments be held universally in the outraged and down trodden South, though in silence and stillness, until the now far-distant day shall arrive for just retribution for Yankee usurpation, oppression and outrages, and for deliverance and vengeance for the now ruined, subjugated and enslaved Southern States! . . . And now with my latest writing and utterance, and with what will be near my last breath, I here repeat and would willingly proclaim my unmitigated hatred to Yankee rule—to all political, social and business connections with Yankees, and the perfidious, malignant and vile Yankee race.[1]

When he lay down his pen, the old fire-eater placed the muzzle of his musket under his chin and blew his brains out.

A Southern Change of Tune

But Ruffin pulled the trigger too soon. Southern states would be free from Yankee rule within a decade. The institution of slavery did not endure, "but southerners' racial beliefs and habits did. . . . The white ex-Confederate South proved much more successful in guarding this sacred realm" during Reconstruction than during war.[2] Confederates who proclaimed slavery the deciding issue for secession and war changed their story. Slavery was "trivialized as the cause of the war in favor of such things as tariff disputes, control of investment banking and the means of wealth, cultural differences, and the conflict between industrial and agricultural societies."[3]

Alexander Stephens, author of the infamous Cornerstone Speech, who said in 1861 that "that the negro is not equal to the white man; that slavery—subordination to the superior race—is his natural and normal condition," now argued that the war was not about slavery, that "it had its origins in opposing principles. . . . It was a strife between the principles of Federation, on the one side, and Centralism, or Consolidation on the other." He concluded that the American Civil War "represented a struggle between 'the friends of Constitutional liberty' and 'the Demon of Centralism, Absolutism, [and] Despotism!'"[4]

Jefferson Davis changed his belief that the slavery was necessary for the Confederacy's claim to exist and the reason for secession. The revisionist Davis wrote:

> The Southern States and Southern people have been sedulously represented as "propagandists" of slavery and the Northern as the champions of universal freedom . . ." and "the attentive reader . . . will already found enough evidence to discern the falsehood of these representations, and to perceive that, to whatever extent the question of slavery may have served as an occasion, it was far from being the cause for the conflict.[5]

Instead of being about slavery, the Confederate cause was

mythologized as a lost one: the term "Lost Cause" coined by William Pollard in 1866, which "touching almost every aspect of the struggle, originated in Southern rationalizations of the war."[6] By 1877 Southerners took as much pride in the Lost Cause as Northerners took in Appomattox.[7] As Alan Nolen writes, "Leaders of such a catastrophe must account for themselves. Justification is necessary. Those who followed their leaders into the catastrophe required similar rationalization."[8] But honesty and introspection of the real causes was not part of the myth.

Southerners elevated the Lost Cause to the level of a religion that proclaimed the Southern cause as holy. The defeated Confederacy became a national version of Christ, crucified but triumphant over death and the Union. In the new religion,

> orthodoxy mattered, both in civil and religious terms: the public symbols of sacrifice were etched into the Southern landscape in the numerous statues, monuments, and consecrated grounds; on the lips of political leaders who reminded their neighbors of that sacrifice and how close they came to suffering the ultimate defeat of Yankee and black rule; in the books and articles they read, primers for remembrance, Aesop's fables for the masses, with the moral always evident and always the same.[9]

In the Lost Cause, Southerners mythologized and "made sacred the Southern way of life, laying the foundation for a Southern culture religion, a regional faith based upon Dixie's wartime experience."[10] In September 1906 Lawrence Griffith told a meeting of United Confederate Veterans that when they returned home they would find that "there was born in the South a new religion."[11] The Lost Cause took on "the proportions of a heroic legend, a Southern Götterdämmerung with Robert E. Lee as a latter-day Siegfried."[12] It was was replete with all the signs, symbols, and rituals of religion:

> This worship of the Immortal Confederacy had its foundation in myth of the Lost Cause. . . . When it reached fruition in the 1880s its votaries not only pledged their allegiance to the Lost

Cause, but they also elevated it above the realm of common patriotic impulse, making it perform a clearly religious function. . . . The Stars and Bars, "Dixie," and the army's gray jacket became religious emblems, symbolic of a holy cause and of the sacrifices made on its behalf. Confederate heroes also functioned as sacred symbols: Lee and Davis emerged as Christ figures, the common soldier attained sainthood, and Southern women became Marys who guarded the tomb of the Confederacy and heralded its resurrection.[13]

Jefferson Davis became an incarnational figure in this new faith. The president so maligned during the war became its Christ figure. Southerners believed "was the sacrifice selected—by the North or by Providence—as the price for Southern atonement. Pastors theologized about his 'passion' and described Davis as a 'vicarious victim' . . . who stood mute as Northerners 'laid on him the falsely alleged iniquities of us all.'"[14] Instead of a traitor, Davis became a martyr wrongly condemned. A 1923 song about Davis repeated the theme: "Jefferson Davis Still we honor thee! / Our Lamb victorious, who for us endur'd a cross of martyrdom / a crown of thorns, soul's Gethsemane, a nation's hate, A dungeon's gloom! Another God in chains."[15]

The myth of the Noble South painted a picture of slavery being benevolent as Southerners contended that slaves liked their status. They echoed Hiram Tibbetts's words to his brother in 1842: "If only the abolitionists could see how happy our people are. . . . The idea of unhappiness would never enter the mind of any one witnessing their enjoyments,"[16] and Davis's response to the Emancipation Proclamation, calling the slaves "peaceful and contented laborers."[17]

The romantic images of the Lost Cause were conveyed to the American public as fact by writers and Hollywood producers. Thomas Dixon Jr.'s 1905 play and novel *The Clansman* became D. W. Griffith's 1915 film epic *The Birth of a Nation* started the nationwide trend. The film was a groundbreaking event in American cinematography that portrayed white Southerners as nobly fighting against Yankee invaders, rapacious Blacks, and bloodsucking carpetbaggers. After Woodrow Wilson, the first president from the South since Zachary Taylor, screened it in White House, Wilson proclaimed, "It is like writing history with lightening, and one of my regrets it is so horribly true."[18]

The film was very popular in Northern cities and in the West, where it "generated its largest profits," and in areas where war's memory had long since faded. "Patrons were likely dazzled by Griffith's technical skill and masterful staging and little bothered by his racism."[19] The crowds that clamored for seats to *The Birth of a Nation* "were not only a testimony to the director's artistic genius, but also evidence of a lack of interested in solving the nation's racial problems."[20]

Non-Southerners "willingly adopted and even enhanced the southern memory of the war and the Reconstruction era." Some, like Henry Cabot Lodge, condemned "the tendency of northerners to accept uncritically the southern perspective on the war and Reconstruction."[21] But the myth of the Noble South appealed to Northerners who shared Southern views amid waves of immigrants and free Blacks. Northerners "cherished the manufactured South precisely because it was not the North: a genteel, rural, homogenous, and harmonious region of languid days and starry nights where people moved as softly as the breeze on a summer evening and where paternalism counted more that profit."[22] In a New York showing of Griffiths's film, "people were moved to cheers, hisses, laughter, and tears, apparently unconscious, and subdued by the intense interest of the play." They "clapped when the masked riders took vengeance on the Negroes," and "when the hero refused to shake the hand of a mulatto."[23] The film added to the movement in the North and West to form what became known as "sundown towns," where Blacks were driven out or were specifically built to keep Blacks and other minorities out.

The Birth of a Nation remained the most popular film in America, particularly the South, for the next twenty years. It lost its place when Margaret Mitchell published her epic novel *Gone with the Wind* in 1936. The book sold over seven million copies and Mitchell received a Pulitzer Prize. Producer David O. Selznick purchased the books rights and turned it an epic film production that was released in December 1939, starring some of the biggest names in Hollywood, including Clark Gable, Vivien Leigh, Olivia de Havilland, and Leslie Howard, as well as notable Black actress Hattie McDaniel. Masterfully filmed in color, it smashed box office records and won ten Academy Awards, and it immortalized the antebellum South with images of kind masters, faithful slaves, noble soldiers, and virtuous women, struggling to defend their way of life against the brutal Yankees. "Hollywood gossip columnist Luella Parsons called *Gone with the Wind* 'the best thing since *Birth of a Nation*.'"[24]

Griffith's film was marked by crude racism, but Selznick adopted a more romantic and genteel portrayal of racism than Griffith in *Gone with the Wind*, that of "a paternalistic treatment of slavery that would have pleased the original Lost Cause warriors."[25] The film painted the South after the Civil War as an ideal, with the war a tragedy and Reconstruction a crime. It was a remarkable film of great cinematographic grandeur, and audiences were swept away as they took in its mythical story of the Old South and passing of a society that was one of "wealth and distinction," with attendant "hospitable manners, broad acres, beautiful women and chivalrous men and the faithful old mammies that served them."[26] Gone was any realistic portrayal of the cruelty of slavery and the fact that, immediately after the war, Southern landowners returned to reenslaving Blacks by other means.

In the film's opening title card, filmgoers are reminded of a quaint, peaceful, yet doomed Southern way of life: "There was a land of Cavaliers and Cotton Fields called the Old South . . . Here in this pretty world Gallantry took its last bow . . . Here was the last ever to be seen of Knights and their Ladies Fair, of Master and of Slave . . . Look for it only in books, for it is no more than a dream remembered. A Civilization gone with the wind . . ."[27] In a later title card the film invokes "the tattered Cavaliers [who] came hobbling back to the desolation that had once been a land of grace and plenty" accompanied by "another invader . . . more cruel and viscous than any they had fought . . . the Carpetbagger." These images were portrayed so powerfully that a Philadelphia critic wrote, "Even a dyed-in-the wool Yankee must—and can afford to—give a rebel yell for *Gone with the Wind*."[28]

The myth of the Noble South found its way into Walt Disney's famed 1946 animated film *Song of the South*. Through such films and books, the twin myths of the Noble South and the Lost Cause became part of the national story, such that people in states outside of the region—and even foreigners—came to believe them: "Were a collection of beliefs which influenced views concerning not just the antebellum South, but the economic, cultural, and racial problems of the nation as well. . . . *Birth of a Nation* and *Gone with the Wind* may have been the most remembered of films, but theaters presented a constant stream of similar fare which perpetuated the myth of ambience, racial fidelity, and courtly idealism."[29]

The films also fed into a national mythology that legitimized Jim Crow and racial prejudice against Blacks. "*Birth of a Nation*, the first great epic, valorized the Ku Klux Klan. So did the film verson of *Gone with the Wind*, the first great color feature and still the most successful film of all time. No longer were secessionists villains; now abolitionists played that role."[30] Griffith's cinematographic masterpiece "lionized the first Ku Klux Klan (1865–75) as the savior of white southern civilization and fueled a nationwide Klan revival. Near the end of the nadir in 1936, *Gone with the Wind* sold a million hardbound books in its first month; the book and the resulting film, the highest-grossing movie of all times, further convinced whites that noncitizenship was appropriate for African Americans."[31]

The most powerful effect of the films was their propaganda value, which shaped the views of millions of people who had little or no contact with Blacks and whose "introduction to African-American history was molded on as much by cinematic fiction as by personal contact and knowledge."[32] It would not be until the late 1940s and the 1950s when Hollywood producers released *The Foxes of Harrow* (1947), *A Band of Angels* (1956), and *Shenandoah* (1965) that films portraying the dark side of slavery began to appear. *To Kill a Mockingbird* (1964) helped many to see the injustice and violence of Jim Crow; Mel Brooks's *Blazing Saddles* (1974), which became a beloved cult classic, used comedy to expose racism; *Glory* (1989) portrayed the sacrifice of valiant Black soldiers of the Fifty-Fourth Massachusetts Regiment at Fort Wagoner, while *A Soldier's Story* (1984), a murder mystery in an all-Black unit on a base in the Deep South in 1944, depicted Black soldiers in the segregated army of World War II. Steven Spielberg's *The Color Purple* (1985) depicted the life of two Black teenage girls in abusive homes in 1920s Georgia, while *Django Unchained* (2012) showed the violence of plantation slavery and the interstate slave trade. Television began to retell the evils of slavery in *The Diary of Miss Jane Pittman* (1974), the story of a former slave recounting her life during the civil rights movement, and Alex Haley's masterpiece miniseries *Roots* (1977). Since those early productions, many television shows and movies have broken new ground for Black actors in nonstereotyped leading roles, making many household names with strong voices for civil rights.

The Divide

The Lost Cause comforted and inspired Southerners following the war: "It defended the old order, including slavery (on the grounds of white supremacy) and in Pollard's case even predicted that the superior virtues of cause it to rise ineluctably from the ashes of its unworthy defeat."[33] The myth paved the way for over a century of second-class citizenship for Blacks, deprived of the vote and forced into "separate but equal" schools, hospitals, and recreational centers, as the KKK intimidated, persecuted, attacked, and lynched Blacks.

However, many Union veterans fought the Lost Causers to the day they died. Members of the Grand Army of the Republic, the first truly national veteran's organization and the first to admit Black soldiers as equals, continued their fight to keep the public fixed on the reason for war. They point out the profound difference between what they and the Confederates fought:

> The Society of the Army of the Tennessee described the war as a struggle "that involved the life of the Nation, the preservation of the Union, the triumph of liberty and the death of slavery. They had fought every battle . . . from the firing on the Union flag Fort Sumter to the surrender of Lee at Appomattox . . . in the cause of human liberty," burying "treason and slavery in the Potter's Field of nations" and "making all our citizens equal before the law, from the gulf to the lakes, and from ocean to ocean."[34]

In 1937 the last great Blue and Gray Reunion was held at Gettysburg. Surviving members of the United Confederate Veterans extended an invitation to the Grand Army of the Republic (GAR) to join them. Members of the GAR's Seventy-First Encampment from Madison, Wisconsin, which included survivors of the immortal Iron Brigade, who sacrificed so much at Gettysburg, adamantly opposed the display of the Confederate Battle flag at the reunion. "No Rebel colors," they shouted. "What sort of compromise is that for Union soldiers but hell and damnation."[35]

Edmund Ruffin outlived Lincoln by a few months. Lincoln was assassinated by John Wilkes Booth on April 14, 1865. To his death by suicide, Ruffin remained bitter and full of hate, but that was not the case with Lincoln, who seemed incapable of hating his enemies. In his second inaugural address, Lincoln spoke in a completely different manner, concluding with these words: "With malice toward none, with charity for all, with firmness in the right as God gives us to see the right, let us strive on to finish the work we are in, to bind up the nation's wounds, to care for him who shall have borne the battle and for his widow and his orphan, to do all which may achieve and cherish a just and lasting peace among ourselves and with all nations."[36]

A New Religion

EPILOGUE

The Past Is Always Present

"We've Got Some Difficult Days Ahead"

One of the tragedies of the Civil War and Reconstruction was how quickly much of the country returned to its previous stances on race and how quickly, first in the South, and later in the North, American Blacks remained persecuted outcasts after emancipation and the passage of the Thirteenth, Fourteenth, and Fifteenth Amendments and the Civil Rights Act of 1875. Frederick Douglass had predicted such an occurrence as early as December 1862 when he remarked:

> Slavery has existed in this country too long and has stamped its character too deeply and indelibly to be blotted out in a day or a year, or even a generation. . . . The law and the sword can and will, in the end abolish slavery But law and the sword cannot abolish the malignant slave-holding sentiment which has kept the slave system alive in the country during two centuries. Pride of race, prejudice against color, will raise their hateful clamor for oppression of the Negro as heretofore. The slave having ceased to be the abject slave of a single master, his enemies will endeavor to make him an enemy of society at large.[1]

In a sense the Civil War is the linchpin in our history from colonial times. To confine that history to the war and Reconstruction is to do a disservice to all Americans. What began when the *White Lion* landed the first Blacks at Point Comfort still remains with us.

FIG. 29. Martin Luther King Jr. giving his "I Have a Dream" speech during the March on Washington in Washington DC, August 28, 1963. Photo by Rowland Scherman. U.S. National Archives and Records Administration.

Numerous killings of Blacks by police, vigilantes, and mass murderers set the stage for the reaction when George Floyd was murdered in what amounted to a public police lynching. Protests began, and the violent militaristic reaction by police and the Trump administration to mostly peaceful Black Lives Matter protests over Floyd's murder, shocked the nation and the world. As the Reverend Dr. Martin Luther King Jr. said in the night before he was assassinated, "We've got some difficult days ahead."

The role of institutionalized, state-sponsored racism and malignant religion and ideology wedded to the aspirations of a slave power oligarchy that desired power over the entire nation demonstrate the timeless importance of this part of our history. A new generation of Americans wrestles with rapidly changing racial and religious demographics. Some attempt to restore a world that only exists in the past, using the same arguments of those who asserted that Blacks were subhuman and slavery their appropriate condition. Thus even today Blacks continue to have higher rates of poverty and unemployment, less access to health care and quality public education, and face discrimination in trying to vote.

This is important in our domestic politics, as well as in foreign policy, where the United States and its allies seek solutions to problems that are often based on long-standing cultural, racial, and religious tensions. Our efforts are complicated by the distrust of people subjected to European and American imperialism, which was based on the foundation of white supremacy. The ghosts of American slavery, the Civil War, Reconstruction, Jim Crow, and the fight for civil rights were reawakened with the election of Barack Obama and intensified under President Donald Trump, who during his time in office weaponized racial hatred and division. Our sordid racist past is on display before the entire world. Therefore, this is not only a domestic issue, but a national security threat. It causes our allies to doubt us and our reliability as allies and gives our enemies grist to feed their propaganda machines.

If we forget these lessons, it is quite likely that the American experiment will die. There has always been a tension in defining liberty. Lincoln, through his belief in the "a new birth of freedom" that he so eloquently framed in the Gettysburg Address, helped to move the nation toward an expanded concept of liberty despite the efforts to thwart it. As James McPherson notes, "The tension between negative and positive liberty did not come to an end in the Civil War, of course. That tension has remained a constant of American political and social philosophy. In recent years, with the rise of small-government or antigovernment movements in our politics, there has been a revival of negative liberty."[2]

The revival of negative liberty was a hallmark of Donald Trump's presidency. Even after his election loss to Joe Biden, he attempted to retain office, continually repeating the lie that he won the election in a landslide and that it had been stolen from him. Despite overwhelming evidence to the contrary, and over sixty rejections of his claims from courts up to the U. S. Supreme Court, Trump's most loyal supporters believed him and took action. On January 6, 2021, as Congress met to conduct its largely ceremonial certification of the votes of the Electoral College, nearly fifty thousand of his supporters, many armed for combat, launched an attack on the Capitol. They overwhelmed the Capitol Police and threatened the lives of VP Mike Pence, Speaker of the House Nancy Pelosi, and other senators and members of Congress who were doing their duty. The motivations of the insurgents were the same as the secessionists of 1860: a failure to accept the results of a fair and legal election.

Most of those involved in this insurrection were self-proclaimed militant evangelical Christian nationalists, who advocate the same theocratic beliefs as their Confederate and Jim Crow predecessors, along with neo-Nazis and white supremacists. In their ranks were a large number of former military personnel or police officers belonging to self-proclaimed militias who had sworn loyalty to President Trump. Three police officers died, 140 were wounded, and 4 attackers, too, died. Watching it was like watching the attacks on Black communities described in this book. Even though Trump has left office,

A New Religion

his militant true believers will remain an entrenched political force in U.S. politics, well capable of political armed insurgency, much like the KKK, the White League, White Liners, and Red Shirts who conducted an armed insurgency against the United States for over fifty years after the Civil War. The FBI and Justice Department believe that they are more of a threat than foreign terrorists including Al-Qaeda and the Islamic State.

The divide will not just magically disappear, so it is important to tell the truth and not mythologize the Civil War by whitewashing the evil of slavery or sugar-coating Southern gallantry while neglecting that of Union soldiers, or forgetting the war's human cost and, most important, the reason it was fought. We must do like Ken Burns, who wrote:

> After the South's surrender at Appomattox we conspired to cloak the Civil War in bloodless, gallant myth, obscuring its causes and its great ennobling outcome—the survival of the Union and the freeing of four million Americans and their descendants from bondage. We struggled to rewrite our history to emphasize the gallantry of the wars' top-down heroes, while ignoring the equally important bottom-up stories of privates and slaves. We changed the irredeemable, as the historian David Blight argues, into positive, inspiring stories.[3]

In the end the Union was preserved. Reconciliation between the North and South was, to some degree, achieved. However, the continuance of racism and discrimination through the black codes and Jim Crow laws stained the honor of the nation. The lack of repentance of those who shamelessly promoted the Lost Cause and its defenders continues. As Allen Guelzo writes about the importance of both reconciliation and repentance to Frederick Douglass after the war:

> Douglass wanted the South not only to admit that it had lost, but also that it had deserved to lose. "The South has a past not to be contemplated with pleasure, but with a shudder," he wrote in 1870. More than a decade later, Douglass was still

not satisfied: "Whatever else I may forget, I shall never forget the difference between those who fought to save the Republic and those who fought to destroy it."[4]

Likewise, the imperfect but reunited Union was all that stood in the way of Nazi Germany in the dark days of early 1942. Had the South won, as many European leaders of that day openly or secretly desired, there would have been nothing to stand in the way of Hitler and his legions, or in the way of Soviet Communism during the Cold War.

The attempts of former presidents George W. Bush and Barack Obama to portray the military response against Al-Qaeda and the invasion of Iraq as "a war against terrorism—not as a war against Arabs, nor, more generally, against Muslims" fell on deaf ears in much of the Muslim world.[5] Many Muslims saw it as a continuation of the Crusades, proving that the past is always present.

In our secular culture, we forget the primal importance of religion. We fail to realize that for many religion is a part of their culture even if they live secular lives, is a bedrock in times of tumult. In tough times is far easier for people to fall back on the simple aspects of faith and myth rather than seek difficult answers to their questions. For Americans this has often played out in our individual dramas of faith, sin, redemption and salvation. However, as in the antebellum period, that faith has again become a political weapon. "But," writes British historian and military theorist B. H. Liddell-Hart, "one should still be able to appreciate the point of view of those who fear the consequences. Faith matters so much in times of crisis. One must have gone deep into history before reaching the conviction that truth matters more."[6]

The controversies and conflicts brought on by the ideological, social, and religious divides in the antebellum United States provide us with historical examples of religion hijacked for racist political and economic ends. We see much of the same language and motivation at play in our time. Once again the issues center on racism, faith, culture and the political arguments regarding how far freedom and liberty extend. The examples drawn from our American experience can be instructive to all involved in policy making. They show the necessity to understand just how the various aspects of conflicts are interconnected, and how they cannot be disconnected without severe repercussions. As Samuel Huntington writes:

> People do not live by reason alone. They cannot calculate and act rationally in pursuit of their self-interest until they define their self. Interest politics presupposes identity. In times of rapid social change established identities dissolve, the self must be redefined, and new identities created. For people facing the need to determine Who am I? Where do I belong? Religion provides compelling answers. . . . In this process people rediscover or create new historical identities. Whatever universalist goals they may have, religions give people identity by positing a basic distinction between believers and non-believers, between a superior in-group and a different and inferior out-group.[7]

By studying our history and popular mythology that surrounds it, Americans can better understand themselves and the world. By studying the Civil War era, we can see how racism, religion, and ideology linked to political agendas can be forces for good or evil. Our Civil War history and that of Europe in the twentieth century shows "that societies can break, democracies can fall, ethics can collapse, and ordinary men can find themselves standing over death pits with guns in their hands. It would serve us well to understand why."[8]

Racism and race hatred fuel the worst aspects of religious intolerance. Authoritarian ideologues fuse them with a ruthless drive for political power. History shows the result in crimes against humanity where the damage to the victims, the perpetrators, and society as a whole is felt for generations. By drawing on those lessons, we can use them to better guide policy when dealing with domestic politics or conflicts between other nations and peoples.

NOTES

Preface

1. Snyder, *On Tyranny*, 63.
2. Bok, *Lying*, 18.
3. Loewen and Sebasta, *Confederate and Neo-Confederate Reader*, 3.
4. "Hermeneutics," Stanford Encyclopedia of Philosophy, accessed July 20, 2020, http://Plato.stanford.edu/entries/hermeneutics/#Textline.
5. Tuchman, *Practicing History*, 268.
6. Thucydides, *History of the Peloponnesian War*, 48.
7. Breisach, *Historiography*, 3.
8. Murray, *Past as Prologue*, 2–3.
9 Trudeau, *Like Men of War*, 212.
10. King, "I've Been to the Mountaintop."
11. Hoffer, *True Believer*, 79.
12. Bok, *Lying*, 268.

1. America's Original Sin

1. Zinn, *People's History of the United States*, 12.
2. "Africans in America, the Terrible Transformation," PBS, https://www.pbs.org/wgbh/aia/partl/lnarrl.html (accessed June 18, 2020).
3. Redding, *They Came in Chains*, quoted in Zinn, *People's History of the United States*, 23.
4. Loewen, *Lies My Teacher Told Me*, 6.
5. Kingsbury, *Records of the Virginia Company*, 243.
6. Kolchin, *American Slavery*, 11.
7. "Trans-Atlantic Slave Estimates," Emory Center for Digital Scholarship https://www.slavevoyages.org/assessment/estimates (accessed June 18, 2020).
8. Morgan, *American Slavery, American Freedom*, 84.
9. Morgan, *American Slavery, American Freedom*, 84.
10. Kolchin, *American Slavery*, 10.

11. Morgan, *American Slavery, American Freedom*, 141.

12. Woodard, *American Nations*, 56.

13. Zinn, *People's History of the United States.*

14. Kolchin, *American Slavery*, 16.

15. Kolchin, *American Slavery*, 16.

16. Woodard, *American Nations*, 56.

17. Kolchin, *American Slavery* , 17.

18. Kolchin, *American Slavery*, 18.

19. Zinn, *People's History of the United States*, 31.

20. "Slave Law in Colonial Virginia: A Timeline," www.shsu.edu/~jll004 /vabeachcourse_spring09/bacons_rebellion/slavelawincolonialvirginiatimeline .pdf (accessed November 30, 2021).

21. Woodard, *American Nations*, 83.

22. Levine, *Half Slave and Half Free*, 18–19.

23. Foner, *Forever Free*, 6.

24. Kolchin, *American Slavery*, 20.

25. Zinn, *People's History of the United States*, 28.

26. Kolchin, *American Slavery*, 19–20.

27. Glickman, "War at the Heart of Man," 16.

28. Zinn, *People's History of the United States*, 28.

29. Zinn, *People's History of the United States*, 32.

30. Kolchin, *American Slavery*, 20.

31. Kolchin, *American Slavery*, 20.

32. Glickman, "War at the Heart of Man," 15.

33. Glickman, "War at the Heart of Man," 34.

34. Foner, *Forever Free*, 7.

35. Kolchin, *American Slavery*, 19.

36. Eldid and Lachance, *Note on the Voyage of Venture Smith.*

37. Equiano, *Interesting Narrative.*

38. Foner, *Forever Free*, 8.

39. Woodard, *American Nations*, 82.

40. Morgan, *American Slavery, American Freedom*, 298.

41. Woodard, *American Nations*, 83.

42. Morgan, *American Slavery, American Freedom*, 301.

43. Woodard, *American Nations*, 82.

44. Freehling, *Road to Disunion, Vol. 1*, 214.

45. Woodard, *American Nations*, 84.

46. Freehling, *Road to Disunion, Vol. 1*, 215.

47. Kolchin, *American Slavery*, 26.

48. Freehling, *Road to Disunion, Vol. 1*, 216.

49. Woodard, *American Nations*, 88.

50. Freehling, *Road to Disunion, Vol. 1*, 216.

51. Woodard, *American Nations*, 82.

2. A Struggle to the Death

1. Fuller, *Conduct of War*, 98.

2. Gray, *Another Bloody Century*, 70.

3. Luttwak, *Missing Dimension*, 9.

4. Luttwak, *Missing Dimension*, 9.

5. It is interesting to see conservative Christians who made up much of former president Donald Trump's near-religious cult following before, during, and after his presidency.

6. Phillips, *American Theocracy*, 107.

7. John Fea, "White Evangelicals Fear the Future and Yearn for the Past. Of Course Trump Is Their Hero," usa today, July 8, 2018, https://www.usatoday.com/story/opinion/2018/07/08/evangelicals-support-donald-trump-out-fear-nostalgia-column/748967002/.

8. Hoffer, *True Believer*, 13–14.

9. Fea, "White Evangelicals."

10. Hoffer, *True Believer*, 15.

11. *American Communications Assn. v. Douds*, https://supreme.justia.com/cases/federal/us/339/382/case.html (accessed August 3, 2016).

12. Tuchman, *Practicing History*, 289.

13. Huntington, *Clash of Civilizations*, 28.

14. *Army and Marine Counterinsurgency Field Manual*, 26.

15. Phillips, *American Theocracy*, 143.

16. McGrath, *Christianity's Dangerous Idea*, 164.

17. Gonzalez, *History of Christianity, Vol. 2*, 246.

18. McGrath, *Christianity's Dangerous Idea*, 164.

19. Goldfield, *America Aflame*, 5.

20. Oren, *Power, Faith, and Fantasy*, 130.

21. McPherson, *Battle Cry of Freedom*, 42.

22. Varon, *Disunion!*, 183.

23. McPherson, *Battle Cry of Freedom*, 45.

24. Varon, *Disunion!*, 183.

25. Bush, "State of the Union Address," Washington DC, January 28, 2003, http://www.presidentialrhetoric.com/speeches/01.28.03.html.

26. Phillips, *American Theocracy*, 252.

27. Oren, *Power, Faith, and Fantasy*, 584.

28. Oren, *Power, Faith, and Fantasy*, 130.

29. Zinn, *People's History of the United States*, 312–13.

30. Tuchman, *Practicing History*, 289.

31. Tuchman, *Proud Tower*, loc. 3098.

32. Zinn, *People's History of the United States*, 313.

33. Tuchman, *Proud Tower*, loc. 2807.

34. Hofstadter, *Paranoid Style in American Politics*, 167.

35. Zinn, *People's History of the United States*, 313.

36. Mark Twain, "To the Person Sitting in Darkness," February 1901, http://www.loc.gov/rr/hispanic/1898/twain.html (accessed December 12, 2014).

37. Hofstadter, *Paranoid Style in American Politics*, 183–84.

38. Butler, *War Is a Racket*, loc. 14.

39. *Army and Marine Counterinsurgency Field Manual*, 27.

40. Rubin, "Religion in International Affairs, 20."

41. This is not new, and it is a growing challenge.

42. Rubin, "Religion in International Affairs," 22.

43. Zinni Koltz, *Battle for Peace*, 22.

44. Tuchman, *March of Folly*, 138.

3. I Hate Them with Perfect Hatred

1. Tuchman, *March of Folly*, 138; Gonzalez, *History of Christianity, Vol. 2*, 140.

2. Fuller, *Military History of the Western World*, 72.

3. Rhodes, *Introduction to Military Ethics*, 83.

4. Clausewitz, *On War*, 606.

5. Clausewitz, *On War*, 87–88.

6. Snay, *Gospel of Disunion*, 4.

7. Wilson, *Baptized in Blood*, 2.

8. McGrath, *Christianity's Dangerous Idea*, 164.

9. Gonzalez, *History of Christianity, Vol. 2*, 245.

10. Snay, *Gospel of Disunion*, 8.

11. Faust, *Creation of Confederate Nationalism*, 22.

12. Rable, *God's Almost Chosen Peoples*, 12.

13. Oren, *Power, Faith, and Fantasy*, 130.

14. Goldfield *America Aflame*, 36.

15. Goldfield, *America Aflame*, 37.

16. Levine, *Half Slave and Half Free*, 184.

17. I try to use the term "First Nations," which is used in Canada in lieu of "Native Americans" or "American Indians." I believe the term is more respectful and not pejorative.

18. Goldfield, *America Aflame*, 5. It seems to this author that the current mouthpieces of American Evangelicalism are little different from the evangelicals of the 1840s in their view of nationalism, religion, and racism.

19. Daly, *When Slavery Was Called Freedom*, 33–34.

20. Faust, *Creation of Confederate Nationalism*, 22.

21. Snay, *Gospel of Disunion*, 77.

22. Rable, *God's Almost Chosen Peoples*, 4.

23. Phillips, *American Theocracy*, 143.

24. Fuller, *Conduct of War*, 99.

25. Huntington, *Who Are We?*, 77.

26. Guelzo, *Fateful Lightning*, 95.

27. Luttwak, *Missing Dimension*, 13.

28. Snay, *Gospel of Disunion*, 15.

29. Rable, *God's Almost Chosen Peoples*, 5.

30. Fuller, *Decisive Battles of the U.S.A.*, 174.

31. McPherson, *War That Forged a Nation*, vii.

32. Gray, *Fighting Talk*, 25.

34. Dower, *War without Mercy*, 5.

35. Rubin, "Religion in International Affairs," 33.

36. Rubin, "Religion in International Affairs," 33.

37. Tuchman, *Practicing History*, 289.

4. They Shall Be Your Bond-Men

1. Wightman, "Glory of God," 78.

2. "American Memory and American Women," Law Library of Congress, http://memory.loc.gov/ammem/awhhtml/awlaw3/slavery.html (accessed August 9, 2016).

3. Zinn, *People's History of the United States*, 32.

4. Levine, *Half-Slave and Half-Free*, 19.

5. Foner, *Forever Free*, 6.

6. Levine, *Half-Slave and Half-Free*, 18.

7. Zinn, *People's History of the United States*, 27–28.

8. Zinn, *People's History of the United States*, 28.

9. Levine, *Half-Slave and Half-Free*, 19.

10. Moulton, *Narrative and Testimony*, 24–25.

11. Kolchin, *American Slavery*, 22–23.

12. Foner, *Forever Free*, 6.

13. Foner, *Short History of Reconstruction*, 1.

14. Egnal, *Clash of Extremes*, 26.

15. Foner, *Forever Free*, 7.

16. Patrick Henry, "The Slave-Trade: An Original Letter from Patrick Henry, dated 13 January 1773," *New York Times*, July 9, 1860, https://www.nytimes.com/1860/07/09/archives/the-slavetrade-an-original-letter-from-patrick-henry.html.

17. Levine, *Half Slave and Half Free*, 5.

18. Varon, *Disunion!*, 22, 24.

19. Guelzo, *Fateful Lightning*, 7.

20. Freehling, *Road to Disunion, Vol. 1*, 146.

21. Varon, *Disunion!*, 23.

22. Freehling, *Road to Disunion, Vol. 1*, 147.

23. Varon, *Disunion!*, 23.

24. Freehling, *Road to Disunion, Vol. 1*, 147.

25. McPherson, *War That Forged a Nation*, 7.

26. Varon, *Disunion!*, 23.

27. Varon, *Disunion!*, 24.

28. Varon, *Disunion!*, 24.

29. McCurry, *Confederate Reckoning*, 220.

30. Zinn, *People's History of the United States*, 90–91.

31. Gonzalez, *History of Christianity, Vol. 2*, 250–51.

32. Rable, *God's Almost Chosen Peoples*, 17.

33. Levine, *Half Slave and Half Free*, 8.

34. Zinn, *People's History of the United States*, 171.

35. Ingraham, *Southwest, by a Yankee*, 2:91, quoted in Woodman, *King Cotton and His Retainers*, 135.

36. Foner, *Forever Free*, 13.

37. Zinn, *People's History of the United States*, 171.

38. Potter, *Impending Crisis*, 41.

39. Thornwell, "Rights and the Duties," 52.

40. Potter, *Impending Crisis*, 41.

41. Burns, *Conflict's Acoustic Shadows*, 102.

42. Potter, *Impending Crisis*, 42.

43. Potter, *Impending Crisis*, 42.

44. Wilson, *Baptized in Blood*, 100.

45. Hotze, "Negro's Place in Nature," 215.

46. Levine, *Half Slave and Half Free*, 140.

47. Fitzhugh, *New Haven Lecture 1855*, 135.

48. Fitzhugh, *New Haven Lecture 1855*, 135; Daly, *When Slavery Was Called Freedom*, 63–64.

49. Faust, *Creation of Confederate Nationalism*, 61.

50. Levin, *Half Slave and Half Free*, 140.

51. Levin, *Half Slave and Half Free*, 140.

52. Levin, *Half Slave and Half Free*, 141.

53. McPherson, *Drawn with the Sword*, 50.

54. Levin, *Half Slave and Half Free*, 122.

55. Potter, *Impending Crisis*, 43.

56. McPherson, *Drawn with the Sword*, 16.

57. Egnal, *Clash of Extremes*, 6.

58. Dew, *Apostles of Disunion*, 12.

59. Thomas, *Confederate Nation*, 5.

60. Thomas, *Confederate Nation*, 5.

61. Potter, *Impending Crisis*, 457–58.

62. Freehling, *South vs. The South*, 20.

63. Levine, *Half Slave and Half Free*, 166.

64. Levine, *Half Slave and Half Free*, 166.

65. Goldfield, *America Aflame*, 27.

66. Freehling, *South vs. The South*, 34.

67. Varon, *Disunion!*, 70–71.

68. Goldfield, *America Aflame*, 27.

69. Freehling, *South vs. The South*, 22.

70. Guelzo, *Fateful Lightning*, 50–51.

71. Freehling, *South vs. The South*, 22.

72. Levine, *Half Slave and Half Free*, 169–70.

73. Guelzo, *Fateful Lightning*, 51–52.

74. Freehling, *South vs. The South*, 34.

75. Calhoun is referring to Henry Clay as "Mr. C."

76. Calhoun, "On Abolition Petitions," 31–32.

77. Potter, *Impending Crisis*, 43.

78. Levine, *Half Slave and Half Free*, 169–70.

79. Potter, *Impending Crisis*, 43.

80. Potter, *Impending Crisis*, 43.

81. Potter, *Impending Crisis*, 463.

82. Abrahamson, *Men of Secession and Civil War*, 43–44.

83. Ruffin, *Political Economy of Slavery*.

84. Ruffin, *Political Economy of Slavery*.

85. Thomas, *Confederate Nation*, 1.

86. Freehling, *Road to Disunion, Vol. 1*, 481.

87. Abrahamson, *Men of Secession and Civil War*, 44.

88. Ruffin, *Political Economy of Slavery*.

89. Catton, *Coming Fury*, 314–15.

90. Abrahamson, *Men of Secession and Civil War*, 42.

91. Abrahamson, *Men of Secession and Civil War*, 33.

92. Adam Goodheart, "The Happiest Man in the South," *New York Times*, December 16, 2010, http://opinionator.blogs.nytimes.com/2010/12/16/the-happiest-man-in-the-south/?_r=.

93. Freehling, *Road to Disunion, Vol. 1*, 286.

94. Abrahamson, *Men of Secession and Civil War*, 34.

95. Abrahamson, *Men of Secession and Civil War*, 34.

96. Goodheart, "Happiest Man in the South."

97. Abrahamson, *Men of Secession and Civil War*, 34.

98. Freehling, *Road to Disunion, Vol. 1*, 295.

99. Guelzo, *Fateful Lightning*, 130.

5. The Privilege of Belonging

1. McPherson, *Drawn with Sword*, 50.

2. Van Evrie, "Negroes and Negro Slavery," 75.

3. Levine, *Half Slave and Half Free*, 19.

4. Cartwright, "Diseases and Peculiarities."

5. Cartwright, "Diseases and Peculiarities, 70."

6. Foner, *Free Soil, Free Labor*, 7.

7. It is interesting that same theology used by Northerners to value free labor was the same that motivated Southern white supremacy and slavery was the same Bible.

8. Foner, *Free Soil, Free Labor*, 12–13.

9. Foner, *Free Soil, Free Labor*, 12.

10. McPherson, *Battle Cry of Freedom*, 28.

11. Foner, *Free Soil, Free Labor*, 12.

12. McPherson, *Battle Cry of Freedom*, 196.

13. Guelzo, *Fateful Lightning*, 38.

14. McPherson, *Battle Cry of Freedom*, 28.

15. Foner, *Free Soil, Free Labor*, 16.

16. Foner, *Free Soil, Free Labor*, 16.

17. Guelzo, *Fateful Lightning*, 38.

18. Guelzo, *Fateful Lightning*, 39.

19. Levine, *Half Slave and Half Free*, 44.

20. Egnal, *Clash of Extremes*, 125–26.

21. Korda, *Clouds of Glory*, 203.

22. Deyle, "Domestic Slave Trade," 53.

23. Korda, *Clouds of Glory*, 203.

24. Rankin, *Letters on American Slavery*, 45–46.

25. Egnal, *Clash of Extremes*, 10.

26. Deyle, "Domestic Slave Trade," 53. Deyle's numbers come from the 1860 census.

27. Egnal, *Clash of Extremes*, 54.

28. Foner, *Free Soil, Free Labor*, 48.

29. Levine, *Half Slave and Half Free*, 37.

30. Goldfield, *America Aflame*, 177.

31. McPherson, *Battle Cry of Freedom*, 199.

32. Levine, *Half Slave and Half Free*, 235.

33. Potter, *Impending Crisis*, 397.

34. Davis, *Jefferson Davis*, 258. I used to believe that anyone advocating such policies could never again hold public office. I was wrong.

35. Potter, *Impending Crisis*, 42.

36. Thomas Jefferson, "Letter to John Holmes," April 22, 1824, http://www.loc.gov.exhibits/jefferson/159.html.

37. Grant, *Personal Memoirs*, 243–45.

38. Guelzo, *Fateful Lightning*, 62–63.

39. Guelzo, *Fateful Lightning*, 68.

40. Goldfield, *America Aflame*, 71.

41. "Fugitive Slave Act 1850," Avalon Project, Yale School of Law, http://avalon.law.yale.edu/19th_century/fugitive.asp (accessed December 11, 2014).

42. "Fugitive Slave Act 1850."

43. Goldfield, *America Aflame*, 71.

44. McPherson, *Battle Cry of Freedom*, 80.

45. McPherson, *Battle Cry of Freedom*, 80.

46. Goldfield, *America Aflame*, 72.

47. Goodheart, *1861*, 42.

48. Varon, *Disunion!*, 241.

49. Mayer, *All on Fire*, 442.

50. McPherson, *Battle Cry of Freedom*, 84.

51. Guelzo, *Fateful Lightning*, 73.

52. Guelzo, *Fateful Lightning*, 73.

53. McPherson, *Battle Cry of Freedom*, 84.

54. Steers, *Blood on the Moon*, 33.

55. McPherson, *Battle Cry of Freedom*, 85.

56. Steers, *Blood on the Moon*, 33.

57. Oates, *Approaching Fury*, 94.

58. Guelzo, *Fateful Lightning*, 71.

59. Goldfield, *America Aflame*, 64.

60. Guelzo, *Fateful Lightning*, 71.

6. A Gross Violation of a Sacred Pledge

1. McPherson, *Battle Cry of Freedom*, 123.

2. McPherson, *Battle Cry of Freedom*, 124.

3. Egnal, *Clash of Extremes*, 208.

4. Foner, *Free Soil, Free Labor*, 94.

5. Goldfield, *America Aflame*, 99.

6. Freehling, *Road to Disunion, Vol. 1*, 559.

7. McPherson, *Battle Cry of Freedom*, 126.

8. Zinn, *Other Civil War*, 20.

9. Zinn, *Other Civil War*, 20–21.

10. McPherson, *Battle Cry of Freedom*, 125.

11. Egnal, *Clash of Extremes*, 215. All three were to play key roles in emancipation, abolition, and Reconstruction.

7. I Will Be Heard!

1. Levine, *Half Slave and Half Free*, 93.

2. McGrath, *Christianity's Dangerous Idea*, 324.

3. Freehling, *Road to Disunion, Vol. 1*, 289.

4. Huntington, *Who Are We?*, 77.

5. Levine, *Half Slave and Half Free*, 93.

6. Egnal, *Clash of Extremes*, 125.

7. Mayer, *All on Fire*, 58.

8. Mayer, *All on Fire*, 82.

9. Guelzo, *Fateful Lightning*, 47.

10. Egnal, *Clash of Extremes*, 125–26.

11. Egnal, *Clash of Extremes*, 125.

12. Freehling, *The Road to Disunion, Vol. 1*, 12.

13. Deyle, "Domestic Slave Trade," 57.

14. McGrath, *Christianity's Dangerous Idea*, 324.

15. Rable, *God's Almost Chosen Peoples*, 14.

16. Wills, *Lincoln at Gettysburg*, 108.

17. Rable, *God's Almost Chosen Peoples*, 13.

18. Rable, *God's Almost Chosen Peoples*, 13.

19. Oates, *Approaching Fury*, 36.

20. Stampp, *Causes of the Civil War*, 23.

21. Stampp, *Causes of the Civil War*, 29.

22. Rable, *God's Almost Chosen Peoples*, 13.

23. Goldfield, *America Aflame*, 35. A similar phenomena can be seen in the contemporary religious right's stand on abortion, and liberal or progressive Christian stands on the death penalty, social justice, health care, and civil rights.

24. McBeth, *Baptist Heritage*, 301.

25. McBeth, *Baptist Heritage*, 301.

26. McBeth, *Baptist Heritage*, 384.

27. McBeth, *Baptist Heritage*, 384–85.

28. Goldfield, *America Aflame*, 35.

29. Varon, *Disunion!*, 140.

30. Catton and Catton, *Two Roads to Sumter*, 94.

31. Goldfield, *America Aflame*, 75.

32. Oates, *Approaching Fury*, 120.

33. Catton and Catton, *Two Roads to Sumter*, 94.

34. Goldfield, *America Aflame*, 83.

35. Catton and Catton, *Two Roads to Sumter*, 94.

36. Goldfield, *America Aflame*, 79.

37. Goldfield, *America Aflame*, 79.

38. Goldfield, *America Aflame*, 83.

39. Varon, *Disunion!*, 245.

40. Goldfield, *America Aflame*, 83.

41. Freehling, *Road to Disunion, Vol. 1*, 48.

42. Freehling, *Road to Disunion, Vol. 1*, 49.

43. Varon, *Disunion!*, 245.

44. Blight, *Beyond the Battlefield*, 30.

45. Zinn, *Other Civil War*, 23.

46. Blight, *Beyond the Battlefield*, 31.

47. Blight, *Beyond the Battlefield*, 31.

48. Douglass, *Narrative of the Life*, 118–19.

49. Blight, *Beyond the Battlefield*, 32.

50. Zinn, *Other Civil War*, 24.

51. Blight, *Beyond the Battlefield*, 32.

52. Lowery, *Harriett Tubman*, 198–99.

53. Goldfield, *America Aflame*, 72.

54. Walt Whitman, "Blood Money," March 22, 1850, http://www.whitmanarchive.org/published/periodical/poems/per.00089.

55. Goldfield, *America Aflame*, 13.

56. Rable, *God's Almost Chosen Peoples*, 16.

57. Catton and Catton, *Two Roads to Sumter*, 123.

58. Foner, *Free Soil, Free Labor*, 145.

59. Seward, "Irrepressible Conflict," 71.

60. Keneally, *American Scoundrel*, 206–7.

61. Keneally, *American Scoundrel*, 207.

62. Catton and Catton, *Two Roads to Sumter*, 123.

63. Levine, *Half Slave and Half Free*, 15.

8. An Institution Sanctioned by God

1. Furman, "Exposition of the Views of Baptists."

2. Zinn, *People's History of the United States*, 29–30.

3. Gonzalez, *History of Christianity*, Vol. 2, 219–20. It is interesting to note that American Anglicans used a similar argument to the Nazis, that baptism did not change the nature of a person, meaning that, civilly, even the baptized in a "Christian" nation who were of a different race did not have the protections accorded to whites. With Americans it was Black slaves; with the Nazis it was Jews who had converted to Christianity.

4. Gallagher, *Confederate War*, 67.

5. McGrath, *Christianity's Dangerous Idea*, 324.

6. Daly, *When Slavery Was Called Freedom*, 69.

7. Thomas, *Confederate Nation*, 4.

8. McGrath, *Christianity's Dangerous Idea*, 324.

9. Leland, *Letter of Valediction*, 174, 179.

10. Varon, *Disunion!*, 109.

11. Freehling, *Road to Disunion*, Vol. 1, 29.

12. Freehling, *Road to Disunion*, Vol. 1, 29.

13. Gonzalez, *History of Christianity*, Vol. 2, 251.

14. Thomas, *Confederate Nation*, 22.

15. Thomas, *Confederate Nation*, 22.

16. Daly, *When Slavery Was Called Freedom*, 30.

17. Levine, *Half Slave and Half Free*, 116.

18. Levine, *Half Slave and Half Free*, 116.

19. Daly, *When Slavery Was Called Freedom*, 60.

20. Rable, *God's Almost Chosen Peoples*, 14. This phenomenon has not changed but only gotten worse over the last century and a half. The most popular Evangelical preachers are those who only use Christ as a weapon against adversaries or as a way to become wealthy.

21. Gonzalez, *History of Christianity*, Vol. 2, 251.

22. Rable, *God's Almost Chosen Peoples*, 14.

23. Gonzalez, *History of Christianity, Vol. 2*, 251.

24. McGrath, *Christianity's Dangerous Idea*, 324.

25. Gonzalez, *History of Christianity, Vol. 2*, 251.

26. McBeth, *Baptist Heritage*, 383. John Leland was one of those who worked on this statement.

27. McBeth, *Baptist Heritage*, 384.

28. McBeth, *Baptist Heritage*, 384.

29. McBeth, *Baptist Heritage*, 384.

30. McBeth, *Baptist Heritage*, 384.

31. Shurden, *Not a Silent People*, 58.

32. Shurden, *Not a Silent People*, 58.

33. Gonzalez, *History of Christianity, Vol. 2*, 251.

34. Rable, *God's Almost Chosen Peoples*, 13.

35. Rable, *God's Almost Chosen Peoples*, 14.

36. Daly, *When Slavery Was Called Freedom*, 97.

37. Freehling, *Road to Disunion, Vol. 2*, 460.

38. Rable, *God's Almost Chosen Peoples*, 39.

39. Freehling, *Road to Disunion, Vol. 2*, 462.

40. Daly, *When Slavery Was Called Freedom*, 38.

41. Varon, *Disunion!*, 108.

42. McGrath, *Christianity's Dangerous Idea*, 324. In our day Evangelicals use similar "biblical" arguments in many social causes, especially to discriminate against beliefs, personal, religious, or political of people they oppose, seeking to use government power and law to enforce their religious beliefs and limit the freedoms of others.

9. The Triumphs Rest on Slavery

1. Goldfield, *America Aflame*, 35.

2. Goldfield, *America Aflame*, 36.

3. Goldfield, *America Aflame*, 35.

4. Rable, *God's Almost Chosen Peoples*, 39–40.

5. Rable, *God's Almost Chosen Peoples*, 40.

6. Wightman, "Glory of God."

7. Goldfield, *America Aflame*, 35.

8. Today American churches are not limited to a few large denominations; they are split into many demonstrations, mini-denominations, para-church groups, and those professing no religious preference. It is yet to be seen in the long term how this will affect American politics and society.

9. Davis, *Jefferson Davis*, 258.

10. Fleming, *Disease in the Public Mind*, 194.

11. Goodwin, *Team of Rivals*, 203.

12. Potter, *Impending Crisis*, 340; Holzer, *Lincoln-Douglas Debates*, 55–56.

13. Catton and Catton, *Two Roads to Sumter*, 61.

14. Goodwin, *Team of Rivals*, 203.

15. Goodwin, *Team of Rivals*, 204.

16. Potter, *Impending Crisis*, 342.

17. Zinn, *Other Civil War*, 27–28.

18. Goodwin, *Team of Rivals*, 164.

19. Goodwin, *Team of Rivals*, 167.

20. Goodwin, *Team of Rivals*, 207.

21. Zinn, *Other Civil War*, 28.

10. With God as Our Champion

1. Brinsfield, *Faith in the Fight*, 67.

2. Daly, *When Slavery Was Called Freedom*, 147.

3. Faust, *Creation of Confederate Nationalism*, 27.

4. Gallagher, *Confederate War*, 66–67.

5. Faust, *Creation of Confederate Nationalism*, 32.

6. Daly, *When Slavery Was Called Freedom*, 145.

7. Daly, *When Slavery Was Called Freedom*, 138.

8. McBeth, *Baptist Heritage*, 392–93.

9. Faust, *Creation of Confederate Nationalism*, 32.

10. Faust, *Creation of Confederate Nationalism*, 33.

11. Faust, *Creation of Confederate Nationalism*, 29.

12. Fuller, *Grant and Lee*, 129.

13. Davis, *They Called Him Stonewall*, 192.

14. Faust, *Creation of Confederate Nationalism*, 60.

15. Daly, *When Slavery Was Called Freedom*, 145, 147.

16. Faust, *Creation of Confederate Nationalism*, 33.

17. Faust, *Creation of Confederate Nationalism*, 32.

18. Foote, *Civil War*, 87.

19. Thomas, *Confederate Nation*, 246.

20. Faust, *Creation of Confederate Nationalism*, 30.

21. Faust, *Creation of Confederate Nationalism*, 62.

11. They Have Closed the Heavy Doors

1. Goodheart, "Moses' Last Exodus," 15.

2. Goodwin, *Team of Rivals*, 189.

3. Potter, *Impending Crisis*, 291.

4. Guelzo, *Fateful Lightning*, 91.

5. Guelzo, *Fateful Lightning*, 91–92.

6. Goldfield, *America Aflame*, 142.

7. Levine, *Half Slave and Half Free*, 210.

8. Potter, *Impending Crisis*, 279.

9. Freehling, *Road to Disunion, Vol. 2*, 115.

10. Potter, *Impending Crisis*, 291.

11. Catton and Catton, *Two Roads to Sumter*, 139.

12. Guelzo, *Fateful Lightning*, 93.

13. Goodwin, *Team of Rivals*, 190.

14. Gienapp, "Republican Party and Slave Power," 81.

15. Levine, *Half Slave and Half Free*, 211.

16. Catton and Catton, *Two Roads to Sumter*, 139.

17. Goodwin, *Team of Rivals*, 190.

18. Goodwin, *Team of Rivals*, 190.

19. Gienapp, *Republican Party and Slave Power*, 81.

20. McPherson, *Battle Cry of Freedom*, 181.

21. McPherson, *Battle Cry of Freedom*, 181.

22. Gienapp, *Republican Party and Slave Power*, 82.

12. Portents Hang on All the Arches

1. Levine, *Half Slave and Half Free*, 196.

2. Levine, *Half Slave and Half Free*, 196.

3. Freehling, *Road to Disunion, Vol. 2*, 124.

4. Freehling, *Road to Disunion, Vol. 2*, 125.

5. Freehling, *Road to Disunion, Vol. 2*, 126.

6. Freehling, *Road to Disunion, Vol. 2*, 126.

7. Levine, *Half Slave and Half Free*, 196.

8. McPherson, *Battle Cry of Freedom*, 148.

9. Guelzo, *Fateful Lightning*, 81.

10. McPherson, *Battle Cry of Freedom*, 149.

11. Guelzo, *Fateful Lightning*, 81.

12. Guelzo, *Fateful Lightning*, 81.

13. Oates, *Approaching Fury*, 173.

14. Goldfield, *America Aflame*, 118.

15. Oates, *Approaching Fury*, 181.

16. Potter, *Impending Crisis*, 213–14.

13. General Jackson Is Dead

1. Guelzo, *Fateful Lightning*, 81.

2. Potter, *Impending Crisis*, 300.

3. Potter, *Impending Crisis*, 314.

4. Guelzo, *Fateful Lightning*, 115.

5. Freehling, *Road to Disunion, Vol. 2*, 138.

6. McPherson, *Battle Cry of Freedom*, 165.

7. McPherson, *Battle Cry of Freedom*, 164.

8. Levine, *Half Slave and Half Free*, 211.

9. Goldfield, *America Aflame*, 144.

10. Freehling, *Road to Disunion, Vol. 2*, 138.

11. Potter, *Impending Crisis*, 340.

12. Oates, *Approaching Fury*, 208.

13. McPherson, *Battle Cry of Freedom*, 166.

14. Oates, *Approaching Fury*, 208.

15. McPherson, *Battle Cry of Freedom*, 166.

16. Guelzo, *Fateful Lightning*, 115.

17. Oates, *Approaching Fury*, 210.

18. Oates, *Approaching Fury*, 212–13.

19. McPherson, *Battle Cry of Freedom*, 168.

20. Varon, *Disunion!*, 308

21. Oates, *Approaching Fury*, 215–16.

22. Guelzo, *Fateful Lightning*, 116.

23. Oates, *Approaching Fury*, 216.

24. Potter, *Impending Crisis*, 325.

25. Guelzo, *Fateful Lightning*, 116.

26. McPherson, *Battle Cry of Freedom*, 167.

27. Freehling, *Road to Disunion, Vol. 2*, 140.

28. Levine, *Half Slave and Half Free*, 213.

29. Freehling, *Road to Disunion, Vol. 2*, 142.

30. Fehrenbacher, "Kansas, Republicanism," 94.

31. Potter, *Impending Crisis*, 394.

32. McPherson, *Battle Cry of Freedom*, 213.

33. Goldfield, *America Aflame*, 167.

34. Levine, *Half Slave and Half Free*, 216.

35. Guelzo, *Fateful Lightning*, 121.

36. Catton, *Coming Fury*, 32.

37. McPherson, *Battle Cry of Freedom*, 215.

38. Goldfield, *America Aflame*, 167.

39. Guelzo, *Fateful Lightning*, 121.

40. Goldfield, *America Aflame*, 167.

41. Catton, *Coming Fury*, 46.

42. Potter, *Impending Crisis*, 417. Everett was one of the true treasures of American history and culture. He helped bring back the Greek Revival in architecture and began the rural cemetery movement so people could commemorate their departed loved ones in tranquility, as the Greeks had serene settings. He was a professor, president of Harvard, member of the House and Senate, and diplomat. He was also one of the greatest orators of his time and gave the keynote address at the dedication of the Gettysburg Soldiers Cemetery, where Lincoln gave the much shorter and more famous Gettysburg Address.

43. Catton, *Coming Fury*, 46.

44. Goldfield, *America Aflame*, 168.

45. Potter, *Impending Crisis*, 413.

46. McPherson, *Battle Cry of Freedom*, 216.

47. Catton, *Coming Fury*, 69.

48. Guelzo, *Fateful Lightning*, 121.

14. Cuba Must Be Ours

1. Catton and Catton, *Two Roads to Sumter*, 142.
2. Freehling, *Road to Disunion, Vol. 2*, 145.
3. Catton and Catton, *Two Roads to Sumter*, 142.
4. McPherson, *Battle Cry of Freedom*, 102.
5. Freehling, *Road to Disunion, Vol. 2*, 183.
6. McPherson, *Battle Cry of Freedom*, 103.
7. Freehling, *Road to Disunion, Vol. 2*, 183.
8. McPherson, *Battle Cry of Freedom*, 103.
9. McPherson, *Battle Cry of Freedom*, 104.
10. McPherson, *Battle Cry of Freedom*, 106.
11. Potter, *Impending Crisis*, 181.
12. Keneally, *American Scoundrel*, 44.
13. Pinchon, *Dan Sickles*, 48.
14. Potter, *Impending Crisis*, 190.
15. Keneally, *American Scoundrel*, 45.
16. Pinchon, *Dan Sickles*, 48.
17. Potter, *Impending Crisis*, 193.
18. McPherson, *War That Forged a Nation*, 29.
19. Potter, *Impending Crisis*, 193.

15. The Final Kingdom Has Arisen

1. Goldfield, *America Aflame*, 360.
2. Guelzo, *Fateful Lightning*, 414.
3. Daly, *When Slavery Was Called Freedom*, 147.
4. Daly, *When Slavery Was Called Freedom*, 147–48.
5. Guelzo, *Fateful Lightning*, 416.
6. Goldfield, *America Aflame*, 456.
7. Goldfield, *America Aflame*, 468–69.
8. Daly, *When Slavery Was Called Freedom*, 153.
9. Guelzo, *Fateful Lightning*, 416.
10. Goldfield, *America Aflame*, 457.
11. Catton and Catton, *Two Roads to Sumter*, 144.
12. Gallagher, *Union War*, 47.
13. Abraham Lincoln, "A House Divided," June 16, 1858, https://www.pbs .org/wgbh/ala/part4/4h2934.html.
14. Guelzo, *Fateful Lightning*, 55.
15. Guelzo, *Fateful Lightning*, 55.
16. Gallagher, *Union War*, 46.
17. Gallagher, *Union War*, 47.
18. Gallagher, *Union War*, 47.

19. Wills, *Lincoln at Gettysburg*, 114.

20. Jones, *Life and Letters*, 121.

21. Guelzo, *Robert E. Lee*, 197.

22. Seidule, *Robert E. Lee and Me*, 219.

23. Catton, *Coming Fury*, 46.

24. Freehling, *Road to Disunion, Vol. 2*, 207.

25. Guelzo, *Fateful Lightning*, 81.

26. Freehling, *Road to Disunion, Vol. 2*, 207.

27. Potter, *Impending Crisis*, 211.

28. Freehling, *Road to Disunion, Vol. 2*, 207.

29. Freehling, *Road to Disunion, Vol. 2*, 206.

30. Potter, *Impending Crisis*, 211–12.

31. Freehling, *Road to Disunion, Vol. 2*, 208.

32. *Army and Marine Counterinsurgency Field Manual*, 27.

33. Levine, *Half Slave and Half Free*, 197.

34. Korda, *Clouds of Glory*, xviii.

35. Oates, *Approaching Fury*, 203.

36. Oates, *Approaching Fury*, 284.

37. Korda, *Clouds of Glory*, xxxix.

38. Catton and Catton, *Two Roads to Sumter*, 187.

39. Potter, *Impending Crisis*, 381.

40. Potter, *Impending Crisis*, 375.

41. Catton and Catton, *Two Roads to Sumter*, 187.

42. "The Harper's Ferry Invasion as Party Capital," *Richmond Enquirer*, October 23, 1859.

43. Oates, *Approaching Fury*, 290.

44. Thomas, *Confederate Nation*, 3.

45. McPherson, *Battle Cry of Freedom*, 210.

46. Potter, *Impending Crisis*, 378.

47. Oefinger, *Soldier's General*, 18.

48. Guelzo, *Fateful Lightning*, 119.

16. The South Will Never Submit

1. Potter, *Impending Crisis*, 447.

2. McPherson, *Battle Cry of Freedom*, 229.

3. Goodheart, *1861*, 45.

4. Holzer, *Lincoln and the Power*, 255.

5. Goodwin, *Team of Rivals*, 267.

6. McCurry, *Confederate Reckoning*, 44.

7. Catton and Catton, *Two Roads to Sumter*, 202.

8. Goldfield, *America Aflame*, 168.

9. Goodheart, *1861*, 45.

10. The Democrats elected the first Black president, Barack Obama, 148 years later, as Republicans waged a race war against Obama and his policies, even questioning his citizenship in the "birther" controversy.

11. McPherson, *Battle Cry of Freedom*, 231.

12. Potter, *Impending Crisis*, 432.

13. Goodwin, *Team of Rivals*, 274–75.

14. Goodwin, *Team of Rivals*, 266.

15. Goldfield, *America Aflame*, 168.

16. McPherson, *Battle Cry of Freedom*, 229.

17. Catton, *Coming Fury*, 97.

18. McPherson, *Battle Cry of Freedom*, 230.

19. Daly, *When Slavery Was Called Freedom*, 135.

20. Rable, *God's Almost Chosen Peoples*, 34–35.

21. Daly, *When Slavery Was Called Freedom*, 135.

22. McPherson, *Battle Cry of Freedom*, 232.

23. Oates, *Approaching Fury*, 329.

24. Oates, *Approaching Fury*, 329–30.

25. Catton and Catton, *Two Roads to Sumter*, 211.

26. Levine, *Half Slave and Half Free*, 223.

27. Oates, *Approaching Fury*, 331.

28. Catton and Catton, *Two Roads to Sumter*, 243.

29. Potter, *Impending Crisis*, 447.

30. Oates, *Approaching Fury*, 337.

31. Freehling, *Road to Disunion, Vol. 2*, 338–39.

32. Catton, *Coming Fury*, 119.

33. Potter, *Impending Crisis*, 447.

17. Whom the Gods Intend to Destroy

1. Oates, *Approaching Fury*, 355–56.

2. Goodwin, *Team of Rivals*, 310.

3. Goodwin, *Team of Rivals*, 310.

4. Oates, *Approaching Fury*, 338.

5. Oates, *Approaching Fury*, 338–39.

6. Oates, *Approaching Fury*, 355.

7. Guelzo, *Fateful Lightning*, 134.

8. Oates, *Approaching Fury*, 354–55.

9. Goldfield, *America Aflame*, 184.

10. McPherson, *Drawn with Sword*, 50. These words are little different than the words of many conservative Evangelical Christian pastors, pundits, and politicians today in relation to the legalization of gay marriage.

11. Rable, *God's Almost Chosen Peoples*, 38–39.

12. Holzer, *Lincoln and the Power*, 256.

13. Goodheart, *1861*, 77.

14. Goodheart, *1861*, 77.

15. McPherson, *Battle Cry of Freedom*, 238.

16. Cooper, *We Have the War upon Us*, 75.

17. Catton, *Coming Fury*, 46–47.

18. Catton and Catton, *Two Roads to Sumter*, 250–51.

19. McPherson, *Battle Cry of Freedom*, 237.

20. Freehling, *The Road to Disunion, Vol. 2*, 398.

21. O'Connell, *Fierce Patriot*, 65.

22. Catton and Catton, *Two Roads to Sumter*, 248.

23. "Declaration of the Immediate Causes which Induce and Justify the Secession of South Carolina and the Federal Union," Avalon Project, Yale School of Law, http://avalon.law.yale.edu/19th_century/csa_scarsec.asp (accessed March 24, 2014).

24. Levine, *Half Slave and Half Free*, 251.

25. Levine, *Half Slave and Half Free*, 253.

26. Oates, *Approaching Fury*, 342.

27. Catton, *Coming Fury*, 122.

28. McPherson, *Battle Cry of Freedom*, 238.

29. Dew, *Apostles of Disunion*, 18.

30. Stampp, *Causes of the Civil War*, 189.

31. Catton and Catton, *Two Roads to Sumter*, 250.

32. Dew, *Apostles of Disunion*, 48.

33. Foner, *Free Soil, Free Labor*, 145.

34. Lincoln, "Illinois Farewell Address," 20.

35. Abraham Lincoln, "First Inaugural Address," March 4, 1861, https://www.bartleby,com/124/pres31.html.

36. Oates, *The Approaching Fury*, 429.

37. McPherson, *Drawn With Sword*, 50–51.

38. Henry Alexander H. Stevens, "Cornerstone Speech," March 21, 1861, http://civilwarcauses.org/corner.htm.

39. Oates, *Approaching Fury*, 382.

40. McPherson, *Battle Cry of Freedom*, 244.

41. Dew, *Apostles of Disunion*, 66.

42. Dew, *Apostles of Disunion*, 67.

43. Osborne, *Jubal*, 49.

44. Catton, *Coming Fury*, 365. Ancestors on both sides of my family owned slaves and fought for the Confederacy as members of the Eighth Virginia Cavalry.

45. Goodheart, "Ashen Ruin," 71. Actually, since Lincoln and Congress never recognized the Confederacy as a separate nation but as states in revolt, Tyler was not elected to office in a foreign country.

46. Catton, *Coming Fury*, 365.

47. Potter, *Impending Crisis*, 510.

48. Foote, *Civil War, Vol. 1*, 53.

49. Foote, *Civil War, Vol. 1*, 53.

50. Cooper, *We Have the War upon Us*, 80.

51. Wills, *Lincoln at Gettysburg*, 130–31.

52. Foote, *Civil War, Vol. 1*, 43.

53. Catton and Catton, *Two Roads to Sumter*, 143.

54. Levine, *Half Slave and Half Free*, 253.

18. The Heather Is on Fire

1. Levine, *Half Slave and Half Free*, 236.

2. Cooper, *We Have the War upon Us*, 192.

3. Daly, *When Slavery Was Called Freedom*, 141.

4. Daly, *When Slavery Was Called Freedom*, 138.

5. Wakelyn, "Benjamin Morgan Palmer," 309.

6. Benjamin Palmer, "Thanksgiving Sermon" (November 29, 1860), Civil War Causes, http://civilwarcauses.org/palmer.htm (accessed November 30, 2021).

7. McPherson, *Battle Cry of Freedom*, 273.

8. Osborne, *Jubal*, 52.

9. Osborne, *Jubal*, 52.

10. Boyce, "I Bow to What God Will Do," 9.

11. Levine, *Half Slave and Half Free*, 253–54.

12. Wakelyn, *Benjamin Morgan Palmer*, 309.

13. Rable, *God's Almost Chosen Peoples*, 56.

14. Huntington, *Who Are We?*, 77.

15. Guelzo, *Fateful Lightning*, 415.

16. Guelzo, *Fateful Lightning*, 415.

17. Goldfield, *America Aflame*, 360.

18. Rable, *God's Almost Chosen Peoples*, 337–38.

19. Guelzo, *Fateful Lightning*, 136.

20. Oates, *Approaching Fury*, 367.

21. McPherson, *Battle Cry of Freedom*, 265–66.

22. Keneally, *American Scoundrel*, 211.

23. Catton, *Coming Fury*, 180–81.

24. Catton, *Coming Fury*, 184.

25. Keneally, *American Scoundrel*, 211–12.

26. Potter, *Impending Crisis*, 544.

27. Guelzo, *Fateful Lightning*, 137.

28. Foote, *Civil War, Vol. 1*, 46.

29. Goodwin, *Team of Rivals*, 335.

30. Holzer, *Lincoln*, 80.

31. McPherson, *Battle Cry of Freedom*, 272.

32. Weigley, *Great Civil War*, 20–21.

33. Foote, *Civil War, Vol. 1*, 47.

34. Davis, *Jefferson Davis*, 323.

35. Oates, *Approaching Fury*, 416–17.

36. Weigley, *Great Civil War*, 21.

37. Goldfield, *America Aflame*, 202.

38. Cooper, *We Have the War upon Us*, 270.

39. Doubleday, "From Moultrie to Sumter," 48.

40. McPherson, *Battle Cry of Freedom*, 274.

41. McPherson, *Battle Cry of Freedom*, 274.

42. Oates, *Approaching Fury*, 423.

43. McPherson, *Battle Cry of Freedom*, 274–75.

44. Sickles was a notorious womanizer who murdered David Barton Key, district attorney for Washington DC in February 1858 after he discovered Key having an affair with his wife, shooting him twice in broad daylight across from the White House. Key was a handsome widower, womanizer, and nephew of Francis Scott Key, and his murder trial was the trial of the century, which, because it was the first such event, transmitted almost instantaneously by telegraph, captivated the nation. Sickles employed a dream team of lawyers and was acquitted with great fanfare, but when he publicly welcomed his adulterous wife back home, he lost all public sympathy and became a pariah in Washington. Then as now the adulteress is often treated worse than an adulterer or a murderer. Had Sickles divorced her, he would have been praised.

45. Keneally, *American Scoundrel*, 212.

46. Keneally, *American Scoundrel*, 214.

47. Goldfield, *America Aflame*, 525.

48. Oates, *Approaching Fury*, 421–22.

49. Oates, *Approaching Fury*, 422.

50. Pfanz, *Richard S. Ewell*, 120.

51. Jordan, *Winfield Scott Hancock*, 33.

52. Hancock, *Reminiscences*, 69–70.

53. Thomas, *Robert E. Lee*, 187.

54. Catton, *Coming Fury*, 335.

55. Thomas, *Confederate Nation*, 85.

56. Pryor, *Reading the Man*, 295.

57. Pryor, *Reading the Man*, 295.

58. Rable, *God's Almost Chosen Peoples*, 38.

59. Alexander, *Fighting for the Confederacy*, 24.

60. Alexander, *Fighting for the Confederacy*, 25.

61. Longacre, *Pickett, the Leader of the Charge*, 51.

62. Huntington, *Soldier and the State*, 213.

63. Guelzo, *Gettysburg*, 121.

64. Longacre, *John Buford*, 70.

65. Longacre, *John Buford*, 70.

66. Pryor, *Reading the Man*, 292.

67. Guelzo, *Fateful Lightning*, 140.

68. Smith, *Grant*, 99.

69. Longacre, *Joshua Chamberlain*, 49–50.

70. Guelzo, *Gettysburg*, 139.

71. Smith, *Grant*, 103.

72. Goldfield, *America Aflame*, 205.

73. Holzer and Symonds, New York Times *Complete Civil War*, 75.

74. Goldfield, *America Aflame*, 205.

19. Sound the Loud Timbrel

1. Foner, *Forever Free*, 42.

2. Freehling, *South vs. The South*, 47.

3. Brewster, *Lincoln's Gamble*, 59.

4. Foote, *Civil War*, 531.

5. Sears, *Lincoln's Generals*, 38.

6. McPherson, *Battle Cry of Freedom*, 364.

7. McPherson, *Battle Cry of Freedom*, 504.

8. McPherson, *Tried by War*, 9.

9. Goodwin, *Team of Rivals*, 468.

10. Foner, *Forever Free*, 49.

11. McGovern, *Abraham Lincoln*, 70.

12. McPherson, *Tried by War*, 108.

13. Zinn, *Other Civil War*, 39.

14. Foner, *Forever Free*, 49.

15. Brewster, *Lincoln's Gamble*, 169.

16. Guelzo, *Fateful Lightning*, 184.

17. Foner, *Forever Free*, 49.

18. Douglass, "Philadelphia Speech," 221.

19. Goodwin, *Team of Rivals*, 499.

20. Abraham Lincoln, "The Emancipation Proclamation," January 1, 1863, National Archives and Records Administration, https://www.archives.gov/exhibits /featured-documents/emancipation-proclamation.

21. Lincoln, "Emancipation Proclamation."

22. Brewster, *Lincoln's Gamble*, 244.

23. McPherson, *Battle Cry of Freedom*, 501.

24. Guelzo, *Fateful Lightning*, 180–81.

25. Goldfield, *America Aflame*, 263.

26. Brewster, *Lincoln's Gamble*, 245.

27. McGovern, *Abraham Lincoln*, 78.

28. Witt, *Lincoln's Code*, 186.

29. Witt, *Lincoln's Code*, 181.

30. Witt, *Lincoln's Code*, 218.

31. Guelzo, *Fateful Lightning*, 178.

32. Witt, *Lincoln's Code*, 219.

33. Reichberg, Syse, and Begby, *Ethics of War*, 570.

34. Reichberg, Syse, and Begby, *Ethics of War*, 570.

35. Witt, *Lincoln's Code*, 231.

36. Hartle, *Moral Issues*, 60.

37. Goldfield, *America Aflame*, 263.

38. Guelzo, *Fateful Lightning*, 534.

39. Goldfield, *America Aflame*, 359.

40. Goldfield, *America Aflame*, 358.

41. Wills, *Lincoln at Gettysburg*, 186.

42. Abraham Lincoln, "Second Inaugural Address," March 4, 1861, https://www.bartleby.com/124/pres32.html.

20. I Knew What I Was Fighting For

1. McPherson, *Tried by War*.

2. Goodwin, *Team of Rivals*, 435.

3. McPherson, *Tried by War*, 58.

4. McPherson, *Tried by War*, 58.

5. Goodwin, *Team of Rivals*, 369.

6. Foote, *Civil War, Vol. 2*, 531.

7. McPherson, *Battle Cry of Freedom*, 503.

8. McPherson, *Drawn with the Sword*, 101.

9. Guelzo, *Gettysburg*, 160.

10. Foner, *Forever Free*, 45.

11. Guelzo, *Gettysburg*, 160.

12. Glatthaar, *General Lee's Army*, 313.

13. Guelzo, *Gettysburg*, 160.

14. Goodwin, *Team of Rivals*, 465.

15. Egnal, *Clash of Extremes*, 318.

16. Foner, *Forever Free*, 48.

17. McPherson, *Tried by War*, 159.

18. McPherson, *Drawn with the Sword*, 159.

19. McPherson, *Abraham Lincoln*, 35.

20. Guelzo, *Fateful Lightning*, 381.

21. Dobak, *Freedom by the Sword*, 10.

22. McPherson, *Abraham Lincoln and the Second American Revolution*, 35.

23. Robertson, *Soldiers Blue and Gray*, 31.

24. Dobak, *Freedom by the Sword*, 11.

25. Robertson, *Soldiers Blue and Gray*, 31.

26. Gallagher, *Union War*, 103.

27. Welton, *Union Soldier's Changing Views*, 242, 245.

28. Robertson, *Soldiers Blue and Gray*, 34.

29. Glatthaar, *Black Glory*.

30. McPherson, *Battle Cry of Freedom*, 686.

31. Goldfield, *America Aflame*, 282.

32. Jones, "Free Men of Color," 403.

33. Guelzo, *Fateful Lightning*, 379. These were the First and Third Regiments.

34. Foote, *Civil War, Vol. 2*, 398.

35. Trudeau, *Like Men of War*, 44.

36. Guelzo, *Fateful Lightning*, 379.

37. McPherson, *Battle Cry of Freedom*, 686.

38. McPherson, *Drawn with the Sword*, 101.

39. McPherson, *Battle Cry of Freedom*, 686.

40. Guelzo, *Fateful Lightning*, 380–81.

41. McPherson, *Battle Cry of Freedom*, 686–87.

42. Foote, *Civil War, Vol. 2*, 697.

43. McPherson, *Battle Cry of Freedom*, 686.

44. Welch, "Letter in the *Christian Recorder*," 225–26.

45. Trudeau, *Like Men of War*, 262.

46. Douglass, "Philadelphia Speech," 220–21.

47. Douglass, "Philadelphia Speech," 221.

48. McPherson, *Battle Cry of Freedom*, 634.

49. Trudeau, *Like Men of War*, 58.

50. Gallagher, *Union War*, 97.

51. Trudeau, *Like Men of War*, 59.

52. Gallagher, *Union War*, 92.

53. McPherson, *Drawn with the Sword*, 89 p.

54. Catton, *Stillness at Appomattox*, 227.

55. Berlin, Riedy, and Rowland, *Freedom's Soldiers*, 133–34.

56. Catton, *Stillness at Appomattox*, 249.

57. Foote, *Civil War, Vol. 3*, 537.

58. Wert, *Sword of Lincoln*, 384–85.

59. Foote, *Civil War, Vol. 3*, 537.

60. Robertson, *Soldiers Blue and Gray*, 34; Butler, *Private and Official Correspondence*, 192.

61. Berlin, Riedy, and Rowland, *Freedom's Soldiers*, 135.

62. Weigley, *Great Civil War*, 189.

63. McPherson, *Battle Cry of Freedom*, 566.

64. Goldfield, *America Aflame*, 280.

65. Weigley, *Great Civil War*, 188.

66. Guelzo, *Fateful Lightning*, 377.

67. Guelzo, *Fateful Lightning*, 377.

68. Goldfield, *America Aflame*, 281.

69. Weigley, *Great Civil War*, 189.

70. Dobak, *Freedom by the Sword*, 208.

71. Grant, "Preparing for the Campaigns of '64," 107–8.

72. Foote, *Civil War, Vol. 3*, 111.

73. Guelzo, *Fateful Lightning*, 378.

74. Foote, *Civil War, Vol. 3*, 112.

75. Dobak, *Freedom by the Sword*, 208.

76. Eakin, "Slave Soldiers," 210, 212.

77. Berlin, Riedy, and Rowland, *Freedom's Soldiers*, 47.

78. McPherson, *Abraham Lincoln*, 89; McPherson, *Battle Cry of Freedom*, 769.

79. Glatthaar, *Black Glory*, 138.

80. McPherson, *War That Forged a Nation*, 113.

81. Guelzo, *Fateful Lightning*, 376.

82. Weigley, *Great Civil War*, 192.

83. McPherson, *For Cause and Comrades*, 130.

84. Weigley, *Great Civil War*, 191.

85. Gallagher et al., *American Civil War*, 296.

86. Foote, *Civil War, Vol. 3*, 756.

87. Robertson, *Soldiers Blue and Gray*, 36.

88. Berlin, Riedy, and Rowland, *Freedom's Soldiers*, 47.

89. Berlin, Riedy, and Rowland, *Freedom's Soldiers*, 49–50.

90. Foner, *Forever Free*, 55.

91. Daughan, *If by Sea*, 320.

92. Fields, "African American Soldiers," loc. 624.

93. Fields, "African American Soldiers," loc. 668.

94. McPherson, *War upon the Waters*, 137.

95. Fields, "African American Soldiers," loc. 844.

96. McPherson, *War upon the Waters*, 137.

97. Kraeczynski, "Spanish American War and After," loc. 2842.

98. McCurry, *Confederate Reckoning*, 310.

99. Herrera, *For Liberty and the Republic*, 74.

100. McPherson, *Battle Cry of Freedom*, 832.

101. McCurry, *Confederate Reckoning*, 325.

102. Symonds, *Stonewall of the West*, 188–89.

103. McPherson, *Embattled Rebel*, loc. 2376.

104. Symonds, *Stonewall of the West*, 182.

105. Thomas, *Confederate Nation*, 262.

106. Levine, *Fall of the House of Dixie*, 167.

107. McCurry, *Confederate Reckoning*, 326.

108. Levine, *Fall of the House of Dixie*, 167.

109. Winik, *April 1865*, 53.

110. McCurry, *Confederate Reckoning*, 327.

111. Guelzo, *Fateful Lightning*, 370.

112. Thomas, *Confederate Nation*, 262.

113. McCurry, *Confederate Reckoning*, 327.

114. Symonds, *Stonewall of the West*, 190.

115. Levine, *Fall of the House of Dixie*, 168.

116. Foote, *Civil War, Vol. 3*, 954.

117. McPherson, *Embattled Rebel*, loc. 2376.

118. Symonds, *Stonewall of the West*, 194.

119. Foote, *Civil War, Vol. 3*, 954.

120. Symonds, *Stonewall of the West*, 194.

121. McPherson, *Battle Cry of Freedom*, 833.

122. Thomas, *Confederate Nation*, 262.

123. Symonds, *Stonewall of the West*, 195.

124. McCurry, *Confederate Reckoning*, 329.

125. Guelzo, *Fateful Lightning*, 370.

126. Gallagher, *Confederate War*, 47.

127. McCurry, *Confederate Reckoning*, 330.

128. Davis, *Jefferson Davis*, 598.

129. McCurry, *Confederate Reckoning*, 335.

130. McCurry, *Confederate Reckoning*, 335.

131. Guelzo, *Fateful Lightning*, 370.

132. Lee, "Letter to Hon. Andrew Hunter," 217.

133. Korda, *Clouds of Glory*, 643.

134. McPherson, *Battle Cry of Freedom*, 836.

135. McPherson, *Embattled Rebel*, loc. 2403.

136. Cobb, "Letter to James A. Seddon," 221.

137. Edmondson, *Catherine Edmonston Reflects*.

138. Thomas, *Confederate Nation*, 293.

139. McPherson, *Embattled Rebel*, loc. 2419.

140. McCurry, *Confederate Reckoning*, 337.

141. Stringfellow, "Letter to President Jefferson Davis," 224.

142. Foote, *Civil War, Vol. 3* , 755.

143. Thomas, *Confederate Nation*, 296.

144. McPherson, *Battle Cry of Freedom*, 836.

145. Foote, *The Civil War, Vol. 3*, 755.

146. McPherson, *Battle Cry of Freedom*, 837.

147. McPherson, *Battle Cry of Freedom*, 837.

148. Foote, *Civil War, Vol. 3*, 860.

149. McPherson, *Battle Cry of Freedom*, 835.

150. McCurry, *Confederate Reckoning*, 345.

151. Pryor, *Reading the Man*, 397.

152. Confederate Congress, "General Orders," loc. 4348.

153. McCurry, *Confederate Reckoning*, 351.

154. McPherson, *Embattled Rebel*, loc. 2441.

155. Robertson, *Soldiers Blue and Gray*, 35.

156. Foote, *Civil War, Vol. 3*, 860.

157. Levine, *Half Slave and Half Free*, 241.

158. Guelzo, *Fateful Lightning*, 476.

159. Foote, *Civil War, Vol. 3*, 968.

160. Guelzo, *Fateful Lightning*, 481.

161. McPherson, *Embattled Rebel*, loc. 2510.

162. Catton, *Grant Takes Command*, 411.

163. Levine, *Half Slave and Half Free*, 241–42.

164. Bartlett, "Richmond's Black Residents," 302.

165. Levine, *Fall of the House of Dixie*, 275.

166. Foote, *Civil War, Vol. 3*, 897.

167. Douglass, "Philadelphia Speech," 221.

168. Luke Broadwater, "Senate Confirms First Black Air Force Chief," *New York Times*, June 9, 2020, https://www.nytimes.com/2020/06/09/us/politics/general-charles-brown-air-force.html?referringSource=articleShare.

169. Gallagher, *Union War*, 113.

21. Reconstruction and Redemption

1. Gray, *Fighting Talk*, 14.

2. Liddell-Hart, *Why Don't We Learn From History?*, 86.

3. McPherson, *War That Forged a Nation*, 132.

4. Rhodes, *All for the Union*, 231.

5. Jordan, *Marching Home*, 64.

6. Smith, *Fanny and Joshua*, 180. It is interesting to note that Chamberlain's commentary is directed at Northerners who were even just a few years after the war were glorifying the Confederate leader's exploits. Chamberlain instead directs the attention of his audience, and those covering the speech, to the atrocities committed at the Fort Pillow massacre of 1864 and to the hellish conditions at the Andersonville and Belle Isle prisoner of war camps run by the Confederacy.

7. Jordan, *Marching Home*, 64.

8. Jordan, *Marching Home*, 64.

9. Carpenter, *Sword and Olive Branch*, 7–11.

10. Langguth, *After Lincoln*, 104.

11. Sherman, *Memoirs*, 268.

12. Carpenter, *Sword and Olive Branch*, 83.

13. Foner, *Forever Free*, 17.

14. Egerton, *Wars of Reconstruction*, 80–81.

15. Foner, *Forever Free*, 116.

16. Egerton, *Wars of Reconstruction*, 102–3.

17. Foner, *Forever Free*, 134.

18. Caldwell, "Assassination," 409.

19. Caldwell, "Assassination," 410.

20. Carpenter, *Sword and Olive Branch*, 156.

21. Carpenter, *Sword and Olive Branch*, 156.

22. Budiansky, *Bloody Shirt*, 214–15.

23. Budiansky, *Bloody Shirt*, 214–15; Hoffer, *True Believer*, 106.

24. Perman and Murrell Taylor, *Civil War and Reconstruction*, 323.

25. Perman and Murrell Taylor, *Civil War and Reconstruction*, 323.

26. Foner, *Short History of Reconstruction*, 89.

27. Perman and Murrell Taylor, *Civil War and Reconstruction*, 323.

28. Foner, *Short History of Reconstruction*, 30.

29. Foner, *Forever Free*, 108.

30. Carpenter, *Sword and Olive Branch*, 109.

31. Carpenter, *Sword and Olive Branch*, 10.

32. Perman and Murrell Taylor, *Civil War and Reconstruction*, 323.

33. McPherson, *War That Forged a Nation*, 177.

34. McPherson, *War That Forged a Nation*, 177.

35. Langguth, *After Lincoln*, 119.

36. Langguth, *After Lincoln*, 319.

37. Foner, *Short History of Reconstruction*, 89.

38. McPherson, *War That Forged a Nation*, 175.

39. Goldfield, *America Aflame*, 407.

40. Carpenter, *Sword and Olive Branch*, 93.

41. Melton, *Sherman's Forgotten General.*

42. Guelzo, *Fateful Lightning*, 494.

43. Guelzo, *Fateful Lightning*, 494.

44. Blackmon, *Slavery by Another Name*, 41.

45. Goldfield, *America Aflame*, 411.

46. Kolchin, *American Slavery*, 209.

47. McPherson, *War That Forged a Nation*, 177.

48. Guelzo, *Fateful Lightning*, 491.

49. Jordan, *Marching Home*, 119.

50. Guelzo, *Fateful Lightning*, 489–90.

51. Foner, *Forever Free*, 96.

52. Foner, 96.

53. Jordan, *Marching Home*, 64.

54. Guelzo, *Fateful Lightning*, 491.

55. "Mississippi 's Black Code," loc. 4505.

56. Foner, *Forever Free*, 93–94.

57. Lord, *Past That Would Not Die*, 12.

58. Zinn, *Other Civil War*, 55.

59. Lord, *Past That Would Not Die*, 8.

60. Foner, *Forever Free*, 92.

61. Budiansky, *Red Shirt*, 216.

62. Carpenter, *Sword and Oliver Branch*, 168.

63. This was a very similar system used by the Nazi ss Main Economic and Administrative Office to profit from concentration camp prisoners in World War II.

64. Blackmon, *Slavery by Another Name*, 56.

65. Zinn, *People's History of the United States*, 275.

66. Foner, *Short History of Reconstruction*, 250.

67. Blackmon, *Slavery by Another Name*, 378–79.

68. Blackmon, *Slavery by Another Name*, 378.

69. Blackmon, *Slavery by Another Name*, 379.

70. Foner, *Short History of Reconstruction*, 30.

71. Lord, *Past That Would Not Die*, 11–12.

72. Zinn, *Other Civil War*, 54.

73. McPherson, *War That Forged a Nation*, 178.

74. Foner, *Forever Free*, 162.

75. Perman, "Illegitimacy and Insurgency," 451.

76. Foner, *Forever Free*, 121.

77. Langguth, *After Lincoln*, 232.

78. "Fourteenth Amendment," https://www.law.cornell.edu/constitution /amendmentxiv (accessed June 29, 2015).

79. Carpenter, *Sword and Olive Branch*, 93.

80. Foner, *Forever Free*, 92.

22. The Failure of Will

1. Lane, *Day Freedom Died*, 230.

2. Foner, *Forever Free*, 17.

3. McPherson, *War That Forged a Nation*, 178.

4. Jordan, *Marching Home*, 118.

5. Foner, *Forever Free*, 171.

6. Foner, *Forever Free*, 116.

7. Lane, *Day Freedom Died*, 2.

8. Lane, *Day Freedom Died*, 4.

9. Langguth, *After Lincoln*, 314.

10. Foner, *Forever Free*, 192–93.

11. Flood, *Grant's Final Victory*, 78–79.

12. Langguth, *After Lincoln*, 232.

13. Lord, *Past That Would Not Die*, 11.

14. Langguth, *After Lincoln*, 233.

15. Guelzo, *Fateful Lightning*, 504.

16. Perman, *Illegitimacy and Insurgency*, 458.

17. Goldfield, *Still Fighting the Civil War*, 195.

18. Egnal, *Clash of Extremes*, 337.

19. Egnal, *Clash of Extremes*, 337.

20. Foner, *Forever Free*, 192.

21. Foner, *Forever Free*, 191.

22. Perman, *Illegitimacy and Insurgency*, 459–60.

23. Perman, *Illegitimacy and Insurgency*, 46.

24. Lord, *Past That Would Not Die*, 15.

25. Loewen and Sebesta, *Confederate and Neo-Confederate Reader*, 281.

26. Lemann, *Redemption*, 33.

27. Lemann, *Redemption*, 48–49.

28. Chernow, *Grant*, 655.

29. Budiansky, *Bloody Shirt*, 179.

30. Ames, "Governor Adelbert Ames Deplores Violence," 434.

31. Lord, *Past That Would Not Die*, 17.

32. Lane, *Day Freedom Died*, 243.

33. McPherson, *War That Forged a Nation*, 190.

34. Lord, *Past That Wouldn't Die*, 17.

35. Leman, *Redemption*, 132.

36. Egerton, *Wars of Reconstruction*, 306.

37. Lemann, *Redemption*, 152–53.

38. Lemann, *Redemption*, 164.

39. Chernow, *Grant*, 817.

40. Chernow, *Grant*, 817–18.

41. Lemann, *Redemption*, 202–3.

42. Budiansky, *Bloody Shirt*, 274–75.

43. Lemann, *Redemption*, 204.

44. Egerton, *Wars of Reconstruction*, 342.

45. Lemann, *Redemption*, 206.

46. Foner, *Forever Free*, 151.

47. Perman, "Illegitimacy and Insurgency," 460.

48. Chernow, *Grant*, 755.

49. Langguth, *After Lincoln*, 312.

50. Watson, *Freedom Summer*, 42.

51. Goldfield, *America Aflame*, 493.

52. Lane, *Day Freedom Died*, 91.

53. Goldfield, *America Aflame*, 493.

54. Lane, *Day Freedom Died*, 11.

55. Lane, *Day Freedom Died*, 22.

56. Goldfield, *America Aflame*, 494.

57. Lane, *Day Freedom Died*, 251.

58. Langguth, *After Lincoln*, 314.

59. Goldfield, *American Aflame*, 494.

60. Lane, *Day Freedom Died*, 213.

61. Lane, *Day Freedom Died*, 254.

62. Budiansky, *Bloody Shirt*, 165.

63. Lane, *Day Freedom Died*, 254.

64. McPherson, *War That Forged a Nation*, 191.

65. Gray, *Fighting Talk*, 1.

66. Goldfield, *American Aflame*, 403.

67. Longacre, *Gentleman and Soldier*, 264–65.

68. Foner, *Forever Free*, 197.

69. Longacre, *Gentleman and Soldier*, 265.

70. Longacre, *Gentleman and Soldier*, 276.

71. Longacre, *Gentleman and Soldier*, 274.

72. Budiansky, *Bloody Shirt*, 234–35.

73. Budiansky, *Bloody Shirt*, 236.

74. Budiansky, *Bloody Shirt*, 251.

75. Goldfield, *Still Fighting the Civil War*, 195.

76. Simkins, "Pitchfork Ben Tillman," 169–71.

77. Longacre, *Gentleman and Soldier*, 273.

78. Tillman, "Speech," 3223–24.

79. "'Pitchfork' Ben Tillman," 38–39.

80. Budiansky, *Bloody Shirt*, 231.

81. Budiansky, *Bloody Shirt*, 165–66.

82. Wert, *General James Longstreet*, 413.

83. Robertson, *After the Civil War*, loc. 944.

84. Wert, *General James Longstreet*, 416.

85. Goldfield, *America Aflame*, 497.

86. James Loewen, "The Monument to White Power That Still Stands in New Orleans," History News Network, September 2016, http://historynewsnetwork.org/blog/15366712 (accessed June 21, 2020).

87. Loewen, "Monument to White Power."

88. Zinn, *Other Civil War*, 57.

88. Lane, *Day Freedom Died*, 253.

8. . Lane, *Day Freedom Died*, 253.

90. Guelzo, *Fateful Lightning*, 526.

91. Lane, *Day Freedom Died*, 251.

92. Brands, *American Colossus*, 463–64.

93. *Plessy v. Ferguson*, Cornell Law School Legal Information Institute https://www.law.cornell.edu/supremecourt/text/163/537 (accessed July 14, 2021).

94. Zinn, *Other Civil War*, 58.

95. LaMorte, *School Law*, 300.

96. Zinn, *People's History of the United States*, 204–5.

97. Blackmon, *Slavery by Another Name*, 110.

98. *Plessy v. Ferguson.*

99. Meacham, *Soul of America*, 68–69.

100. Huntington, *Who Are We?*, 54.

101. Goldfield, *Still Fighting the Civil War*, 197.

102. Gonzalez, *History of Christianity, Vol. 2*, 252.

103. Foner, *Forever Free*, 208.

104. Watson, *Freedom Summer*, 46.

105. "Lynching in America: Confronting the Legacy of Racial Terror," Equal Justice Institute, https://lynchinginamerica.eji.org/report/ (accessed July 10, 2020).

106. Lord, *Past That Wouldn't Die*, 22.

107. *Williams v. State of Mississippi*, Cornell Law School Legal Information Institute, https://www.law.cornell.edu/supremecourt/text/170/213 (accessed July 10, 2020).

108. *Williams v. State of Mississippi*.

109. Lord, *Past That Wouldn't Die*, 23.

110. Watson, *Freedom Summer*, 41.

111. Langguth, *After Lincoln*, 338.

112. Zinn, *People's History of the United States*, 200.

113. Lane, *Day Freedom Died*, 253.

114. Lord, *Past That Wouldn't Die*, 25.

115. "Lynching in America"; "Reconstruction in America: Racial Violence after the Civil War," Equal Justice Institute, 2002, https://eji.org/reports/reconstruction-in-america-overview/ (accesssed November 30, 2021).

116. *United States v. Cruikshank*, 92 U.S. 542, 554 (1876).

117. Lord, *Past That Wouldn't Die*, 139.

118. Lord, *Past That Wouldn't Die*, 159.

119. Lord, *Past That Wouldn't Die*, 231. There was a time when I lionized James Meredith, but I can no longer do that. Instead of embracing those who fought for his rights, he abandoned them and supported those who fought against him. Like so many others, then and now, he turned his back on those still discriminated against and excluded for what others sacrificed for him to attend and graduate from Ole Miss.

120. Bass and Nelson, *Orangeburg Massacre*, 11–12.

121. Watson, *Freedom Summer*, 12.

122. Lewis, *Across That Bridge*, 139–40.

123. Egerton, "Terrorized African-Americans."

124. Egerton, "Terrorized African-Americans."

125. Egerton, "Terrorized African-Americans."

126. Lane, *Day Freedom Died*, 254.

127. Lane, *Day Freedom Died*, 254.

128. McPherson, *War That Forged a Nation*, 191.

129. Gray, *Fighting Talk*, 1.

130. Foner, *Forever Free*, 175.

131. Foner, *Forever Free*, 175.

132. Egerton, *Wars of Reconstruction*, 299.

133. Egerton, *Wars of Reconstruction*, 299.

134. Blackmon, *Slavery by Another Name*, 42.

135. Douglass, "Frederick Douglass Assesses," 416–17.

23. A New Religion

1. Edmund Ruffin, "Diary Entry, June 18, 1865," Manuscript Division, Library of Congress, http://blogs.loc.gov/civil-war-voices/about/edmund-ruffin/ (accessed March 24, 2014).

2. Daly, *When Slavery Was Called Freedom*, 148–49.

3. Gallagherand Nolan, *Myth of the Lost Cause*, 15.

4. Dew, *Apostles of Disunion*, 16.

5. Davis, *Rise and Fall*, 76–77.

6. Gallagher and Nolan, *Myth of the Lost Cause*, 12.

7. Millet and Maslowski, *For the Common Defense*, 230.

8. Gallagher and Nolan, *Myth of the Lost Cause*, 12.

9. Goldfield, *Still Fighting the Civil War*, 28.

10. Hunter, *Immortal Confederacy*, 185.

11. Hunter, *Immortal Confederacy*, 185.

12. McPherson, *Battle Cry of Freedom*, 854.

13. Hunter, *Immortal Confederacy*, 186.

14. Hunter, *Immortal Confederacy*, 198.

15. Hunter, *Immortal Confederacy*, 198.

16. Levine, *Half Slave and Half Free*, 106.

17. Gallagher and Nolan, *Myth of the Lost Cause*, 16.

18. Campbell, *Celluloid South*, 58. It must also be remembered that Wilson's administration removed Blacks from the civil service and only allowed them to serve in the navy as mess stewards.

19. Gallagher, *Causes Won, Lost, and Forgotten*, 45.

20. Campbell, *Celluloid South*, 36.

21. Goldfield, *America Aflame*, 529.

22. Goldfield, *America Aflame*, 529–30.

23. Campbell, *Celluloid South*, 60–61.

24. Gallagher, *Causes Won, Lost, and Forgotten*, 46.

25. Gallagher, *Causes Won, Lost, and Forgotten*, 46.

26. Campbell, *Celluloid South*, 138–39.

27. Gallagher, *Causes Won, Lost, and Forgotten*, 49.

28. Campbell, *Celluloid South*, 140.

29. Campbell, *Celluloid South*, 8–29.

30. Loewen and Sebesta, *Confederate and Neo-Confederate Reader*, 282.

31. Loewen, *Sunset Towns*, 40.

32. Campbell, *Celluloid South*, 30.

33. Guelzo, *Fateful Lightning*, 525.

34. Guelzo, *Fateful Lightning*, 532.

35. Guelzo, *Fateful Lightning*, 532.

36. Abraham Lincoln, "Second Inaugural Address," March 4, 1861, https://www.bartleby.com/124/pres32.html.

Epilogue

1. Masur, "Real War," 114.

2. McPherson, *War That Forged a Nation*, 13.

3. Burns, *Conflict's Acoustic Shadows*, 102.

4. Allen C. Guelzo, "A War Lost and Found," *American Interest*, September 1, 2011, http://www.the-american-interest.com/articles/2011/09/01/a-war-lost-and-found/.

5. Lewis, *Crisis of Islam*, xv.

6. Liddell-Hart, *Why Don't We Learn from History?*, loc. 432.

7. Huntington, *Clash of Civilizations*, 97.

8. Snyder, *On Tyranny*, 12.

BIBLIOGRAPHY

Abrahamson, James L. *The Men of Secession and Civil War, 1859–1861*. Wilmington DE: Scholarly Resources, 2000.

"Africans in America: The Terrible Transformation." PBS. Accessed June 18, 2020. https://www.pbs.org/wgbh/aia/part1/1narr1.html.

Alexander, Edward Porter. *Fighting for the Confederacy: The Personal Recollections of General Edward Porter Alexander*. Edited by Gary Gallagher. Chapel Hill: University of North Carolina Press, 1989.

"American Memory and American Women." Law Library of Congress. Accessed August 9, 2016. http://memory.loc.gov/ammem/awhhtml/awlaw3/slavery.html.

American Rhetoric Movie Speeches. "*Judgment at Nuremberg*: Ernst Janning Confesses His Guilt to the Tribunal." Accessed July 18, 2016. http://www.americanrhetoric.com/MovieSpeeches/moviespeechjudgmentatnuremberg1.html.

Ames, Adelbert. "Governor Adelbert Ames Deplores Violence in Mississippi, September 1875." In *The Civil War and Reconstruction Documents and Essays*, 3rd ed., edited by Michael Perman and Amy Murrell Taylor, 433–34. Boston: Wadsworth Cengage Learning, 2011.

Bartlett, A. W. "Richmond's Black Residents Welcome Abraham Lincoln." In *The Civil War and Reconstruction: A Documentary Collection*, edited by William E. Gienapp, 302. New York: W. W. Norton, New York, 2001.

Bass, Jack, and Jack Nelson. *The Orangeburg Massacre*. Macon GA: Mercer University Press, 2002

Berlin, Ira, Joseph P. Riedy, and Leslie S. Rowland, eds. *Freedom's Soldiers: The Black Military Experience in the Civil War*. Cambridge: Cambridge University Press, 1998.

Blackmon, Douglas A. *Slavery by Another Name: The Re-Enslavement of Black Americans from the Civil War to World War II*. New York: Anchor, 2008.

Blight, David W. *Beyond the Battlefield: Race, Memory, and the American Civil War*. Amherst: University of Massachusetts Press, 2002.

Bok, Sissela. *Lying: Moral Choice in Public and Private Life.* 2nd ed. New York: Vintage, 1989.

Boyce, James P. "I Bow to What God Will Do." In *The Routledge Sourcebook of Religion and the American Civil War,* edited by Robert R. Mathisen, 9. New York: Routledge, 2015.

Brands, H. W. *American Colossus: The Triumph of Capitalism, 1865–1900.* New York: Random House, 2011.

Breisach, Ernst. *Historiography: Ancient, Mediaeval, and Modern.* Chicago: University of Chicago Press, 1994.

Brewster, Todd. *Lincoln's Gamble: The Tumultuous Six Months that Gave America the Emancipation Proclamation and Changed the Course of the Civil War.* New York: Scribner, 2014.

Brinsfield, John W., William C. Davis, Benedict Maryniak, and James I. Robertson. *Faith in the Fight: Civil War Chaplains.* Mechanicsburg PA: Stackpole, 2003.

Budiansky, Stephen. *The Bloody Shirt: Terror after Appomattox.* New York: Viking, 2008.

Burns, Ken. "A Conflict's Acoustic Shadows." In *The* New York Times *Disunion: Modern Historians Revisit and Reconsider the Civil War from Lincoln's Election to the Emancipation Proclamation,* 101–3. New York: Black Dog & Leventhal, 2013.

Bush, George W. "State of the Union Address." Washington DC, January 28, 2003. http://www.presidentialrhetoric.com/speeches/01.28.03.html.

Butler, Benjamin F. *The Private and Official Correspondence of General Benjamin F. Butler.* Vol. 5. Norwood MA: Plimpton, 1917.

Caldwell, Margaret Ann. "The Assassination of an African American Political Leader." In *The Civil War and Reconstruction: A Documentary Collection,* edited by William E. Gienapp, 409–10. New York: W. W. Norton, 2001.

Calhoun, John C. "'On Abolition Petitions,' U.S. Senate, February 6, 1837." In *The Confederate and Neo-Confederate Reader: The "Great Truth" about "The Lost Cause,"* edited by James W. Loewen and Edward Sebesta, 30–35. Jackson: University Press of Mississippi, 2010.

Campbell, Edward D. C., Jr. *The Celluloid South: Hollywood and the Southern Myth.* Knowxville: University of Tennessee Press, 1981.

Cartwright, Samuel A. "Diseases and Peculiarities of the Negro Race, 1851." In *The Confederate and Neo-Confederate Reader: The "Great Truth" about "The Lost Cause,"* edited by James W. Loewen and Edward H. Sebesta, 64–70. Jackson: University Press of Mississippi, 2010.

Catton, Bruce. *The Coming Fury.* London: Phoenix, 1961.

———. *Grant Takes Command: 1863–1865.* New York: Back Bay, 1990.

———. *A Stillness at Appomattox.* Garden City NY: Doubleday, 1953.

Catton, William, and Bruce Catton. *Two Roads to Sumter: Abraham Lincoln, Jefferson Davis, and the March to Civil War.* London: Phoenix, 2003.

Clausewitz, Carl von. *On War.* Edited and translated by Michael Howard and Peter Paret. Princeton NJ: Princeton University Press, 1976.

Cleveland, Henry. "Alexander H. Stevens, in Public and Private: With Letters and Speeches, before, during and since the War, Philadelphia 1886." Civil War Causes. Accessed March 24, 2014. http://civilwarcauses.org /corner.htm.

Confederate Congress. "General Orders, No. 14, an Act to Increase the Military Force of the Confederate States, Approved March 13, 1865." In *The Confederate and Neo-Confederate Reader: The "Great Truth" about the "Lost Cause,"* edited by James W. Loewen and Edward H. Sebesta, loc. 4348. Jackson: University Press of Mississippi, 2010. Kindle.

Cooper, William J. *We Have the War upon Us: The Onset of the Civil War, November 1860–April 1861.* New York: Knopf, 2012.

Daly, John Patrick. *When Slavery Was Called Freedom: Evangelicalism, Proslavery, and the Causes of the Civil War.* Lexington: University Press of Kentucky, 2002.

Daughan, George C. *If by Sea: The Forging of the American Navy—From the Revolution to the War of 1812.* New York: Basic Books, 2008.

Davis, Burke. *They Called Him Stonewall: A Life of T. J. Jackson CSA.* New York: Random House, 2000.

Davis, Jefferson. *The Rise and Fall of the Confederate Government.* Vol. 1. New York: D. Appleton, 1881. Kindle.

Davis, William C. *Jefferson Davis: The Man and His Hour.* New York: HarperCollins, 1991.

"Declaration of the Immediate Causes which Induce and Justify the Secession of South Carolina from the Federal Union." Avalon Project, Yale School of Law. Accessed March 24, 2014. http://avalon.law.yale.edu/19th_century /csa_scarsec.asp.

Dew, Charles B. *Apostles of Disunion: Southern Secession Commissioners and the Causes of the Civil War.* Charlottesville: University Press of Virginia, 2001.

Deyle, Steven. "The Domestic Slave Trade." In *Major Problems in the Civil War and Reconstruction: Documents and Essays,* 3rd ed., edited by Michael Perman and Amy Murrell Taylor Wadsworth, 50–63. Boston: Cengage Learning, 2011.

Dobak, William A. *Freedom by the Sword: The U.S. Colored Troops, 1862–1867.* New York: St. John's, 2016.

Doubleday, Abner. "From Moultrie to Sumter." In *Battles and Leaders of the Civil War, Vol. 1,* edited by Robert Underwood Johnson and Clarence Clough, 40–49. Secaucus NJ: Buel Castle, 1983.

Douglass, Frederick. "Frederick Douglass Assesses the Mistakes of Reconstruction (1880)." In *The Civil War and Reconstruction: A Documentary Collection,* edited by William E. Gienapp, 416–17. New York: W. W. Norton, 2001.

———. *Life and Times of Frederick Douglass: His Early Life as a Slave, His Escape From Bondage, and His Complete History.* New York: Collier, 1892.

———. *Narrative of the Life of Frederick Douglass, An American Slave, Written by Himself.* Boston: Anti-Slavery Office, 1845.

————. "Philadelphia Speech of July 6th 1863, Recorded in the *Liberator*." In *The Civil War and Reconstruction: A Documentary Collection*, edited by William E. Gienapp, 220–21. New York: W. W. Norton, 2001.

Dower, John W. *War without Mercy: Race and Power in the Pacific War*. New York: Pantheon, 1986.

Eakin, John R. "The Slave Soldiers, June 8, 1864." In *The Confederate and Neo-Confederate Reader: The "Great Truth" about "The Lost Cause,"* edited by James W. Loewen and Edward H. Sebesta, 209–12. Jackson: University of Mississippi Press, 2010 .

Edmondson, Catherine. "Catherine Edmonston Reflects on the Situation in the Confederacy." In *The Civil War and Reconstruction: A Documentary Collection*, edited by William E. Gienapp, 294–97. New York: W. W. Norton, 2001.

Egerton, Douglas R. *The Wars of Reconstruction: The Brief Violent History of America's Most Progressive Era*. New York: Bloomsbury, 2014.

Egnal, Marc. *Clash of Extremes: The Economic Origins of the Civil War*. New York: Hill & Wang, 2009.

Eldid, David, and Paul Lachance. "A Note on the Voyage of Venture Smith." Slave Voyages. Accessed July 25, 2020. https://www.slavevoyages.org/voyage/essays#interpretation/a-note-on-the-voyage-of-venture-smith/3/en/.

Equiano, Olaudah. *The Interesting Narrative of the Life of Olaudah Equiano, Or Gustavus Vassa, the African, Written by Himself*. Accessed July 25, 2020. https://www.gutenberg.org/files/15399/15399-h/15399-h.htm.

Faust, Drew Gilpin. *The Creation of Confederate Nationalism: Ideology and Identity in the Civil War South*. Baton Rouge: Louisiana State University Press, 1988.

Fea, John. *Believe Me: The Evangelical Raod to Donald Trump*. Grand Rapids MI: William B. Eerdman's, 2018.

Fehrenbacher, Don E. "Kansas, Republicanism, and the Crisis of the Union." In *The Civil War and Reconstruction, Documents and Essays*, 3rd ed., edited by Michael Perman and Amy Murrell Taylor Wadsworth, 86–89. Boston: Cengage Learning, 2011.

Fields, Elizabeth Arnett. "African American Soldiers before the Civil War." In *A Historic Context for the African American Military Experience—Before the Civil War, Blacks in the Union and Confederate Armies, Buffalo Soldier, Scouts, Spanish American War, World War I and II*. Washington DC: U.S. Department of Defense, U.S. Army Corps of Engineers, 1998. Kindle.

Fitzhugh, George. "New Haven Lecture, 1855." In *The Approaching Fury: Voices From the Storm, 1820–1861*, edited by Stephen B. Oates, 135. Lincoln: University of Nebraska Press, 1997.

Fleming, Thomas. *A Disease in the Public Mind: A New Understanding of Why We Fought the Civil War*. New York: Da Capo, 2013.

Foner, Eric. *Free Soil, Free Labor, Free Men: The Ideology of the Republican Party before the Civil War*. Oxford: Oxford University Press, 1995.

———. *Forever Free: The Story of Emancipation and Reconstruction.* New York: Vintage, 2005.

———. *A Short History of Reconstruction.* New York: Harper & Row, 1990.

Foote, Shelby. *The Civil War: A Narrative, Volume 1: Fort Sumter to Perryville.* New York: Random House, 1963.

Fourteenth Amendment to the U.S. Constitution. Accessed June 29, 2015. https://www.law.cornell.edu/constitution/amendmentxiv.

Freehling, William W. *The Road to Disunion, Volume 1: Secessionists at Bay.* Oxford: Oxford University Press, 1990.

———. *The Road to Disunion, Volume 2: Secessionists Triumphant, 1854–1861.* Oxford: Oxford University Press, 2007.

———. *The South vs. The South: How Anti-Confederate Southerners Shaped the Course of the Civil War.* Oxford: Oxford University Press, 2001.

"Fugitive Slave Act of 1850." Avalon Project, Yale School of Law. Accessed December 11, 2015. http://avalon.law.yale.edu/19th_century/fugitive.asp.

Fuller, J. F. C. *A Military History of the Western World: Volume Two, From the Defeat of the Spanish Armada to Waterloo.* New York: Minerva, 1955.

Fuller, J. F. C. *The Conduct of War, 1789–1961.* New York: Da Capo, 1992.

———. *Decisive Battles of the U.S.A., 1776–1918.* Lincoln: University of Nebraska Press, 2007.

———. *Grant and Lee: A Study in Personality and Generalship.* Bloomington: Indiana University Press, 1957.

Furman, Richard. "Exposition of the Views of Baptists, Relative to the Coloured Population in the United States May 28th 1823." In *A Communication to the Governor of South Carolina.* Charleston SC: A. E. Miller, 1838. http://faceweb.furman.edu/~benson/docs/rcd-fmn1.htm (accessed July 15, 2016).

Gallagher, Gary W. *Causes Won, Lost, and Forgotten: How Hollywood and Popular Art Shape What We Know about the Civil War.* Chapel Hill: University of North Carolina Press, 2008.

———. *The Confederate War: How Popular Will, Nationalism, and Military Strategy Could Not Stave Off Defeat.* Cambridge MA: Harvard University Press, 1999.

———. *The Union War.* Cambridge MA: Harvard University Press, 2011.

Gallagher, Gary W., and Alan T. Nolan, eds. *The Myth of the Lost Cause and Civil War History.* Bloomington: Indiana University Press, 2000.

Gallagher, Gary, Stephen Engle, Robert K. Krick, and Joseph T. Glatthaar, eds. *The American Civil War: The Mighty Scourge of War.* Oxford: Oxford University Press, 2003.

Gienapp, William. "The Republican Party and Slave Power." In *The Civil War and Reconstruction: Documents and Essays,* 3rd ed., edited by Michael Perman and Amy Murrell Taylor, 74–86. Boston: Cengage Learning, 2011.

Glatthaar, Joseph T. *General Lee's Army from Victory to Collapse.* New York: Free Press, 2008.

Glickman, Jessica A. "A War at the Heart of Man: The Structure and Construction of Ships Bound for Africa." PhD diss., University of Rhode Island, 2015.

Goldfield, David. *America Aflame: How the Civil War Created a Nation.* New York: Bloomsbury, 2011.

———. *Still Fighting the Civil War: The American South and Southern History.* Baton Rouge: Louisiana State University Press, 2002.

Gonzalez, Justo L. *The History of Christianity, Vol. 2: The Reformation to the Present Day.* San Francisco: Harper & Row, 1985.

Goodheart, Adam. *1861: The Civil War Awakening.* New York: Vintage, 2011.

———. "The Ashen Ruin." In *Disunion, 106 Articles from the* New York Times *Opinionator: Modern Historians Revisit and Reconsider the Civil War from Lincoln's Election to the Emancipation Proclamation,* edited by Ted Widmer, 67–71. New York: Black Dog & Leventhal, 2013.

———. "Moses' Last Exodus." In *Disunion, 106 Articles from the* New York Times *Opinionator: Modern Historians Revisit and Reconsider the Civil War from Lincoln's Election to the Emancipation Proclamation,* edited by Ted Widmer, 13–16. New York: Black Dog & Leventhal, 2013.

Goodwin, Doris Kearns. *Team of Rivals: The Political Genius of Abraham Lincoln.* New York: Simon & Schuster, 2005.

Grant, Ulysses S. *Personal Memoirs of U.S. Grant.* New York: Charles L. Webster, 1885–86.

———. "Preparing for the Campaigns of '64." In *Battles and Leaders of the Civil War, Volume IV: Retreat with Honor,* edited by Robert Underwood Johnson and Clarence Clough, 97–117. Secaucus NJ: Buel Castle, 2010.

Gray, Colin S. *Fighting Talk: Forty Maxims on War, Peace, and Strategy.* Dulles VA: Potomac, 2009.

Guelzo, Allen C. *Fateful Lightning: A New History of the Civil War Era and Reconstruction.* Oxford: Oxford University Press, 2012.

———. *Gettysburg: The Last Invasion.* New York: Vintage, 2013.

———. *Robert E. Lee: A Life.* New York, Knopf, 2021.

———. "A War Lost and Found." *American Interest,* September 1, 2011. http://www.the-american-interest.com/articles/2011/09/01/a-war-lost-and-found/.

Hancock, Almira. *Reminiscences of Winfield Scott Hancock.* New York: Charles L. Webster, 1887.

"The Harper's Ferry Invasion as Party Capital." *Richmond Enquirer,* October 23, 1859. In *The Civil War and Reconstruction: A Documentary Collection,* edited by William E. Gienapp, 54. New York: W. W. Norton, 2001.

Hartle, Anthony E. *Moral Issues in Military Decision-Making.* Lawrence: University Press of Kansas, 1989.

"Hermenutics." Stanford Encyclopedia of Philosophy. Accessed July 20, 2020 http://Plato.stanford.edu/entries/hermeneutics/#Textline.

Herrera, Riccardo. *For Liberty and the Republic: The American Citizen as Soldier, 1775–1861.* New York: New York University Press, 2015.

Hitler, Adolf. *Mein Kampf.* Translated by James Murphy. Munich: Franz Eher Nachfolger GmbH, 1925.

Hoffer, Eric. *The True Believer: Thoughts on the Nature of Mass Movements.* New York: HarperCollins, 1951.

Hofstadter, Richard. *The Paranoid Style in American Politics.* New York: Vintage, 2008.

Holzer, Harold. *Lincoln and the Power of the Press: The War for Public Opinion.* New York: Simon & Schuster, 2014.

_____. *The Lincoln-Douglas Debates: The First Complete Unexpurgated Text.* New York: HarperCollins, 1993.

———. *Lincoln: How Abraham Lincoln Ended Slavery in America.* New York: Newmarket, 2012.

Holzer, Harold, and Craig L. Symonds, eds. *The* New York Times *Complete Civil War, 1861–1865.* New York: Black Dog & Leventhal, 2010.

Hotze, Henry. "The Negro's Place in Nature: December 10, 1863." In *The Confederate and Neo-Confederate Reader: The "Great Truth" about "The Lost Cause,"* 213–17. Jackson: University Press of Mississippi, 2010.

Hunter, Lloyd. "The Immortal Confederacy: Another Look at the Lost Cause Religion." In *The Myth of the Lost Cause and Civil War*, edited by Gary W. Gallagher and Alan T. Nolan, 185–218. Bloomington: Indiana University Press, 2000.

Huntington, Samuel P. *The Clash of Civilizations and the Remaking of the World Order.* New York: Touchstone, 1997.

———. *The Soldier and the State: The Theory and Politics of Civil-Military Relations.* Cambridge MA: Belknap Press of Harvard University Press, 1957.

———. *Who Are We? America's Great Debate.* London: Free Press, 2004.

Ingraham, Joseph Holt. *The Southwest, by a Yankee.* Vol. 2. New York: Harper, 1835.

Jefferson, Thomas. "Letter to John Holmes, April 22, 1824." Accessed November 30, 2021. www.loc.gov/exhibits/jefferson/159.html.

Jones, J. William. *Life and Letters of Robert E. Lee, Soldier and Man.* New York: Neale, 1906.

Jones, Terry L. "The Free Men of Color Go to War." In *Disunion, 106 Articles from the* New York Times *Opinionator: Modern Historians Revisit and Reconsider the Civil War from Lincoln's Election to the Emancipation Proclamation,* edited by Ted Widmer, 401–5. New York: Black Dog & Leventhal, 2013.

Jordan, David M. *Winfield Scott Hancock: A Soldier's Life.* Bloomington: Indiana University Press, 1988.

Keneally, Thomas. *American Scoundrel: The Life of the Notorious Civil War General Dan Sickles.* New York: Anchor, 2003.

King, Martin Luther, Jr. "I've Been to the Mountaintop." April 3, 1968. Research and Education Institute at Stanford University. https://kinginstitute.stanford.edu/king-papers/documents/ive-been-mountaintop-address-delivered-bishop-charles-mason-temple.

Kingsbury, Susan Myra, ed. *The Records of the Virginia Company of London.* Vol. 3. Washington DC: United States Government Printing Office, 1933.

Kipling, Rudyard. "The White Man's Burden: The United States and the Philippine Islands." 1899. Accessed August 6, 2016. https://public.wsu.edu/ ~brians/world_civ/worldcivreader/world_civ_reader_2/kipling.html.

Kolchin, Peter. *American Slavery: 1689–1877.* New York: Hill & Wang, 2003.

Korda, Michael. *Clouds of Glory: The Life and Legend of Robert E. Lee.* New York: HarperCollins, 2014.

Kraeczynski, Keith. "The Spanish-American War and After." In *A Historic Context for the African American Military Experience—Before the Civil War Blacks in the Union and Confederate Armies, Buffalo Soldier, Scouts, Spanish American War, World War I and II,* loc. 2842. Washington DC: U.S. Department of Defense, U.S. Army Corps of Engineers, 1998. Kindle.

Lee, Robert E. "Letter to Hon. Andrew Hunter, January 11, 1865." In *The Confederate and Neo-Confederate Reader: The "Great Truth" about "The Lost Cause,"* edited by James W. Loewen and Edward H. Sebesta, 216–18. Jackson: University of Mississippi Press, 2010.

Levine, Bruce. *The Fall of the House of Dixie: The Civil War and the Social Revolution That Transformed the South.* New York: Random House, 2014.

———. *Half Slave and Half Free: The Roots of the Civil War.* Rev. ed. New York: Hill & Wang, 1995.

Lewis, Bernard. *The Crisis of Islam: Holy War and Unholy Terror.* New York: Random House, 2003.

Lewis, John, with Brenda Jones. *Across That Bridge: Life Lessons and a Vision for Change.* New York: Hyperion, 2012.

Lincoln, Abraham. "Abraham Lincoln's Illinois Farewell Address, February 11, 1861." In *The Routledge Sourcebook of Religion and the American Civil War,* edited by Robert R. Mathise, 20. New York: Routledge, 2015.

———. "The Emancipation Proclamation." January 1, 1863. National Archives and Records Administration. http://www.archives.gov/exhibits/featured _documents/emancipation_proclamation/transcript.html.

———. "First Inaugural Address." March 4, 1861. Bartleby. www.bartleby.com /124/pres31.html.

———. "A House Divided." June 16, 1858. PBS. www.pbs.org/wgbh/ala/part4 /4h2934.html.

———. "Second Inaugural Address." March 4, 1865. Bartleby. www.bartleby .com/124/pres32.html.

Linson, Desiree D. "Vice Admiral Samuel Gravely: Leadership by Example." Master's thesis, Air War College, 1998.

Longacre, Edward G. *John Buford: A Military Biography.* Cambridge MA: Da Capo, 2003.

———. *Joshua Chamberlain: The Soldier and the Man.* Conshohocken PA: Combined, 1999.

Longacre, Edward G. "The Monument to White Power That Still Stands in New Orleans." History News Network. Accessed November 30, 2021. http://historynewsnetwork.org/blog/15366712.

———. *Pickett, the Leader of the Charge: A Biography of General George E. Pickett, CSA.* Shippensburg PA: White Mane, 1995.

Loewen, James. *Lies My Teacher Told Me.* New York: Simon & Schuster, 2007.

———. *Sunset Towns: The Hidden Dimension of American Racism.* New York: Touchstone, 2005.

Loewen, James W., and Edward H. Sebesta, eds. *The Confederate and Neo-Confederate Reader: The "Great Truth" about "The Lost Cause."* Jackson: University Press of Mississippi, 2010.

Lowery, Beverly. *Harriet Tubman: Imagining a Life.* New York: Doubleday, 2007.

Luttwak, Edward. "The Missing Dimension." In *Religion: The Missing Dimension of Statecraft,* edited by Douglas Johnston and Cynthia Sampson, 7–19. Oxford: Oxford University Press, 1994.

"Lynching in America: Confronting the Legacy of Racial Terror." Equal Justice Institute. Accessed July 10, 2020. https://lynchinginamerica.eji.org/report/.

Masur, Louis. *"The Real War Will Never Get in the Books": Selections from Writers during the Civil War.* Oxford: Oxford University Press, 1996.

Mayer, Henry. *All on Fire: William Lloyd Garrison and the Abolition of Slavery.* New York: W. W. Norton, 1998.

McBeth, H. Leon. *The Baptist Heritage.* Nashville TN: Broadman, 1987.

McCurry, Stephanie. *Confederate Reckoning: Power and Politics in the Civil War South.* Cambridge MA: Harvard University Press, 2010.

McGovern, George. *Abraham Lincoln.* New York: Henry Holt, 2009.

McGrath, Alister. *Abraham Lincoln and the Second American Revolution.* Oxford: Oxford University Press, 1992.

———. *Christianity's Dangerous Idea: The Protestant Revolution, A History from the Sixteenth Century to the Twenty-First.* New York: HarperCollins, 2007.McPherson, James. *The Battle Cry of Freedom: The Civil War Era.* Oxford: Oxford University Press, 1988.

———. *Drawn with the Sword: Reflections on the American Civil War.* Oxford: Oxford University Press, 1996.

———. *For Cause and Comrades.* Oxford: Oxford University Press, 1998.

———. *Tried by War: Abraham Lincoln as Commander in Chief.* New York: Penguin, 2008.

———. *The War That Forged a Nation: Why the Civil War Still Matters.* Oxford: Oxford University Press, 2015.

Meacham, John. *The Soul of America: The Battle for Our Better Angels.* New York: Random House, 2018.

"Mississippi's Black Code, November 24–29, 1865." In *The Confederate and Neo-Confederate Reader: The "Great Truth" about the "Lost Cause,"* edited by James

W. Loewen and Edward H. Sebesta, 237–39. Jackson: University Press of Mississippi, 2010.

Morgan, Edmund S. *American Slavery, American Freedom.* New York: W. W. Norton, 1975.

Moulton, Horace. "Narrative and Testimony of Rev. Horace Moulton." In *American Slavery as It Is: Selections from the Testimony of a Thousand Witnesses,* edited by Theodore Dwight Weld, 18–30. New York: Dover, [1839] 2018.

Murray, Williamson, ed. *The Past as Prologue: The Importance of History to the Military Professional.* New York: Cambridge University Press, 2006.

Oates, Stephen B., ed. *The Approaching Fury: Voices of the Storm, 1820–1861.* Lincoln: University of Nebraska Press, 1997.

O'Connell, Robert L. *Fierce Patriot: The Tangled Lives of William Tecumseh Sherman.* New York: Random House, 2013.

Oefinger, John C., ed. *A Soldier's General: The Civil War Letters of Major General Lafayette McLaws.* Chapel Hill: University of North Carolina Press, 2002.

Oren, Michael. *Power, Faith, and Fantasy: America and the Middle East, 1776 to the Present.* New York: W. W. Norton, 2007.

Osborne, Charles C. *Jubal: The Life and Times of General Jubal A. Earl, CSA.* Chapel Hill NC: Algonquin, 1992.

Palmer, Benjamin M. "Thanksgiving Sermon." November, 29, 1860. Civil War Causes. http://civilwarcauses.org/palmer.htm.

Perman, Michael. "Illegitimacy and Insurgency in the Reconstructed South." In *Major Problems of the Civil War and Reconstruction: Documents and Essays,* edited by Michael Perlman and Murrell Taylor Wadsworth, 460. Boston: Cengage Learning, 2011.

Pfanz, Donald. *Richard S. Ewell: A Soldier's Life.* Chapel Hill: University of North Carolina Press, 1998.

Phillips, Kevin. *American Theocracy: The Peril and Politics of Radical Religion, Oil and Borrowed Money in the Twenty-First Century.* New York: Viking, 2006.

Pinchon, Edgcumb. *Dan Sickles: Hero of Gettysburg and "Yankee King of Spain."* Garden City NY: Doubleday, Doran, 1945.

"'Pitchfork' Ben Tillman: The Most Lionized Figure in South Carolina History." *Journal of Blacks in Higher Education* 58 (Winter 2007–8): 38–39.

Plessy v. Ferguson. Cornell Law School Legal Information Institute. Accessed July 7, 2020. https://www.law.cornell.edu/supremecourt/text/163/537.

Potter, David M. *The Impending Crisis: America before the Civil War, 1848–1861.* Completed and edited by Don E. Fehrenbacher. New York: HarperCollins, 1976.

Pryor, Elizabeth Brown. *Reading the Man: A Portrait of Robert E. Lee through His Private Letters.* New York: Penguin, 2007.

Rable, George C. *God's Almost Chosen Peoples: A Religious History of the American Civil War.* Chapel Hill: University of North Carolina Press, 2010.

"Reconstruction in America: Racial Violence after the Civil War." Equal Justice Institute. Accessed November 30, 2021. https://eji.org/reports/reconstruction-in-america-overview/.

Redding, J. Saunders. *They Came in Chains: Americans from Africa.* Rev. ed. New York: Lippincott,1973.

Reichberg, Gregory M., Henrik Syse, and Endre Begby. *The Ethics of War: Classic and Contemporary Readings.* Malden MA: Blackwell 2006.

Rhodes, Bill. *An Introduction to Military Ethics: A Reference Handbook.* Santa Barbara CA: Praeger Security International, 2009.

Robertson, James I. *Soldiers Blue and Gray.* Columbia: University of South Carolina Press, 1998.

Rubin, Barry. "Religion in International Affairs." In *Religion: The Missing Dimension of Statecraft,* edited by Douglas Johnson and Cynthia Sampson, 20–37. Oxford: Oxford University Press, 1994.

Ruffin, Edmund. "Diary Entry for June 18, 1865." Manuscript Division, Library of Congress. Accessed November 30, 2021. http://blogs.loc.gov/civil-war-voices/about/edmund-ruffin/.

———. *The Political Economy of Slavery.* Washington DC: L. Towers [1857?].

Sears, Stephen. "Lincoln and McClellan." In *Lincoln's Generals,* edited by Gabor S. Boritt, 1–51. Lincoln: University of Nebraska Press, 2010.

Seidule, Ty. *Robert E. Lee and Me: A Southerner's Reckoning with the Myth of the Lost Cause.* New York: St. Martin's, 2020.

Seward, William H. "The Irrepressible Conflict." In *The Civil War and Reconstruction: Documents and Essays,* 3rd ed., edited by Michael Perman and Amy Murrell Taylor, 70–72. Boston: Cengage Learning, 2011.

Sherman, William T. *The Memoirs of General William T. Sherman.* Toronto: HarperTorch Classics, 2014.

Shurden, Walter B. *Not a Silent People: The Controversies That Have Shaped Southern Baptists.* Nashville TN: Broadman, 1972.

Simkins, Francis Butler. *Pitchfork Ben Tillman, South Carolinian.* Baton Rouge: Louisiana State University Press, 1944.

"1641 Massachusetts Body of Liberties." Online Library of Liberty. Accessed July 22, 2020. https://oll.libertyfund.org/pages/1641-massachusetts-body-of-liberties.

"Slave Law in Colonial Virginia: A Timeline." Sam Houston State University. Accessed November 30, 2021. www.shsu.edu/~jll004/vabeachcourse_spring09/bacons_rebellion/slavelawincolonialvirginiatimeline.pdf.

Smith, Diane Monroe. *Fanny and Joshua: The Enigmatic Lives of France's Caroline Adams and Joshua Lawrence Chamberlain.* Gettysburg PA: Thomas, 1999.

Smith, Jean Edward. *Grant.* New York: Simon & Schuster, 2001.

Snay, Mitchell. *The Gospel of Disunion: Religion and Separatism in the Antebellum South.* Chapel Hill: University of North Carolina Press, 1993.

Stampp, Kenneth M., ed. *The Causes of the Civil War*. Rev. ed. New York: Touchstone, 1992.

Steers, Edward, Jr. *Blood on the Moon: The Assassination of Abraham Lincoln*. Lexington: University of Kentucky Press, 2001.

Stringfellow, J. H. "Letter to President Jefferson Davis, February 8, 1865." In *The Confederate and Neo-Confederate Reader: The "Great Truth" about "The Lost Cause,"* edited by James W. Loewen and Edward H. Sebesta, 223–27. Jackson: University of Mississippi Press, 2010.

Symonds, Craig L. *Stonewall of the West: Patrick Cleburne and the Civil War*. Lawrence: University Press of Kansas, 1997.

Thomas, Emory. *The Confederate Nation, 1861–1865*. New York: Harper Perennial, 1979.

———. *Robert E. Lee*. New York: W. W. Norton, 1995.

Thornwell, James H. "The Rights and the Duties of the Masters, May 26, 1850." In *The Confederate and Neo-Confederate Reader: The "Great Truth" about "The Lost Cause,"* edited by James W. Loewen and Edward H. Sebesta, 50–54. Jackson: University Press of Mississippi, 2010.

Thucydides. *History of the Peloponnesian War*. Translated by Rex Warner. London: Penguin, 1954.

Tillman, Benjamin. "Speech of Senator Benjamin R. Tillman." Congressional Record, 56th Cong., 1st sess. Reprinted in *Document Sets for the South in U. S. History*, edited by Richard Purday, 3223–24. Lexington MA: D. C. Heath, 1991.

"Trans-Atlantic Slave Estimates." Slave Voyages, Emory Center for Digital Scholarship. Accessed June 18, 2020. https://www.slavevoyages.org/assessment/estimates.

Trudeau, Noah Andre. *Like Men of War: Black Troops in the Civil War, 1862–1865*. New York: Back Bay, 1998.

Tuchman, Barbara. *The March of Folly: From Troy to Vietnam*. New York: Ballantine, 1984.

———. *Practicing History*. New York: Knopf, 1981.

———. *The Proud Tower: A Portrait of the World Before the War, 1890–1914*. New York: Random House, 2008.

Twain, Mark. "To the Person Sitting in Darkness" (February 1901). The World of 1898: The Spanish American War, Library of Congress. Accessed December 12, 2014. http://www.loc.gov/rr/hispanic/1898/twain.html.

U.S. Army. *The Army and Marine Counterinsurgency Field Manual*, FM 3–24 MCWP 3–33.5. With a foreword by Gen. David A. Petraeus and Gen. James Amos. Old Saybrook CT: Konecky & Konecky, 2007.

Van Evrie, J. H. "Negroes and Negro Slavery: The First an Inferior Race—The Latter, Its Normal Condition, 1861." In *The Confederate and Neo-Confederate Reader: The "Great Truth" about "The Lost Cause,"* edited by James W. Loewen and Edward H. Sebesta, 73–79. Jackson: University Press of Mississippi, 2010.

Varon, Elizabeth R. *Disunion! The Coming of the American Civil War, 1789–1858*. Chapel Hill: University of North Carolina Press, 2008.

Vidor, King, dir. *Gone with the Wind*. Metro-Goldwyn-Mayer, 1939.

Wakelyn, John L. "Benjamin Morgan Palmer." In *Leaders of the American Civil War: A Biographical and Historiographical Dictionary*, edited by Charles F. Ritter and Jon L. Wakelyn, 306–14. Westport CT: Greenwood, 1998.

Weigley, Russell F. *A Great Civil War: A Military and Political History, 1861–1865*. Bloomington: Indiana University Press, 2000.

Welch, Isaiah H. "Letter in the *Christian Recorder*, 24 October 1863." In *The Civil War and Reconstruction: A Documentary Collection*, edited by William E. Gienapp, 225–26. New York: W. W. Norton, 2001.

Welton, Chauncey B. "A Union Soldier's Changing Views on Emancipation." In *The Civil War and Reconstruction: A Documentary Collection*, edited by William Gienapp, 242–45. New York: W. W. Norton, 2001.

Wert, Jeffry. *The Sword of Lincoln: The Army of the Potomac*. New York: Simon & Schuster, 2005.

Whitman, Walt. "Blood Money." March 22, 1850. Walt Whitman Archive. http://www.whitmanarchive.org/published/periodical/poems/per.00089.

Wightman, John T. "The Glory of God, the Defense of the South—July 28, 1861." In *The Routledge Sourcebook of Religion and the American Civil War*, edited by Robert R. Mathisen, 77–78. New York: Routledge, 2015.

Williams v. State of Mississippi. April 25, 1898. Cornell Law School Legal Information Institute. https://www.law.cornell.edu/supremecourt/text/170/213.

Wills, Garry. *Lincoln at Gettysburg: The Words That Remade America*. New York: Simon & Schuster, 1992.

Winik, Jay. *April 1865: The Month That Saved America*. New York: HarperCollins, 2002.

Wilson, Charles Reagan. *Baptized in Blood: The Religion of the Lost Cause, 1865–1920*. Athens: University of Georgia Press, 1980.

Witt, John Fabian. *Lincoln's Code: The Laws of War in American History*. New York: Free Press, 2012.

Woodard, Colin. *American Nations: A History of the Eleven Rival Regional Cultures of North America*. New York: Penguin, 2011.

Zinn, Howard. *The Other Civil War: Slavery and Struggle in Civil War America*. New York: Harper Perennial, 2011.

———. *A People's History of the United States*. New York: Harper Perennial, 1999.

Zinni, Tony, and Tony Koltz. *The Battle for Peace: A Frontline Vision of America's Power and Purpose*. New York: Palgrave Macmillan, 2006.

INDEX

abolition, 52, 254, 266; Evangelical proponents of, 35, 84, 164, 186; gradual, 47, 50, 68, 112, 155, 167, 169, 172, 185, 196, 211; war aims and, 247. *See also* emancipation

abolitionist movement, 55, 90; Blacks in, 93; Christians in, 84, 87, 91; Republican Party and, 96

abolitionists, 12, 90, 96, 107, 194; British, 52, 89; Christian supporters of, 88–89, 106, 147; Emancipation Proclamation and, 210; Frederick Douglass and, 87, 94; Fugitive Slave Act of 1850 and, 77–78; immigrants and, 98; John Brown, 149; militant, 123; in myths of Lost Cause and Noble South, 325, 328; Northern Democrats and, 98, 106; religion and, 39, 82, 84; Republican Party and, 88, 96–97, 291, 319; Southern churches' views of, 103–5, 164, 177; Southern opponents' views of, 34, 55, 57, 59–60, 62, 79; U.S. mail used by, 58; William Lloyd Garrison, 59, 86–87, 255

Adams, Henry, 277

Adams, John, 49, 180

Adams, John Quincy, 49, 58

Africans, 3–4, 8–10, 14, 42, 46, 139, 220

Alabama, 18, 68, 123, 136, 166, 253, 256

American exceptionalism, 23, 25–26, 29, 31, 113

American Museum, 12

American Party, 154

American Revolution, 4, 7, 14, 231

American Slavery as It Is (Grimke-Weld), 91

Ames, Adelbert, 254, 263, 278–80, 284

Appomattox VA, 242, 248, 279, 292, 295, 324, 329, 335

Army and Marine Corps Counterinsurgency Manual, 22

Atlantic Monthly, 28, 218

Austin, Lloyd, 245

Axe Handle Sunday, 312

Banks, Nathaniel, 215–16

Barbados, 7, 14–16

Barksdale, William, 130

Barnett, Ross, 313–14

Battle for Liberty Place, 300

Battle of Battery Wagner, 212, 217

Battle of First Bull Run, 42

Battle of Fort Sumter, 19, 63, 141, 174, 176, 178, 180, 182–87, 191, 194, 321, 330

Battle of Franklin, 237

Battle of Gettysburg, 183, 190, 283, 300

Battle of Little Round Top, 249

Battle of Milliken's Bend, 219, 221

Battle of Petersburg, 222

Battle of Port Hudson, 215, 228

Battle of Saltville, 223

Battle of the Crater, 222

Battle of Vicksburg, 233

Beauregard, P. T. G., 184–85, 222, 243

Beckwith, J. R., 288

Bell, John, 136, 155, 157, 159

Benjamin, Judah, 165

Benning, Henry, 171–72

the Bible: amendment, 180; as condemnation of slavery, 35, 47, 87; Confederate nationalism and, 36, 103, 105, 108, 115, 177; as defense of slavery, 96, 178; Douglass on, 94; justification for racism and slavery in, 33, 37, 68, 101, 106, 114, 315; Lincoln on, 207

Index